This impressive collection assembles a stellar international team of experts to discuss developments in police education. Perry Stanislas, a leading authority on community relations and police training, has achieved wonders in bringing together a truly global perspective on an issue that is the bedrock of police professionalization. It will be of value to practitioners, policy-makers, researchers, educators, and all who are concerned about a pivotal institution.

Robert Reiner, Emeritus Professor of Criminology, LSE, UK

This is an excellent text that provides a careful analysis of the professionalization agenda in policing across the world. This book is a crucial source for anyone interested in examining the demands on policing and the attempts of police training and education to prepare police personnel for the unique challenges they face.

Dr Stephen Tong, Director of Policing,
Canterbury Christ Church University, UK

This book gives recognition to the crucial role played by education and training in all aspects of policing. Whether it is in the context of police officers' skills and competencies, police reform, the professionalization of policing, or trends in police organizations globally, the contributors have something interesting and significant to say about it. For anyone who wants to understand where the future of policing lies, this is an essential text.

Professor Kenneth B. Scott, Centre for Criminal Justice and Police Studies,
University of the West of Scotland, UK

International Perspectives on Police Education and Training

Training and education constitutes the backbone of a significant amount of police activity and expenditure in developing the most important resources involved in policing work. It also involves an array of actors and agencies, such as educational institutions which have a long and important relationship with police organizations.

This book examines the role of education and training in the development of police in the contemporary world. Bringing together specialist scholars and practitioners from around the world, the book examines training methods in the UK, the USA, Australia, Canada, China, France, Hungary, India, the Netherlands, St Lucia and Sweden.

The book throws light on important aspects of public service policing, and new areas of public and private provision, through the lens of training and development. It will be of interest to policing scholars and those involved in professional and organizational development worldwide.

Perry Stanislas has over 30 years international experience in non-state and state policing. He was the first full-time civilian policy advisor for a police organization specializing in human resource management and quality of service.

Routledge frontiers of criminal justice

1 **Sex Offenders: Punish, Help, Change or Control?**
Theory, policy and practice explored
Edited by Jo Brayford, Francis Cowe and John Deering

2 **Building Justice in Post-Transition Europe**
Processes of criminalisation within Central and Eastern European societies
Edited by Kay Goodall, Margaret Malloch and Bill Munro

3 **Technocrime, Policing and Surveillance**
Edited by Stéphane Leman-Langlois

4 **Youth Justice in Context**
Community, compliance and young people
Mairead Seymour

5 **Women, Punishment and Social Justice**
Human rights and penal practices
Margaret Malloch and Gill McIvor

6 **Handbook of Policing, Ethics and Professional Standards**
Edited by Allyson MacVean, Peter Spindler and Charlotte Solf

7 **Contrasts in Punishment**
An explanation of Anglophone excess and Nordic exceptionalism
John Pratt and Anna Eriksson

8 **Victims of Environmental Harm**
Rights, recognition and redress under national and international law
Matthew Hall

9 **Doing Probation Work**
Identity in a criminal justice occupation
Rob C. Mawby and Anne Worrall

10 **Justice Reinvestment**
    Can the criminal justice system deliver more for less?
    Chris Fox, Kevin Albertson and Kevin Wong

11 **Epidemiological Criminology**
    Theory to practice
    Edited by Eve Waltermaurer and Timothy A. Akers

12 **Policing Cities**
    Urban securitization and regulation in a twenty-first century world
    Edited by Randy K. Lippert and Kevin Walby

13 **Restorative Justice in Transition**
    Kerry Clamp

14 **International Perspectives on Police Education and Training**
    Edited by Perry Stanislas

International Perspectives on Police Education and Training

Edited by Perry Stanislas

Routledge
Taylor & Francis Group

LONDON AND NEW YORK

First published 2014
by Routledge
2 Park Square, Milton Park, Abingdon, Oxfordshire OX14 4RN

and by Routledge
711 Third Avenue, New York, NY 10017

First issued in paperback 2015

Routledge is an imprint of the Taylor & Francis Group, an informa business

British Library Cataloguing in Publication Data
A catalogue record for this book is available from the British Library

Library of Congress Cataloging-in-Publication Data
International perspectives on police education and training/[edited by]
Perry Stanislas.
 pages cm. – (Routledge frontiers of criminal justice.)
 1. Police–Study and teaching. 2. Police training. I. Stanislas, Perry.
 HV7923.I58 2014
 363.2'2–dc23
                                                                  2013014393

ISBN 13: 978-1-138-92242-6 (pbk)
ISBN 13: 978-0-415-63218-8 (hbk)

Typeset in Times New Roman
by Wearset Ltd, Boldon, Tyne and Wear

Contents

List of figures		xii
List of tables		xiii
Notes on contributors		xv

1 **Introduction: police education and training in context**   1
P. STANISLAS

PART I
The determinants of police training and education   21

2 **An overview of police training in the United States,
historical development, current trends and critical issues:
the evidence**   23
M. BERLIN

3 **Police training and education and university collaboration
in Australia**   42
T. GREEN AND R. WOOLSTON

4 **The challenges and dilemmas facing university-based police
education in Britain**   57
P. STANISLAS

5 **Perspectives on police training and education: the Canadian
experience**   72
S. WYATT AND N. BELL

6 **Constructing comparative competency profiles: the
Netherlands experience**   90
H. PEETERS

PART II
Preparing for police work   115

7   Police training and reform in India: bringing
     knowledge-based learning to the Indian Police Service   117
     P. NEYROUD AND N. WAIN

8   Fire-arms and self-defense training in Sweden   128
     J. BERTILSSON AND P. FREDRIKSSON

9   Police use-of-force issues in Canada   138
     A. ARSENAULT AND T. HINTON

10 How violence comes to French police: the role of violence in
     the socialization and training of the French police   158
     C. MOREAU DE BELLAING

PART III
**Police reform and training in developing and
post-Communist societies**   173

11 Police training and education in Hungary   175
     F. SÁNDOR

12 A review of police education and training in China   193
     Y. TINGYOU

13 Transforming St Lucian policing through recruit training in
     a context of high crime   209
     P. STANISLAS

PART IV
Contemporary developments in policing and training   235

14 Getting back to Peel: PCSO training in England and Wales   237
     A. CRISP

15 New perspectives on police education and training: lessons
     from the private security sector   254
     A. WAKEFIELD AND M. BUTTON

16 Police training in America: changes in the new millennium 274
A. CHAPPELL

17 Conclusion 289
P. STANISLAS

Index 314

Figures

3.1 Joint management structure   49
3.2 Teaching staff   51
13.1 Recruit responses to selected questions   226
15.1 Brooks' (2010) integrated science of security framework   263

Tables

2.1	Types of police academies	24
2.2	Topics included in basic training of state and local law enforcement	27
2.3	Percentage of academies	28
2.4	Percentage of academies employing	30
2.5	Percentage of academies using scenarios	31
2.6	Topics and percentage of academies	35
3.1	Associated Degree in Policing Practice (ADPP) full-time on campus	45
5.1	Seneca basic police training program	86
6.1	Similarities between characteristics of professions	91
6.2	Equivalence of levels	92
6.3	Distinctive core processes of police profession	92
6.4	Typology of generic distinctions	94
6.5	Template of generic distinctions between competency levels, still to be specified as policing competencies	96–97
6.6	Particular competence feature	98
6.7	An operational emergency response competence (EQF4)	99
6.8	A tactical emergency response competence (EQF6)	100
6.9	An operational law enforcement competence (EQF4)	101
6.10	A tactical law enforcement competence (EQF6)	102
6.11	A strategic law enforcement competence (EQF7)	103
6.12	An operational criminal investigation competence (EQF4)	104
6.13	A tactical criminal investigation competence (EQF6)	105
6.14	A strategic criminal investigation competence (EQF7)	106
6.15	Assessment criteria corresponding with learning outcomes (examples)	108
6.16	Assessment matrix re. work experience at a Bachelor's level of policing (EQF6)	109
6.17	Comparing competencies	111
11.1	Basic training modules	180
11.2	Special courses for handlers of dogs	181
13.1	Educational qualifications of Cohort One	212

13.2   Educational qualification of Cohort Two   212
13.3   Training syllabus   216
13.4   Module 6 Traffic   217
13.5   Responses to Question 5b   220
14.1   Original structure of the foundation degree in policing
        incorporating IPLDP   242
14.2   Original structure for the UCPD for police community
        support officers   243
15.1   Security 'traditionalists' versus 'modern entrepreneurs'   257
15.2   The state of training for key security occupations pre- and
        post 2001 legislation   267

Contributors

Al Arsenault is a retired constable from Vancouver Police with 27 years experience. He earned a BSc Hons from McMaster University in Geography and Geology (1977) and a BEd from Queen's University in Geography and Physical Education (1978). He is an expert in the martial arts and non-firearm weaponry and has trained and educated others globally. He is also a published author and film-maker. He was presented with the 'Shield of Merit' in 1980 for being the top recruit. In 2005 he was chosen as the 'Police Officer of the Year'. He co-founded Police Judo which he continues to teach at Simon Frazer University and the Justice Institute British Columbia. He is currently writing a book on police judo and the history and development of this model of training.

Nick Bell has been in the emergency management field for over 13 years. He started his career in the Ministry of Forests Protection Branch in British Columbia. In 2003 he was hired by West Vancouver Police department and has spent the past nine years working in law enforcement. He is currently an acting sergeant instructing at the police academy. Nick has a BA in Anthropology from the University of Victoria and a master's degree in Disaster and Emergency Management from Royal Roads University. He is currently pursuing postgraduate work in the field of international criminal law through the University of London.

Michael Berlin, JD, PhD, is Director of the Criminal Justice Graduate Program and Assistant Professor at Coppin State University in Baltimore, Maryland. He previously served as a Professor of Criminal Justice at Baltimore City Community College. He is an attorney with more than 20 years' experience in private practice and is a former Baltimore Police Officer. He served as an instructor at the International Law Enforcement Academy in Roswell, New Mexico, where he taught police supervisors from around the world. He was named instructor of the year by the Maryland Police Training Commission in 2003 and received the Distinguished Graduate Faculty Award from Coppin State University in 2012. His recent publications include *Crime Scene Searches and the Fourth Amendment* and *The Evolution, Decline and Nascent Transformation of Community Policing in the United States: 1980–2010*.

Johan Bertilsson is a sergeant and also a self-defence, firearms and tactics instructor. From 2005 he has been employed as Chief Self-Defence Instructor at Skåne County Police Department in the Swedish National Police Force. Since 2009 he has been a PhD student at the Department of Clinical Sciences at Lund University. His research interests include perceptive, cognitive and motor skill performance influenced by prior training and the effects of psychological and physical stress.

Mark Button is Professor of Criminology and Director of the Centre for Counter Fraud Studies at the Institute of Criminal Justice Studies, University of Portsmouth. He has written extensively on counter fraud and private policing issues, publishing many articles and chapters, and completing six books with one forthcoming. He completed his undergraduate studies at the University of Exeter, his master's at the University of Warwick and his doctorate at the London School of Economics.

Allison Chappell, PhD, is Associate Professor in the Department of Sociology and Criminal Justice, Old Dominion University in Norfolk, Virginia. She earned her PhD in Sociology from the University of Florida in 2005. She conducts research in the areas of policing and juvenile delinquency. Her work has appeared in journals such as *Journal of Contemporary Ethnography*, *Crime and Delinquency* and *Justice Quarterly*.

Annette Crisp is Senior Lecturer at De Montfort University in the Community and Criminal Justice Department. With a background in both public and private sectors she has specific expertise and research interest in the impact of complex systems on the organization, management and training of police officers and members of the wider police family. Having audited the IPLDP for the Home Office she has subsequently developed and taught on training programmes for senior officers, PCSOs and constables.

Peter Fredriksson is a sergeant and has worked as both firefighter and paramedic before working as a police officer. He is a tactics, firearms and self-defence instructor and developer of strategies concerning tactics and training in the Skåne County Police Department. His research interests include performance influenced by psychological and physical stress and ways to conceptualize needed adaptation for such situations.

Tracey Green has 22 years police experience as a sworn officer in the UK. She has extensive experience in the areas of serious and serial criminal investigation, in particular homicide, drug and police corruption. Since joining Charles Sturt University, Professor Green has been a strong advocate of policing as a profession and collaboration between law enforcement agencies and education and research related to policing. She has been instrumental in the development of postgraduate courses in the areas of investigation, intelligence, terrorism and police leadership.

Toby Hinton is a sergeant with the Vancouver City Police Department with 24 years of experience of street-level policing. He works in the notorious Downtown Eastside of Vancouver and is currently a beat patrol team sergeant. He has a BA in Political Science and Criminology from Simon Fraser University in British Columbia. He has a black belt in judo and is one of the instructors for VPD Police Judo, Simon Frazer University Police Judo, and the Justice Institute of British Columbia Police Judo program.

Cédric Moreau de Bellaing received his PhD in political science in Sciences Po Paris. He is now Assistant Professor in Political Science and Sociology of Law at the École Normale Supérieure in Paris. His research fields include police institutions, law, violence, war and peace.

Peter Neyroud, CBE, QPM, is a well-known former Chief Constable and Chief Executive of the National Police Improvement Agency. He most recently led the Home Office Review of Police Leadership and Training, more commonly known as the Neyroud Report (2011), and has written widely on policing matters. He holds several academic positions. He is a visiting professor at the University of Chester, a visiting fellow at Nuffield College Oxford and a research associate at the Centre for Criminology, University of Oxford.

Harry Peeters, PhD, retired from the Police Academy of the Netherlands in April 2013 after decades of experience as a police educator, trainer, consultant and academic. He has worked around the world and for numerous policing agencies including Interpol and was the programme director of the MSc in Policing in collaboration with Canterbury Christ Church University, UK. He has written and presented a large number of technical reports and papers in various European countries and elsewhere in the world.

Fórizs Sándor, PhD, is Professor at the National University of Public Services and a retired brigadier-general in the Hungarian Police. He has been a member of the Scientific Council of the doctoral school of the Zrínyi Miklós National University of Defence (currently the Faculty of Military Sciences and Officer Training, National University of Public Service). His area of interest is police education and training in the European Union countries and developments in EU policing.

Perry Stanislas, PhD, has over 30 years international experience in non-state and state policing. He was the first full-time civilian policy advisor for a police organization specializing in human resource management and quality of service. Perry was a key leader of 'Towards 2000', a major total quality police change programme. He received his PhD from the London School of Economics and is Senior Lecturer at De Montfort University. His areas of interest are domestic and international policing with an emphasis on the developing world. He has been published in *Safer Communities Journal* and *Interventions*: *An International Journal of Postcolonial Thought*.

Yang Tingyou, PhD, graduated from Sichuan International Studies University in 1990 and since then has taught college-level English and Police English at Sichuan Police College and is Associate Professor. She also teaches 'peacekeeping' to police officers in Sichuan Province and has published approximately 20 provincial-level papers on matters related to police education and training. She also participated in the state-level research programme 'Practical English' Multimedia Software Development in 1999.

Neil Wain is a former assistant chief constable with Greater Manchester Police. He is currently resident scholar at the Jerry Lee Centre of Criminology at Cambridge University. He has delivered police training programmes in the UK, US and Caribbean, most recently as Joint Director of the Indian Police Service Mid-Career Training Programme. He is the vice president of the British Society of Evidence Based Policing (www.sebp.police.uk), which, as part of its aims, seeks to facilitate a partnership between researchers, academics and police practitioners.

Alison Wakefield, PhD, is Senior Lecturer in Security Risk Management at the Institute of Criminal Justice Studies, University of Portsmouth, and a director of the Security Institute. Her publications include *Selling Security: The Private Policing of Public Space* (Willan Publishing, 2003); *The Sage Dictionary of Policing*, edited with Jenny Fleming (Sage, 2009); and *Ethical and Social Perspectives on Situational Crime Prevention*, edited with Andrew von Hirsch and David Garland (Hart Publishing, 2000).

Rosemary Woolston is Assistant Professor and head of school of Policing Studies at Charles Sturt University, Australia. Prior to joining the university she was a detective sergeant with the New South Wales Police and is experienced in generalist and specialist policing areas. She has extensive experience in the field of child protection. She has lectured on Police Practicum subjects within the Diploma of Policing Practice and coordinated investigations, child protection, domestic violence and mental health subjects within the Bachelor of Policing (Investigations).

Stu Wyatt is a police officer of 25 years in the Province of British Columbia, Canada and has served in a variety of sections including Training, Recruiting and Forensic Identification. He recently completed a 4½ year assignment at the Justice Institute of British Columbia – Police Academy, as a legal instructor. He has an extensive interest in forensic investigation and has authored *Forensic DNA Evidence: Investigative Procedures for Law Enforcement* (Ministry of Advanced Education, 2001). He has lectured on forensic evidence in numerous places including Santiago, Chile.

1 Introduction

Police education and training in context

P. Stanislas

All around the world police leaders and their organizations face problems with improving aspects of their performance. On occasions these issues can involve relatively minor improvements or adjustments in practice, while in other instances organizational and performance problems can be more widespread and potentially endemic, requiring a number of interventions or strategies to bring about meaningful change and improved outcomes. Another set of factors in understanding the processes linking demands for change in police practice and outcomes are the key actors involved in this process both locally and internationally. This book critically examines the role of police training, education and development and organizational change and the key stakeholders involved. This collection of essays explores practices in police training and education drawn from around the world and the factors which are changing them, and provides a lens for understanding important developments, similarities, and differences in world policing.

While some policing jurisdictions may face relatively straightforward challenges in improving their organizations' performance, other difficulties faced by police leaders are more complex, as highlighted by the following instance.

In 2008 a beleaguered Jamaican Deputy Commissioner of Police announced his support for training and education to increase the awareness and sensitivity of his officers towards social diversity and human rights (*Jamaican Gleaner* 2008). The recognition of these previously unrecognized needs came as a result of the Jamaican police becoming central characters in an international controversy about homophobia, driven primarily by Western activists (Stanislas 2013). The increase in popular homophobia, which emerged in Jamaica since the late 1980s, fuelled by the emergence of AIDS (Carr 2003) and more importantly the impact of globalism and rising poverty (Stanislas 2013) is witnessed in the increased intolerance against the Jamaican gay and lesbian population. The Jamaican police has been criticized for the important role it plays in reproducing these attitudes, as illustrated by its treatment of victims of homophobic-based crimes.

The problems experienced by the Jamaican police leadership are compounded by dissatisfaction from wide sections of society about the quality of policing received (Jones 2003), characterized by a history of police violence and human rights abuses which has earned it a poor reputation (Manning 2007; *Jamaican Gleaner* 2011). Many of these issues have a human resource management component in terms of remedies, which is highlighted by Harriot (2009) and in the various chapters of this book, but more specifically a training and education dimension in terms of philosophies of policing, issues around citizenship, social diversity and inclusion and the use of force inter alia.

The Jamaican example illustrates how local and transnational pressures are paramount in creating the environment contemporary police organizations have to negotiate and the important role those involved in police education and training potentially play in this process. The greater awareness of the experiences of citizens around the world of unsatisfactory police performance is highlighted in the International Victimization Crime Survey (IVCS) and the growth of its use, and similar types of research (Mawby and Walklate 1994; Zvekic 1998). Initially an initiative of the Dutch Justice Ministry, the IVCS, which first gained popularity in North America and Western Europe, is now being embraced around the world to include developing nations and those in transition, as an important means to gauge public experiences of criminal victimization and the criminal justice system (Zvekic 1998; Alvazzi del Frate 2003). Countries as diverse as former communist nations to those in the African southern hemisphere are increasingly subjecting their police organizations to critical scrutiny and demanding higher standards, as Kratcoski and Das (2007: 5) explain:

> As societies are getting developed in civilization, freedoms, education and in communication, the expectation from police organizations, which are the organs of state, increases. Especially the society is not only expecting the police to do its basic duties, but also expecting him to carry these out with tolerance [in a] kindly way.

The sentiments of Kratcoski and Das are reinforced by international standards promoted by influential transnational bodies such as the United Nations (see Cheah 1997; Painter and Farrington 1999) which can serve as a resource for those seeking to bring about reform in their countries.

The training and education of police officers is not only important in the context of preparing the police to respond to a variety of contemporary changes, but is significant in terms of the sheer scale and amount of time, personnel and other resources it takes up and the various forms training and education can take. This is particularly pronounced in countries with long histories of political stability, economic prosperity, and with advanced policing systems (Hinton and Newburn 2009; Kratcoski and Das 2007). Mawby (2007), for example, notes that in many countries enhanced training and education in how to respond effectively to victims now constitutes a standard feature of the preparation of police officers. However, even in poor parts of the world where police organizations suffer from lack of material resources, training and education activities can still take up a considerable amount of resources. This is illustrated in Jones and

Satchell's (2009) review of the growing training and education infrastructure for police and public safety officials in the English-speaking Caribbean and Latin America, while Munanura (2007) informs us that the Masindi Police Training School in Uganda has a staff of 56, of which 36 are trainers.

The decentralized and devolved character of decision-making around police education and training in many western liberal democratic policing systems, makes it difficult to ascertain how much of the police budget is spent on these activities (Jarvis 1992; Brew 1995). Even though Kratcoski and Das (2007: 13) have noted that in some countries the amount spent on formal training and education by the police is mandated by legislation, calculating the financial and resource costs of training, education, and development activities is further complicated by the fact that many wanting to join the police may privately pursue education or similar development activities independently to prepare themselves or throughout their policing career (Marenin 2007; Cordner and Shain 2011). The notion of making those wanting to join the police responsible for their initial pre-entry education and training, and the financial costs involved, is a model gaining increased attention in England and Wales (Wood and Tong 2010; Patterson 2011) and already established in parts of Canada and the US (Cordner and Shain 2011: 282).

In Hungary the practice of making recruits pay for their initial training if they fail to remain with the police for a stipulated period enables the Hungarian police to recoup its initial outlay (Sándor, this collection). This practice addresses one dimension of an important debate about police training and education practice in parts of the world (Reaves 2009; Cordner and Shain 2011: 282). The change to a pre-employment model of police education and training in England has been driven by efforts to reduce costs which is one dimension of various discourses calling for major reform of the British police (O'Malley 1997; Loveday 2006).

The issue of managing and evaluating resources involved in achieving desired outcomes is an increasingly important aspect of the work of police managers around the world (O'Malley 1997; McLaughlin 2007). The area of police human resources management is an important focus for these concerns. Veic and Mraovic (2007) highlight the work of the Croatian Police's Department of Professional Improvement and Specialization. The DPIS is responsible for identifying police education and training needs and how they can be best met. A glimpse into the potential resources implications of training for advanced policing systems can be inferred from the remarks of Kratcoski and Das (2007: 5):

> Those in specialized crime control units might receive advanced training in cybercrime, narcotics, juvenile crime, arson investigations, forgery, organized crimes, and vice-related or violent crime. For others, advanced training might be technical, related to advance photography, computer skills, or new types of equipment for traffic control. The topics covered in the advanced training often were expansions of the more general knowledge provided in earlier courses.

Many of the types of training and education mentioned above are also provided in the policing systems of the former communist European nation of Hungary which has a comprehensive provision of education and training for police officers and civilians, working for the police and public security and emergency response services, and examined by Sándor in Chapter 11. The cost of training and education provision in a relatively small country like Hungary is potentially very expensive and compares favourably with some of the more advanced policing training systems in the world.

Definition of education and training

A crucial issue central to the development of police officers is the type of informational and other inputs provided to help them effectively carry out their various functions. Training is generally defined as formal activities designed to improve human performance in carrying out specific functions, and as a result improve the efficiency of the role holder (Kirkpatrick 1998). This process usually entails passing on skills and knowledge by more experienced practitioners to those less familiar with relevant requirements. The basic elements of a good training programme have been described as consisting of, in the first instance, planned achievable learning activities with clear objectives. These can include theoretical, behavioural, and applied elements which are measurable (Kirkpatrick 1998: 12; Knowles *et al.* 2005). Learning is informed by an appropriate syllabus and taught by experienced and appropriately qualified tutors (Laird 1985: 285–287; Kirkpatrick 1998: 74–75).

A final characteristic of effective training and education is that programmes have systems of assessment and evaluation to ensure learning outcomes have been achieved (Laird 1985: 267; Rowe and Garland 2007). This process is multidimensional and can consist of assessing whether training and education programmes meet their learning objectives, in terms of students or trainees being able to demonstrate their improved understanding and abilities periodically, throughout the training programme or at its conclusion. It can also include the contribution of such inputs to the improved capacity of individuals to achieve organizational goals. How learning demonstrated in classrooms or other learning environments transfers to the actual work place is fundamental to this form of evaluation (Laird 1985: 267–272; Werth 2009). By the same token, how work experience is accredited in order to qualify for further development is another dimension of this process which is addressed by Peeters in his chapter.

Training has traditionally been viewed as being concerned with a narrow body of knowledge or skills, such as understanding appropriate legislation and how to apply it by police recruits (Birzer 2003). Training also provides psychological and emotional benefits in helping recruits identify with and feel part of the recruiting organization (Conser and Russell 2003) which is one phase of a longer socialization process (Fielding 1986; Conti 2006). The essential characteristics of education can be viewed as the provision of a body of knowledge designed to shape the individual's understanding and decision-making (Laird

1985; Roberg *et al.* 2002). Another precise definition of education is offered by Jarvis (2010: 41) as a 'planned series of incidents having a humanistic basis directed to the participants learning and understanding'. In its essence education seeks to improve and expand the knowledge and cognitive skills of the subject through planned interventions (Kratcoski and Das 2007: 4).

Conventional thinking about the preparation for police work defines the activities and processes involved under the rubric of training, characterized by a top-down approach to the transmission of knowledge and skills (Birzer 2003; Conser and Russell 2003). This conceptualization has been challenged (Jarvis 1992; Brew 1995; Conser and Russell 2003: 233). These authors argue that policing involves much more than passively applying precepts and practices taught in training, and can entail activities which are traditionally defined as educational in character. Examples of this are the use of analytical reasoning and problem-solving in resolving disputes. What links training and education for authors such as Laird (1985), Birzer (2003) and Wood and Tong (2008: 302) is the utilization of appropriate learning methods that complement the needs of target groups and the specific outcomes in question. This view has important implications for the role of tutors/instructors and how they perform their role and the pedagogic techniques relied on. Laird, Birzer and others reject the traditional training versus education dichotomy and adopt a more pragmatic and contingent view around the best technical means to produce desired outcomes.

The image of the trainer/educator coming from this view is an informed and flexible practitioner able to utilize various approaches and techniques ranging from traditional lectures, student-centred approaches, discussions, group work, role play and simulations, and use of technology and equipment (see Jarvis 2010, Sheldon and Wright 2010). Interestingly, despite the array of methods of delivery available to modern trainers and educators, which include the use of internet and distance learning (Cordner and Shain 2011), instructor-led programmes, according to US research continues to be a popular form of learning (Knowles *et al.* 2005: 296). However, as Cordner and Shain (2011: 282) note worries about costs is increasing the popularity of these alternative forms of delivery. The role and importance of the trainer transcends issues of style and methods of delivery. Trainers are very important role models and leaders and play a crucial role in the psychological conditioning and socialization of police officers, as highlighted by Moreau de Bellaing in his chapter.

Contemporary thinking emphasizes the overlapping and complementary nature of training and educational activities, which for Kratcoski and Das (2007) reflects the changing nature of police work. Contemporary policing according to them is carried out by knowledge workers, more so than skilled workers involved in routine and predictable work tasks and environments. However, a significant amount of all police work involves carrying out routine and predictable activities such as taking statements, compiling case files, and keeping or updating records (Rogers and Lewis 2007). Given the role of policing within the system of criminal justice administration in any country, these types of tasks and the bureaucratic aspects of police work are unlikely to change and may well be increasing in parts of the world (see Berlin and Chappell's chapters in this volume; Neyroud 2011: 41). Improving policing standards also too often means increasing paperwork and administration for police personnel. Kratcoski and Das are correct in that important aspects of contemporary policing require new skills and abilities in, for example, understanding other societies, systems, and practices. This can be seen in the area of policing transnational crime and terrorism in particular (Bowling and Sheptycki 2010). The chapter by Neyroud and Wain examines some of these issues and the role of an important training programme for middle-ranking officers in the Indian Police Service which is delivered in different parts of the world. Similar concerns inform the education and training of police and public security officials in China as described by Tingyou in her chapter.

The importance of police education and training

It is perhaps indicative of the difference between the status of police education and training as an area of research compared to its importance in practical terms (Jarvis 1992: 407) that very little is known about the amount of police resources that are dedicated to training and educating its personnel (Cebulla *et al.* 2007: 3). This is particularly pertinent in the area of recruit training which is the most intensive form of police training and of longer duration (Berlin, this collection). The importance of education and training as a generic area of activity is illustrated in the US context by Knowles *et al.* (2005: 297), who trace the growth of the training sector in the last three decades into what at the time of writing had become a US$30 billion industry, with 15 million employees participating in 1.7 million courses. It is the desire to throw light on the importance of education and training activities in the area of policing, in order to start exploring these and other pertinent issues, that this book finds its purpose. Education and training is a fundamental and significant activity in the preparation and ongoing development of the police, from entry ranks to those responsible for supervision, management, and leadership of the police organization. It is also important for the growing number of civilian staff who are playing an increasingly important role in policing in many jurisdictions around the world, and other areas of public and private safety (Loveday 2006; Paterson 2011). Wakefield and Button highlight the importance of ex-police and military personnel to the British private security industry in their chapter, given the superior levels of training they receive compared to other sources of personnel.

Training and educational activities not only appear to draw heavily on domestic resources, they also constitute a key element in international development funding of government and agencies (Bayley 2006; Hinton and Newburn 2009). Examples of this are assisting the establishment of new police organizations in previously war-torn countries such as Serbia or Somalia or introducing democratic policing in former communist countries (Zvekic 1998: 206; Brogden and Nijhar 2005: 193–198). Martin (1998) in his study of international funding in the area of criminal justice reform, notes that in countries such as Russia the majority of funding, running into millions of US dollars, has gone to reforming the police at the expense of other institutions and agencies (see Beck and Chistyakova 2002, and Sándor ibid.).

While the expenditure on police development activities is increasingly becoming an important matter, in some jurisdictions (Cordner and Shain 2011, Paterson 2011), one area which has not gained such attention is the issue of the evaluation of the effectiveness of training and education. Outside a small number of studies carried out largely in the US (see Marion 1998; Werth 2009; Carlan 2007) and in Britain (Wood and Tong 2010; Heslop 2011) there is very little research about the effectiveness of these activities, compared to the amount of it that takes place in police organizations around the world. One of the important issues these studies highlight is the differences in the subjective evaluation of police officers in terms of the impact education and training activities have on them as individuals. Another is the problem of assessing objectively changes in how the police perform their tasks (Paterson 2011: 293). Assessing competency in practice according to Jarvis (2010: 237) is a very difficult task. He uses the use of judgement to illustrate his point and argues that what makes a good prac-titioner is often their understanding of knowing when *not* to act in many instances. Competency-based systems of evaluation according to Jarvis are very poor at assessing the competence of non-action. Werth (2009) throws light on some of the important challenges involved in measuring the effectiveness of training interventions given the complex number of variables which impact on how police officers perceive and respond to issues. These issues are highlighted in Moreau de Bellaing's chapter on training police in France in the use of viol-ence and Arsenault and Hinton's chapter on self-defence training in Canada.

Notions of training and education in many societies are infused with modern-ist assumptions about the nature of knowledge and the capacity to solve human problems (Blaschek 1992; O'Malley 1999). These notions are playfully exposed by a veteran training colleague, who had the habit of pre-empting individuals in conversation, in anticipation of a problem being posed, by saying 'Of course training is the answer – what is the question?' At the root of this provocative remark is a critique of the fetishism of training for training's sake without con-sideration of its appropriateness for particular problems or other ways of achiev-ing desired outcomes. This observation is not unique to policing but a reflection of a broader management and political culture driven by the desire for visible action (Laird 1985: 61; Brew 1995: 3–5). As Laird (1985) points out an important precondition in using training interventions, as a means to address per-formance issues, is the recognition and distinction that needs to be made between genuine training issues and problems that have their roots elsewhere.

Institutional and organizational culture(s) and police education and training

A good example of the way training is often utilized as an inappropriate remedy for organizational problems can be seen in the MacPherson Report (1999) heralded as a groundbreaking document in which the London Metropolitan police was described as institutionally racist. MacPherson's explanation of institutional racism is not rooted in the personal or group attitudes of police officers themselves but viewed largely as a product of police practices routinely carried out without much thought (Singh 2000; Rowe and Garland 2007). Despite this, improved training in racial awareness and social diversity is one of the primary recommendations coming from the inquiry (MacPherson 1999, Chapter 47). MacPherson is not alone in the conspicuous silence among key stakeholders about remedies that address institutional racism, both in its routine and non-routine and newer forms (see Stanislas 2013). The most obvious being the practices which result in ethnic minority youth disproportionately being the subject of police surveillance and control in the form of stop and search, which has increased since the terrorist attacks of 2005 (Spalek 2008; see Chappell, Chapter 16).

The attempt to eliminate racial prejudice has driven the development of important aspects of police training and development in the UK and the US and is explored by Stanislas in Chapter 4. These are also issues of sensitivity which police training seeks to address in China (see Tingyou, Chapter 12), and in Hungary (Sándor, Chapter 11) and other countries with histories of ethnic tensions. Developing an appreciation of what training cannot achieve is as important as an emphasis on what it can achieve (Laird 1985: 61–65). These types of considerations are particularly important in countries trying to reform their police organizations where structural inequalities are closely linked to how policing has developed and is carried out (Zvekic 1999; Hinton and Newburn 2009: 12). In Northern Ireland transformation of the police is linked to efforts to increase the representation of the excluded Catholic community throughout society (Brogden and Nijhar 2005: 210–216). While training and education interventions may play a crucial role in transforming police organizations trying to address particular issues, in others their effectiveness is contingent on more fundamental changes elsewhere.

The issue of institutional practices is intrinsically related to the vexed question of organizational cultures and how formal training and education impacts on how the police carry out their various tasks (Wilson 1978; Grimshaw and Jefferson 1987). The answer to this type of question would to a significant degree depend on what role the individual police officer is expected to carry out, and the counter-prevailing forces and factors working against them complying with taught practice (Cummings and Huse 1989: 420–431). Despite the variety of training and education that takes place within many police organizations or is received by their personnel, the issue of institutional and cultural constraints and their impact on behaviour has been discussed most widely in relation to the norms which shape the work of frontline patrol or 'street cops' who carry out police work that the public are most familiar with (Wilson 1978; Grimshaw and Jefferson 1987). These researchers' findings indicate a two-tier system of education and training for the new police recruit. The first and formal phase takes place primarily in training establishments, under the guidance of instructors and tutors (Chappell 2008). The second and most important phase is provided by experienced officers on the ground, into how to carry out 'real police work' and the values and practices that inform this worldview (Grimshaw and Jefferson 1987: 124–128; Conti 2006).

The prevailing view is that the occupational culture of the street cops is more influential in the transmission of knowledge and skills, in most key areas, than that received formally. However, these findings are relatively dated and suggest a stable and unchanging work environment and an occupational culture which is capable of co-opting new challenges within a traditional paradigm of the world. This way of viewing police occupational culture conjures up an image of a relatively insulated village largely untouched by the changes of the outside postmodern world described by so many (Reiner 1992; McLaughlin and Murji 1999). It also posits an unchanging image of police recruits, and those who supervise them to a lesser extent, who seamlessly fit into this world. This popular representation of police occupational culture has been questioned by Janet Chan (2005) who introduces a plurality of occupational cultures within the police organization each susceptible to change under appropriate conditions.

Chan's observations notwithstanding, the formal training and education of police officers and its benefits may be more clearly discernible in societies with weaker policing traditions, where widespread dissatisfaction exists about police practice among officers themselves and other stakeholders. Unlike their counterparts in more affluent parts of the world, police officers in other regions, such as South Asian and many African countries, where policing is seen as a low status occupation, police officers are less content, poorly paid and resourced, and forced to work in substandard conditions (Onoja 2005; Brogden and Nijhar 2005: 165–167). They may also have had less quality training (Van Zant 2005). In these circumstances new training regimes may serve more than instrumental purposes, but also represent efforts to improve the social standing of the police by inculcating new values and be positively embraced by officers as highlighted in Stanislas' case study on recruit training reform in St Lucia.

Lessons from Australia highlight that, even in a prosperous country, transformation in policing practice was an outcome of a national scandal about corruption in the New South Wales Police (Woods 1997; Chan and Dixon 2007). The controversy brought to light a dysfunctional police culture throughout the entire organization (Chan and Dixon 2007). Education and training played a critical role, along with other important reforms, in improving the NSWP which is examined by Green and Woolston in their chapter.

The international sharing of experience and learning

The sharing of experiences between police from different parts of the world has been an important feature of modern policing and can be seen in the events that led up to the creation of Interpol and the work of international professional associations (Pustinev 2002: 89; Andreas and Nadelmann 2006). Organizations such as the International Association of Police Chiefs play a particularly important role in influencing police practice worldwide. The sharing of information is particularly important in terms of disseminating ideas around training and educational matters and can take a number of forms. It can include officers attending educational and training events in countries outside of their own, or formal educational courses at universities (Bowling 2010: 76; Tingyou, Chapter 12). Employing consultants or seconding specialist training officers is another way in which ideas can be gained from other police organizations or bodies (Brew 1995: 11; Bayley 2006). A good example of the high value placed on sharing experience and facilitating policy transfer can be seen in the International Specialized Police Training Centre in Poland, which was established to achieve these objectives (Ptywaczewski 2007). The creation of the European Police Academy is another example of an agency which came about due to the desire to facilitate the transfer of knowledge and to harmonize teaching content and standards for Central European countries (Jarvis 2010: 222–223). Other more obvious ways information can be shared in the 'information society' are books produced by specialist policing or educational publishers, academic and professional journals, and the use of internet and open or distance learning methods (Osborne and Thomas 2003).

Stakeholders and key actors in police training and education

Training and education constitutes the backbone of a significant amount of police activity in developing the most important resources involved in policing work: its personnel. Just as the work of the visible police officer is supported by a host of other personnel, training and education of police officers involves an array of actors and agencies, such as educational institutions, many of whom have a long and important relationship with police organizations. The best example of this is the FBI, one of the premier law enforcement agencies in the world and its longstanding relationship with institutions of higher education and research (Jones 2008). The type of stakeholders involved in police education and training according to Brew (1995) can include:

- Teachers and academics
- Researchers and those involved in curriculum development
- Administrators involved in policy development, course management
- Brokers and those involved in finding the best deal in terms of types of courses, programmes to meet staff needs
- Managers of resources (financial and personnel)
- Change agents, promoting and driving changes in practice
- Advisors, providing support to management and staff
- Counsellors, to help staff and managers deal with difficulties
- Consultants, to provide expertise in supporting teams of staff or managers on specific problems and issues
- Evaluators and regulators to assist in judging the quality of practice
- Appraisers who assist in evaluating staff performance and future needs
- Publishers who produce materials to support teaching and learning
- Disseminators who spread ideas and materials.

This book seeks to elucidate the importance of education, training, and development of police and the agencies and personnel involved in this area of activity. The chapters explore practice from around the world and the range of stakeholders involved in the education and training of police, public, and private security personnel. One of the omissions of the book is the lack of contributions in the areas of the teaching of scientific and technology matters. The hope of the author is that by raising the profile of the issue of the training and education of the aforementioned groups more contributions, especially in specialist fields, will be forthcoming. A sound start in documenting the types of technologies used in policing for education and training purposes is Foster (2004) and Sheldon and Wright (2010).

This book is organized around eight core themes which are highlighted below in the form of questions which, when taken together, help to provide a comprehensive framework for exploration of some of the most pressing issues in the historical and contemporary discussions around police training, education, and development.

1 What is education, training, and development? What are their benefits and limitations?

The processes used to facilitate the transfer of knowledge, understanding, and skills constitute the central concern of this collection. Stanislas' chapter explores the debate around police training versus police education and highlights that an important dimension of this debate is its link to deeper concerns about the occupational status of policing, which is an unresolved issue in many places around the world. Is policing to be considered a craft informed by an apprenticeship model (Jarvis 2010: 236) or is it a profession characterized by accredited forms of higher education as a precondition for entry and continuing education and development throughout a working career (Neyroud 2011)? In Western, and many other countries, these issues are part of an ongoing and evolving debate while, in other parts of the world, similar concerns are often hidden or implicit in other popular conversations. In the developing world issues around poor police performance, low levels of remuneration, and the calibre of recruits is often a localized manifestation of a historical and global discussion about the status of policing as an occupation (Emsley 2005: 77–79; Neyroud 2011: 29–31). In Hungary many of the key issues at the heart of this debate appear to be resolved around the view that policing is a professional activity requiring accredited and appropriately qualified graduates and postgraduates. These debates parallel those in the private security industry, albeit less well developed, which are explored in Wakefield and Button's chapter.

As many contributors illustrate in different ways the calls for higher levels of education for police officers takes place in a broader context of an increasingly educated population with greater access to higher education. As populations and professions increase their levels of education and training the police are held to similar expectations (Kratcoski and Das 2007: 5). This is highlighted in

Stanislas' chapters on the role of higher education and policing in Britain and the Eastern Caribbean country of St Lucia.

Proponents of the craft model of policing view formal training as potentially useful in many areas such as understanding procedural, mechanistic, and similar aspects of the job. However, the usefulness of formal training is viewed to be naturally limited given the inherent differences between where, what, and how issues are taught, compared to the social learning at the coal face. An important precondition for effective training is selection systems used to initially select appropriate individuals and screen out undesirables. These matters are addressed by Green and Woolston and Stanislas in their chapters, and touched on by Vargas (cited by Kratcoski and Das 2007: 7):

> It is very difficult to determine if a candidate has the strong moral character to be a good police officer, and it was also observed that no amount of training in ethics related to policing will change a person of low moral character.

The limits of training and education shaped by the personality of the individual is of particular importance in the teaching police the use of violence, where worries around the excessive use of force is an area of great sensitivity in many parts of the world and is examined by Arsenault and Hinton in the context of Canada, and Moreau de Bellaing in his ethnography of police training in France, and Bertilsson and Fredriksson in their chapter on firearms training in Sweden. By the same token, as pointed out by some of these authors, issues around personality may also feature in the reluctance to use force where appropriate with a number of adverse consequences.

2 Who is involved in the education and training of the police and public and private security officials?

Who is involved in the education and training of police personnel in the first instance is shaped by the type of police organization. In many poor parts of the world police training has been historically monopolized by police personnel, with the minor involvement of other professionals such as a nurse to teach first aid (Sinclair 2006). This type of limited outside involvement has been the traditional practice in Caribbean countries, with the exception of senior officers who receive training from abroad (Lee and Punch 2004; Bowling 2010). The numbers of actors involved in police training, both local and international in origin, has increased in these parts of the world (Bayley 2006: 7; Neyroud 2011: 126). Stanislas' chapter on St Lucia highlights the role of a private American college on the island and a number of other influences, which have contributed in creating greater openness and participation in police training.

In the wealthier countries of North America, Britain and parts of Western Europe there is a wider number of actors involved in the education and training process ranging from educational institutions, community and voluntary organizations, to name a few (and highlighted by Berlin and Chappell in this collection). The Chinese police have a unique relationship with local community security organizations who are often involved in co-delivery of police training (Tingyou ibid.), while in Japan there appears to be a practice of limiting the involvement of non-police personnel to the teaching of very specialist subjects, as opposed to any positive value placed on widening participation in itself (Das and Pinto 2007). One of the most important sets of institutional relationships in this generic area is that involving police training authorities and institutions of higher education and research. Green and Woolston's chapter charts the partnership between Charles Sturt University and the NSW police in Australia, and critically examines some important issues around developing durable working relationships. Bell and Wyatt in their chapter highlight the unique features of some Canadian private colleges and the type of specialist facilities they possess, which has earned them the recognition of official police training establishments; and illustrate some of the most advanced practices in world policing with significant import for non-state providers of police training and related services.

An important development over the last couple of decades in the area of policing has been the growth of the global private sector which can be seen in countries as diverse as Britain, Hungary, and South Africa (see Boda forthcoming, 1998; Bowling and Sheptycki 2010). However, very little is known about the education and training of private security personnel and the factors that influence and inform it, and if the Canadian lessons highlighted by Bell and Wyatt are taken, what is the potential scope for growth of this sector and the type of training and physical resources inter alia required to support it. Wakefield and Button's chapter examines private security training and is a welcome contribution to this growing area of interest. A final relatively new area of policing in terms of research and discussion is the growth of policing auxiliaries, who support the work of regular police officers, and exist in many parts of the world. Crisp explores the developments which brought into existence Police Community Safety Officers in England and Wales and the training and education they receive.

3 What are the dominant factors, and actors, that drive and inform police training and education policy and practice?

The influences that drive police training and education are often multidimensional in character and interrelated. Political factors are some of the most important in shaping government's attitude to the police and other public security officials' performance. This can be seen most clearly where countries are undergoing whole-scale political transformation, which is highlighted in the chapter on China. Political considerations and influences can be traced in the case studies of most contributors in this collection. Allison Chappell examines the development in the area of police education and training in the US over the decades and how, since the terrorist attacks of 9/11, the issue of protecting the homeland has become an important priority in police and public safety training with a range of adverse consequences. Individual initiative and leadership can also play a crucial role as highlighted in the St Lucian instance with import for the development of police officers.

Legislation is another important driver for education and training, with import for others involved in public and private security. It can have its source in domestic legislation as highlighted in Crisp's chapter on the formation and development of PCSOs and has a significant role in outlining the standards required in training private security personnel and highlighted in Wakefield and Button's case study. Both Chappell and Arsenault and Hinton remind us in their chapters that another source of legal influence on training requirements relates to matters of legal liability, covering a range of issues from discrimination, quality of service, or health and safety matters, which have become increasingly important concerns for police decision-makers in many parts of the world (see Baker forthcoming).

4 How is education and training of police and security personnel delivered? What does it consist of and where does it take place?

The most common forms of police training takes the form of unit based inputs or modular type courses that cover specific subjects which can combine several types of teaching in class and in the field. Other types of in-service training usually takes place in state run police training or specialists centres and are largely practice based and can consist of how to use equipment such as weapons, or vehicles, and techniques in carrying out difficult tasks (Neyroud 2011: 94–95). Recruit training in many countries can combine all of the aforementioned in terms of how it is delivered and where. Not all training is carried out on police premises: correspondence courses are popular in many countries in the world such as China, according to Tingyou in her chapter, which has adopted an approach to training and education utilizing a wide range of methods including encouraging and supporting self-schooling in the form of study groups where recruits teach each other.

Higher education institutions are increasingly providing education and training for police and security personnel at all levels in many parts of the world and, as illustrated in several case studies in the book, is a trend which is likely to grow. These institutions are intrinsically linked to debates around the professionalization of the police, which is examined by Berlin in the US, Green and Woolston in Australia, and Sándor in Hungary. Finally, unique features of countries often have import for specific elements of training content and where it is carried out. For example, compulsory sea swimming for St Lucian police recruits reflects the the island's small size, limited water-based rescue services, and that the police are likely to be first responders to many water-based incidents.

5 Who is the target for police education and training?

Most police officers will be the target for continuing training and education in one form of another some of which is mandatory. In the case of new recruits their ability to successfully negotiate basic training is fundamental to their ability to join the police organization as full members of the occupation. Once established, officers may undergo periodic training to update skills and knowledge and more specialist training for specific areas of work or if they seek promotion to higher rank (Sándor's and Wain and Neyroud's chapters). According to the occupational profiles developed by Peeters, all roles within the police organization require forms of continuing training and education. In the Hungarian system, examined by Sándor, police and civilian staff are required to undergo mandatory training and education from entry grades through a pathway into more career opportunities and specialisms, most of which require higher education qualifications.

6 How do historical and cultural factors shape reform and the kind of training and education provided?

The role that historical and cultural factors play in shaping policing and the subsequent training police receive in a given country can be seen in one way or another in all the case studies in the book. In some countries, their unique histories of conflict and social transformation have led to police and criminal justice reform playing a central role in creating new societies and notions of social order. This can be clearly seen in the Communist state of China and its policing reforms. Similar problems are evident in efforts to eradicate a colonial police heritage in St Lucia in order to respond to a new environment. In these societies police training has a salient position in improving the technical competence of the new police charged with meeting the expectations of an empowered citizenry but, also, in exemplifying new norms.

7 How are training outcomes assessed?

Policing scholars have long noted the difficulties in measuring the outcome of policing interventions and strategies. Sherman (2003) highlights this difficulty in areas such as crime prevention, while Werth (2009) and others have demonstrated similar problems in other areas of police work. Similar issues are explored in Chapter 5 in the areas of training and education which are compounded by the limited amount of time and effort spent on carrying out research on how to improve measurement in these areas. The search for measurement can potentially create disparate interpretations as in training in the use of violence as highlighted by Moreau de Bellaing, where effectiveness is potentially a highly disputed concept depending where one stands amongst a range of police views or the perceptions of those being policed.

8 Trends in future police training and education

Trying to establish clear patterns in international practice is not a straightforward affair. What is clear is the drive to improve, modernize, or professionalize the police in many countries around the world where training and education plays an important role. This is witnessed by an increasing presence of universities and other educational institutions in this process and potentially includes professional bodies. These trends parallel those taking place in the world of adult and further education in many countries (Osborne and Thomas 2003). Police organizations are placing greater emphasis on international education and transnational elements to their development activities. While part of this is shaped by jurisdictions contributing to international policing efforts under the rubric of transnational bodies or bi-lateral agreements (Bowling and Sheptycki 2010), the numbers of police personnel spending time in countries other than their own for development and work purposes is increasing. Another shared concern for police leaders around the world is the issue of finance and budgets (see Baker ibid.). Concerns about costs in all likelihood will continue to drive the development of distance and electronic learning methods both for domestic and international consumption. The types of practical benefits and savings reported by Wyatt and Bell in Canada, gained by the use of electronic based learning, almost guarantees this. Of particular interest here is whether the concerns for value for money and reduced public spending in countries such as the US and UK will result in reductions in the amounts spent on police education, training, and development. Berlin, in his chapter, offers a pessimistic prognosis in the case of the former. The indication provided by Chappell is that government priorities around securing the homeland from terrorism in the US may well drive the costs of training up or increase this priority at the expense of other areas of importance. Even in the less well-off countries of the English-speaking Caribbean countries of Jamaica and St Lucia, worries about crime and its impact on society, and particularly the national image in relatively small tourism-based economies, in all likelihood will contribute to continual searches for training-led remedies for improving the police. This form of intervention is cheaper and more politically rewarding, at least in the short term, than more fundamental system-wide organizational change. In India which historically spends a miniscule amount on police training, according to Neyroud and Wain, faces a particularly difficult challenge in balancing its economic and regional ambitions while maintaining its traditional attitude to spending on the police.

Book structure

The book is organized in four parts. Part I examines the factors that shape the content and design of contemporary police training, the actors involved and their relationships, and some of the debates informing the evolution of police education and training. Key amongst these is the issue of the status of policing and its relationship to institutions of higher education. Part II of the book examines the issue of preparing police officers for specific areas of police work. These case studies cover the areas of recruit police education, preparing officers for the use of violence, self-defence training, and the use of firearms. Also covered is the training and education of middle-ranking officers preparing for senior leadership. Part III of the book examines the historical and political influences driving the reform of police education and training in several countries undergoing major changes. Part IV explores contemporary developments in public policing with import for the private sector and the future character of police training around the world.

Conclusion

An important consideration of contributors to this collection is an examination of the various constraints and challenges that shape the training and education process. While police organizations around the world differ in terms of their own unique histories, political and cultural traditions, geographical challenges and other constraints, policing at its core consists of a set of shared activities which includes routine administrative work, carrying out regular or ad hoc patrolling of geographical areas, investigating crime and bringing suspects to court usually against their will (Zvekic 1998). This similarity in terms of functions and the way work is carried out provides the opportunity to explore the role education and training plays in policing across the world. This collection brings together specialist scholars and practitioners who throw light on important aspects of public service policing, and new areas of public and private provision, through the lens of training and development. It seeks to open the topic up to a much wider audience given the important issues explored in the book, and reflected in the diversity of contributors and topics they cover.

To proponents of a contemporary view of policing, there are very few limits or negatives associated with higher and continuing education and development. This view is shared by all the contributors to this collection. This does not suggest that they adopt an uncritical view of various ideas, designs or programmes and strategies that informs training, education, and development practices around the world. On the contrary, such an optimistic view of education and training is indicative of their underlying humanism and their view of human beings' social and learning potential, which underpins prevailing thinking on adult and continuing education and underpins the ethos of this book.

Bibliography

Alvazzi del Frate, A. (2003) *The Voices of the Victims of Crime: Estimating the True Level of Conventional Crime*, www.unodc.org/pdf/crime/forum/forum3_note4.pdf (accessed 12 February 2010).

Andreas, P. and Nadelmann, E.A. (2006) *Policing the Globe Criminalization and Crime Control in International Relations in International Relations*, Oxford University Press.

Baker, B (ed.) (forthcoming), Interviews with Global Leaders in Policing, Florida: CRC Press.

Bayley, D. (2006) Changing the Guard: Developing Democratic Policing Abroad, New York: Oxford University Press.

Beck, A. and Chistyakova, Y. (2002) 'Crime and Policing in Post-Soviet Societies: Bridging the Police/Public Divide', *Policing and Society*, 12(2): 123–137.

Beckford, M. (2012) *Cameron Urged to Get a Grip on Police Racism Allegations*, 9 April, www.telegraph.co.uk (accessed 10 April 2010).

Birzer, M.L. (2003) 'The Theory of Andragogy Applied to Police Training', *Policing: An International Journal of Police Strategies and Management*, 26(1): 29–42.

Blaschek, H. (1992) 'Austria Case Study' in P. Jarvis (ed.) *Perspectives on Adult Education and Training in Europe*, London: National Institute of Adult Continuing Education.

Bola, J. (forthcoming) 'Interview with Police Lieutenant General Dr Joseph Bencze, High Commissioner, Hungarian National Police', in B Baker (ed.) *Interview with Global Leader in Policing.*

Bowling, B. (2010) Caribbean Policing the Caribbean: Transnational Security Cooperation in Practice, Oxford: Oxford University Press.

Bowling, B. and Sheptycki, J. (2010) *Global Policing*, London: Sage Publication.

Brew, A. (1995) 'Directions in Staff Development', The Society for Research into Higher Education and Open University Press.

Brogden, M. and Nijhar, P. (2005) *Community Policing, National and International Models and Approaches*, Devon: Willan Publishing, Collumpton.

Carlan, P.E. (2007) 'The Criminal Justice Degree and Policing: Conceptual Development or Occupational Primer', *Policing an International Journal of Police Strategies and Management*, 30(4): 608–619.

Carr, R. (2003) 'On Judgements: Poverty, Sexuality-Based Violence and Human Rights in 21st Century Jamaica', The Caribbean Journal of Social Work, 2(7): 71–87.

Chan, J. (1996) 'Changing Police Culture', *British Journal of Criminology*, 36(1): 109–134.

Chan, J. and Dixon, D. (2007) 'The Politics of Police Reform: Ten Years After the Royal Commission into the New South Wales Police', *Criminology and Criminal Justice*, 7(4): 443–468.

Chappell, A.T. (2008) 'Police Academy Training: Comparing Across Curricula', *Policing an International: Journal of Police Strategies and Management*, 31(1): 36–56.

Cheah, P. (1997) 'Posit(ion)ing Human Rights in the Current Global Conjuncture', *Public Culture*, 9(2): 233–266.

Conti, N. (2006) 'Role Call: Preprofessional Socialization into Police Culture', *Policing and Society: An International Journal of Research and Policy*, 6(3): 221–242.

Conser, J.A. and Russell, G.A. (2000) *Law Enforcement in the United States*, Maryland: Aspen Publishing.

Cordner, G. and Shain, C. (2011) 'The Changing Landscape of Police Education and Training', *Police Practice and Research*, 12(4): 281–285.

Cummings, T. and Huse, E (1989) *Organisation Development and Change*, 4th Edition, New York: West Publishing.

Das, D.K. and Pinto, N.W. (2007) 'A Comparative Account of Police Training in Four Countries' in D.K. Das and P.C. Kratcoski, *Police Education and Training in a Global World.*

Emsley, C. (2005) 'The Birth and Development of the Police' in T. Newburn (ed.) *Handbook of Policing*, Cullumpton: Willan Publishing.

Fielding, N. (1986) 'Evaluating the Role of Training in Police Socialization: A British Example', *Journal of Community Psychology*, 14(3): 319–330.

Foster, R. (2004) *Police Technology*, Indiana: Pearson Press.

Garland, J., Rowe, M., and Johnson, S. (2002). *Police Community and Race Relations Training: An Evaluation*, University of Leicester.

Grimshaw, R. and Jefferson, T. (1987) *Interpreting Police Work*, London: Allen Unwin.

Harriot, A. (2009) Controlling Violent Crime Model and Policy Options, Grace Kennedy Foundation Lecture, Jamaica.

Heslop, R. (2011) 'Reproducing Police Culture in a British University: Findings from an Exploratory Case Study of Police Foundation Degrees', *Police, Practice and Research*, 12(4): 1–15.

Hinton, M.S. and Newburn, T. (2009) http://policing.oxfordjournals.org/content/5/4/377. extract, *Policing Developing Democracies*, Abingdon: Routledge.

Jamaican Gleaner (2008) Shields, Backs Sensitivity Training for Police Force, February 19, www.jamaican.gleaner.com (accessed 5 April 2012).

Jamaican Gleaner (2011) *Letter of the Day: The Police Must Improve Human Rights Record*, 6 January, www.jamican-gleaner.com (accessed 5 April 2012).

Jarvis, P. (1992) Perspectives on Adult Education and Training in Europe, National Institute of Adult Continuing Education.

Jarvis, P. (2010) Adult Education and Lifelong Learning, Theory and Practice, 4th edn, London: Routledge.

Jones, M. and Satchell, N. (2009) Data Gathering on Police Officers and Civil Service Training Courses in the Caribbean Region, prepared for Organisation of American States.

Jones, R. (2008) The FBI: A History, Yale University Press.

Kirkpatrick, D.L. (1998) *Techniques for Evaluating Training Programs*, San Francisco: Berrett Koehler.

Knowles, M.S. and Holton, E.F., and Swanson, R.A. (2005) *The Adult Learner. The Definitive Classic in Adult Education and Human Resource Development*, Amsterdam: Elsevier.

Kratcoski, P.C. and Das, D.K. (2007) Police Education and Training in a Global World, Plymouth: Lexington Books.

Laird, D. (1985) Approaches to Training and Development, 2nd edn., New York: Addison Wesley.

Lee, M. and Punch, M. (2004) 'Policing By Degrees: Police Officers' Experiences of University Education', *Policing and Society*, 14(3): 233–249.

Lewis, P. (2012) Police Inspector Latest to be Arrested for Alleged Racism, *Guardian*, 27 April.

Loveday, B. (2006) 'Workforce Modernisation: Implications for the Police Service of England and Wales', *The Police Journal*, 79: 105–123.

Manning, G. (2007) Police Excesses Worst in 2007, Jamaican Gleaner, 30 September, www.jamaican-gleaner.com (accessed 5 April 2012).

Marenin, O. (1998) 'United States Police Assistance to Emerging Democracies', *Policing and Society: An International Journal*, 8: 153–167.

Marion, N. (1998) 'Police Academy Training: Are We Teaching Recruits What They Need to Know', Policing: An International Journal of Police Strategies and Management, 21(1): 54–79.

Mawby, I.R. (2007) 'Public Sector Services and the Victims of Crime' in S. Walklate (ed.) *Handbook of Victims and Victim ology*, Devon: Willan Publishing.

Mawby, I.R. and Walklate, S. (1994) Critical Victim ology, London: Sage.

McLaughlin, E. (2007) *The New Policing*, London: Sage.

McLaughlin, E. and Murji, K. (1999) 'The Postmodern Condition of the Police', *The Liverpool Law Review*, 21: 217–240.

O'Malley, P. (1997) 'Policing, Politics and Postmodernity', *Social and Legal Studies*, 6(3): 363–381.

Osborne, M. and Thomas, E. (2003) *Lifelong Learning in a Changing Continent: Continuing Education in the Universities of Europe*, National Institute of Adult Continuing Education (England and Wales).

Painter, K. and Farrington, D. (1999) 'Criminal Victimization in a Caribbean Family', *International Review of Victim ology*, 6(1): 1–16.

Paterson, C. (2011) 'Adding Value? A Review of the International Literature on the Role of Higher Education in Police Training and Education', *Police Practice and Research*, 12(4): 286–297.

Ptywaczewski, W. (2007) 'Polish Police Training System and the Current Crime Threat' in P. Kratcoski and D. Das.

Reaves, B.A. (2009) *State and Local Law Enforcement Agencies Training Academies (2006)*, Bureau of Justice Statistics, Special Report.

Reiner, R. (1992) 'Policing a Postmodern Society', *The Modern Law*, 55(6): 761–781.

Roberg, R., Kuykendall, J. and Cordner, G. (2005) *Police and Society*, Edition 8, Los Angeles: Roxburg Publishing.

Rogers, C. and Lewis, R. (2007) *Introduction to Policework*, Devon: Willan Publishing.

Rowe, M. and Garland, J. (2007) 'Police Diversity Training: A Silver Bullet Tarnished?' in M. Rowe (ed.) *Policing Beyond Macpherson*, Cullompton: Willan.

Sheldon, B. and Wright, P. (2010) Policing and Technology: Policing Matters, Exeter: Learning Matters.

Sheptycki, J.W.E. (1998) 'Postmodernism and Transnationalization', *British Journal of Criminology*, 38(3).

Sherman, L. (2003) (ed.) *Evidence-Based Crime Prevention*, London: Taylor Francis.

Sinclair, G. (2006) *At the End of the Line, Colonial Policing and the Imperial Endgame 1945–80*, Manchester: Manchester University Press.

Singh, G. (2000) 'The Context and Concept of Institutional Racism' in A. Marlow and B. Loveday (eds.) After MacPherson: Policing After the Stephen Lawrence Inquiry, Dorset: Russell House Publishing.

Spalek, B. (2009) *Communities, Identities and Crime*, Bristol: The Policy Press.

Stanislas, P. (2013) 'Policing Violent Homophobia in the Caribbean and the British Caribbean Disaspora: Postcolonical Discourses and the Limits of Postmodernity', *International Journal of Postcolonial Studies*, Published Online May 8, DOI: 10.1080/1369801X.2013.798134.

Van Zant, E. (2005) 'Better Policing: Tackling The Problems Besetting The Bangladeshi Police Services Means Overcoming A Long History And Great Shortage Of Funds', Asian Development Bank Review, May.

Veic, P. and Mraovic, I.C. (2003) 'Police Training and Education: The Croatian Perspective' in P.C. Kratcoski and and D.K. Das (eds.).

Werth, E.P. (2009) 'Student Perception of Learning through a Problem-Based Learning Exercise: An Exploratory Study', *Policing: An International Journal of Police Strategies and Management*, 32(1): 21–37.

Wilson, J.Q. (1978) *Varieties of Police Behaviors: The Management of Law and Order in Eight Communities*, Harvard University Press.

Wood, D. and Tong, S. (2008) 'The Future of Initial Police Training: A University Perspective', *International Journal of Police Science and Management*, 11(3): 113–131.

Woods, J.R.T. (1997) *Royal Commission into the New South Wales Police*, Final Report Volume 1, Corruption, The Government of the State of New South Wales.

World Bank (2007) 'Crime, Violence, and Development: Trends, Costs, Policy Options in the Caribbean'. A Report by The United Nations Office of Drugs and Crime and the Latin America and Caribbean Region, March.

Zvekic, U. (1998) 'Policing and Attitude Towards Police in Countries in Transition: Preliminary Results of the International Crime Victim Survey', *Policing and Society: An International Journal of Research and Policy*, 8(2): 205–224.

Part I

The determinants of police training and education

2 An overview of police training in the United States, historical development, current trends and critical issues

The evidence

M. Berlin

This chapter provides an overview of police training in the United States. It examines the historical development of police training and discusses changes in training associated with the political, reform and community policing eras. It examines current trends and issues in law-enforcement education and training and considers the role of police training in advancing both traditional and contemporary policing strategies.

The chapter looks at contemporary police training in terms of goals and objectives, standards, oversight, curricula, content, instructional delivery and environment. It discusses the uneasy coexistence of reform and community policing era components in contemporary approaches to training. It looks at potential benefits and obstacles to the role of higher education in police training and considers different models of police and college/university partnership. The chapter concludes with a discussion of the most critical issues facing law-enforcement training today. These issues include the need to reconcile conflicts between traditional enforcement and community-centered policing through the strategic integration of training and departmental philosophy, as well as the need to maintain standards and introduce innovation in light of budget cuts occasioned by the recent economic crisis.

Police training in the US must be understood within the context of the legal, governmental and political framework in which police service is delivered. Unlike many other nations, the US has no national police department, and policing is the responsibility of state and local governments. The vast majority of policing in the US is local. The US Bureau of Justice Statistics indicates that there are 12,575 police departments at the city, county or town level (Reaves 2010). There are also approximately 3,012 sheriffs' departments, many of which are full-service law enforcement agencies, frequently found in rural and suburban jurisdictions. Municipal sheriffs' offices tend to be primarily responsible for providing courthouse security, staffing local jails or detention centres and service of warrants and court documents. In addition, there are 49 state police agencies for a total of 15,636 state and local police agencies (Reaves 2010).

Local control of policing is ensured through the appointment of the police chief by elected local government leaders, typically mayors or county executives.

In some instances, local legislative bodies such as city or county councils may control the appointment process. Sheriffs are elected public officials. As a result of their appointment powers, local political elected officials often play a critical role in the decision to implement policing strategies, thereby at least indirectly influencing training.

There are 648 state and local training academies (Reaves 2009) which can be categorized as follows: operated by academic institutions (two and four year colleges), municipal academies, sheriffs' academies, multi-agency academies, State police academies, POST academies, county police academies and other academies.

A greater number of academies of a particular type does not necessarily correlate to a greater number of cadets. For example, municipal academies tend to be far larger than academies operated by academic institutions.

State and local police agencies provide a variety of different types of training including entrance-level academy training, field training, in-service training, leadership/management training and a wide range of specialized training. More time and resources are devoted to entrance-level training than any other type of training. Average entrance-level training in 2006 was 761 hours or 19 weeks, not including field training. County/Municipal academies typically run longer, from 800 to 1,000 hours. POST (Police Officers Standards Commissions) Academies tend to be shorter at 604 hours. About one-third of academies require mandatory field training. Field training ranges from 225 to 1,678 hours with an average of 453 hours. The actual number of academy graduates who undergo field training may be higher, as some police departments require that new hires from unaffiliated college and university academies complete field training (Reaves 2009).

Local police training is typically regulated at the state level by a POST which mandates curriculum objectives and sets minimum performance standards for trainees. POST commissions had their origins in the early 1900s during the reform era of policing and have grown substantially over the past 100 years.

POST commissions often certify police academies and establish minimum requirements for those seeking to enter the profession. Many also provide for instructor certification and academy audits and inspections. The directors of police training commissions are frequently appointed by state governors.

Table 2.1 Types of police academies

Number	Types of police academies	Percentage
292	Operated by Academic Institutions (2 and 4 year colleges)	45
143	Municipal Academies	22
57	Sheriff's Academies	9
54	Multi-Agency Academies	8
44	State Police Academies	7
25	POST Academies	4
19	County Police Academies	3
14	Other Academies	2
Total		**100**

The historical evolution of policing provides a useful framework for understanding contemporary approaches to police training. Kelling and Moore (1988) summarize salient features of the three 'eras' of policing. Each era is characterized by differences in public perception of the primary sources of police legitimacy and authority and view of the police function, as well as differences in organizational design, external relationships between the police and the community (how police are summoned and the police resources allocated), inter alia.

The political era dates from the introduction of municipal police forces in the 1840s through the early 1900s. The political era was characterized by close ties between police commanders and local political leaders and was noted for its corruption. Police patrolled on foot, had frequent face to face contact with citizens and conducted rudimentary investigations. Police received little, if any, training during the political era. White (2007: 37) indicates that from 'the mid-nineteenth century to the early twentieth century [policing] was marked by very little professionalism, as police were essentially political appointees with no training and no-pre-service or in-service standards of conduct'. As a result of the lack of formalized training, 'new officers learned how to do the job from more senior personnel'. While there is some evidence to suggest that the New York City Police Department (NYPD) began training officers in the later part of the nineteenth century, the extent of that training appears to be limited (Grammage 1963).

The reform era took hold in the 1930s, reached its peak between the 1950s and 1960s, and began its decline in the 1970s. The reform era was characterized by a 'professional crime fighting' approach, relying upon routine patrol and quick response to calls for service and criminal investigations. The reform era was both a reaction to the corruption of the political era and an outgrowth of the trend toward scientific management (Kelling and Moore 1988). Both policing and police organizations became more professional and sophisticated during the reform era.

August Vollmer, a police chief and the first professor of Police Administration, is credited with establishing the first formal in-service training school for police officers. The school, which was founded in Berkeley, California in 1908 offered courses in law, first aid and photography (Gammage 1963). New York followed with a formal academy the following year, as did at least eight additional cities over the next decade. The FBI established a 12-week National Academy for the training of city, county and state police training officers in 1935. By 1959, all cities with a population over 250,000 had a recruit training program. Over half of cities with a population under 25,000 did not have a training program (Grammage 1963). Recruit training during this period followed a traditional, legalistic model consistent with the values of the reform era (Kelling and Moore 1988; Chappell 2008).

Police training literature from the late 1950s through the mid-1970s generally reflects the professional approach of the reform era and highlighted in the work of Frost (1959) and. Gammage (1963) and Harrison's (1964) *How to Teach Police Subjects: Theory and Practice*. The latter is a good example of a reform-era instructor's guide.

By today's standards, the language of these works appears stilted, and the approach to training seems legalistic and technical. They display a remarkable degree of sophistication and include significant coverage of instructional methodology, including a combination of lecture, demonstrations, field trips, roleplays, laboratories, conferences and discussion and appear to reflect educational theory of the time. Many of the issues and much of subject matter discussed in these works remain relevant to police academy curriculum and instruction today.

The community policing era began in the early 1980s in response both to rising crime and decreasing citizen satisfaction with the police. Oliver (2004) categorizes the new era of community policing as falling within three 'generations:' innovation (1979–1986), diffusion (1987–1994) and institutionalization (1995-present). The innovation generation included early foot patrol experiments, Goldstein's (1990) early work on problem-oriented policing and Wilson and Kelling's (1982) *Broken Windows* theory, focused on attention to quality of life offenses as a means of reducing crime and citizen fear.

The next generation of community policing, the diffusion generation, began in the mid-1980s. It was marked by the diffusion of community policing to medium and large metropolitan law enforcement agencies throughout the US (Oliver 2004). Community policing efforts during this period were generally, although not always, grant funded and involved multiple components, such as specialized units, foot patrol, partnership efforts and problem-solving. The third generation of community policing, which began in the mid-1990s and remains ongoing today, is characterized by its institutionalization of community policing and spread to small town and rural police agencies. During this period community policing became widespread and tended to involve multiple strategies such as improved police–citizen communication and community partnerships, increased attention to quality of life offenses and targeted enforcement of violent drug offenders. Despite clear evidence of extensive implementation of community policing, 'the ultimate and widespread institutionalization of community policing still remains somewhat uncertain' (Zaho *et al.* 1999: 89). Rank-and-file officers never entirely 'bought' into it, nor did management (Lurigio and Rosenbaum 1994).

Although community policing has been in existence for over 30 years, it has no commonly accepted definition. This lack of consensus has profound implications for training Cordner (2001) and others suggest that the broad range of concepts and activities associated with community policing require that it be defined on multiple levels.

Contemporary law-enforcement training reflects a mix of 'traditional' reform-era professional policing, coupled with more recent approaches to policing, particularly community policing, and to a lesser extent, CompStat (Reaves 2009) provides a summary of topics covered in entrance-level state and local law-enforcement training. He groups report groups topics into several broad categories: operations, weapons/self-defence, legal, self-improvement, community policing inter alia a variety of special topics – and breaks down the percentage of academies covering each topic and the median number of instructional hours allotted.

Table 2.2 Topics included in basic training of state and local law enforcement

Training academies, 2006

Topics	% academies with training	Median hours instruction
Operations		
Report writing	100	20 hours
Patrol	99	40 hours
Investigations	99	40 hours
Basic first aid/CPR	99	24 hours
Emergency Vehicle Operations	97	40 hours
Computers/Information Systems	58	8 hours
Weapons/self-defence		
Self-defence	99	51 hours
Firearms skills	98	60 hours
Non-lethal weapons	98	12 hours
Legal		
Criminal law	100	36 hours
Constitutional law	98	12 hours
History of law enforcement	84	4 hours
Self-improvement		
Ethics and integrity	100	8 hours
Health and fitness	96	46 hours
Stress prevention/management	87	5 hours
Basic foreign language	36	16 hours
Community Policing		
Cultural diversity	98	11 hours
Basic strategies	92	8 hours
Mediation skills/conflict management	88	8 hours
Special topics		
Domestic violence	99	14 hours
Juveniles	99	8 hours
Domestic preparedness	88	8 hours
Hate crimes/bias crimes	87	4 hours

The above list is not exhaustive, and many state and local law-enforcement agencies include additional topics in entrance-level training. The remarkably high percentage of academies covering operational, weapons/self-defence and legal aspects of training, as well as the comparatively high median number of instructional hours allotted to these subjects, reflects the continuing influence of the reform era. While approximately 90 per cent of state and local police training academies cover many of the community policing and special topics areas, the number of hours allocated to these areas is far fewer than the traditional topics. Analysis of a community policing curriculum requires far more than a comparison of the number of hours allocated to specific topics. Differences in instructors, instructional content, instructional methodology and academy environment must also be considered.

Much of the current police training literature arises from issues relating to community policing. Palmiotto (2000), Peak and Glensor (2004), Chappell *et al.* (2005, 2011) all address changes in training associated with community policing. These changes generally fall within three broad areas: changes in curricula/content; changes in instructional design, delivery and methodology; and changes in training environment. I address each of these areas in turn, following a brief discussion of the purposes of training.

Training is recognized as an essential means of transferring knowledge, skills and abilities (Goldstein 1993). It also plays a critical role in transmission of organizational values and organizational socialization (chapter one). As a result of developments during the reform era, police agencies recognize the value of training, particularly in areas such as law and procedures, report writing, patrol, arrest and control techniques, etc. Training in these and other subjects has grown substantially from the 1960s to the present. Much of the recent training literature focuses on entrance-level community policing training.

Curriculum development and content for entrance-level training involve input from many sources and are guided by a variety of mandates and processes. Reaves' (2009) report indicates that curriculum development includes input from academy staff's, 67 per cent subject matter experts, 53 per cent job task and needs analyses, 50 per cent departmental objectives, 46 per cent and legislative or regulatory mandates (45 per cent). 95 per cent of training academies follow state mandates to develop their curriculum (Reaves 2009). In many instances, these mandates are extensive. For example, the Maryland Police and Correctional Training Commission sets forth 16 terminal training objectives and several hundred enabling training objectives, all of which must be successfully completed for certification as a police officer.

Over 90 per cent of police academies included community policing in entrance-level training in 2006 (Reaves 2009). Table 2.3 shows community policing topics covered in state and local law-enforcement academies curriculum in 2006 and the percent of academies covering these topics:

Table 2.3 Percentage of academies

Topic	Percentage of academies
Identifying community problems	85
History of community policing	83
Environmental crime analysis	62
Prioritizing crime/disorder problems	62
Using problem-solving models	60
Organizing/mobilizing community	54
Assessing response effectiveness	45
Creating problem-solving teams	43
Analysing crime/calls for service data	38
Using crime mapping to analyse problems	36
Applying research methods to study crime.	35

While the range of topics associated with community policing appears quite broad, the hours devoted to these topics are limited. Median hours for community policing training totaled approximately 27 hours, broken into the following categories: cultural diversity 11 hours taught by 98 per cent of academies; basic strategies, eight hours taught by 98 per cent of academies; mediation skills/ conflict management eight hours taught by 88 per cent of academies; special training concerning juveniles, eight hours, 99 per cent of academies and hate/ bias crime, four hours, 87 per cent of academies (Reaves 2009).

Palmiotto (2000: 262) advanced three broad guidelines for the content of community policing training. First, he argues that 'Police officers should possess a sense of social history', which will contribute to an understanding of the current mission and goals of policing. Next, he indicates that 'police officers should have a sense of how societies function' and a basic understanding of crime, victimization, incarceration rates, poverty and quality of life issues. Finally, he states, 'police officers should be equipped with the skills and knowledge for incorporating community policing in their work in the field'.

Palmiotto *et al.* (2000) developed a model community policing curriculum based upon these guidelines. The curriculum incorporates the philosophy, mission, values and organizational structure of the individual department, the history of policing and the fundamentals of problem-oriented and community-oriented policing, including police discretion, ethics, misconduct inter alia. Palmiotto *et al.* (2000) further indicate that changes in police operations to reflect community policing cannot be made without education and training. Brown (1989) and Palmiotto (2000) further suggest that entrance-level and in-service community policing training should expose officers to community policing programs and activities and address diversity. Given the strained history of police – minority community relationships in the US, diversity and multi-cultural instruction are almost universally covered in entrance-level police academy instruction. The content and delivery of the instruction however varies significantly among agencies.

Entrance-level training often seeks to develop interpersonal communication and problem-solving skills in an effort to give officers the ability to function properly in the field (Meese 1993). One approach developed by Thompson termed 'verbal judo' which involves the use of interpersonal skills as a tactic to reduce the likelihood of a physical confrontation. Chief Leonard Hamm, former Baltimore Police Commissioner from 2004 to 2007 and Director of the Education and Training Division from 1991–1993, views interpersonal skills and personal integrity as core training and management issues. He believes the academy needs to develop and teach a curriculum that speaks to the moral standards society expects of officers. It needs to produce professionals who will be able to communicate effectively in assisting citizens to and to learn not to take things personally. One way to achieve this goal is through after-action reviews and use of case studies as a teaching tool in entrance-level, in-service and supervisory training every time an 'officer tarnishes the badge' (Interview 2012).

Peak and Glensor (2004) represent the majority view, which advises that community policing needs to be infused through the training curriculum. They indicate that traditional academy courses such as the history of policing, patrol procedures, and crime prevention need to be revamped to include community-oriented policing concepts. Chappell (Chappell *et al.* 2005, 2011; Chappell 2008) also argues that community policing needs to be integrated throughout the curriculum and cite the new Los Angeles Police Department training program as a promising approach (Glenn *et al.* 2003).

Palmiotto *et al.* (2000) cite Perez (1993), who argues that community policing must become the accepted and orthodox way of policing. Academy training provides an opportunity to transmit explicit and implicit values, both formally and informally, and is a valuable means of organizational socialization (Berlin 2006). Issues of organizational socialization and culture extend far beyond the training academy and encompass every level of a police department.

Palmiotto (2000) and others argue that the goals and objectives of community policing require a different approach to training than traditional policing. Arguably, traditional training would benefit from this new approach, as well. Traditional police training in past decades was largely centred upon a pedagogical, lecture-based approach. Community policing proposes a largely androgogical approach, relying on adult learning techniques where recruits take responsibility for their own learning (Knowles 1973, see Stanislas Chapter 13). The instructor teaches the student in a respectful atmosphere characterized by mutual trust and respect. Community policing involves experiential activities beyond lecture, and include role plays, case studies, group presentations, simulations and other in-class exercises and assignments (Bennett and Hess 1996). Problem-based learning, a developing adult instructional methodology, involves a team-based approach to learning. Trainees are required to work together in teams to find solutions to problems they are likely to encounter in the field (Werth 2011). While lecture is probably overused, it continues to play an important role in transmitting knowledge and information.

The *Bureau of Justice Statistics State and Local Law Enforcement Training Academies, 2002* report reveals that a significant minority of academies incorporate community policing training methods that take learning outside the classroom (Hickman 2005). These methods include:

Table 2.4 Percentage academies employing

Training method	Percentage of academies employing
Mock scenarios	46
Work with a community policing officer	21
Develop community project	9
Conduct community survey	7
Problem solving project	7

Table 2.5 Percentage of academies using scenarios

Type of training	Percentage of academies using scenarios
Arrest Control Tactics	93
Self-defence	91
Verbal tactics	87
Use-of-force continuum	86
Firearms	84
Non-lethal weapons	76
Threat assessment	73
Simunitions	64
Firearms Training Simulator	62

Reaves (2009) report on State and Local Law Enforcement Training Agencies, 2006 reveals that reality-based (mock) scenarios, which can be enacted both inside and outside of the classroom, are used extensively by state and local academies in entrance-level training:

Chappell *et al.* (2005) indicate that an ideal police training curriculum must contextualize instruction. They explore the LAPD approach to training, which is based upon the philosophy that training must reflect as closely as possible the actual working conditions for which recruits are being prepared (Chappell *et al.* 2005: 60). An analysis of Los Angeles police training for the Rand Corporation by Glenn *et al.* (2003) indicates that LAPD training involves four key processes: (1) conceptualize the learning; (2) integrate key topics throughout the curriculum; (3) build the scenario; and (4) conduct a thorough debriefing after the scenario. Integration of the curriculum is achieved by building the training scenarios around core values or key themes. Staff design curricula and build scenarios. Students join with staff in debriefing the scenarios.

There appears to be a growing awareness of the importance of the academy training environment in general and the potential consequences of the stressful paramilitary-style training environment in particular. Considerable controversy surrounds the issue of whether and to what extent the training academy should be modeled along the lines of the 'highly stressful' paramilitary environment, as opposed to the 'less stressful' academic environment. The decision whether to adopt a paramilitary model, a collegiate style, or an approach that mixes the two has significant implications for organizational socialization, as well as for curriculum and instruction. Roberg and Kuykendall (1990) raised the issue of academy training environments over 20 years ago. Chappell *et al.* (2009) addresses the adverse consequences of the paramilitary model in terms of its emphasis on positional authority, discipline and deference inter alia (see Chappell, Chapter 16).

My research (Berlin 2006) on community policing in New Haven, Connecticut and Richmond, Virginia from the mid-1990s to the early 2000s afforded me the opportunity to investigate changes in police training associated with broad implementation of community policing. I examined changes in the areas of academy curricula/content, instructional delivery and training environment.

New Haven and Richmond began implementation of community policing at roughly the same time in 1989. Community policing was implemented in both cities for the same general reasons: to improve relationships between the police and the community and to reduce crime. There were specific differences unique to each city based upon local concerns and personalities. Community policing in New Haven was perceived as a means of addressing past complaints of police abuse and indifference. In Richmond, it was perceived as a means of improving communication and access between the police and the community.

These differences, coupled with the differing priorities of the chiefs in the two cities, helped shape both the curriculum and training environment of the academies.

New Haven and Richmond revised both entrance-level and in-service training to facilitate implementation of community policing. Both cities also offered other additional specialized community policing training. Training was used to convey important theoretical and practical aspects of community policing to rank and file and to articulate and transmit the principles and values of community policing to all members of both departments. New Haven completely overhauled its entrance-level training, while Richmond updated its training to incorporate community policing.

The changes in New Haven, particularly with regard to entrance-level training, represented a profound departure from the past. The department hired a civilian director, who changed the tone of the academy from a paramilitary to a collegiate environment and revised entrance-level training to emphasize academics, problem-solving, interpersonal skills and other aspects of community policing. Sensitivity, diversity and other community policing related subjects were infused throughout the curriculum. The New Haven academy curricula was designed to get students out of the classroom and into the community, and required community service.

Management raised concerns that the emphasis on community policing occurred at the expense of tactical training, resulting in unprepared and ill-equipped recruits. Academy staff were aware of these concerns and indicated to the contrary that recruits received substantial physical and tactical training. While these concerns probably contributed to management and possibly rank-and-file resistance to community policing, they did not prevent successful implementation of community policing in New Haven.

Richmond also made significant and very visible changes with regard to training. The bureau entered into a partnership with Virginia Union University, a traditionally black college, to construct a new, state of the art, grant funded training facility on the university's campus. Recruit training was revised to be consistent with community policing. Topics covered included cultural diversity, cultural sensitivity, communications, interpersonal skills and problem solving. A civilian director of the academy was later jointly appointed by the police department and the University and served as Chair of the Criminal Justice Program. A Richmond police lieutenant oversaw day-to-day operations at the academy. An eight-hour block of instruction specifically devoted to community policing, which incorporated the history and social context of policing, was added and aspects of community policing infused in the curriculum. In addition to lecture, adult learning techniques, including use of case studies and extensive class discussion were employed. Recruits discussed the reasons why they chose to become police officers, including issues of excitement and adventure, life experience, diversity, ethnicity, class differences and upward mobility.

The academy in Richmond instituted a three-level approach to training. Phase one involved a strong emphasis on close supervision and military discipline. During the second phase, community policing content was added, and the supervision and discipline relaxed somewhat. During the final phase, recruits were treated more like police officers and expected to take responsibility for class leadership and exercise discretion consistent with community policing. Members of the bureau believed that the department did a good job training professional officers and teaching community policing. Unlike New Haven, Richmond did not change its fundamental paramilitary approach to training and continued to strongly emphasize a professional model.

Training played a critical role in providing recruits and in-service personnel with knowledge and understanding of community policing in both departments. The different approaches to training reflected the philosophy and values of the respective chiefs. Training was consistent with the strategic approach to policing in both cities.

As community policing continued its gradual expansion in the mid-1990s, a new movement, CompStat, was simultaneously developing and expanding at a rapid rate. CompStat (short for computer statistics) is a management process that consists of five basic elements: (1) specific objectives; (2) accurate and timely intelligence; (3) effective tactics; (4) rapid deployment of personnel and resources; and (5) relentless assessment and follow-up (McDonald 2001: 263, 2002).

CompStat was developed by Jack Maple, a New York Transit Police Lieutenant, and William Bratton, Chief of the New York Transit Police Department (Dussault 1999). It was adopted by the NYPD after Bratton was appointed Police Commissioner in 1994. Crime fell dramatically in the following decade. Weisburd, Mastrofski *et al.* (2004) trace the rapid growth of CompStat and indicate that by 1999, 32.6 per cent of all large police agencies had implemented CompStat and another 25.6 per cent of large police agencies were planning its implementation.

CompStat does not address the police–community relationship or other aspects of community policing. Nevertheless, many proponents of CompStat argue that the two approaches are not mutually exclusive and can be implemented simultaneously. Willis, Kochel and Mastrofski (2010b) find some evidence of co-implementation within the same agency. In fact, they argue that maximizing the benefits of reform requires integrating CompStat and community policing and make recommendations toward this end (Willis, Kochel and Mastrofski 2010a). Their recommendations include, among others: (1) harnessing community policing values, goals and practices in CompStat; and (2) committing substantial resources to crime analysis, training in problem-oriented policing, problem solving and building partnerships. A debate exists within the literature as to whether CompStat represents a new era of policing (Walsh 2001) or whether it is simply an administrative tool or innovation (Moore 2003).

Criticisms of CompStat include its adverse impact on police-community relationships, internal police management issues and alleged falsification of crime data (Eterno and Silverman 2010). Perhaps, the most controversial aspect of CompStat is 'zero-tolerance' policing, typically involving aggressive enforcement of 'minor' offenses such as disorderly conduct and other 'quality of life' offenses. Community policing focused on abating quality of life issues and problems. Only when abatement was not successful did the police turn to enforcement, arrest and citation (Berlin 2012). Quality of life offenses lend themselves to discretionary enforcement. CompStat removed much of that discretion and replaced it with a policy of arrest and citation.

Departments adopting CompStat need to design training which defines and explains the elements of CompStat, describes the goals and objectives of CompStat and clarifies both the officer's role in CompStat and agency expectations (O'Keefe 2004). The NYPD, which credits CompStat with a 75 per cent reduction in homicides, indicates that it provides only 1.5 hours of entry-level training on CompStat (Glenn *et al.* 2003). This figure may not include potentially relevant lessons in crime mapping, problem solving and related topics.

Arguably, police training should cover the knowledge and skills that will be used in the field. If a department's primary interest is in aggressive enforcement and crime control, training should stress the professional model of policing and those elements of a community policing curriculum such as interpersonal skills which would be relevant to effective policing. Realistically, few agencies are likely to admit that they are not concerned with the community and terminate community policing entirely. Boba *et al.* (2010) suggest an integrated problem-solving approach as a way to involve officers in street level problem solving, while leaving more complex issues to commanders. This represents a promising approach to integrating CompStat and community policing and is consistent with the recommendations of Willis, Kochel and Mastrofski (2010a). It also overcomes the rigid, top-down approach of CompStat and allows for some creativity and discretion on the part of the officer.

Homeland security and anti-terrorism related responsibilities assumed by local police since September 11, 2001, represent a further challenge for police training. Already busy training schedules had to be expanded or modified to include newly mandated state POST training material. Overall, 90 per cent of state and local police training academies covered terrorism related topics in 2006. These topics and the percentage of academies covering them are as follows.

On the one hand, increased militarization associated with anti-terrorism operations goes against many of the principles of community policing (see Chappell, Chapter 16). On the other hand, law enforcement and homeland security officials believe that intelligence is the key to preventing and disrupting terrorist activities.

Table 2.6 Topics and percentage of academies

Topic	Percentage
Response to weapons of mass destruction	70
Understanding the nature of terrorism	62
Relevant federal, state and local agencies	57
Interagency information sharing	44
Intelligence gathering	44
Role of anti-terrorist task forces	35
Related technology/equipment	33
Post-incident stabilization of the community	31
Intelligence analysis	26

At present, there is growing attention to a new approach in policing, 'intelligence-led policing' (Peterson 2005). In essence, intelligence-led policing employs a problem-solving approach based upon the 'intelligence cycle' to identify and target threats. The importance of problem-solving, critical thinking skills, intelligence analysis and social science principles opens the door to an expanded role for higher education in police training. However, the evidence on the benefits of higher education for police and police training is mixed (White 2007; Stanislas, Chapter 4).

As Bureau of Justice Statistics data indicate, 45 per cent of existing training academies are operated by two and four-year colleges and universities. These academies are responsible for training 35 per cent of all police recruits (Reaves 2009). Many are non-credit academies located on or near the college campus. Recruits, who generally pay tuition and fees, are often are part of a cohort group which trains together and is segregated from traditional students. Instructors are often current or retired law enforcement officers working on a part-time basis. College faculty may (or may not) teach a variety of subject matter at the academy. One of the advantages of college academies is their relatively low costs, compared to other types of academies. Costs per recruit range from $7,400 for college and university academies to $27,000 for municipal academies and $52,700 for county academies (Reaves 2009). There are vast differences among the college and university/academy arrangements, and more research needs to be done to fully understand these arrangements.

Comparatively little is known about existing partnership or contractual relationships between training academies and colleges and universities. For example, many local community colleges in the Baltimore, Maryland metropolitan area have arrangements with large municipal, county and specialized academies. Depending upon the arrangement, college faculty teach law, human relations, community policing and other social science subject matter to police recruits attending the academy. College faculty members may also assist with curriculum development and provide training workshops to sworn academy instructional staff. While it is clear that higher education has a lot to offer police education and training, it is not clear that higher education is in a position to reform police training (Bayley 2011; see Stanislas, Chapter 4).

Budget cuts

One of the most critical issues facing law-enforcement training today is the difficulty of maintaining standards and introducing innovation in light of drastic budget cuts. The recent economic crisis has significantly limited the availability of resources for local law enforcement. The nature and extent of budget cuts vary substantially between jurisdictions. Some city, town and municipal departments such as Camden, New Jersey have shut down and their responsibilities have been assumed by county police or sheriffs' departments. Other departments have laid off significant percentages of their force. Hiring has ceased or been drastically reduced at many departments, and training facilities have closed or scaled back. The economic crisis is ongoing, and the full extent of its impact has yet to be determined.

The impact on policing of the 'Great Recession' of 2008, euphemistically referred to as an 'economic downturn', has been documented by the popular media and official sources. It has also been the subject of study by numerous academic bodies, professional organizations and the US Government. The Police Executive Research Forum (PERF 2010), the International Association of Chiefs of Police (IACP 2011) and the US Department of Justice Office of Community Oriented Policing Services (COPS 2011) all explored the impact of current and projected budget cuts. PERF surveyed 608 police agencies concerning economic challenges facing their departments and the steps the agencies are taking to confront these challenges (PERF 2010). PERF found that 6 per cent of agencies have reduced or terminated training. According to the PERF (2010) survey, 22 per cent of respondents indicated they laid off employees as a result of decreasing budgets (PERF 2010). The IACP reports that 60 per cent of police agencies have to reduce training. The Major Cities Chiefs Association (MCCA 2010) found that 52 per cent of agencies surveyed had laid off sworn officers, 48 per cent had reduced training, 39 per cent reduced community policing, 34 per cent reduced narcotics enforcement and 22 per cent reduced school resource officers. Maintaining training standards and introducing innovation in light of drastic budget cuts is clearly a critical issue for both law-enforcement agencies and the public they serve.

Conclusion

Contemporary police training in the US reflects a mix of traditional reform era and community policing and incorporates more recent developments such as CompStat, crime mapping and post 9/11 homeland security strategies. Police have always confronted potentially conflicting priorities of enforcement, service and order maintenance. The growth of community policing in the 1980s and 1990s brought a more balanced approach to what had previously been a heavy emphasis on enforcement. By the late 1990s, the balance began shifting back toward enforcement in response to political demands for crime control. After 9/11, homeland security and anti-terrorism responsibilities further contributed to the shift back toward enforcement. Although community policing subject matter is included in most current police academy training, many academies continue to emphasize a traditional crime-fighting approach to policing, supplemented by CompStat and other technological advances.

Community policing and CompStat-enhanced traditional policing have developed and operated, by and large, along parallel tracks with little direct interaction. Much of the community policing practice and related training literature pays scant attention to the shift back toward an enforcement orientation. Similarly, the comstat literature and practice barely acknowledges the role of community policing. This disconnect has profound implications in the field and for training. Integrating the two approaches is critical. Officers must have a clear understanding of what is expected of them and be able to balance their community service and law-enforcement roles.

The design and delivery of entrance-level training is, in fact, far more sophisticated than is generally known. Police academy curriculum, instruction and outcomes assessment, are certainly more regulated and arguably more sophisticated than traditional higher education, especially in the 'liberal arts'. In addition to the broad range of content already covered and the extensive instructional methodologies already in use, academy curricula and methodology continue to develop. Recent developments include problem-based learning and use of online resources to supplement classroom instruction.

Clearly, there is room for improvement in police academy training, White (2007) and others suggest, more attention needs to be paid to cover human relations, communications, and other topics associated with community policing. Additional coverage of discretion, ethics, juvenile justice, cyber-crime and policing strategies is also warranted. Quality coverage of these topics would seem relatively easy to accomplish, given sufficient time and resources. However, several words of caution with respect to academy curriculum and content are necessary. Academies often attempt to teach too much. A wide range of subject matter to meet state POST mandates and address current issues compete for limited slots in the curriculum. While one solution might be to lengthen training, current budget constraints make this option extremely unlikely. Resources and time for training will likely remain major issues for the foreseeable future.

More problematic is the paramilitary approach to police training and organizational socialization issues. Compelling arguments have been made that a high stress paramilitary approach results in rigid, mechanistic officers unsuitable for community policing activities and inculcated an 'us vs. them' mentality. On the other hand, a typical collegiate environment may not necessarily be ideal for police training. A certain amount of discipline, professionalism and teamwork are essential to good policing.

Closely related to academy approach, stress levels and officer socialization are issues associated with authority, use of coercive force and the danger inherent in police work. Effective training must address these issues without overemphasizing the danger. These issues must be addressed in police training and a balance needs to be struck between higher stress paramilitary approaches and lower-stress collegiate approaches.

Police academy training must reconcile apparent conflicts between traditional enforcement and community-oriented strategies, incorporate new technologies and address developing issues through the strategic integration of training, departmental philosophy, leadership and management. Training must be consistent with an honest assessment of departmental priorities, including externally imposed priorities, and allocate an appropriate balance of time and resources to each priority. In the final analysis, training must prepare officers to perform the tasks necessary to accomplish the core mission of the department.

References

Bayley, D.H. (2011) 'Et Tu Brute: Are Police Agencies Managed Better Or Worse Than Universities?', *Police Practice and Research*, 12(4): 313–316.

Bennett, W.W. and Hess, K.M. (1996) *Management And Supervision In Law Enforcement*, 2nd edn, Minneapolis/St. Paul, MN: West Publishing Company.

Berlin, M.M. (2006) 'Implementing Community Policing: Case Studies Of New Haven, Connecticut And Richmond, Virginia', Unpublished doctoral dissertation, University of Maryland Baltimore County, Baltimore, Maryland.

Berlin, M.M. (2012) 'The Evolution, Decline And Nascent Transformation Of Community Policing In The United States: 1980–2010', in D. Palmer, M.M. Berlin and D.K. Das (eds) *The Global Environment of Policing*, 27–48, Boca Raton, FL: CRC Press Taylor and Francis Group.

Bittner, E. (1970) *The Functions Of The Police In Modern Society*, Cambridge, MA: Oelgeschlager, Gunn and Hain.

Boba, R., Wycoff, L. and Santos, R. (2010) 'Advancing CompStat practices: The stratified model of problem solving, analysis and accountability', in *Implementing And Institutionalizing CompStat In* Maryland, College Park, Maryland: Institute for Governmental Service and Research.

Brown, L.P. (1989) 'Community Policing: A Practical Guide for Police Officials', *Perspectives on Policing*, 12 (No. NCJ 118001), Washington, DC: National Institute of Justice, US Department of Justice and the Program in Criminal Justice Policy and Management, John F. Kennedy School of Government, Harvard University.

Chappell, A.T. (2008) 'Police Academy Training: Comparing Across Curricula', *Policing An International Journal of Police Strategies and Management*, 3(1), DOI 10.1108136951081082567.

Chappell, A.T. and Lanza-Kaduce, L. (2009) 'Police academy socialization: Understanding the lessons learned in a paramilitary-bureaucratic organization', *Journal of Contemporary Ethnography*, DOI: 10.11770891241609342230.

Chappell, A.T., Lanza-Kaduxe, L. and Johnston, D.H. (2005) 'Law Enforcement Training: Changes And Challenges', in R.G. Dunham and G.P. Alpert (eds), *Critical Issues In Policing: Contemporary Readings*, 71–88, Long Grove, IL: Waveland Press.

Chappell, A.T., Lanza-Kaduxe, L., and Johnston, D.H. (2011) 'Law Enforcement Training: Changes And Challenges', in R.G. Dunham and G.P. Alpert (eds), *Critical Issues In Policing: Contemporary Readings*, 52–70, Long Grove, IL: Waveland Press.

COPS (Office of Community Oriented Policing Services) 'The Impact of the Economic Downturn on American Police Agencies: A Report of the COPS Office', Washington, DC: US Department of Justice, October 2011

Cordner, G.W. (2001) 'Community policing: Elements and effects', in R.G. Dunham and G.P. Alpert (eds) *Critical Issues In Policing: Contemporary Readings*, 493–510, Prospect Heights, IL: Waveland Press.

Dussault, R. (1999) 'Jack Maple: Betting on Intelligence', Government Technology. (1 March 1999).

Eck, J.E. and Spelman, W. (1989) 'Problem-Solving, Problem-Oriented Policing In Newport News', in R.G. Durham and G.P. Alpert (eds), *Critical Issues In Policing: Contemporary Readings*, 489–503, Prospects Heights, IL: Waveland Press.

Eterno, J. and Silverman, E. (2010) 'The Trouble With CompStat: Pressure On NYPD Commanders Endangered The Integrity Of Crime Stats', New York Daily News. [Electronic version]. (15 February 2010).

Frost, T. (1959) *A Forward Look In Police Education*, Springfield, IL.: Charles C. Thomas Publisher.

Gammage, A. (1963) *Police Training In The United States*, Springfield, IL.: Charles C. Thomas Publisher.

Glenn, R.W., Panitch, B.R., Barnes-Proby, D., Williams, E. Christian, J. and Lewis, Matthew W. *et al.* (2003) *Training The 21st Century Police Officer: Redefining Police Professionalism For The Los Angeles Police Department*, Santa Monica, CA: RAND.

Goldstein, H. (1990) *Problem Oriented Policing*, Philadelphia: Temple University Press.

Goldstein, I.L. (1993) *Training In Organizations*, (3rd edn), Pacific Grove, CA: Brooks/Cole Publishing Company.

Hamm, L. personal conversation, 11 October 2012.

Harrison, L.H. (1964) *How To Teach Police Subjects: Theory And Practice*, Springfield, IL.: Charles C. Thomas Publisher.

Hickman, M.J. (2005*)* State And Local Law Enforcement Academies, 2002*, Washington, DC: Bureau of Justice Statistics, Office of Justice Programs, US Department of Justice, www.ojp.usdoj.gov/bjs/.

International Association of Chiefs of Police (2010) *Policing In The 21st Century: Preliminary Survey Results*, Alexandria, Virginia: International Association of Chiefs of Police.

Kelling, G.L. and Moore, M.H. (1988) 'The Evolving Strategy of Policing', *Perspectives on Policing*, 4 (No. NCJ 114213). Washington, D.C.: National Institute of Justice, US Department of Justice, and the Program in Criminal Justice Policy and Management, John F. Kennedy School of Government, Harvard University.

Knowles, M. (1973) *The Adult Learner: A Neglected Species*, Houston, TX: Gulf Publishing Company.

Lurigio, A.J. and Rosenbaum, D.P. (1994) 'The impact of community policing on police personnel: A review of the literature', in D.P. Rosenbaum (ed.), *The Challenge Of Community Policy: Testing The Promises*, 147–163, Thousand Oaks, CA: Sage Publications.

Major Cities Chiefs Association (2011) *Police Economic Challenges Survey Results*, Sun Valley, Idaho: Major Cities Chiefs Association (unpublished).

McDonald, P. (2001) 'COP. CompStat, And The New Professionalism Mutual Support Or Counter-productivity', in R.G. Dunham and G.P. Alpert (eds), *Critical Issues In Policing: Contemporary Readings*, 4th edn, Prospect Heights, IL: Waveland Press.

McDonald, P. (2002) *Managing police operations: Implementing the New York crime control model–CompStat*. Belmont, CA: Wadsworth/Thompson Learning.

Meese, E., III. (1993, January) 'Community policing and the police officer', *Perspectives On Policing*, 15 (No. NCJ 139164), Washington, DC: Department of Justice, National Institute of Justice.

Miller, L.S. and Hess, K.M. (1998) *The police in the community: Strategies for the 21st Century*, 2nd edn, Belmont, CA: Wadsworth Publishing Company.

Moore, M. (2003) Sizing Up Compstat: An Important Administrative Innovation In Policing, in T. Newburn, ed, *Policing Key Readings*, Devon, UK: Willan Publishing.

National Advisory Commission On Civil Disorders (1968) *Report Of The National Advisory Commission On Civil Disorders*, New York: E.P. Dutton.

O'Keefe, J (2004) *Protecting The Republic: The Education And Training Of American Police Officers*, Upper Saddle River, NJ: Pearson Prentice Hall.

Oliver, W.M. (2004) *Community-Oriented Policing: A Systemic Approach To Policing* (3rd edn, Upper Saddle River, NJ: Pearson Prentice Hall.

Palmiotto, M.J. (2000) *Community Policing: A Policing Strategy For The 21st Century*, Gaithersburg, MD: Aspen Publishers, Inc.

Palmiotto, M.J., Birzer, M.L. and Unnithan, P.N. (2000) 'Training In Community Policing: A Suggested Curriculum', *Policing: An International Journal of Police Strategies and Management, 23*(1): 1363–951X.

Peak, K.J. (1997) *Policing America: Methods, issues, challenges*, 2nd edn, Upper Saddle River, NJ: Prentice Hall.

Peak, K.J. (2006) *Policing America: Methods, Issues, Challenges*, 5th edn, Upper Saddle River, NJ: Pearson Prentice Hall.

Peak, K.J. and Glensor, R.W. (2004) *Community Policing And Problem Solving: Strategies And Practices* (4th edn), Upper Saddle River, NJ: Pearson Prentice Hall.

Perez, M.B. (1993) 'IACP Offers Training In Community-Oriented Policing', *The Police Chief*, 39–40.

Police Executive Research Forum (PERF) (2010) 'Is the Economic Downturn Fundamentally Changing How We Police?', *Critical Issues in Policing Series*, vol. 16, Washington, D.C.: Police Executive Research Forum.

Peterson, M. (2005*) Intelligence-Led Policing: The New Intelligence Architecture*. NCJ 210681 Washington, DC: US Department of Justice, Office of Justice Programs, Bureau of Justice Assistance and the International Association of Chiefs of Police.

Reaves, B.A. (2009) *State And Local Law Enforcement Academies, 2006*. Washington, DC: Bureau of Justice Statistics, Office of Justice Programs, US Department of Justice www.ojp.usdoj.gov/bjs/abstract/slleta06.htm.

Reaves, B.A. (2010) *Local Police Departments, 2007*, Washington, DC: Bureau of Justice Statistics, Office of Justice Programs, US Department of Justice www.ojp.usdoj.gov/bjs/abstract/slleta06.htm, http://bjs.ojp.usdoj.gov/content/pub/pdf/lpd07.pdf.

Roberg, R.R. and Kuykendall, J. (1993) *Police and Society*. Belmont CA: Wadsworth Publishing Company.

Sadd, S. and Grinc, R. (1994) 'Innovative Neighborhood Oriented Policing: An Evaluation Of Community Police Programs In Eight Cities', in D.P. Rosenbaum (ed.), *The Challenge Of Community Policy: Testing The* Promises, 27–52, Thousand Oaks, CA: Sage Publications.

Skolnick, J.H, and Bayley, D.H. (1988) *Community Policing: Issues And Practices Around The World*, Washington, DC: US Department of Justice.

Skolnick, J.H. and Fyfe, J.J. (1993) *Above The Law Police And The Excessive Use Of Force*, New York: Free Press.

Trojanowicz, R.C. and Bucquerox, B. (1990) *Community Policing: A Contemporary Perspective*, Cincinnati, OH: Anderson.

Walsh, W. (2001) 'CompStat An Analysis Of An Emerging Paradigm', in R.G. Dunham and G.P. Alpert (eds.), *Critical Issues In Policing: Contemporary Readings*, 5th edn, Longrove, IL: Waveland Press.

Weisburd, D., Mastrofski, S., Greenspan, R. and Willis, J. (2004) *The Growth Of Compstat In American Policing*, Washington, DC: Police Foundation.

Weisburd, D., Mastrofski, S., McNally, A, Greenspan, R. and Willis, J. (2003) 'Reforming To Preserve: Compstat And Strategic Problem Solving In American Policing', in T. Newburn (ed.). *Policing key readings.* Devon, U.K.: Willan Publishing.

Werth, E.P. (2011) 'Scenario Training In Police Academies: Developing Students' Higher Level Thinking Skills', *Police Practice And Research*, 12(4): 325–340.

White, M.D. (2007) *Current Issues And Controversies In Policing*, Boston: Pearson.

Willis, J., Kochel, T. and Mastrofski, S. (2010b) *The Co-Implementation Of CompStat And Community Policing: A National Assessment*, Washington, DC: Office of Community Oriented Policing Services, US Department of Justice.

Willis, J., Mastrofski, S. and Kochel, T. (2010a) *Maximizing The Benefits Of Reform: Integrating Compstat And Community Policing In America*, Washington, DC Office of Community Oriented Policing Services, US Department of Justice.

Willis, J., Mastrofski, S. and Weisburd, D. (2003) *CompStat In Practice: An In-Depth Analysis Of Three Cities*, Washington, DC: Police Foundation.

Wilson, J.Q. and Kelling, G.L. (1982) 'Broken Windows: The Police And Neighborhood Safety', *Atlantic Monthly*, 29–38.

Zhao, J., Lovrich, N.P. and Thurman, Q. (1999) The Status Of Community Policing In American Cities: Facilitators And Impediments Revisited, [Electronic version]. *Policing: An International Journal Of Police Strategies And Management, 22*(1): 74–92.

3 Police training and education and university collaboration in Australia

T. Green and R. Woolston

Introduction

Australian policing is characterized by the six states and two territory police agencies which make up the Commonwealth of Australia. In addition to state policing, the Australian Federal Police has responsibility for policing a range of national crime types, border control and international liaison. The New South Wales Police Force (NSWPF) is the largest police force of the six states, with a population of approximately 7.3 million people and a police force of over 16,000 members.[1] Charles Sturt University (CSU) is a large regional university within New South Wales (NSW) with over 45,000 students, two-thirds of whom are enrolled in study by distance education. Currently, one in seven CSU students are studying programs in policing/law enforcement. This chapter provides an overview of the police recruit education and training program in NSW, which is jointly developed and delivered in partnership by the NSWPF and CSU. This collaborative arrangement is discussed, highlighting the strengths and challenges facing partnerships between police and tertiary providers, who strive to suitably prepare new police officers for contemporary policing roles.

History

Police recruit education and training in NSW has developed significantly from its inception in the late nineteenth century, when introductory police training consisted of only a few days instruction. Today, recruit education involves the undertaking and successful completion of an Associate Degree program collaboratively developed and delivered by the NSWPF and CSU.

In 1998, the joint tertiary/police model (the Diploma of Policing Practice [DPP] the Associate Degree in Policing Practice [ADPP]),[2] the subject of this chapter, superseded the previous police recruit training program. The DPP was introduced in response to findings and recommendations arising from the Wood Commission into allegations of corruption within the NSWPF (chapter one). Justice Wood, the presiding judge (1997: 542) recommended that a tertiary level degree should be introduced as a pre-requisite for all new police recruits prior to attending the Police Academy (Wimshurst and Ransley 2007). Woods' recommendations (1997), whilst non-specific, were based on what he perceived to be a requirement for raising the educational standards of police, to better prepare them for dealing with complex situations and decision-making. He also recommended that police students needed to be exposed to a broader general education, providing them with alternative perspectives and views on contemporary issues which would make them more open to the values of the community in which they would police. Woods' (1997) findings were similar to those of previous commissions of inquiry within Australia (Fitzgerald 1989; Lusher 1981) which also suggested that tertiary education for policing, not only at the recruit level, was necessary if the police were to meet contemporary policing expectations. Earlier efforts to embrace higher education in police recruit training in Queensland following the Fitzgerald Report (1989) had ended in controversy because the police felt the program did not suitably prepare police recruits, while the academics involved felt that the benefits of a liberal education were being ignored (Wimshurst and Ransley 2007).

Learning from the Queensland experience, NSWPF determined that they would adopt a professional policing model of higher education, focused on the science of policing rather than a broader liberal education (Bradley 1996; Higgs *et al.* 2009). This approach was deliberately designed to ensure that the police retained a high level of involvement in the design and application of the curriculum. The move to a collaborative policing education model was also supported by the NSWPF Association who saw the move to be a positive one against which they could leverage on the 'professionalization' of the police force for better terms and conditions.[3]

Following a detailed tendering process, the NSWPF entered into a partnership with CSU for the joint development and delivery of the Diploma of Policing Practice (DPP). CSU were well placed to successfully tender to work with NSW Police, having already determined to develop the discipline of policing. CSU had previously demonstrated their commitment to work collaboratively with the NSWPF and since 1993 had been jointly delivering the Diploma of Policing which was the requirement for all NSW police to be promoted to the rank of Senior Constable. Furthermore, CSU had also developed and delivered a Bachelor of Policing/Bachelor of Policing (Investigations) for serving police. These qualifications were delivered outside NSW to police from other regions within Australia and international police forces (Chambers 2004).

The model proposed by Justice Wood (Wood 1997) of acquiring a tertiary qualification as a pre-requisite to attending the Police Academy was not entirely rejected but modified, resulting in an alternative professional policing model (Bradley 1996). The alternative adopted combined knowledge and skills in a policing context at the Police Academy, rather than a separation of academic study conducted at a university and what is often perceived as 'real policing' learnt elsewhere. Additionally, studies extended into the probationary year and culminated in the awarding of the Diploma of Policing Practice (Chambers 2004). As a result, CSU located the School of Policing Studies at the NSW Police Academy, and collaboratively the NSWPF and CSU developed and delivered the recruit education and training program, a model which has been criticized by some as displacing the liberal education model recommended by Wood (Wimshurst and Ransley 2007: 120) but which has formed the basis of an arrangement that continues to the present day.

The Associate Degree Policing Practice (ADPP)

The ADPP is designed to meet the educational needs of entry-level police officers and is the primary entry pathway[4] for recruits into the NSWPF. It is compulsory for all new police to undertake the program, with the exception of a small number of police rejoining the force or joining the NSWPF as transferees from other states through a mobility program. The ADPP focuses on foundation studies and developing knowledge and skills necessary for policing modern society (Corboy 2008). The residential phase of the program is delivered from the NSWPF Academy where the CSU School of Policing Studies is co-located in the same buildings alongside the police.

Being a university accredited associate degree the award is governed and shaped by university policies and procedures. The entire program is developed and delivered jointly by the NSWPF and CSU, with the exception of operational safety (firearms, tasers, handcuffs, etc.) which is delivered solely by the police. The program is delivered on a trimester-based calendar;[5] the first two trimesters[6] are delivered at the NSWP Academy in Goulburn with an 80-hour field placement at a Local Area Command (police station) during the session break. The three remaining trimesters are delivered by distance education whilst the police officers are working as probationary constables under the tutelage and guidance of police in the field. At the successful completion of their studies students graduate with an Associate Degree in Policing Practice and are confirmed to the rank of constable.

ADPP course structure – probationary constable at end of trimester 2, constable at end of trimester 5

The ADPP is divided into two distinct phases, for the first two trimesters ADPP students are not employees of the NSWPF. They become employees on successful completion of trimesters 1 and 2 plus a professional suitability requirement which results in students becoming eligible to be attested as a probationary constable. All probationary constables remain enrolled as university students to the point of completion of their studies in trimester 5. This is also the completion of their one year probationary period and confirmation in the role of constable. The fact that the students are not employed by the NSWPF for the first nine months of their studies enables the police to monitor students' behaviour and progress as prospective police employees for the full period prior to making an offer of employment.

The offer of employment will only be forthcoming if the student meets all the academic requirements including their practical assessments as well as maintaining 'police suitability' requirements which include appropriate standards of conduct.[7]

Table 3.1 Associated Degree in Policing Practice (ADPP) full-time on campus

NSW police college		ATTESTATION	Distance education			CONFIRMATION & GRADUATION
Trimester 1	*Trimester 2*		*Trimester 3*	*Trimester 4*	*Trimester 5*	
PPP111 (4) – Simulated Policing (Acquiring Confidence)	PPP121 (4) – Simulating Policing (Acquiring Competence)		PPP231 (8) – Session 3 Police Practicum	PPP241 (8) – Session 4 Police Practicum	PPP251 (8) – Session 5 Police Practicum	
PPP112 (8) – Police as Investigators 1	PPP122 (8) – Police as Investigators 2		PPP232 (8) – Police as Investigators 3	PPP242 (8) – Problem-oriented Policing and Vulnerable Populations	PPP252 (8) – Ethical Values and Leadership	
PPP113 (8) – Communication in Policing	PPP123 (8) – Ethical Reasoning and Policing					
PPP114 (8) – Criminal Justice and Policing	PPP124 (8) – Policing and Road Safety					
PPP115 (8) – Police, Crime and Society 1	PPP125 (8) – Police, Crime and Society 2					
PPP116 (4) – Operational Safety and Tactics 1	PPP126 (4) – Operational Safety and Tactics 2					
At the conclusion of session 1 all students will be required to undertake an 80 hour placement in a Local Area Command (LAC)						

Why a collaborative model?

The model proposed by CSU to the NSWPF was one of full collaboration at every stage. CSU is recognized as the 'University for the Professions' and has a long history of working with professional groups in practice-based education (Higgs, Loftus and Trede 2010). This collaborative approach was adopted with the policing program which was modeled to ensure that there was no separation of the various elements of education and training required to prepare a police recruit. Wood (1997) and his predecessors espoused the values of a university experience and a liberal education, which reflected their own education within the legal profession. The approach adopted by CSU and the NSWPF however, better reflected the adult learning requirements of the students recruited from very diverse backgrounds and ages (*Review of the Diploma of Policing Practice: Final report* 2002). It was recognized that these people already had significant life experience and required a professional policing education designed to prepare them for their role as police officers. Despite being university students, they are students who want to be police officers and therefore their preparation should be practice based and holistic. Separating the academic knowledge and core skills of decision-making, analysis and critical thinking from operational safety and tactics type preparation is counterproductive and not in accordance with practice based education pedagogy (Chapter 1; Garbett 2004; Higgs *et al.* 2010).

Collaboration at every step

The collaborative model is adopted from the beginning of the recruitment process through the design, development and delivery, continuing to the evaluation and review of the program. At the earliest stage of the process, CSU and NSWPF marketing strategies are employed to promote the ADPP as the entry pathway to the NSWPF. CSU's Division of Marketing works with NSWPF recruitment to identify and target marketing opportunities, including online and media advertising. With NSW spanning an area of 800,000 square kilometers and CSU being a large rural provider of education, there is also a focus on non-metropolitan and rural areas.

One of the most successful strategies to engage new recruits to the NSWPF has been to provide a joint CSU/NSWPF 'road show', which promotes policing as a career and explains what is involved when studying the ADPP. The NSW Police Academy also holds an open day for the public, during which various specialist groups within the police provide displays. Police recruitment and CSU staff provide information on the ADPP to prospective applicants.

Once attracted to the career of policing, NSWPF applicants must firstly apply to CSU to determine their academic eligibility to enroll in the program. This is an online process in which applicants provide CSU with information relating to their academic qualifications. There are a number of varying academic entry categories including, but not limited to, previous tertiary studies, completion of the

High School Certificate with good grades or trade qualifications, as well as some areas of relevant work experience. If applicants are deemed academically unsuitable, CSU provides a tertiary level 'bridging program' which if successfully completed meets the requirements for academic entry while also providing students with the necessary academic skills to undertake studies at associate degree level. Levels of education vary from students who enter the program with a PhD through to those students who did not complete their secondary schooling but who have excellent life skills and gain entry via the bridging program. Having achieved academic suitability applicants undergo what is collectively recognized as police 'professional suitability' including:

- medical examinations;
- criminal and driving history checks;
- interview at place of residence;
- proof of age, citizenship/residency;
- driver's license;
- swimming, first aid and typing certificates.

Having completed all of the above, applicants reach the final stages of fitness testing and psychological examination, following which they are placed into a 'pool' of eligible applicants waiting for an offer to be made to commence the ADPP. This entire process can take as little as four months or more than a year depending on the applicant's situation. Importantly, the flow of students into the ADPP is restricted to ensure that only the number required by the NSWPF to meet their establishment needs are granted entry to the program.

This is not a generic program with open entry and those students who meet all of the requirements of the program to the point of attestation whilst retaining professional suitability will be offered a job. Issues of retaining the currency (Heslop and White 2011) of the learning prevent a greater number of applicants being granted admission than are likely to be offered employment. The challenges associated with this process will be discussed further on.

Once students commence study in the program, they are taught by both NSWPF and CSU staff. As the ADPP is a recognized university award there is a requirement for all staff teaching on the ADPP to be accredited to teach by the University. In order for this to happen NSWPF teaching staff undergoes annual accreditation conducted by the Principal of the Academy and the Head of School, Policing Studies. Academic accreditation relies on staff undertaking continued professional development which includes tertiary studies, research and rotations within operational policing to ensure currency with policing practice (Heslop and White 2011). Furthermore, CSU and the NSWPF have developed a staff teaching development program which is undertaken by CSU and NSWPF staff and delivered at the academy by both police and academic teaching staff. CSU staff are also required as a condition of employment to engage in professional development, including periods of time spent as an observer at a police station to establish and maintain currency of practice (Higgs *et al.* 2010). This is critical because, unlike other professions such as nursing and teaching where academics can return to the profession for periods of time or re-accreditation, such a provision does not exist in policing (Heslop and White 2011).

In order for CSU academic staff to teach on the ADPP and be co-located at the police academy they must also be deemed 'professionally suitable' by the NSWPF. This involves primarily a criminal history check and a professional suitability assessment to teach on the program.

Curriculum is jointly designed, developed, delivered, assessed and evaluated by teaching teams which consist of both police and academics. Learning is facilitated primarily through tutorials[8] developed in accordance with adult learning principles. The tutorials are delivered by both CSU staff (many of whom are suitably qualified ex-police from a wide variety of backgrounds and police forces, nationally and internationally) and serving police officers with subject matter expertise, with the exception of the weapons and tactics subject which is taught only by specially qualified police instructors.

A broad spectrum of assessment methodologies are utilized to engage the wide variety of learning styles within the student body including: tutorial participation; written (essay format) and oral presentation; written examinations; and demonstration of practice in a simulated policing environment.

Evaluation of the curriculum is ongoing with a major review every four years in line with university policy. This involves a team of teaching staff from both organizations, being assigned the task of evaluating the curriculum and the learning outcomes, incorporating feedback from students as well as field based learning officers and police commanders.

What is the management structure?

Whilst the ADPP is a university program and award, there is an extensive and detailed contract between CSU and the NSWPF which provides the detail for the governance for the contract agreement. To maintain quality assurance of processes, a variety of committees exist to monitor performance of all parties to the agreement. All committees have an equal representation of NSWPF staff and CSU staff with equal voting rights with each committee meeting a minimum, three times a year.

The Board of Management is the body responsible for the strategic planning and management of the ADPP. The position of Chair is independent of both organizations and previous high-profile personalities have included the Australian Governor General, Quentin Bryce, Mr Hugh Mackay, esteemed author and social commentator, Mr Steven Lowey (Westfield Corporation) and currently Mr Alan Joyce (CEO Qantas airlines). All ADPP committees report to this board which has strategic responsibility for the program including the financial delegation of funds, approval of the curriculum and entry requirements, plus dispute resolution between the parties should any occur.

The courses committee is responsible for the quality of content and continuous improvement in the development and delivery of the ADPP. This

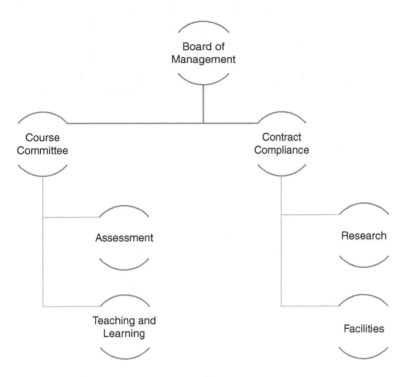

Figure 3.1 Joint management structure.

committee is comprised of senior police, CSU staff, representatives from the Police Association and operational policing. In addition to reporting to the Board of Management, courses committee reports internally in the university to faculty level committees.

The role of the Contract Agreement Performance Review Committee (CAPRC) is to review all aspects of performance of each party against the criteria outlined under the contract agreement. This includes acknowledging positive performance as well as reviewing areas of poor performance. The ADPP Assessment Committee has the important role of verifying the assessment practices and student results in the ADPP, ensuring the assessment process is fair, equitable and transparent. This committee, which is comprised of subject coordinators from CSU and the police and senior academy management staff from both organizations, meets at the end of each session and also reports directly to Faculty as well as the ADPP Board of Management.

Other joint committees include:

- the Teaching Development Advisory Committee, which oversees the development and delivery of staff development in teaching and learning in the ADPP;

- the Research Development Advisory Committee, which oversees the development, direction and review of policing related research, with a focus on enhancing the ADPP curriculum and delivery;
- the Facilities Maintenance and Infrastructure Committee (FMIC), which provides advice on the use and improvement of facilities and the use of CSU's infrastructure contribution for future infrastructure development at the Police Academy.

What are the funding arrangements?

Funding arrangements for the ADPP are quite unique and are based on an 'employee reserved' basis which is different from the usual Australian university fee arrangement for undergraduate students which are supported by the Commonwealth. Students in Australia are entitled to a Commonwealth Grant Scheme (CGS) place which supports approximately half of the cost of their education paid directly to the University and the students accumulate a debt for the remaining half, which they gradually repay once their income reaches an affordable threshold. As the ADPP is linked to restricted employment within the NSWPF and entry is limited to those people who have met the entry requirements for NSWPF, the Commonwealth determined that CGS places could not be made available for this program to recruit police for which the State already provides funding. It was therefore determined to enroll the students in a specific category of full-fee paying 'employee reserved' students on a fee basis equivalent to a normal CGS funded university fee. The fees pay for the university teaching of the program, effectively halving the cost of the police component whilst increasing the educational levels of the recruits. Additional financial benefits to the police include contributions to library holdings, research funding and staff development.

ADPP students are not employees of the NSWPF until the point of attestation (end of trimester 2), when they are employed but remain enrolled for a further six subjects throughout their probationary year. ADPP students can therefore defer their fee payments until they are employed by the NSWPF and are entitled to the same government study support payments as other tertiary students. In addition, the students can apply for a scholarship payment to assist with living expenses prior to them being employed. This scholarship fund is financed by the NSWPF but administered by CSU; it is allocated on a 'needs basis' with those students demonstrating greater needs receiving a higher value scholarship.

Challenges!

The influence of politics

As previously mentioned in this chapter, the ADPP only enrolls the number of students (allowing for attrition) as is required to meet the staffing needs (authorized strength) of the NSWPF at the point of attestation (Chambers 2004, Corboy

2008). Calculating this number is a difficult process which requires estimations to be made in terms of students not progressing at the normal rate in the program or students withdrawing due to personal, academic or professional suitability issues. In addition police salary increases, changes to police policies and election promises all impact on attrition numbers (Chambers 2004, Kennedy 2004, Wood 1997). The impact can include significant financial implications if too many students successfully complete semester two and become eligible for employment. Measures to manage the numbers have included delaying the start of trimesters and at worst delaying student progression towards attestation. Such outcomes are complex and demanding for all parties involved, especially the students. Student intake numbers vary depending on the needs of the NSWPF. For example, in the period 2009–2011 trimester intake numbers have been as high as 978 and as low as 20, with an average cohort size of 444. Clearly the implications for recruiting and teaching such fluctuating numbers has created a need for some very innovative initiatives including a huge range of casual staff, development of a second campus and students and staff all working split shift rosters.

Teaching staff

Teaching the ADPP with appropriate, adequately trained staff can be challenging for both CSU and the NSWPF. The contract requires for the program to be co-delivered at 50:50 by CSU and NSWPF. The two main factors that impact on the ability of both organizations to provide appropriate staff and teach half of the program are:

- the fluctuating numbers of students;
- the geographical location of the Police Academy.

First, in terms of response to the fluctuating numbers, it is more difficult for CSU to identify and maintain adequate staffing numbers because unlike the police who can undertake periods of rotation to other areas of policing when student numbers are low, university staff cannot be redeployed into other areas of the

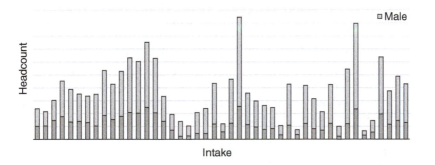

Figure 3.2 Teaching staff.

university. CSU therefore has a large pool of casual teaching staff who can be employed on short-term contracts. Some of the casual staff are drawn from serving police who have appropriate tertiary qualifications and currency to teach the new recruits. For the NSWPF the issue is recruiting operational police from the field, with little or no teaching experience to teach on the program. As a result, there is a strong requirement for an induction and mentoring program which aims to provide maximum support and guidance to new staff from both organizations (Corboy 2008; Wood 1997).

The second factor impacting on the availability of suitable staff is the geographical location of the Police Academy. Located in Goulburn, a small country town which is approximately two and a half hours drive from the city of Sydney, the academy attracts staff and their families who permanently relocate. There is no tenure policy in the NSWPF in terms of teaching staff at the academy and some staff have been teaching for almost 20 years. This raises the issue of operational currency and limited turnover of staff. In addition the majority of the NSW population live on the east coast, enjoying temperate climates and high employment, there is a resistance to relocate, even short term, to inland rural locations (Mackay 2010).

Diversity

Being a multicultural society the diversity of the NSW Police Force is incredibly important and the ADPP has been a major factor in increasing the number of women, aboriginal and CALD students. In the past three years, students from 71 countries have progressed through the program into the NSW Police Force. There is a strong focus on equity and every effort is made to ensure that the ADPP is accessible to the broadest range of the community as possible. In relation to gender, most cohorts average between 23–30 percent females, and the average for that same three year period being 27 percent. Ages range from 18 years to 60 years with the average age for that same period being 27 years. There are no age or height restrictions, provided the recruit meets the physical testing and medical requirements. To encourage people to join the NSWPF, CSU and NSWPF jointly have established a number of initiatives to ensure that there are pathways to encourage and assist in making the program accessible. The key initiatives are:

- Distance education pathway for trimester 1 (studying part time) to encourage mature people and women who may not choose to be away from home for prolonged periods;
- Provision of a bridging program to ensure a pathway for mature people and to provide the necessary study skills required;
- Study skill support for those who have not been in formal education for a long time;
- Programs for Aboriginal applicants via TAFE NSW to provide a supported pathway into policing;

- English language standards higher than those of normal university, which ensures a better chance of success (and support to meet those standards);
- Two university 'feeder' programs which allow students the opportunity to complete a degree and join the ADPP at the midpoint of their study.

Expectations of the probationary constable

From a curriculum perspective, the challenges lie in the ability to develop the first trimester of the curricula to be flexible for delivery by face-to-face full time and distance education, part time. The distance education pathway provides the NSWPF with a large number of mature people with life experience. Most continue to work or manage families whilst undertaking this first part of the program. There are limited periods of residential teaching but the majority is delivered online. The challenge is to ensure these students are not disadvantaged by studying via distance. In addition, students undertaking their studies through the feeder pathways (the university studies undertaken on other campuses) also need to be integrated into the ADPP at trimester 2 (pre-attestation). This transition begins with these students participating in the distance education residential schools, however, ensuring all students achieve the same level commencing trimester 2 remains an ongoing challenge. In addition, as with many professional education programs there is an expectation that the 'novice' practitioner should be able to complete all tasks and have the knowledge of the expert practitioner (Higgs *et al.* 2010).

Indicators of success

One of the strongest indicators of success of this collaborative arrangement is the duration and enduring nature of the partnership. The ADPP (then DPP) was first introduced in 1998 with a contract period of three years. This contract was extended and an interim contract awarded until January 2006 when a new contact was negotiated for an initial five-year period, with a further five-year extension. A review conducted in 2011 confirming the ongoing contract which is due to expire in December 2015, when the NSWPF will be required to re-tender. During the past 14 years the program has 'weathered' changes in State and Federal government, several changes in the Commissioner of the NSWPF and significant changes in senior management of both CSU and the NSWPF. Throughout the extraordinary fluctuation of student numbers and external demands upon the program, there has never been an occasion when the program has failed to meet the intake numbers required by the country's largest police force. In the same period, other Australian states have struggled to secure recruits through traditional police employment recruitment pathways, resorting amongst other things to importing experienced police from the UK to meet their needs.

During the duration of the contract each of the chairs of the Board of Management have acknowledged the sound working relationship which exists between both organizations and several have extended their period as Chair of the Board of Management for more than one term. The joint commitment to the success of the program and the degree of flexibility demonstrated to meet the needs of the program have provided the foundations of a very robust relationship.[9]

In addition the partnership between the NSWPF and CSU was subject to inspection by the Australian Universities Quality Assurance (AUQA) who were until 2012 responsible for the quality assurance of all Australian University providers. The AUQA inspection determined:

> It is evident that issues in combining academic and very specific professional education and training requirements have been thoroughly worked through and addressed by both parties. These requirements include the need for great flexibility in academic staffing, due to substantial variations in the size of entering cohorts. The current partnership agreement is the product of an extended period of collaborative provision and, in the view of the Audit Panel, is a model of good practice.
>
> AUQA commends CSU, with the New South Wales Police Force, for their management and operation of a successful partnership in police education.
>
> The Audit Panel considers that this model of partnership in professional education is an exemplar for other partnerships.
>
> (AUQA 2010: 25)

Conclusion

Reviews of the ADPP program reveal that the collaborative model provides the police with the ownership and control they need, whilst the recruits benefit from a training and education program which prepares them for policing, applying a policing science model (Bradley 1996; Higgs *et al.* 2009; Neyroud 2011; Wimshurst and Ransley 2007; Winsor 2012). Police commanders are generally very satisfied with the level of recruit. Feedback for improvements is continually driven back to the program. Unlike others, where the education and practice models are separated from one another, this integrated and compulsory approach to police recruit education seems to endure the many pitfalls which have been the downfall of other efforts to bring police training and higher education into a relationship (Heslop 2011; Kennedy 2004; Lee and Punch 2004).

Notes

1 The average length of service for male officers is 14 years and the average length of service for female officers is seven years.
2 In 2005 the DPP was replaced by the ADPP based on recommendations from the New South Wales Police Ministerial Working Party on Recruitment, Training and Retention (Anderson, 2003). The curriculum underwent minor modifications but maintained the same structure and delivery modes.

3 NSW Police negotiated a pay rise in response to the introduction of a tertiary award for recruitment and remain the highest paid officers in Australia by a considerable margin.
4 There are two tertiary 'feeder' pathways. These pathways provide younger applicants an opportunity to go firstly to university and study two thirds of a degree in criminology and related areas before joining other students at the police academy to continue their studies in the ADPP and to complete their degree.
5 There is a new intake of students three times a year with each of the three trimesters being approximately 16 weeks duration.
6 The first session is also delivered by distance education over two trimesters.
7 This process has been colloquially referred to by police as 'the longest job interview ever' and includes fitness, criminal history, misconduct or inappropriate behavior.
8 Tutorials comprise groups of approximately 20 students who work with a tutor in class exploring in greater detail the material from the Master Lectures.
9 Evidence of similar relationship can be seen between Leicestershire Constabulary and De Montfort University which has survived changes of police leaders, financial cutbacks and recruitment freezes etc., demonstrating a commitment to partnership uncommon in most parts of Britain.

References

Anderson, P. (2003) *Ministerial Working Party on Recruitment, Training and Retention: A Report on the Review of the Diploma of Policing Practice 2002*, Sydney: New South Wales State Government.

Australian Universities Quality Agency (AUQA) *Report of an Audit of Charles Sturt University*, January 2010.

Bradley, D. (1996) 'Contemporary police education in Australia', in D. Chappell and P. Wilson (eds) *Australian policing: Contemporary issues*, 2: 85–110, Sydney: Butterworths.

Chambers, R. (2004) 'Collaborative police education – A report', paper presented at the World Association for Collaborative Education.

Corboy, M. (2008) Operation Viente: A review of the NSW police education and training command. Unpublished Unpublished report.

Fitzgerald, G.E. (1989) *Report of a Commission of Inquiry Pursuant to Orders In Council*.

Garbett, R. (2004) 'The role of practitioners in developing professional knowledge and practice', in J. Higgs, B. Richardson and M. Abrandt Dahlgren (eds), *Developing Practice Knowledge, For Health Professionals*, pp. 165–184, London: Butterworth-Heinemann.

Heslop, R. (2011) 'Reproducing police culture in a British university: Findings from an exploratory case study of police foundation degrees', *Police Practice and Research*, 12(4): 298–312.

Heslop, R. and White, D. (2011) 'What is the attraction of nurse training as a model for professional education? An analysis of field and habitus in the construction of curricula for nurse, teacher and police officer training', paper presented at the Critical Perspectives on Professional Learning, Fifth Annual Conference. Retrieved from www.leeds.ac.uk/medicine/meu/events/pll11-docs/White-Heslop.pdf.

Higgs, J., Loftus, S. and Trede, F. (2010) 'Education for Future Practice', in J. Higgs, D. Fish, I. Goulter, S. Loftus, J. Reid and F. Trede (eds), *Practice, Education Work and Society: Education for Future Practice*, 3(3): 3–15. Rotterdam: Sense.

Higgs, J., McAllister, L. and Whiteford, G. (2009) 'The practice and praxis of professional decision making', in B. Green (ed.), *Understanding and researching professional practice*, Rotterdam, the Netherlands: Sense Publishers.

Kennedy, G.A. (2004) *Royal commission into whether there has been corrupt or criminal conduct by any Western Australian Police Officer*, Australia: Perth.

Lee, M. and Punch, M. (2004) 'Policing by degrees: Police officers' experience of University Education', *Policing and Society*, 14(3): 233–249.

Lusher, E.A. (1981) *Commission to inquire into New South Wales Police Administration*, Sydney: Government Printer.

Mackay, H. (2010) *Advance Australia ... Where?* Sydney: Hachette.

Neyroud, P. (2011) *Review of Police Leadership and Training*, London: Home Office.

Review of the Diploma of Policing Practice: Final report. (2002). Unpublished Unpublished report.

Wimshurst, K. and Ransley, J. (2007) 'Police Education and the University Sector: Contrasting Models from the Australian Experience', *Journal of Criminal Justice Education*, 18(1): 106–122.

Winsor, T. (2012) *Independent Review of Police Officers and Staff Remuneration and Conditions*.

Wood, J.R.T. (1997) 'Royal Commission into the New South Wales Police Service: Final report', *Corruption*, vol. 1: Sydney: The Government of New South Wales.

4 The challenges and dilemmas facing university-based police education in Britain

P. Stanislas

Introduction

This chapter examines the role of higher education institutions (HEIs) in police education and training as well as the factors which have contributed to their emergence and centrality to debates around police reform. The chapter is exploratory in character, given that the involvement of HEIs in the training and education of police recruits in Britain is still relatively new, with universities such as Portsmouth, De Montfort, and others taking the lead in the area (Shepard 2003; Wood and Tong 2010). By studying the experiences of countries such as the United States and Australia, who are more advanced in these working relations, the chapter identifies core issues which can assist research and practice within the British context. An important aim of the chapter is to assist in directing future research around university-based policing programmes, contribute to the emerging literature, and sensitize researchers to some of the issues involved.

Historical and international context

The first university-based policing programme was created by Police Chief and Professor August Vollmer in 1916. He was a key figure in the movement for reform and higher education in policing, who started a policing course at the University of California, Berkeley (Mahony and Prenzler 1996; Kakar 1998). Vollmer was an exemplar for many important ideas which was to influence police thinking internationally and contemporaneously. First, in emphasizing the importance of higher education for police officers. Second, in highlighting the significance of graduate recruitment; and third in demonstrating the relationship between professional policing and criminology. The driving force behind the creation of university-based police education was the need to modernize police organizations, to be able to meet the complexities of contemporary society, which in Vollmer's view traditional police academy-based training was unable to do.

In Australia and the US public controversy around police corruption, the quality of recruits, and poor performance were critical in providing impetus for growing demands for change (Mahony and Prenzler 1996; Woods 1997). Historically, and across many parts of the world, policing was viewed as an occupation that required very little educational or even training requirements compared to other areas of public activity (Kakar 1998; Emersley 2005). This was particularly important in terms of the backgrounds of police recruits who came predominantly from the lower classes. Many of those posted to the colonies were of particularly poor quality, which had an adverse effect on how policing developed in these countries (Paterson 2011: 294; Stanislas forthcoming).

The military model and police training academies

The military model has been traditionally utilized to explain the ethos of policing organizations (Mahony and Prenzler 1996). One of the core underlying assumptions of this view is the belief that the police are a classic Weberian bureaucratic and authoritarian-type institution (Reiner 1992). In accordance with this view is the importance of compliance with the decisions of senior officers (Chappell 2008: 38). These militaristic characteristics of the police can also be seen by its historical recruitment patterns and high visibility in postcolonial police organizations (Bankole 1999). Accordingly, one of the key functions of police training is to reinforce the aforementioned norms (Birzer 2003; Chappell 2008).

Police training and education has historically been delivered at police training academies run by senior police officers and training instructors. The content of this training consists largely of legal knowledge and various procedural competencies and basic policing skills (Mahony and Prenzler 1996: 109; Roberg 2004). Police training academies have been described as being semi-military in character and detached from public life (Carlan 2007; Chappell 2008). This is highlighted by the militaristic-type paraphernalia seen in many of them, marching drills, and recruit inspections that replicate the military model of socialization (Marion 1998). Another important aspect of this approach is a pedagogy which emphasizes learning by rote and a reliance on didactic techniques (Birzer 2003; Paterson 2011: 292).

The ethos of police training academies has been reinforced by the composition of training staff who traditionally are veteran officers and predominantly white males. Historically training officers were not recruited because of their abilities as teachers/trainers or sensitivity to contemporary public concerns around racism or sexism (Marion 1988: 75). However, as Bayley (2011) notes this type of practice is common to many organizations, universities included, and not unique to policing. One of the criticisms levelled at police instructors is that they reinforce negative aspects of the informal police culture; especially the notions of 'them and us' where the public are seen in opposition to the police (Marion 1998: 74; Chan and Dixon 2007). Despite these criticisms police academies are viewed as crucial institutions in training police officers, as opposed to places of education (Marion 1998: 60; White 2006: 392; Werth 2009). The continued importance of the academy in police training in the development of practical job-related competencies is stressed by many authors (Mahony and Prenzler 1996: 236–237; Carlan 2007).

An important defence for the military model and its approach to education and training is provided by Cowper (2000) who maintains much of the criticism levelled at this paradigm is rooted in misrepresentation. Cowper suggests that while military organizations by their nature are based on the subordination to command principle, this does not undermine the requirements for military personnel to be analytical and flexible in the field. Similar observations can be made regarding police work and something well known to experienced police trainers (Roberg *et al.* 2002). Cowper's observations gives support to the traditional selection criteria used in choosing police trainers where the importance of operational experience outweighs other considerations (Marion 1998; Chan and Dixon 2003: 134). The potential bias of critics towards the conventional model of police training is also seen in the failure to recognize that police practices are not immune from change and illustrated by the selection, training, and education of contemporary police training staff; and the support provided to them in areas such as race and community relations and other areas of policing (Oakley 1990; Blakemore *et al.* 1995).

Professionalization

Professionalization of occupations is characterized at a bare minimum by several key features according to Houle (1980). The first is the identification of clear occupational standards for how tasks are carried out. Second, in efforts to improve the status of the occupation and the processes of how individuals enter and progress through it; and finally increased autonomy and self-regulation. HEIs played a central role in debates about professionalization and improving the police in the US (Carter *et al.* 1990; Mahony and Prenzler 1996), Australia (Chan and Dixon 2007; Wimshurst and Ransley 2007) and Canada (Froyland 1991). An ambitious project of professionalizing the police and some of the issues entailed are addressed by Neyroud (2011) in the British context which will be examined below.

Wimshurst and Ransley identify two types of moves towards professionalization that involve HEIs. The first they term 'emerging professionalism' which is characterized by the adoption of liberal arts components in police training and the second they describe as 'full professionalism' which is associated with the development of special policing programmes or qualifications that are taught by policing specialists. In the latter model, the police are dominant in their relationships with universities. Professionalization has long been viewed as critical in changing the attitudes and behaviour of police officers and in improving the occupation's status (Carter *et al.* 1989; Chan and Dixon 2007). However, Wimshurst and Ransley (2007: 17) argue that these two goals are in conflict insofar as while an improvement in status may accompany a move towards professionalization, there is little evidence to suggest that it leads to a significant change in police behaviour in itself.

Government commissions and inquiries have played an important role in improving the type of education received by police officers and discussions about professionalization. This can be seen in the Australian and US context and in the case of the latter led to the creation of the Law Enforcement Education

Programme (LEEP) which provided federal funds for higher education for police officers (Froyland 2005: 19). The number of police officers receiving higher education has not been widespread, despite the number of HEIs in the US that provide programmes for police personnel (see Reaves 2006; Wood and Tong 2008: 297). This is illustrated by the fact that only 16 per cent of state police agencies in that country require a two-year college degree and four per cent require a four-year Bachelors degree as a mandatory entry requirement (Marion 1998: 75; Roberg 2004; Chappell 2008: 44). These figures demonstrate the resilience of traditional attitudes towards police recruitment practices in the US, and the conservative interests that maintain them.

Benefits of higher education for police recruits

Those advocating the perceived advantages of university-based education include important players in the police education/training decision-making process. This can include: police administrators, i.e. chief officers and their political superiors, police managers, recruits and academics (Kalka 1998; Carlan 2007; Wimshurst and Ransley 2007). Tracing the development of university-based provision Mahony and Prenzler (1996), Carlan (2007), and Wimshurst and Ransley (2007) maintain that the involvement of HEIs in the delivery of education has been viewed by many police administrators as a crucial means in exposing police recruits to liberal values. This is seen as important in developing effective human relations in areas such as communication and complex problem-solving, as highlighted in Peeters' chapter. At the same time police student officers are able to acquire knowledge about society and those they will come in contact with through social science-based education (Marion 1998: 65; Kratcoski and Das 2007; Stanislas, Chapter 13).

There are several strands of dissent coming from academics who view the relationship between HEIs and police organizations as potentially problematic. A specific concern which has drawn critical attention is the neo-liberal thinking shaping contemporary higher education environment in the US. Teixera (2006) highlights the adverse impacts neo-liberal values have had on universities in eroding their traditional roles with import for university-based police programmes (Barnett 2006; Wimshurst and Ransley 2007: 120). Teixera notes how economic forces are having important consequences for notions of classic liberal education which underpins the arguments of proponents of HEIs in police education and training. A more pedestrian, but important, set of concerns exist around the practical implications and problems around developing education and training-based partnerships and reconciling the various interests involved (Wood and Tong 2010).

The empirical evidence and methodological challenges

Despite the numerous claims made for university-based police education and its perceived superiority to police academy-based learning, in particular subject and skill areas, the evidence as it presently stands is not convincing (Kakar 1998; Marion 1998; Carlan 2007; Neyroud 2011: 33; Paterson 2011). Proper evaluation of both university and academy-based learning has lagged behind the development and implementation of these programmes, even in the US which has been at the forefront of these debates (Marion 1998; Carlan 2007; Rowe and Garland 2007). In Australia important reforms have resulted in the greater involvement of HEIs in police education and have been hailed as a success in changing particular attitudes and behaviour (Chan and Dixon 2007; Stanislas, Chapter 1). It is difficult however to establish any clear causal relationship between identifiable changes in police conduct and performance and the involvement of HEIs, given the large number of reforms simultaneously introduced by the Woods' Commission (Woods 1997). This type of conundrum has implications for any number of complex organizational problems.

The attitude of police recruits to higher education is one area which has been documented by American researchers. Carlan (2007) found that higher education, according to experienced police officers, improved their knowledge and skills in a number of areas. He also found that the criminal justice degree programme (examined in the study) was pertinent to real policing, contrary to commonly held belief, and provided police officers with greater resources in carrying out their work. Chappell (2008) on the other hand found little difference between the class-based performance of police students on a new Community Orientated Policing programme, run by a HEI, and those who attended a similar programme delivered at a police training academy. The former consisted of many new ideas around policing diverse communities, and the issues involved and not dissimilar to many university-run courses (Marion 1998: 63–64; Garland *et al.* 2002: 20–23; Stanislas 2009). Marion (1998) found that diversity-based programmes were better received by police students on university courses than those at police academies, and the attitudes of teachers/instructors and learning environment were crucial factors in shaping this outcome. This does not suggest that receptiveness to the programme necessarily translates into better outcomes (Werth 2009).

Kakar's (1998) study on the impact of higher education on officers and their performance found police officers who were college or university educated rated themselves significantly higher on several important performance criteria than those trained in the conventional manner. An example of this is in the areas of leadership skills and negotiating diversity. An important finding in Kaka's study is that police officers with graduate education had less tolerance about inequality and discrimination. They also used their discretion in more productive ways (Paterson 2011: 293). These officers also experienced higher levels of frustration and lower levels of job satisfaction. The latter finding supports those from other studies (Mahony and Prenzler 1996: 287; Roberg 2004: 3) and a view articulated by police union representatives that university education led to dysfunctional outcomes producing officers who were more questioning (see Fielding 1986). Another important and related finding from Carlan's (2007) study is that police officers with higher levels of education, i.e. post degree qualifications, found university-based education the most useful due to their longer policing experience and specific organizational roles (see Paterson 2011).

While the US studies, cited for the most part, do not all focus primarily on the effectiveness of university-based police education, they all touch on this issue in various ways or have import for understanding some of the difficulties in question. See Roberg (2004) and Paterson's (2011) review of several studies. Ascertaining the effectiveness of university-based learning on police officers is fraught with methodological challenges. In the first instance, attempting to solicit the opinions of new recruits about the efficacy of university-based learning on future performance is difficult, given they are not in the position to realistically comment on how useful their education is for practical policing at that stage in their career (Roberg 2004: 4; Carlan 2007; Stanislas 2009). A different problem presents itself with experienced officers in the form of 'memory lag' given the gap which exists between the time when they concluded their basic training, participating in research, and being able to link specific learning to particular outcomes (Garland *et al.* 2002: 13; Carlan 2007: 618; Werth 2009: 24).

The difficulty of evaluating how class-based learning translates to work practices is one conceded by researchers, given the intrinsic nature of police work; in particular its variety, unpredictability, and the difficulties in isolating discrete influencing factors (Kakar 1996; Garland *et al.* 2002; Werth 2009). For this reason Kakar utilizes the self-evaluation survey method which it is argued is a relatively reliable approach and superior than the sole reliance on supervisory evaluation techniques. The effectiveness of this method is supported by a body of research which demonstrates the closeness of findings derived by its use to other forms of evaluation, including the use of polygraph tests (Kakar 1996: 638). Werth (2009) advances a potentially useful set of methodologies. He calls for the use of multiple assessment tools, that can include self-assessment surveys, experiments to test knowledge and skills, and peer assessments, which can also include multi agency partners involved in particular areas. The results of these findings can be triangulated to develop a more comprehensive and reliable data set.

Another consideration in thinking about research in these areas raised by Fielding (1986) concerns the time period required to study changes in police recruit behaviour. Fielding concludes that over the duration of years the socialization of police officers results in shifting attitudes from the public service orientation, developed at training school, to a more self-interested and instrumental orientation. This can manifest in attitudes about not 'rocking the boat' or the desire for 'an easy life'. Importantly, he stresses that the periods of one year, five, and ten are the crucial points in measuring attitudinal change.

Universities and police education and training in Britain

Some British universities have a long relationship with the police service. Public concerns around corruption and poor performance highlighted by the 1960 Royal

Commission on the Police, stimulated growing efforts to improve the training of officers (Reiner 1992: 764; Lee and Punch 2004). This led to, in some instances, the police working in conjunction with local HEIs to develop graduate programmes. In Essex Constabulary the first step in this process were police officers being funded to study social science degrees (Lee and Punch 2004: 238). The frustration of police leaders in their efforts to introduce degree education for police officers is touched on by Wood and Tong (2008: 297). Universities have played an important role in assisting police constabularies in developing their own training programmes and supporting aspects of their work. An example of this was the role of Manchester University in the evaluation and development of Manchester Police's community relations training during the 1960s (Shaw 1987).

The murder of Stephen Lawrence and the subsequent MacPherson inquiry in 1999 (Stanislas, Chapter 1), along with the fall out of the Secret Policeman documentary which gave graphic illustration of the deep-seated racism of some police recruits, forced the issue of the training and the type of recruit coming into the police service back onto the public agenda (White 2006: 393; Rowe and Garland 2007: 44). What was particularly disturbing about the former is the impression given in the documentary of the police trainer supporting the racist diatribe being expressed by recruits, and the apparent victimization of a lone Asian police probationer. These incidents and the furore that followed served to reinforce growing worries about institutionalized police racism amongst the public, government, and important regulatory bodies. Many related matters were to constitute important areas of focus of Her Majesty's Inspectorate of the Constabulary (2002) in its call for professionalization and the modernization of the British police service. The report drew attention to police recruitment and entry requirements and the type of education received at police training centres (Marion 1998; Carlan 2007). Specific problem areas were identified, such as the excessive emphasis on knowledge-based training and in particular legal matters. Also highlighted was the little amount of time spent or available for developing police probationers' understanding, and to apply reflective learning to a range of social issues pertinent to contemporary police work (HMIC 2002: 46).

While falling short of calling for full-blown involvement of HEIs in police training, the HMIC gave plenty indications of its feelings on the matter in terms of case studies of good practice highlighted in its report. For example, it cites the National Police Training Centre in Warrington, where police probationers studied alongside non-policing students on academic and vocational courses. This interaction between police probationers and the public is represented as a positive development in changing the insularity and exclusionary nature of traditional police training (Marion 1998: 72; Garland *et al.* 2002: 15–16). The insularity of police training, particularly in the areas of understanding and respecting social diversity,[1] constituted an area requiring serious action for the HMIC. The report recommended greater participation of members of the community in police probationer training, the use of community placements allowing probationers to work with, for example, the mentally ill, as a means to improve their understanding and practice (see Marion 1998). An important departure from previous thought was the HMIC's view that the interaction and learning derived from the involvement of the community in police education does not have to be reduced solely to operational requirements (HMIC 2002: 49; White 2006: 393).

Many of the issues raised by the HMIC[2] were reinforced by the Commission for Racial Equality's formal investigation into the police service of England and Wales (CRE 2005). Chiefly amongst these was evidence of an unhealthy learning environment in many police training centres which were characterized by bullying of minority probationers. Attitudes towards racial equality were found that ranged from indifference to hostility, along with poor standards of training officers, many of whom it is suggested lacked appropriate training for their role (CRE 2005: 70; HMIC 2002: 49). The CRE also expressed concern about the lack of representation of ethnic minority staff as in-force trainers and the failure of many police organizations to employ external consultants, academic trainers, and HEIs in delivering their programmes. Two national police training establishments, the Metropolitan Police Hendon training school and The Central Police Training and Development Authority, were cited as poor examples in this regard (CRE 2005: 84).

The foundation degree in policing

The Department of Education and Skills White Paper entitled *The Future of Higher Education* (2003) outlined the importance of higher education in modernizing the public services. The Foundation Degree (FD) established in 2000 was a result of the DES White paper (DES 2003: 47). The two-year qualification, which has been at the centre of controversy given its classification as a degree (Smith and Betts 2003: 225–227), combines six months of university-based academic education with work-based learning (Stanislas 2009; Heslop 2011). The FD can be tailored to meet the needs of various occupations. In terms of policing it encompasses the legal, procedural, and basic policing skills training found on traditional courses with a much larger social science component around matters relating to diversity, working with vulnerable and hard to reach communities (Stanislas 2009: 105; Heslop 2011: 5).[3]

While little evaluation of the FD has taken place some of the following problems have been identified with much wider import. First, the liberal ethos of HEIs is an important characteristic that has made them an attractive alternative to police training centres. What this actually means for minority and non-mainstream police students and their experiences with HEIs is under-researched, but there is growing recognition that universities inter alia are not immune from institutionalized racism and other bias (Law *et al.* 2004; Howson 2009). The experiences of police FD students portrayed by Heslop (2011: 7) raises important questions about cultural and institutional biases of HEIs and how they disadvantage those from non-traditional student groups. He identifies several practices of teaching staff and administrators which negatively stigmatized police students undermining many of the purported benefits of university-based recruit education. Despite the importance of issues of discrimination and diversity in the call for greater involvement of HEIs in police recruit training and education, the track records of HEIs on these matters appear be of little consideration in police decision-making when forming partnerships, which seem more driven by financial issues and matters of practical convenience (see Smith and Betts 2003).

Second, the lack of time available for learning on residential-based police training courses is not addressed by the designers of the police FD. The HMIC (2002: 44) notes that the structure and time pressures on residentially-based police training programmes, largely shaped by financial concerns, limits the flexibility available to trainers and course designers. The writer's experience of having taught on both residentially-based courses and the FD suggests that moving courses to universities does not change the constraints and pressures placed on students and teaching staff with import for the quality of teaching and learning (Garland *et al.* 2002: 27). The university experience for both parties on these types of courses is not the same as traditional academic programmes. See Smith and Betts (2003), Wood and Tong (2010).

Modernization, professionalization, and HEIs

The modernization and professionalization of the British police service constitutes a prominent set of themes in several HMIC reports and from others calling for reform (Loveday 2006; see Waters 2007). One issue at the heart of these discussions is the occupational status of the contemporary police, which is viewed in premodern terms by many (Loveday 2006; Stanislas 2013). One of the strongest advocates of the professional model is Stone (2009: 10) who maintains:

> Policing and nursing are the last two apprenticeship schemes in the country. Like nursing, learning on the job is vital for police officers. However, if officers are to have the capacity to think developed to the maximum, then police leaders need to learn from nursing how to introduce Higher Education qualifications as a basic requirement for officers.

Numerous public professionals who work closely with the police require higher education qualifications, such as social workers (HMIC 2002; Stone 2009). While many of the mechanistic functions of policing may not require a degree education, the same may not be said for other important aspects of the role (see Werth 2009; Paterson 2011). Despite the greater demands of contemporary police work, the title of Hayne's (2009) article 'Boffin Bobbies' written for the police trade magazine, *Police Review*, demonstrates the traditional commitment to a lay police organization in the way it handles the issue of police education. One police officer who is cited in the article comments: 'I could have gone to university, but decided not to. Would a history degree have made me a better officer? Absolutely not' (cited in Haynes 2009: 18).

Opposition to changing educational entry requirements has come from the Police Federation, which has historically acted as an obstacle to modernization (O'Malley 1997: 365; Loveday 2006: 106). A particularly specious line of argument advanced by the Federation given its track record on racism (Hopkins 2000), and others, is that the introduction of higher educational requirements adversely affects the recruitment of ethnic minority officers (Neyroud 2011: 82–83).[4] Those advocating greater professionalization have been weakened in the absence of a body responsible for setting national educational standards for the police service, as found in various professions (Collier 2010). Quasi-government agencies such as the National Police Improvement Association lacked the authority of a professional standard-setting body (*Guardian* 26 July 2010).

For advocates of police professionalization support for their agenda is potentially strengthened by one influential strand of neo-liberal thinking (see O'Malley 1997; Loveday 2006) where the calls for higher and more formal levels of education and accreditation is not directed at the traditional police workforce. In the mind of important opinion-formers increasing the number of civilian staff is the future of the British police service, in terms of greater civilianization of core policing functions (Loveday 2006: 107–109; see Crisp, Chapter 14); along with the growth of the private security sector and the granting of legal powers to a range of groups to carry out investigatory and other policing functions (Slack 2012). According to this view the police are characterized as a very expensive, antiquated (if not arrogant), and increasingly ineffective public service indifferent to taxpayers' needs. Loveday (2006) takes the view that concerns about public finances are changing the government's attitude towards the police, and creating the conditions for what he paints as an inevitable conflict about fundamental and radical reform. The selection of Tom Winsor, the first civilian to be appointed the HMIC's Chief Inspector, and the controversy surrounding the decision (Beckford 2012) can be read as a clear indicator of the government's attitude to the type of changes the police service needs to undergo.

The Neyroud Report and the future of police education and development

Many of the aforementioned concerns and challenges facing British police leaders constitute central themes in the Neyroud Report (2011). The context for the report is the coalition government entering office and inheriting an unprecedented budget deficit caused by the spending policies of the previous Labour administration. The government immediately launched a *Comprehensive Spending Review*, whose findings were published in October 2010 (Bloxham and Barrett 2010). The *Review* announced the need for major cutbacks in public spending, and a projected 20 per cent cut to the central government grant to the 43 police forces in England and Wales. This indicated not only an immediate reduction in police funding; it was also clearly communicated that the public services were from now on operating in a new and less generous funding environment (Neyroud 2011).

Several months earlier the Home Office published its White Paper on *Policing in the 21st Century* (Home Office 2010), where it revealed some of the most radical proposals for change in half a century. The most controversial of which is the creation of directly elected local Police and Crime Commissioners with the power to hire and dismiss chief constables, moving power away from the centre. A central theme running through the report was the renewed importance of value for money given the contemporary funding environment.

Neyroud's review of police leadership and training encompassed entry requirements and training of new recruits to the development of senior managers, leaders, and the needs of the modern police organization. The report recommendations represent a fundamental overhaul of existing practices, arrangements, and thinking about important issues concerning police human resource management. Four specific recommendations from the report are pertinent to the discussion: first, Neyroud calls for the full professionalization of the police which in his view is critical to improving its status, clarifying areas of accountability, and meeting public expectations. Second, he recommends the establishment of a single professional chartered body responsible for important aspects of policing (Neyroud 2011: 47–48). Third, this body would be responsible for setting national standards, especially as it relates to entry and progression within the police service, eliminating important discrepancies that presently exist (Neyroud 2011: 133). Neyroud specifically calls for a new pre-entry national qualification and a new qualification for police managers. Finally, the report recommends that police training and education be devolved outside the police training establishment, which is already occurring in some areas and police forces, and delivered in two principle ways: via partnerships of providers, where HEIs play a pivotal role, and specialist police training centres, teaching subjects such as surveillance and operational matters (Neyroud 2011: 87–89). The government's recent announcement of its intention to form the professional body called for by Neyroud, and some of the obvious corollaries coming from this decision (Home Office 2011), in concert with others, suggests a significant change in the policing environment, which could not have been predicted by the most optimistic supporter of police reform five, never mind ten, years ago. The new national strategic agenda for British policing appears to have been set.

Conclusion

The role of higher education in the development of police officers has a relatively long history in many Western countries in various forms, but in the US and UK its role in recruit education has been more of a passing phase, as opposed to a significant change in practice by police organizations. Recent developments in Britain offer new and potentially unprecedented opportunities for HEIs to play a major role in the education of police officers at all levels. However, while there are promising pieces of evidence of the personal and other benefits derived by police officers from higher education in various roles and capacities, the evidence base regarding its effectiveness in too many areas is conspicuous by its absence.

This is particularly important given concerns around value for money, and other similar measures, while not unfamiliar, will increasingly inform the decision-making of police managers and leaders (Neyroud 2011). Moreover, the claims made by academics and HEIs about their provision must be empirically grounded or sufficiently qualified in preserving academic and professional integrity. In addition, Teixera (2006) reminds us of the dangers of neo-liberal values on HEIs and its potential to reduce them to simply commercial operators in the market place at the expense of important values fundamental to their role. Bayley (2011) and Heslop (2011) in different ways highlight some of the important discrepancies between the claims of universities and their actual practices which give food for thought. If HEIs are to become a standard feature in the arrangements for the development of British police officers, and indeed they have a lot to offer, researchers in this and related areas will have to play a critical role in keeping them there or elucidating more clearly what their role can or should be.

Notes

1 Stanislas (2013) demonstrates police leadership's inability to handle complex matters when competing claims with potentially equal merit are made by disadvantaged groups which call for police intervention. Even with better education and training police decision-makers are prone to acting in predetermined ways in important instances.
2 The HMIC is one of the most influential bodies in the governance and structure of the police service of England and Wales reporting to the Home Office responsible for policing.
3 The take up of the FD has dropped over the last couple of years from approximately 16 forces to about half that number in 2012 and in many ways follows the US pattern.
4 The notion that lower educational qualifications serve the interest of ethnic communities is an odd one and, the writer suggests, is self-serving in protecting the interests of white majority officers, or those protecting the status quo. White majority officers are more likely to come into contact with ethnic communities in Britain than a minuscule number of ethnic officers. The notion that ethnic minority officers are the source or catalyst of cultural change within the police is questionable (see Cashmore 2002). Improving the quality of white majority officers invariably will have potentially better outcomes for minority communities, even if it reduces the number of ethnic officers who apply.

Bibliography

Bankole, C. (1999) 'Postcolonial Policing Systems', in I. Mawby (ed.) *Policing across the World: Issues for the Twenty-First Century*, London: UCL Press.
Barnett, R. (2006) *Re-Shaping the University: New relations between Research, Scholarship and Teaching*, Maidenhead: Society for Research into Higher Education and the Open University Press.
Bayley, D. (2011) 'Et Tu Brute: Are Police Agencies managed Better or Worse than Universities?', *Police, Practice and Research*, 12(4).
Beckford, M. (2012) *MPs Likely To Try To Block Tom Winsor's Appointment As Police Watchdog*, www.telegraph.co.uk, 9 June. Accessed 20 June 2012.
Birzer, M. (2003) 'The Theory of Andragogy applied to Police Training', *Policing: An International Journal of Police Strategies and Management*, 26(1): 29–42.
Blakemore, J., Barlow, D., and Padgett, D. (1995) 'From Classroom To The Community: Introducing Process In Police Diversity Training', *Police Studies*, XVIII(1).

Bloxham, A. and Barrett, D. (2010) *Spending Review: What it means for the home office*, www.telegraph.co.uk, 20 October 2010. Accessed 19 June 2012.

Carlan, E.P. (2007) 'The Criminal Justice Degree and Policing: Conceptual Development or Occupational Primer', *Policing an International Journal of Police Strategies and Management*, 30(4): 608–619.

Carter, D., Sapp, D., and Allen, D. (1990) 'The Evolution of Higher Education in Law Enforcement: Preliminary findings from a National Survey', *Journal of Crime Justice Education*, 1(1) 59–86.

Chan, J. and Dixon, D. (2007) 'The politics of Police Reform: Ten years after the Royal Commission into the New South Wales Police', *Criminology and Criminal Justice*, 7(4): 443–468.

Chappell, A. (2008) 'Police Academy Training: Comparing across Curricula', *Policing: an International Journal of Police Strategies and Management*, 31(1): 36–56.

Collier, R. (2010) *Men, Law and Gender: Essays on the Man Of Law*, London: Routledge.

Commission for Racial Equality (2005) *The Police Service in England and Wales, Final Report of a Formal Investigation*. London: CRE.

Conser, J.A. and Russell, G.A. (2000) *Law Enforcement in the United States*, Gaitherburg, Maryland: Aspen Publishing.

Cowper, T. (2000) 'The Myth of the "Military Model" of Leadership in Law Enforcement', *Police Quarterly*, 3(3): 451–464.

Department of Education and Science (2003*) The Future of Higher Education*, London: HMSO, CMD 5735.

Emsley, C. (2005) 'The Birth and Development of the Police', in T. Newburn (ed.), *The Handbook of Policing*, Cullompton: Willan Publishing.

Fielding, N. (1986) 'Evaluating the Role of Training in Police Socialisation: A British Example', *Journal of Community Psychology*, 14(3): 319–330.

Froyland, D.I. (1991) Police university education: Expectations for a changing world, Phd Thesis, Canada: Simon Fraser University.

Garland, J., Rowe, M., and Johnson, S. (2002) *Police Community and Race Relations Training: An Evaluation*, Leicester: University of Leicester.

Grimshaw, R. and Jefferson, T. (1987) *Interpreting Police Work*, London: Allen Unwin.

Guardian (2010) Government to Phase Out, NPIA & SOCA, 26 July.

Haynes, C. (2009) 'Boffin Bobbies: Should university degrees or their equivalent become a basic requirement for officer recruits?', *Police Review*, 6 March.

Her Majesty's Inspectorate of Constabulary (2002) *Training Matters*, London: HMSO.

Heslop, R. (2011) 'Reproducing Police Culture in a British University: Findings from an exploratory case study of police foundation degrees', *Police, Practice and Research*, 12(4): 1–15.

Home Office (2011) *Home secretary outlines plans for new police professional body*, Press Release 15 December 2011, www.homeoffice.co.uk. Accessed 5 January 2012.

Hopkins, N. (2000) *Stop whining Lawrence Judge tells the Met*, www.theguardian.co.uk, 18 February. Accessed 21 June 2011.

Houle, C. (1980) *Continuing learning in the professions*, San Francisco, California: Jossey-Bass.

Howson, C. (2009) 'Crabs in a barrel: Race, class and widening participation', in C. Howson and M. Salah (eds) *Europe's established and emerging immigrant communities*.

Kakar, S.N. (1998) 'Self-Evaluations of police performance: an analysis of the relationship between police officers' educational level and job performance', *Policing an International Journal of Police Strategies and Management*, 21(4): 632–647.

Law, I., Phillips, D., and Turney, L. (2004) *Institutional Racism in Higher Education*, London: Trentham Books.

Lee, M. and Punch, M. (2004) 'Policing by degrees: Police officers' experiences of university education', *Policing and Society*, 14(3): 233–249.

Loveday, B. (2006) 'Workforce modernisation: Implications for the police service of England and Wales', *The Police Journal*, 79: 105–123.

Mahony, D. and Prenzler, T. (1996) 'Police Studies, the University and the Police Service: An Australian Study', *Journal of Criminal Justice Education*, 18(1): 106–122.

Marion, N. (1998) 'Police Academy training: Are we teaching recruits what they need to know', *Policing: An International Journal of Police Strategies and Management*, 21(1): 54–79.

O'Malley, P. (1997) 'Policing, Politics and Postmodernity', *Social and Legal Studies*, 6(3): 363–381.

Neyroud, P. (2011) *Review of Police Leadership and Training*, London: HMSO.

Reaves, B. (2009) State and Local Law Enforcement Agencies Training Academies 2006, *Bureau of Justice Statistics*, Special Report.

Reiner, R. (1992) 'Policing a Postmodern Society', *The Modern Law Review*, 55(6): 761–781.

Roberg, R., Kuykendall, J., and Cordner, G. (2005) *Police and Society*, 3rd edn, Los Angeles, CA: Roxbury Publishing.

Roberg, R. (2004) 'Higher Education and Policing: Where Are We Now?', *Policing: An International Journal of Police Management and Strategy*, 27(4): 469–486.

Rowe, M. and Garland, D. (2007) 'Police diversity training: A silver bullet tarnished', in M. Rowe (ed.) *Policing After Macpherson*, London: Willan.

Shaw. W.J. (1987) 'Planning and Implementing Race Relations Seminars: The Holly Royde Experience', in J. Shaw, P. Nordlie and R. Shapiro (eds) *Strategies for Improving Race Relations*, Manchester: Manchester University Press.

Shepard, J. (2003) 'Why I believe universities could help transform the police service', *Times Higher Education*, 25 July.

Slack, J. (2012) *Jacqui's 'Civilian Snoopers' Given Yet More Power: Warning as 'Busybody' Numbers Surge*, www.dailymail.co.uk. Accessed 9 July 2012.

Smith, R. and Betts, M. (2003) 'Partnership and consortia approach to United Kingdom Foundation Degrees: A case study of benefits and pitfalls', *Journal of Vocational Education and Training*, 55(2): 223–240.

Stanislas, P. (2009) 'Policing Experiences and Perceptions of New Communities in Britain', in C. Howson and M. Sallah (eds) *Europe's Established and Emerging Immigrant Communities*, London: Trentham Books.

Stone, R. (2009) *The Stephen Lawrence Review: An independent commentary to mark the 10th Anniversary of the Stephen Lawrence Inquiry*. London: Uniting Britain Trust.

Teixeira, N.P. (2006) *Markets in Higher Education: Can We Still Learn From Economics Founding Fathers?*, Centre for Studies in Higher Education, University of California, Berkley, Research and Occasional Paper Series CSHE 406.

Waters, I. (2007) 'Policing, Modernity and Postmodernity', *Policing and Society*, 7(3): 257–278.

Werth, P. (2009) 'Student perception of learning through a problem-based learning exercise: An exploratory study', *Policing: An International Journal of Police Strategies and Management*, 32(1): 21–37.

White, D. (2006) 'A Conceptual Analysis of the Hidden Curriculum of Police Training in England and Wales', *Policing and Society*, 16(4): 386–404.

Wimshurst, K. and Ransley, J. (2007) 'Police Education and the University Sector: Contrasting Models from Australian Experience', *Journal of Criminal Justice Education*, 18(1): 106–122.

Wood, D. and Tong, S. (2008) 'The Future of Initial Police Training: A University Perspective', *International Journal of Police Science and Management*, 11(3): 113–131.

Woods, T.R.J. (1997) Royal Commission into the New South Wales Police, Final Report 1, Corruption.

5 Perspectives on police training and education

The Canadian experience

S. Wyatt and N. Bell

Introduction

Many scholars have commented on the fact that the "public are the police and the police are the public". This is no different in Canada. Tens of thousands of citizens every year decide that they want to become police officers. Of those tens of thousands, thousands make it through the rigorous selection process and start a career as either a federal, provincial, or municipal police officer. The process from hiring to operational police officer is as diverse as Canada's many regions. This chapter will explore the training that new police officers receive. Specifically, it will provide an overview of the different policing models and how they inform the training of newly hired police officers. The role of colleges in the training of police recruits will also be explored. Examples will be used to show how in some regions of Canada colleges have become active partners in the training of new police officers.

Canadian nation state

The task environment within which Canadian policing operates is varied given Canada is geographically the second largest nation in the world encompassing 9,984,670 km² divided into ten provinces and three territories. The majority of the Canadian population, approximately 35,000,000 as of 2012, is concentrated within 50 km of the Canadian/USA border at the 49th parallel. Policing must be delivered in one of the two official languages in Canada, English or French. Police service delivery ranges from officers posted in rural detachments in Northern Canada to major metropolitan cities including Toronto, Ontario, Montreal, Quebec and Vancouver, British Columbia.

Federalist government

In Canada the Constitution Act (1982) delineates the division of powers between the provinces and the federal government. As such the "Administration of Justice", which includes responsibility for policing, is the responsibility of the ten provincial governments. The three Territorial governments operate differently from provincial governments, and as such no independent police agencies exist in the Yukon territories, Northwest Territories or Nunavut, which are all policed federally by the RCMP. Canada's Police Organizations include a total of 222 police services:

- one Police Service with national scope: RCMP
- three Provincial Police Services: Royal Newfoundland Constabulary, Sûreté du Québec and Ontario Provincial Police
- over 150 Municipal Police Services
- over 50 First Nations Police Services
- 12 very large Police Services (over 1000 employees)
- 15 large Police Services (300–999 employees)
- 27 medium Police Services (100–299 employees)
- 65 small Police Services (25–99 employees)
- 103 very small Police Services (under 25 employees)

Selection process for police officers in Canada

In order to have a better perspective on recruit training in Canada, a brief over-view of the selection and hiring of police officers is required. Throughout Canada there are many different standards and ideas around the hiring of police officers. This is reflected in the different models of recruit training that will be explored further in the chapter. For the most part, police agencies require a basic set of pre-requisites. Those are based around the individual's legal status, their age, physical health, and their education. Building on those basic requirements, police agencies look for personality criteria such as integrity and trust. Below is an outline of the Vancouver Police Department's criteria for the hiring of new police recruits.

Qualifications

Basic qualifications

The VPD's basic requirements include (VPDa, 2013):

- minimum 19 years of age
- excellent character
- physically fit and in excellent health
- Canadian Citizen or Permanent Resident
- Grade 12 diploma or equivalent, plus a minimum 30 credits of academic post-secondary education from a recognized university or college, e.g., eco-nomics, social sciences, history, or literature (credits must be directly trans-ferable to an approved post-secondary institution; consult the British Columbia Transfer Guide for assistance)
- no criminal convictions, no adult criminal charges pending

- no history of improper conduct, poor employment, military, educational, or driving record that would affect your suitability for policing duties
- a valid Class 5 driver's license with a good driving record
- be able to type a minimum of 25 words per minute
- meet the visual acuity and hearing standards

Preferred qualifications

- a degree or diploma in any field of study
- knowledge of a second language or culture
- community volunteer experience
- work experience in a supervisory capacity and/or having significant interaction with the public

IPAR

The VPD has four core values:

- Integrity
- Professionalism
- Accountability
- Respect

These core values can't be taught in any school, and they are non-negotiable for our applicants. Without these it would be impossible to have a successful career with the VPD.

Policing service delivery models

As cited by Griffiths (2011: 79) "just as important as recruiting qualified people to become police officers is training them well." As such police recruit training is delivered in either *pre-employment* or *post-employment* models depending on the province. There are three main models of policing in Canada. The only federally mandated police force is the Royal Canadian Mounted Police (RCMP). Given that there is only one federal policing agency, one would assume that each province would in turn have a provincial policing agency. This is not the case, only a few provinces in Canada have their own provincial police agencies. For the purpose of this chapter, the Ontario Provincial Police (OPP) will represent the provincially mandated police departments. Finally, Canada has municipal police departments established in all of the Provinces. These are municipally governed agencies that deliver policing services to municipalities throughout Canada. The municipal policing example used for this chapter is the region of British Columbia known as the Lower Mainland. This region has a relatively dense population of municipal policing agencies.

This section will start with brief overview of the federal, provincial, and municipal policing models. Thereafter each model will be expanded upon, highlighting the recruit training standards and procedures.

RCMP (National Federal Policing)

While the Royal Canadian Mounted Police (RCMP) is Canada's National Federal police force, it uniquely provides policing services at the federal, provincial, and municipal level. Provincial and Municipal police services performed by the RCMP is done so under contract with various provincial governments or Municipalities. As a result many Provinces will have a mix of RCM and independent police agencies operating side by side.

The training of RCMP officers is centralized at the RCMP training Depot in Regina, Saskatchewan. Advanced Police training centres are also operated by the RCMP at the Canadian Police College in Ottawa Ontario (www.cpc.ca) and the Pacific Region Training Centre in Chilliwack, British Columbia.

Training in the RCMP is accomplished through a cadet training program. This is a pre-employment training. Selected cadets attend the RCMP training center in Regina Saskatchewan (Depot) to complete a 24-week training program. Cadets do not become members of the RCMP until successful completion of the program.

Provincial policing (Ontario Provincial Police)

Policing in the province of Ontario is primarily provided by the Ontario Provincial Police (OPP), though a number of regional and independent police agencies such as Toronto City police exist. In Ontario, individuals interested in becoming a police officer can complete a provincially recognized two year "Police Foundations program" at various colleges, for example (www.senecac.on.ca). Successful completion of the program permits individuals to take a provincial exam, which if completed successfully makes them eligible for employment in any police agency in Ontario with the exception of the RCMP.

Upon being employed by a police agency, candidates are sent for further training at the Ontario Police College (OPC). The recruits attend a 12 week training program at the OPC. Once this training is complete, the recruits attend further training at the Provincial Police Academy prior to graduation.

Municipal police agencies

There are 12 municipal police agencies located in the Lower Mainland of Vancouver and Victoria. All of these police agencies train their recruits at the same police academy, located at the Justice Institute of British Columbia (JIBC) in New Westminster. The JIBC applies a block training process. Recruits spend two periods of time training at the JIBC and a further and longer period training at their respective municipal departments. This allows for each municipal agency to adapt the training to meet the specific demands of their respective communities.

Aboriginal police

Prior to colonization, Canada was inhabited by many different aboriginal bands. Each band lived on their ancestral lands, surviving off the land. The arrival of Europeans resulted in a dramatic change in the lives of aboriginals. The Canadian Constitution recognizes three groups of aboriginal people: First Nations, Métis, and Inuit. These are three distinct peoples with unique histories, languages, cultural practices, and beliefs. Currently, there are approximately 1,172,790 aboriginals in Canada (Statistics Canada, 2006).

The policing of these aboriginal people and communities have taken many different forms. The RCMP is contracted by many aboriginal communities to be their police force. Some provincial and municipal agencies also have policing contracts with these communities. Another approach has been for the aboriginal communities to establish their own police force.

Public Safety Canada established an aboriginal policing program, in order to fund the development and creation of aboriginal policing agencies (Public Safety Canada, 2013). The First Nations Policing Program (FNPP) provides financial contributions for policing in First Nation and Inuit communities that is dedicated and responsive to the communities they serve and respect cultural and linguistic diversities. Highlights in 2010–2011 included funding for:

- 168 policing service agreements;
- Policing services to 408 First Nation and Inuit communities (total population 327,430); and
- 1240 police officers.

The Stl'at'imx (pronounced Stat lee im) Tribal police are an excellent example of an aboriginal community that has developed their own police force. Since 1986, the Stl'at'imx people have had some form of security force in their community. What was a security program has developed into an independent and fully recognized policing agency. This police service is modeled on the structure of an independent municipal police department, with governance provided by a police board whose members are selected from the communities served. Police officers recruited by the police boards are either experienced officers or graduates from the Police Academy of the Justice Institute of BC (Ministry of Justice, 2013). All officers are appointed under the Police Act. In 2010, the Stl'at'imx Tribal Police had an authorized strength of ten police officers. The Stl'at'imx police officers train side-by-side with other municipal police officers at the Justice Institute of British Columbia. The tribal police officers receive the same amount of training and are required to meet the same standards as any other police office in the province of British Columbia. There is currently one First Nations Administered Policing Service in British Columbia: Stl'atl'imx Tribal Police.

Now that an overview has been provided, a more detailed examination of each of these recruit training systems will follow.

Royal Canadian Mounted Police

The RCMP has its roots in the later 1800s with the creation of the North-West Mounted Police. In 1873, the North-West Mounted Police (NWMP) was created by an act of parliament (RCMPa, 2012). Parliament was concerned with the lawless environment taking hold in western Canada. The first patrol by the Mounted Police was targeted at whisky traders on the shores of Lake Winnipeg (Nora and Kelly, 1973). Parliament's goal was to establish a force that could enforce the laws of the country and ensure order was maintained in the region. The NWMP's manpower grew reaching approximately 1000 men by 1896 (RCMPb, 2012). While the NWMP was policing western Canada, the Dominion police force was policing most of eastern Canada. The modern RCMP was born in 1920 when parliament merged both the NWMP and the Dominion police force (RCMPc, 2012).

The RCMP is the Canadian national police service and an agency of the Ministry of Public Safety Canada (RCMPd, 2012). The RCMP's model of police is relatively unique in the world. This is due to the fact that the RCMP is a national, federal, provincial, and municipal policing body. Although there are no other police agencies that provide federal policing, provincial and municipal policing is carried out on a contract basis, with some areas opting for other suppliers of policing services.

The RCMP is responsible for all federal policing services. Federal policing deals with policing strategies and issues that have national consequences. This includes areas such as anti-terrorism and border security to name a few. Provincially, the RCMP polices eight provinces and three territories. Provincial policing is carried out on a contract basis. This results in each province having the option to either contract the RCMP for their policing needs or seek the services of another policing agency. The majority of provinces and territories have opted for the RCMP. Examples of provinces that have other arrangements are Ontario and Quebec. Each of these provinces has established their own provincial police forces, with the Ontario Provincial Police (OPP) policing Ontario and the Sûreté du Québec (SQ). They police more than 190 municipalities, 184 aboriginal communities, and three international airports (RCMPe, 2012).

The RCMP's headquarters are located in Ottawa, the capital of Canada. The RCMP is divided into 15 divisions, with each province and territory being roughly a separate division (RCMPf, 2012). Once a person is hired and trained by the RCMP, they can expect to work in multiple divisions and in both federal and provincial policing. Police officers can move from division to division, depending on the manpower requirements and career aspiration of each police officer. A difference worth noting between the RCMP and municipal models is career progression. In the majority of municipal departments, officers that are promoted or who gain experience in a different field rotate back to the general patrol division. In the RCMP, officers who obtain a level of specialization or experience may stay in that position for the rest of their careers, never rotating back to general patrol duties. Some argue that this results in the RCMP patrol divisions being less experienced.

The recruitment of further RCMP officers is a task carried out by all divisions throughout the country. Recruiting sessions take place in every province and territory. The RCMP's basic entry standards are similar to all police agencies in Canada. The only difference is the lack of post-secondary education. Most police agencies currently require a certain amount of post-secondary credits or vocational training. The RCMP's requirements are as follows: (a) a Canadian citizen, (b) be of good character, (c) be proficient in either French or English, (d) have a Canadian High School Diploma or equivalent, (e) possess a valid unrestricted Canadian driver's license, (f) meet the medical/health standards, (g) be willing to relocate anywhere in Canada, and (h) be physically fit (RCMPg, 2012). Having met the minimum standards, applicants have to successfully complete a series of physical and psychological tests. This process is similar to the application process for any policing agency within Canada.

Even though the RCMP delivers a huge variety of services, their recruit training is delivered from one central facility, referrrd to as "depot". Since 1885, every police recruit in the RCMP has completed their basic recruit training at depot, located in Regina, Saskatchewan (RCMPg, 2012). Depot is not an integrated learning institution. Similar to other police academies throughout the country, the education of new RCMP recruits is carried out outside of the mainstreams of adult education (Mckenna, 1998). The program for training new RCMP police officers is referred to as the "Cadet Training Program" (CTP). This is a residential program, where cadets live and attend classes on the same campus.

The Cadet Training Program takes 24 weeks for successful candidates to complete (RCMPh, 2012). Given that Canada is a bilingual country, the training is provided in both French and English. The RCMP utilizes the troop division for organizing recruits. Each troop contains 32 cadets.

The RCMP base their training around the CAPRA operational model. This stands for Clients, Acquiring and analyzing information, Partnership, Response, and Assessment for continuous improvement. Each component of this model is applied to the different areas of instruction delivered to the cadets. The cadet training incorporates this operational model with a competency based approach to cadet learning.

Training at depot is based around problem solving (RCMPi, 2012). Given the fact that the RCMP deploy police officers in major cities and isolated communities, the training is based around acquiring skills as a "generalist" (Sewell, 2010). The CTP has a total of 785 hours of instructions. Those hours are allocated in the following way:

- Applied Police Sciences: 373 hours
- Police Defensive Tactics: 75 hours
- Fitness and Lifestyle: 45 hours
- Firearms: 64 hours
- Police Driving: 65 hours
- Drill, Deportment, and Tactics: 48 hours
- Detachment visits, exams, etc.: 115 hours

Applied Police Sciences dominates the training schedule, with approximately half the instructional hours. This is where the cadets learn all of the basic police skills of investigation and interacting with the public. This can be everything from legal studies, to using the radio, to dealing with a distressed victim. The rest of the cadet training program is based around much more specific skills, such as driving and shooting.

Once cadets have completed their 24-week training course, they graduate from depot. They are officially offered a job with the RCMP and are posted to one of the hundreds of RCMP detachments across the country. The training does not stop for cadets. Once the cadets are assigned to a detachment, they take part in the six-month Field Coaching Program. This program places cadets with experienced officers. These field trainers monitor the cadet's development and coach them through the variety of situations that a patrol officer might be faced with. As one senior officer stated "we need to invest in the first six months of a 35 year career" (RCMPj, 2012). This program of mentoring or coaching by experienced police officers is a common practice among the police agencies.

Once the cadet has successfully completed the Field Coaching period, they leave the constraints of cadet life behind them. They now operate as normal RCMP police officers. Their training now takes the form of "advanced police training". The RCMP has recently gone through some transition with the advanced training approach. Historically, advanced training was delivered face-to-face either at a regional training center or at the Canadian Police College in Ottawa. Delivering ongoing training in this fashion is extremely expensive. Expenses included travel, accommodation, wages, and overtime for the officers filling the vacant spots. Recently, the RCMP has implemented an online distance learning approach to their advanced police training. Although the RCMP started using computer based training in the 1990s, recent technological innovations have allowed this program to mushroom. They have partnered with Canada's leading online police training company, Canadian Police Knowledge Network (CPKN), to develop and run many of their courses. Lisa Gillis, the manager of the RCMP's technology assisted learning unit stated that "e-Learning delivers a lot of advantages, both at organizational and learner levels. Apart from the obvious financial benefits, online courses increase the accessibility, timeliness, and reach of training" (CPKN, 2012). One can see that a major motivation for further expansion of the online delivery of advanced training is a financial saving. An internal review of training expenses by the RCMP concluded that they were able to deliver 43 percent of their training for just 1 percent of the budget by using online learning programs (CPKN, 2012). These benefits are important in increasing the popularity of this form of training and education delivery elsewhere around the world, as highlighted by Stanislas in Chapter 1.

Through all of these developments and changes, one constant remains. Every new police officer serving in the RCMP has been trained in depot. All have been part of a cadet troop, spending their early weeks of their careers marching around the historic Regina grounds. Recent developments in e-learning are starting to affect this old institution. Lately online learning has been blended with the tried and tested cadet training program. Although technology may bring some changes, depot will continue to have its influence on the RCMP members of the future.

Ontario

Police Recruit Training for Ontario's provincial, regional, First Nations, and municipal police agencies is centralized at the Ontario Police College (OPC), located in Aylmer, Ontario. This training is delivered via a post-employment model which requires all recruits to have been hired and sworn in by an authorized police agency in Ontario. This is similar to other municipal agencies throughout Canada. The training is conducted in a residential model, similar to the RCMP. Recruits reside in cohorts within the campus, living and learning with the same group of recruits.

Every police officer hired in the province of Ontario goes through the same 12-week basic training program. This program has academic, physical, and mental components. The goal of this 12-week training is to provide the recruits with the basic knowledge in order to progress towards an end goal of being a frontline police officer. The core components of the training are:

- Crime Prevention
- Law Enforcement
- Assistance to Victims of Crime
- Public Order Maintenance
- Emergency Response

Essential knowledge and skills are developed through simulation exercises, classroom discussion, and case studies. The major topics covered during the recruit training are:

- Biker enforcement
- Community policing
- Counter terrorism
- CPIC
- Critical incident stress management
- Death notification
- Defensive tactics
- Domestic violence
- Drill
- Diversity and professional practice
- Elder abuse
- EMO – IMS100
- Ethics
- Evidence
- Federal statutes

- Infectious disease
- Leadership
- Provincial statutes
- Race relations
- Special Investigations Unit
- Taser
- Traffic
- Use of force (see Arsenault chapter)
- Victims

Applied police learning

Students must complete a series of cumulative written tests and final examinations. A mark of 75 percent per subject is required. In order to retake, students cannot fail more than two academic subjects and are allowed one opportunity to rewrite each of the two failed subjects within six months at the request of their police service.

Practical training

Students must meet required standards in a series of tests that may include judgment and proficiency. Students not successfully completing any of the following subject areas must be re-examined/tested at the request of their police service within six months, unless special consideration is obtained from the Director. Defensive Tactics:

- Defensive tactics
- Firearms
- Officer safety/tactical communication

This standardized approach ensures that all police recruits receive the same foundational training in the basics of policing. Once the recruit has successfully completed the 12-week Ontario Police College course, they are dispatched to their respective agencies for further training. The Ontario Provincial Police conduct another five weeks of training at their police academy, the Provincial Police Academy. At the completion of this five week training period, recruits are placed on attachment throughout the province of Ontario for further mentorship.

Municipal police training (British Columbia)

In the province of British Columbia policing is provided by both the RCMP and 12 Independent police agencies ranging in size from 20 members in the municipality of Oak Bay to approximate 1200 members of the Vancouver Police. Again, the province of British Columbia contracts with the RCMP to provide police services throughout most of central and Northern British Columbia, in addition to Municipalities which contracts the RCMP to provide policing in lieu of establishing or operating an Independent Agency.

The Justice Institute of British Columbia – Police Academy provides centralized and standardized police training for the 12 independent municipal agencies in addition to advanced programs training on select topics. In this model, police recruits are screened and hired by an independent police agency and sent to the police academy as sworn police officers. The program is approximately 38 weeks of training divided into three modules of academic and applied knowledge training, practical field training, and then further academic applied knowledge training.

The JIBC also provides advanced training in select topics, such as forensic DNA evidence investigations, sexual assault investigations as well as others. Municipal police officers in BC can also attend training programs offered at the Canadian Police College and the Pacific Region Training centre.

Police training curriculum

The Police training curriculum in Canada is largely standardized, encompassing the following topics:

- Criminal law
- Applicable provincial statutes
- Firearms training
- Driver training and emergency vehicle operation
- Investigation and patrol techniques and strategies
- Diversity training
- Physical training and use of force skills
- Critical incident de-escalation
- Community policing techniques
- Problem Oriented Policing models, CAPRA, etc.
- Other specific training programs as mandated by provincial governments or determined by geographical location

Police Recruit Training for BC's independent municipal police agencies, transit police and First Nations police is provided by the Police Academy, Justice Institute of BC (JIBC).

The Police Academy delivers a block system of recruit training in which the 13–17-week field practicum (at the recruit's police service) is sandwiched between the theoretical and practical training components of Block I (13 weeks) and Block III (eight weeks), that are held at the Justice Institute of BC in New Westminster. The Police Recruit Training program is *post-employment* and all recruits must be hired and sworn in by a BC police agency prior to attending the program. Although it is *post-employment* training, recruits are required to pay a tuition fee of $9500 for the nine-month program. The Police Academy has four to six intakes a year, depending on demand, and currently between 140 and 180 recruits graduate annually. The Academy's police recruit training program consists of a mix of theory and practice and includes realistic simulations in which actors are employed; an approach which is popular in world policing training practice (See Moreau de Bellaing and Tingyou chapters).

College approach

Post-employment police training is not the only model being used within Canada. There are a growing number of provinces and colleges that offer police recruit training from a post-secondary institution. The majority of these colleges offer a multi-month program to anyone accepted by the college. Once a student graduates with their certificate or diploma, they then apply directly to the police agencies. This allows the police agencies to pass on some of the training costs to the colleges. The two programs that will be examined in greater detail are the programs at Holland College in Prince Edward Island and Seneca College in Ontario.

Although these colleges operate as post-secondary institutions, the selection process for the policing programs are often more extensive. Generally, educational grades are the most important information considered by post-secondary institutions in informing their acceptance decisions. The college-based policing programs tend to be more rigorous around establishing applicants' core competencies in key areas, and often use written aptitude and communication tests to supplement their requirements for higher educational entry requirements. Below is an example of the Seneca College prerequisites for their policing program.

Atlantic Police College

As previously mentioned, Canada offers a great amount of diversity in both its approach to policing and also in the training of new police officers. The Atlantic Police Academy (APA) is another example of the diversity that exists. Unlike the central approach of the RCMP or the regional approach to recruit training as in the Lower Mainland of Vancouver, the Atlantic region of Canada has taken an educational institution approach. Instead of hiring the police officers and then following them through their training, the Atlantic region places the onus on the potential recruit to obtain the training themselves.

The APA is recognized by the Canadian Chiefs of Police as a certified police training facility. It is one of very few academies or colleges in Canada to obtain this recognition. It is based in Prince Edward Island (PEI). PEI is located on the eastern coast of Canada, in the region referred to as the Maritimes. Until recently, the island was cut off from the rest of the country. A new bridge has meant that the large island is much easier to access. The Atlantic Police College is a division of Holland College. Holland College is a respected post-secondary institution that not only trains future police officers, but also other law enforcement professionals, and firefighters inter alia. In 2011, the academy completed a multi-million dollar upgrade, resulting in the development of industry leading facilities (Holland College, 2012b). The academy's driving, shooting, and simulation facilities were upgraded. The mission of the APA is to:

> ...provide timely, contemporary law enforcement training, education and development from basic to advanced levels. Today's law enforcement professional is challenged in the acquisition of a wide variety of skills necessary in a fast-changing society. The Atlantic Police Academy provides the means to obtain those necessary skills.
>
> (Prince Edward Island 2012a: 1)

The main difference between the Atlantic Police College (APC) and other police recruit training models that have been reviewed up to this point is how students enroll for basic training. Although the training models have been slightly different, up to this point the recruits have gone through a hiring process prior to enrolling into the training. Without being hired the recruit could not take the course at either the RCMP's depot or the Lower Mainland's JIBC. This is different at the APA. There they accept application much the same as any post-secondary institution. The students do not apply to specific police departments but apply to Holland College. When accepted into the program, the students are only accepted into a certificate program and are not guaranteed any sort of employment as a police officer upon graduation.

The application process to the academy is relatively similar to the application processes of police departments within Canada. The process for the APA includes a physical test, medical examination, written test, criminal background check, and background investigation (Holland College 2012a). This application is much more rigorous than a regular Canadian college application. Once accepted into the police academy, the students take part in a 35-week residential training program. The length of the program is similar to those across Canada. The program is based around a multi-disciplinary approach. The following are the courses that are offered during the certificate program (Holland College 2012c):

Law: Criminal Code and Federal Statutes I
Law: Criminal Code and Federal Statutes II
Principles of Traffic Services
Psychology: Police Applied Social Sciences
Sociology: Police Applied Social Sciences and Community Based Policing
Criminal Investigations I
Criminal Investigations II
Police Vehicle Operations and Speed Measurement Devices
Police Reporting Systems and Computer Literacy
Occupational Safety for Police

Professional Patrol Tactics
Intervention and Use of Force: Restraints and Intermediate Weapons
Judgmental Use of Force Simulation Training
Police Firearms Proficiency and Tactical Training
Police Physical Abilities Development
On the Job Training/Workplace Experience Program

Unlike many of the other police academies in Canada, the APA takes a standard educational approach to the course content. That is to say that the police academy process is broken down into courses, similar to an academic degree or certificate. Recruits take each of the courses, which consist of lectures, activities, assignments, and examination. As they complete each course, they move closer to obtaining a certificate. This multi-course approach is different to the other major Canadian police academies. The majority of academies are less formally structured, with more flow between subjects. The actual content of the training is very similar to other police academies throughout Canada, with a blending of tactical skills and investigative techniques.

Although the APA is not affiliated with any specific police department, it does have regional recognition for its recruit program. The largest police force in the province, which is the Charlottetown Police Department, list the APA as their main source of applicants (Charlottetown Police, 2012. The majority of police services in Canada recognize the APA as an accredited training facility. This allows graduates from this program to apply to many police departments throughout Canada.

Although recruit training is their main function, advanced and in-service training is also delivered at the APA. With the recent upgrades to their facilities, the academy is well suited for advanced courses in all of the major policing areas. Holland College has also recently built a relationship with the Canadian Police Knowledge Network (CPKN). CPKN is Canada's leading online police education institution (CPKN, 2012). They are located on Prince Edward Island, thus the association with Holland College and the Atlantic Police Academy is a natural fit. This association allows the APA to be at the forefront of police education.

Seneca College

Program description

The police foundations program is intended to provide potential police recruits with a comprehensive education combining legal education with practical skill development. The program meets the standards as set by the Provincial Ministry of Training, Colleges, and Universities in Ontario.

The objectives of the program include the ability to:

- Act in a manner consistent with all relevant law and legislation, and professional, organizational, and ethical standards.

- Communicate accurately, persuasively, and credibly to develop effective working relationships with individuals, groups, and multidisciplinary teams in order to achieve goals.
- Apply knowledge of basic concepts of psychology, sociology, and criminology when interacting with peers, supervisors, other professionals, victims, suspects/offenders, and the public.
- Document, prepare, and assist in the presentation of court cases in compliance with criminal and provincial law, rules of evidence, and the Charter of Rights and Freedom.
- Assess the use of police powers.
- Initiate, promote, and facilitate partnerships to meet community policing and security needs.
- Assess the relationship of policing services to other participants in the criminal justice system and other community service agencies.
- Make sound decisions based on an evaluation of situations.
- Cope with stress and optimize fitness and wellness.
- Apply fundamental concepts of political science, law and legislative policy making, and public administration to the provision of police services.
- Assess information-gathering skills used in basic investigative techniques.
- Assess crisis intervention strategies.
- Develop strategies to assist crime victims to meet their needs.

The Seneca program blends college-level education courses with police specific practical application courses. This allows students to have both a solid academic foundation, as well as much more practical experience in the skills required to be a police officer. The Seneca program is based on the completion of four semesters. Much like any post-secondary institutions, the semesters build on themselves, with the most complex material presented in the last semester.

Below is an example of one of the courses for one of the semesters within the policing program. You can see this blending of academic and police specific programs.

College English

Table 5.1 Seneca basic police training program

ICA001	Introduction to Computers and Applications	2
LAW120	Criminal Law and the Charter of Rights and Freedoms	4
LAW130	Criminal Justice System and Community Services	4
LAW140	Law Enforcement Communications	4
LAW150	Fitness and Lifestyle Management I	2
PSY100	Introduction to Psychology	

The future of recruit training within Canada

The training of police recruits is an essential task within policing. There is a never-ending cycle of new police officers entering the hundreds of different agencies within the Canadian policing community. There have been some significant developments in the training of recruits in recent years. One of these developments has been the impact that the Police Sector Counsel has had on training.

Police Sector Counsel

Recently efforts have been initiated by the federal government through the "Police Sector Council" (PSC or SC) to develop a nationally standardized police training curriculum (taking into account regional differences where necessary). This initiative is still under development

Policing in Canada is a dynamic and diverse sector where many different police organizations work to keep Canadians safe. Different police organizations exist, each with their own jurisdiction, to serve and protect the various regions of Canada. The country is vast and different areas require different types of policing services. The most recent research conducted by the SC in relation to recruit training involved the identification of a competency-based framework for policing. This was a three-year project that brought together policing agencies throughout Canada. By identifying the competencies within policing, institutions that train police recruits are able to work together to develop their curriculum to match these demands.

National e-learning projects

The other major trend in recruit training and in police training within Canada is the implementation and development of online training. Online-based education has developed in leaps and bounds throughout the world. The policing community is no exception to this rule. Online-based training is being incorporated into all levels of policing training.

Since 2007, the Police Sector Council and the Canadian Police Knowledge Network (CPKN) have collaborated to produce e-learning courses that meet the training needs of the national police community. Funded through the Government of Canada's Sector Council Program, courses are selected for relevance to a frontline police audience and are delivered in both official languages. On release, each course is offered at no cost to members of the Canadian police community for a designated Learning and Evaluation period. L and E events not only provide frontline personnel with free access to priority training, but are also an effective means of assessing and advancing online police training. The national e-learning initiative is an important component of PSC's mandate to implement innovative, practical solutions to human resource planning and management challenges.

Examples of programs delivered by CPKN include: Human Trafficking, Preventing Officer-Involved Collisions and Critical Incident Stress Management in addition to a host of other offerings. Although much of the online-based training is not geared towards recruit training, there are some courses currently delivered to recruits through an online platform. For example, at the JIBC recruits currently receive their training for Incident Command systems through an online course.

Conclusion

Canada is a huge country with many different regions and territories. The demands of policing such a large and unique environment have resulted in the development of hundreds of different policing agencies. Currently there are three major models of police recruit training in Canada. Some policing agencies, such as the RCMP, have a central police academy. These central academies train all new police recruits for one agency. Another approach is to have a multi-agency police academy, which can be found at both the provincial and municipal level. These police academies provide a standardized training system to a variety of policing agencies. This results in police recruits from different police agencies training together prior to returning to their respective agencies. This is seen in British Columbia and Ontario. The final option is a post-secondary police academy. These police academies are based within established colleges. These academies carry out police recruit training prior to the recruits being hired as police officers. Recruits successfully complete the college-based training and then hope to apply those skills in a successful application to a police agency of their choice. Each of these different approaches has advantages and disadvantages. The variety of regions within Canada means that a standard approach is extremely hard to accomplish. Recent developments in online learning and competency-based training may result in future collaboration and standardization within Canada's recruit training community.

References

Canadian Police Knowledge Network (2012), retrieved from: www.cpkn.ca/about.

Charlottetown Police (2012), retrieved from: www.charlottetownpolice.com/recruitment.

Government of British Columbia, Ministry of Justice (2013), retrieved from: www.pssg. gov.bc.ca/policeservices/firstnations/index.htm.

Government of Canada, Public Safety (2013), retrieved from: www.publicsafety.gc.ca/ prg/le/ap/1index-eng.aspx.

Government of Prince Edward Island (2012), retrieved from: www.gov.pe.ca/infopei/ index.php3?number=252&lang=e.

Griffiths, Curt (2011), Canadian Criminal Justice: A primer (4th edition), Nelson Education Ltd, Canada.

Holland College (2012a), retrieved from: www.hollandcollege.com/admissions/full_ time_programs/police_science_cadet/.

Holland College (2012b), retrieved from: www.hollandcollege.com/atlantic_police_ academy/.

Holland College (2012c), retrieved from: www.hollandcollege.com/admissions/full_time_programs/police_science_cadet/.

Kelly, Nora and Kelly, William (1973) The Royal Canadian Mounted Police: A century of History, Hurtig Publishers, Edmonton, Alberta.

McKenna, Paul (1998) Foundations of Policing in Canada, Prentice-Hall Canada Inc., Scarborough, Ontario.

Nancoo, Stephen (2004) Contemporary Issues in Canadian Policing, Canadian Educators' Press, Mississauga, Ontario.

Seagrave, Jayne (1997) Introduction to Policing in Canada, Prentice-Hall Canada Inc., Scarborough, Ontario.

Sewell, John (2010) The Real Story: Policing in Canada, James Lorimer & Company ltd., Publishers, Toronto.

Statistics Canada, 2006 census (2013), retrieved from: http://www12.statcan.ca/census-recensement/2006/rt-td/ap-pa-eng.cfm.

Vancouver Police Department (2013), retrieved from: http://vancouver.ca/police/recruiting/police-officers/index.html.

6 Constructing comparative competency profiles

The Netherlands experience

H. Peeters

The subject of this chapter is related to work carried out on behalf of the Police Academy of the Netherlands (The Academy). The idea to develop comparative competency profiles irrespective of type of education or occupation arose eight years ago when the Academy participated in setting up a new system of police training in Guatemala (Alvarez 2004–2007), based on universal principles of work-related education but nonetheless tailor-made. Recently, three similar endeavours have been successfully completed. One initiative consisted of matching police tasks and corresponding educational levels between six Dutch Caribbean islands because of their new constitutional framework (Boersen *et al.* 2010), the other involved reviewing the ten-year-old occupational profiles of the Dutch Police by the Dutch Police Education Council (POR). Recently I transformed the reviewed occupational profiles into a set of qualification profiles for the Academy as a basis for curriculum development (Peeters 2012).

An important set of lessons learnt from these undertakings is that – at first – it is crucial to distinguish between the remit of the organization on one hand and the remit of the educational institute on the other in order to bring both worlds transparently together – later on (Nijhof *et al.* 2010). The organization should be centrally involved in the development of both an occupational and a competency profile, the institute in conceiving both a qualification and a curriculum profile. Such a 'division of labour' should not prevent a smooth convergence between these profiles. If the participation of those in the field is overlooked, the study programme will fail to capture crucial insights and information and lack acceptance from key stakeholders. Conversely, if you give the field a decisive say in qualifications and curriculum criteria, the programme will suffer from the limited frame of reference of professionals with outdated ideas and it will miss the indispensable academic dimension (Grotendorst *et al.* 2002). These and related considerations are important in developing working partnerships (see Green and Woolston chapter). Clear definitions are vital. In this case, definitions of the four different profiles that I examine are (Nijhof *et al.* 2010):

- an occupational profile should bear the marks of recent and future influences of societal developments in order to produce the characteristic essentials of the responsibilities and tasks of the particular profession.

- a competency profile should refer to the integration of knowledge, abilities and attitudes that are needed to act and behave adequately at work.
- a qualification profile should describe the level and criteria of examinations that will yield a particular certificate (see Sándor ibid.).
- a curriculum profile should consist of components such as terms, learning outcomes, credits, ways of teaching, learning and tutoring.

Competencies as a bridge between occupational profiles and qualification profiles

Let us assume that the societal influences on the occupation in question have been properly mapped in sessions with the input of professionals only, the academics are only facilitators in this phase, and the outcome of this collaboration is a clear picture of the challenges laying ahead in terms of occupational activities[1] (Nijhof *et al.* 2010). We then can proceed with the tricky procedure of formulating the required competencies. Tricky, because at this point in the process professionals are inclined to recite what they have learned previously. Police officers too are inclined to formulate possibly outdated competencies in terms of what or how to learn often reinforced by occupational culture (Stanislas, Chapter 1), not in terms of what is needed to demonstrate competent behaviour at work (Stam *et al.* 2007). In order to prevent professionals from reciting a lot of rather vague notions of academic know-how[2] the institute's facilitator should encourage professionals to formulate the required competencies in terms of 's/he should be able to…' (Den Boer and Peeters 2007). Such a procedure will result in a list of activities and a set of competencies needed to carry out tasks adequately. What still has to be figured out though is what levels of work have been identified by the professionals, implicitly or explicitly, and how these levels relate to qualification levels. In other words, how to correlate occupational levels and qualification levels (Peeters 2010). Moreover, the typical features of a particular profession should catch the eye (Peeters 2011). So far this should be sufficient, if it comes to innovation, but over and above this it is my ambition to present a universal model that could connect the characteristics of any type of profession to any type of education. The guiding assumption is that each profession consists of three main layers: implementation, organization and governance[3] (Mintzberg 1983). In policing terms this equates with the operational, tactical, and strategic layer. See Table 6.1.

Table 6.1 Similarities between characteristics of professions

Any profession	Police profession
• Implementation Layer ∿∿	• Operational Layer
• Organisation Layer ∿∿	• Tactical Layer
• Governance Layer ∿∿	• Strategic Layer

These levels can be differentiated, but in the rough they respectively come down to address either 'what', 'how' or 'why' questions, or to carrying out things, arranging things or directing things. The next assumption is that these occupational levels are more or less equivalent to respectively intermediate vocational, higher professional, and academic-professional levels (Twijnstra Gudde Management Consultancy 2007). This is highlighted in Table 6.2

Table 6.2 outlines a generic picture that for the sake of clarity has to be specified by the unique features of the profession in question[4] (Meerdink *et al.* 1999). In line with Stanislas' earlier observations the 'core' processes of the policing profession are more or less similar all over the world, namely serving the public by quickly responding to incidents, by enforcing the law and by investigating crimes (Stanislas ibid.).[5] In fact emergency response is or can be an ad hoc mixture of police services, law enforcement and criminal investigation. That leads to Table 6.3.

Now that we have connected specific levels of work to specific levels of qualification itemized in three processes of policing, we can make use of the terminology that connects all these elements, namely the competency concept. Thus, competency profiles act as intermediary between occupational profiles and qualification profiles (Peeters 2009). For 'daily police work' the competency profiles indicate what particular level of performance can be expected with regard to a particular process; for 'the institute' the competency profiles provide a frame of reference from which comparable assessment criteria and comparable learning outcomes can be deduced. To be sure that the profession remains at the heart of the comparisons the competency breakdown used by CEPOL[6] (IJzerman 2003) might be useful. CEPOL's competency framework – a further elaborated version of a competency model by the German scholars Frei, Baitsch and Bunk (Bunk 1990) – divides competencies into four categories: professional, contextual, social and individual.[7] The focus is on the profession and on the context that affects its functioning in terms of interactions and personal input.

Table 6.2 Equivalence of levels

Generic characteristics of a (police) profession	Qualification levels
• Implementation/Operations $\approx$ = 'what' = carrying out • Organisation/Tactics $\approx$ = 'how' = arranging • Governance/Strategies $\approx$ = 'why' = directing	• Intermediate Vocational • Higher Professional • Academic Professional

Table 6.3 Distinctive core processes of police profession

Operational level	Tactical level	Strategic level
• Emergency Response • Law Enforcement • Criminal Investigation	• Emergency Response • Law Enforcement • Criminal Investigation	• Emergency Response • Law Enforcement • Criminal Investigation

From generic competencies towards specific competencies

Before explaining these comparable outcomes and the relationship between levels of police work and corresponding qualification levels, in advancing my aim in developing an universal approach, I am obliged to sketch a 'generic' distinction between intermediate vocational, higher professional and academic-professional levels of competencies.[8] For instance, under what circumstances do you have to show your professional competencies: within a stable, an unpredictable or an unfamiliar situation? This is only one of the generic components in the range from a vocational level up to an academic level: the higher the complexity of the situation, the higher the level of required competencies. Table 6.4 shows a typology of generic characteristics based on experience and eclectic gathering.

In Table 6.5 I have transformed this typology into a template of generic distinctions between competencies at each level. For instance, if it comes to a time-scale, the factor 'medium term' appears in a generic competency as: 'converting environmental developments into medium term police proposals'.

The words in italics indicate where, generally speaking, the differences lie with respect to the determining level.

Each of the 16 competencies refers to a particular feature, whereas a horizontal comparison per number indicates the different qualification level of that particular feature. The essentials of each feature can be summarized in Table 6.6 as follows, highlighted in italics:

The generic character of the template of competency levels and its contracted version aim at heeding several functions:

- diploma-equivalence between different educational programmes
- translation of generic competencies into specific competencies
- consistency between programmes of the same field
- visibility of differences in qualification levels
- a compact set of competencies, divided into categories introduced by CEPOL
- a frame of reference for curriculum construction
- a frame of reference for assessment criteria

With regard to police education the template can be used for converting generic competencies into specific policing competencies. Within the context of the chapter 'specific' means that not only the core processes of policing have to be addressed, but also different levels of work in line with different levels of education. For the sake of international analogy the generic competencies (as shown in the template) as well as specific policing competencies will be compared with the learning outcomes of the European Qualifications Framework for lifelong learning, abbreviated as EQF (European Commission 2010). Each of the following diagrams contains a full description of the EQF descriptors in question and a classification of competencies according to the categories used by CEPOL. For

Table 6.4 Typology of generic distinctions

Level ⇧ ⇨	Intermediate vocational	Higher professional	Academic professional
Category			
Situation	• Stable Environment	• Changeable Environment	• Unfamiliar Environment
Resources	• Applying Factors	• Analysing Patterns	• Researching Patterns
Activities	• Applying Limited Resources	• Applying a Wide Range of Resources	• Considering a Wide Range of Resources
Timescale Attitude	• Context-Bound Instruments	• Using Instruments in other Contexts	• Inventing Instruments for other Contexts
	• Limited Deployable	• Widely Deployable	• Specialized Deployable
	• Performing Duties	• Considering Duties	• Conceptualizing Duties
	• Separate Actions	• Integrated Actions	• Multidisciplinary Approach
	• External Cooperation	• External Coordination	• Dealing with Authorities
	• Concrete Activities	• Complex Activities	• Uncertain Activities
	• Short Term	• Medium Term	• Long Term
	• Actions	• Tactics	• Strategies
	• Result-Oriented	• Application Oriented	• Reflection-Oriented
	• Following Instructions	• Enterprising	• Inquiring
	• Supervising the Work of Others	• Supervising Development of Others	• Supervising Strategic Performance of Others

instance, at qualification level 4, one of the EQF descriptors requires that you should be able to 'supervize the (evaluation and improvement of) routine work of others'. In terms of the template this particular EQF 4 learning outcome is comparable with 'social' competency number 11, namely 'reporting on one's conduct and the conduct of others'. See Table 6.5. In terms of policing this means that the police officer 'should be able to deliver a sound report of his or her interventions or those of colleagues'.

Table 6.7 illustrates the similarities between generic, specific and EQF-competencies by connecting EQF-descriptors and generic as well as policing competencies to a particular level of work and education in relation to a particular policing process. In this case the level of work is operational, the level of education is intermediate vocational and the particular policing process is emergency response.

The lines in italics illustrate which generic competency or which specific policing competency relates to which EQF-descriptor and which CEPOL-category, not only with regard to Table 6.7 but also with regard to Tables 6.8–6.14.

The following diagrams are constructed in a similar way, i.e. containing EQF-descriptors that are similar to both generic and policing competencies with reference to a particular level of work and education in relation to a particular policing process. In this case the level of work is tactical, the level of education is higher professional and the particular policing process remains emergency response. In this instance, see Table 6.8, many of the competences required are similar to those involved in national disaster response work (see Sándor chapter).

The next three illustrations, Tables 6.9–6.11, refer to the policing process of law enforcement instead of emergency response. Table 6.9 addresses the operational layer, situated at an intermediate vocational level of qualification, Table 6.10 addresses the tactical layer situated at a higher professional level of qualification and Table 6.11 addresses the strategic layer, situated at an academic-professional level of qualification (see Neyroud and Wain chapter, Sándor ibid.).

Finally, three examples relating to the policing task of criminal investigation instead of law enforcement or emergency response. The examples refer to three EQF-levels level 4, 6 and 7. They are again related to the three different layers of operation, tactics, and strategies in conformance with the corresponding educational levels: an intermediate vocational level, a higher professional level and an academic-professional level.

Again the competencies are divided into the CEPOL-categories, this time respectively social, professional and contextual competencies.

The connection between levels of work and levels of education – which in case of policing means expertize at an operational level related to an intermediate vocational level (see Moreau de Bellaing, Wakefield and Button chapters), expertize at a tactical level related to a higher professional level and expertize at a strategic level related to an academic-professional level (see Neyroud and Wain, and Sándor chapters) can also be applied to distinguish levels of competencies needed for managing the main processes of policing. An operational level of policing requires another qualification level

Table 6.5 Template of generic distinctions between competency levels, still to be specified as policing competencies

Competencies		Intermediate Vocational Education/EQF4	Higher Professional Education/EQF5/6	Academic-Professional Education/EQF7/8
Professional	1	Operating in *rather complex situations*, i.e. stable but possibly dangerous and stressful situations	Operating in *complex* situations, i.e. unexpected situations with a lot of influences	Operating in unfamiliar situations from an *interdisciplinary perspective* in both an academic and professional sense
	2	Acting *relatively independently within prescriptions*	*Weighing* tasks, means, powers and *acting independently*	Combining *independent research with societal relevance*
	3	Performing result-oriented and *systematically*	Recognizing and *analysing* patterns and trends, applying research findings	*Generalizing* practical results and findings into a conceptual approach
	4	Suggesting and implementing *elements* of an operating procedure	Drawing up, implementing and evaluating an *entire* operating procedure	Converting academic research into *strategies or scenarios*
Contextual	5	Gearing activities to those of other organizational units	Directing and coordinating (multidisciplinary) activities inside and outside the organization	*Dealing with* and reporting to *authorities*
	6	Applying *limited* resources/disciplines	Applying *a wide range of* resources/disciplines	*Considering a wide range of resources/disciplines*
	7	Taking initiatives and *responsibility, also for other people*	*Considering societal developments, positions, interests*	*Researching societal trends* and assessing their practical relevance
	8	Spotting and *mapping signals* from the environment	Converting environmental developments into *medium term policy proposals*	Converting environmental developments into *long term policy proposals*

Social	9	Supervising the routine work of colleagues and coaching them with regard to the profession	Supervising the professional development of colleagues and managing internal and external relationships	Supervising the strategic performance of colleagues and realising acceptance of research findings and recommendations
	10	Cooperating in operations with colleagues, partners and organizations	Cooperating in operations and policies with colleagues, partners and organizations	Cooperating in policies and strategies with authorities and academics
	11	Reporting on one's own conduct and the conduct of others	Communicating operational plans in an understandable way (internally and externally) also in a foreign language	Giving substantiated advice and accounting for it, also in a foreign language
	12	Dealing with diversity of standards and values of persons	Dealing with diversity of standards and values within and between organizations	Dealing with cultural differences within and between countries
Individual	13	Taking a particular point of view and coping with feedback	Deploying what has been learned in another context	Reflecting on theory and practice, leading to conceptualization and new knowledge
	14	Delivering unusual solutions for problems in a qualitative or effective way	(Creative) advising with regard to the profession and utilizing obtained advice in a flexible way	(Creative) strategic advising about implications of social dynamics.
	15	Gathering, elaborating and organizing information	Assessing the relevance of information and resources	Keeping up with one's specialist academic literature and assessing its actual value
	16	Exploiting experience for future performance	Creating durable conditions for an effective handling of issues	Contributing to a scientific development of the particular academic field

Notes

1 Characterizations must not be seen as strict 'partitions' between the different competency levels, but as 'applying' for the most part.

2 The competencies refer to initial training programmes. For post-initial programmes the competencies of the intermediate vocational level can sometimes shift up somewhat to the higher professional level and the latter ones to the academic-professional level.

3 A horizontal comparison per number indicates the differences between the levels at one glance.

of steering competencies than a tactical or strategic level of policing. In this context Robert Quinn's typology of management roles comes in handy (Quinn 2003), because its features can be incorporated into the three different levels of competency profiles. For Quinn a 'master manager' (as he calls it) should be able to switch between eight different roles as a result of the combination of two different styles, namely flexibility or control versus two different situations, namely internal or external. The present and future competency profiles for leading positions within the Dutch police are built upon this device (Peeters 2009).

I will illustrate this by a few competencies out of the profile for an operational police manager, to be positioned at EQF level 5. Similar illustrations could be given with regard to competencies of police managers in tactical or strategic positions.

For instance, in a role as stimulator – being flexible internally – a leader should encourage team-building and participatory decision-making. For the operational police manager this has been translated into the professional competency 'to combine individual talents in order to form focused teams', for example an arrest team, a riot squad or a SWAT team. The template's generic competency behind this is 'implementing an entire operating procedure'.

In a role as mediator – being flexible externally – a leader should 'build and maintain a power base and negotiate on deployment, agreements and ideas'. For the operational police manager this has been translated into the contextual competency 'to translate wishes of clients into possible activities for the organization', for example addressing neighbourhood complaints by a particular community policing approach. The template's generic competency behind this is 'considering societal interests'.

Table 6.6 Particular competence feature

Category	No	Feature and level of competencies
Professional	1	Complexity of the *situation*
	2	Degree of *independency*
	3	*Methodical* dimension
	4	Degree of *induction/deduction/deconstruction*
Contextual	5	*Positioning* towards partners
	6	Handling *instruments/disciplines* as to nature or volume
	7	Considering *societal developments*
	8	*Converting environmental developments* in terms of span or scope
Social	9	Level and nature of *relational management*
	10	Level and nature of *cooperation*
	11	*Communicative ability* in terms of scope
	12	Dealing with *diversity* in terms of scope
Individual	13	*Taking a stand (point)* in terms of depth or scope
	14	Level, creativity, ingenuity, flexibility of *advice*
	15	Degree of utilizing type of *information*
	16	Scope of results of *own input*

Table 6.7 An operational emergency response competence (EQF4)

Level of work		Operations
Competencies		*Intermediate vocational education related to emergency response*
EQF 4 Descriptors		Factual and theoretical knowledge in broad contexts • Cognitive and practical skills to generate solutions to specific problems • Self-management within guidelines of contexts that are predictable but changeable • *Supervising the (evaluation and improvement of) routine work of others*
Professional	Generic	Operating in rather complex situations, i.e. stable but possibly dangerous and stressful
	Specific	Being able to operate on call in a stable but possibly critical situation
Contextual	Generic	Gearing activities to those of other organizational units
	Specific	Being able to assess whether persons or activities have to be transferred to a colleague
Social	Generic	*Reporting on one's own conduct and the conduct of others*
	Specific	*Being able to deliver a sound report of own interventions or interventions by colleagues*
Individual	Generic	Taking a particular point of view and coping with feedback
	Specific	Being able to review one's own police performance and to amend it, if necessary

Table 6.8 A tactical emergency response competence (EQF6)

Level of work		Tactics
Competencies		*Higher professional education related to emergency response*
EQF 6 Descriptors		• Advanced knowledge, involving a critical understanding of theories and principles • Advanced innovative skills to solve complex and unpredictable problems • *Managing complex activities or projects, taking responsibility for decision-making* • Taking responsibility for managing professional development of individuals and groups
Professional	Generic	Operating in complex situations, i.e. unexpected situations with a lot of influences
	Specific	Being able to operate with regard to violent incidents and unforeseen calamities
Contextual	Generic	*Directing and coordinating (multidisciplinary) activities inside and outside the organization*
	Specific	*Being able to coordinate police response and the assistance of emergency services*
Social	Generic	Managing internal and external relationships
	Specific	Being able to deal evenly with conflicts between several parties, also in mass gatherings
Individual	Generic	Deploying what has been learned in another context
	Specific	Being able to apply protocols in combination with intelligent action

Table 6.9 An operational law enforcement competence (EQF4)

Level of work		Operations
Competencies		*Intermediate vocational education related to law enforcement*
EQF 4 Descriptors		• Factual and theoretical knowledge in broad contexts • Cognitive and practical skills to generate solutions to specific problems • *Self-management within guidelines of contexts that are predictable but changeable* • Supervising the (evaluation and improvement of) routine work of others
Professional	*Generic*	*Acting relatively independent within prescriptions*
	Specific	*Being able to execute police powers proportionally within the boundaries of laws and rules*
Contextual	*Generic*	Applying limited resources/disciplines
	Specific	Being able to apply some fields of law
Social	*Generic*	Dealing with diversity of standards and values of persons
	Specific	Being able to consider cultural standards of colleagues and the public
Individual	*Generic*	Exploiting experience for future performance
	Specific	Being able to make own policing experiences subject of discussion

Table 6.10 A tactical law enforcement competence (EQF6)

Level of work		Tactics
Competencies		*Higher professional education related to law enforcement*
EQF 6 Descriptors		• Advanced knowledge, involving a critical understanding of theories and principles • Advanced innovative skills to solve complex and unpredictable problems • Managing complex activities or projects, taking responsibility for decision-making • *Taking responsibility for managing professional development of individuals & groups*
Professional	Generic	Drawing up, implementing and evaluating an entire operating procedure
	Specific	Being able to develop, conduct and evaluate a plan for a high-risk operation
Contextual	Generic	Applying a wide range of resources/disciplines
	Specific	Being able to organize interventions in both a geographical and functional respect
Social	Generic	Cooperating in operations and policies with colleagues, partners and institutions
	Specific	Being able to build and maintain a network for community policing
Individual	Generic	*(Creatively)advising with regard to the profession and utilizing obtained advice*
	Specific	*Being able to advise partners and chiefs with regard to a law enforcement approach*

Table 6.11 A strategic law enforcement competence (EQF7)

Level of work		Strategies
Competencies		*Academic professional education related to law enforcement*
EQF 7 Descriptors		• Highly specialized knowledge as the basis for original thinking and/or research
		• *Specialised problem-solving skills to develop and integrate (new) knowledge*
		• Managing complex and unpredictable contexts that require new strategic approaches
		• Taking responsibility for contributing to professional knowledge and practice and/or for reviewing the strategic performance of teams
Professional	Generic	Generalizing practical results and findings into a conceptual approach
	Specific	Being able to draft policing strategies based on information of traditional and new media
Contextual	Generic	Dealing with and reporting to authorities
	Specific	Being able to account for law enforcement actions of the force towards authorities
Social	Generic	Cooperating in policies and strategies with authorities and academics
	Specific	Being able to network in government circles
Individual	*Generic*	*Reflecting on theory and practice, leading to conceptualization and new knowledge*
	Specific	*Being able to translate evaluations of public order policing into original policing methods*

Table 6.12 An operational criminal investigation competence (EQF4)

Level of work		Operations
Competencies		*Intermediate vocational education related to criminal investigation*
EQF 4 Descriptors		• Factual and theoretical knowledge in broad contexts • Cognitive and practical skills to generate solutions to specific problems • Self-management within guidelines of contexts that are predictable but changeable • *Supervising the (evaluation and improvement of) routine work of others*
Professional	Generic	Suggesting and implementing elements of an operating procedure
	Specific	Being able to carry out elementary measures at a scene of crime
Contextual	Generic	Spotting and mapping signals from the environment
	Specific	Being able to structure facts and circumstances or to connect suspects and offences
Social	*Generic*	*Coaching colleagues with regard to the profession*
	Specific	*Being able to support colleagues during a criminal investigation*
Individual	Generic	Gathering, elaborating and organizing information
	Specific	Being able to collect and structure tactical and forensic evidence

Table 6.13 A tactical criminal investigation competence (EQF6)

Level of work	Competencies	Tactics
		Higher professional education related to criminal investigation
EQF 6 Descriptors		• Advanced knowledge, involving a critical understanding of theories and principles • Advanced innovative skills to solve complex and unpredictable problems • Managing complex activities or projects, taking responsibility for decision-making • Taking responsibility for managing professional development of individuals & groups
Professional	Generic Specific	Recognizing and analysing patterns and trends, applying research findings Being able to make an operational and strategic crime analysis
Contextual	Generic Specific	Considering societal developments, positions, interests Being able to consider social, administrative and judicial influences on crime investigation
Social	Generic Specific	Communicating operational plans in an understandable way (internally and externally) Being able to share 'intelligence'
Individual	Generic Specific	Assessing the relevance of information and resources Being able to assess the relevance and sensitivity of sharing 'intelligence'

Table 6.14 A strategic criminal investigation competence (EQF7)

Level of work		Strategies
Competencies		*Academic professional education related to criminal investigation*
EQF 7 Descriptors		• *Highly specialized knowledge as the basis for original thinking and/or research* • Specialized problem-solving skills to develop and integrate (new) knowledge • Managing complex and unpredictable contexts that require new strategic approaches • Taking responsibility for contributing to professional knowledge and practice and/or for reviewing the strategic performance of teams
Professional	Generic	Converting academic research into strategies or scenarios
	Specific	Being able to develop, perform and evaluate alternative investigation scenarios
Contextual	Generic	*Researching societal trends and assessing their practical relevance*
	Specific	*Being able to use specialised 'intelligence' for predicting probable crime hot spots*
Social	Generic	Dealing with cultural differences within and between countries
	Specific	Being able to collaborate in an international and multicultural joint investigation team
Individual	Generic	Contributing to a scientific development of the particular academic field
	Specific	Being able to contribute to a body of knowledge of crime science

I will give a final example from the control category, which is a favourite category in the world of policing as a logical consequence of their legal position in
law enforcement. In a role as coordinator of internal affairs, a leader should be
'good at planning, organizing and controlling'. The profile for the operational
police manager refers to 'recognizing processes within a team and being able to
influence these' as a social competency. The template's generic competency
behind this is 'managing internal relationships'.

In terms of EQF level 5 these examples with regard to the operational police
manager are congruous with the descriptor: 'taking responsibility for managing
professional development of individual and groups'.

So far I presented competency profiles divided into four core categories of
each profession as the bridge between occupational and qualification levels. In
addition to that, the template's 16 generic competencies of each level can also
function as a framework for required learning outcomes and for criteria to assess
them. This is about the transfer of qualification profiles into learning outcomes
for modules of a curriculum. To illustrate this, I will give some examples at EQF
master's level 7 with respect to the four different categories: professional, contextual, social and individual. These learning outcomes and assessment criteria
(see italics in the diagram) stem from modules of the MSc in Policing programme that we delivered in collaboration with Canterbury Christ Church University (Bryant and Peeters 2007).

Coming full circle

Finally, the template's 16 generic competencies (Table 6.15) can also be used as
anchor points for the assessment of work experience in relation to a particular
qualification level (Peeters 2004). As such it is important to stress that the EQF
descriptors systematically refer to both 'work and study contexts'. I am ending
now where I started, namely from curriculum and qualification profiles back to
occupational and competency profiles.

Table 6.16 – again divided into four categories – describes the criteria for
assessing work experience at Bachelor's level, i.e. EQF level 6, in order to
enable police officers that lack a Bachelor's diploma to study at Master's level.
Without a competency approach it would be very difficult to make a reliable
comparison between the level of qualification gained from work experience and
the corresponding educational level (Peeters 2009).

We ask applicants to describe their work experience in terms of their role and
responsibility in policing situations. The description should incorporate competencies at a Bachelor's level as this is the entry requirement for a particular Master's
programme. This device enables the applicants to formulate their policing experience in terms of activities and competencies that resemble the ones described in the
modules of the Bachelor programme. The Dutch Police Academy supports the
applicants by clarifying the characteristics of a Bachelor's level, supported by
examples related to policing. For instance, we expect them to have worked under
'complex' circumstances, but what does that mean with regard to policing at a

Table 6.15 Assessment criteria corresponding with learning outcomes (examples)

Competencies	A strategic approach to interagency policing re. crime analysis
Learning outcome (professional)	Evaluate the utility of a number of concepts of crime analysis related to community policing
Assessment criterion	Academic research should also draws upon experiences of the organization involved
Generic competency	Combining independent research with societal relevance
EQF 7 Descriptors	Specialized problem-solving skills required in research in order to integrate knowledge from different fields.
Competencies	A strategic approach to interagency policing re interdisciplinary interactions
Learning outcome (contextual)	Analyse and discern relevant variables in the interaction between the police and their environment
Assessment criterion	The review should consider two distinct academic bodies of knowledge as they relate to each other
Generic competency	Considering a wide range of resources/disciplines
EQF 7 Descriptors	Critical awareness of knowledge issues in a field and at the interface between different fields
Competencies	Police and society/perceptions and strategies re. international aspects
Learning outcome (social)	Stand up for a methodologically sound opinion on research findings, reflecting both sides of the picture: the societal demands of policing and the legitimacy of the response
Assessment criterion	Essay judged on comparative perspectives: e.g. present versus future state of affairs
Generic competency	Realizing acceptance of research findings and recommendations
EQF 7 Descriptors	Manage and transform work or study contexts that are complex, unpredictable and require new strategic approaches
Competencies	Dissertation (master thesis) re. report and viva
Learning outcome (individual)	Critically review work in relation to the objectives of the study and assess the implications for policing within the societal context
Assessment criterion	The dissertation should consider political or ethical factors that might arise, e.g. the interests of the police organization versus delivering autonomous conclusions
Generic competency	Reflecting on theory and practice leading to conceptualization and new knowledge
EQF 7 Descriptors	Highly specialized knowledge, some of which is at the forefront of knowledge in a field of work or study as the basis for original thinking and/or research

Table 6.16 Assessment matrix re. work experience at a Bachelor's level of policing (EQF6)

I PROFESSIONAL Competencies	Complex Situation/Many Influences	Check on Judicial Correctness	Analytical Skills: Recognition of Patterns	Integral (Tactical) Approach
II CONTEXTUAL Competencies	Coordination/External Networking	In Command of Operations	Taking Policy Initiatives	Judging Situations/Positions/Interests
III SOCIAL Competencies	Managing Internal/External Relations	Autonomy in Decision-Making	(De-) Briefing Strategies	Empathy within Context of Situation or Investigation
IV INDIVIDUAL Competencies	Generating New Creative Information	Assessing Relevancy of Information	Transfer of One's Experiences	Creating Effective Conditions for Others

Bachelor's level? We suggest examples of policing or criminal investigation in an unsettled environment, requiring the deployment of a variety of means or involving many influences such as frantic circumstances, serious organized crime, media pressure, unwilling witnesses or important missing clues. Comparable suggestions are given with respect to 16 criteria that represent a Bachelor's level of policing. They are brought together in a diagram, i.e. the Assessment Matrix that our Accreditation for Prior Learning (APL) Bureau applies to the description of work experience by the candidates. Their chief officers have to vouch for the authenticity of the portfolios. More than one hundred police officers have been assessed along these lines. A few police officers were refused admittance to a Master's study due to insufficient evidence of competencies. Some of them had to fulfil additional requirements, like being interviewed or completing a particular exam.

Summary

Table 6.17 presents a summarizing framework of the comparisons I made as to visualize how competency profiles – irrespective of particular profession – can function as a link between the generic as well as specific characteristics of occupational profiles and the corresponding levels of qualification profiles also in terms of the learning outcomes of EQF, (as shown in columns 1, 2 and 6). The generic characteristics refer to the professional layers implementation, organization and governance; the specific characteristics to the corresponding operational, tactical and strategic level of policing and its core processes, namely reactive policing, law enforcement and criminal investigation. The columns 2, 3 and 4 of the diagram show that curriculum profiles cover more aspects than a qualification profile, such as the assessment of learning outcomes and the ratio behind the classification of competencies (in this case the CEPOL-categories); or a more detailed arrangement of competencies (in this instance Quinn's configuration of management roles, symbolized by a cross). Moreover, the assessment of a certain level of work experience can be taken at different levels of qualification along the lines of the division of CEPOL-competencies, abbreviated as P, C, S and I (see column 5).

Conclusion

The ambition of the chapter was to explore the possibility of developing a universal approach to the construction of comparable competency frameworks for any type of training or profession. The line of thought was how to relate generic features of (different layers) of an occupation to equivalent characteristics of (levels) of an educational programme. The degree of abstraction allowed for a specification of occupational layers as well as a systematic elaboration of generic competencies into specific ones, in this case for the purpose of police training in relation to (managing) the police profession. The concept of competencies not only appeared to act as a bridge between occupational profiles and qualification profiles but also as intermediary between profiles and learning outcomes of modules, between learning outcomes and assessment criteria and – the other way around – between levels of training and performance at work.

Table 6.17 Comparing competencies

Occupational profiles/levels	Curriculum profiles	Management levels	Assessment learning outcomes levels	Assessment levels of work experience	EQF levels
	Qualification profiles/levels				
Implementation	Intermediate Vocational	Operational	Operational	Operational	EQF 4/5
Re. Police: Operational layer • Emergency Response • Law Enforcement • Criminal Investigation	COMPETENCY PROFILES • Professional (P) • Contextual (C) • Social (S) • Individual (I)	Operational P Quinn C S I	Operational P C S I	Operational P C S I	EQF4=implementation EQF5 (here)=managing implementation
Organisation Re. Police: Tactical layer • Emergency Response • Law Enforcement • Criminal Investigation	Higher Professional COMPETENCY PROFILES • Professional (P) • Contextual (C) • Social (S) • Individual (I)	Tactical P Quinn C S I	Tactical P C S I	Tactical P C S I	EQF 5/6 EQF5 (here)=preliminary phase of EQF6 or short cycle of a bachelor EQF6=bachelor
Governance Re. Police: Strategic layer • Emergency Response • Law Enforcement • Criminal Investigation	Academic Professional COMPETENCY PROFILES • Professional (P) • Contextual (C) • Social (S) • Individual (I)	Strategic P Quinn C S I	Strategic P C S I	Strategic P C S I	EQF 7/8 EQF7=Master EQF8=doctorate
1	2	3	4	5	6

Notes

1 This was the result of research underlying the POR-report on reviewing occupational profiles in collaboration with police professionals, i.e. on the basis of interviews, a survey and conferences.
2 My experience with the development of the new Dutch Police Training in 2002. For instance, participating police officers mention the importance of statistic knowledge instead of indicating what aspects of statistics are needed to perform a certain task.
3 Mintzberg distinguishes five basic components of an organization, namely the operating core, the strategic apex, the middle line, the techno-structure and support staff. The operating core refers to the implementation layer, the strategic apex is similar to the governance layer, whereas the middle line functions as the organizational link between them. In terms of the core business of a profession they are the key players. Analysts of the techno-structure and support staff have a sustaining function.
4 For instance, the key functions of a public manager entail (factual and emotional) engagement in public matters, policy-making and management of public–private relations. In this case competencies of four different Dutch bachelor's curricula for public administration have been related to these core processes.
5 If one has a look at police laws of arbitrary countries, it turns out that – in spite of the great variety of police structures – policing tasks come down to response to emergencies (in terms of service or repression), to enforcing laws (e.g. regarding traffic, public order) and to investigating crimes.
6 CEPOL is a French acronym for Collège Européen de Police (European Police College).
7 Elaborated by CEPOL in a Competency Profile for Senior Police Officers (Brekelmans *et al.* 2006).
8 These distinctions are to be regarded as generalizations of the diversity of educational levels in different countries. They relate to the descriptors of the European Qualifications Framework (EQF). Amongst others EQF 4 refers to an intermediate vocational level, EQF 5 and 6 to a higher professional level and EQF 7 and 8 to an academic (professional) level.

Bibliography

Alvarez, C. (2004–2007) Project Leader of Curriculum Innovation ANPC (*Proyecto de Innovación Curricular APNC – Academica Policia Nacional Civil*), Collaboration of Police Academy of the Netherlands, Leiden University of Applied Sciences, Saxion University of Applied Sciences, National Civil Police Academy of Guatemala, Guatemala City.
Boersen, H., Martina, R., Mensen, H., De Witte, P., Peeters, H. and Van Gendt, K, (2010) Invulling RW 40: gezamenlijk voorzien in politieonderwijs SXM/BES (Implementation of Art. 40 Empire Law 40: Providing Police Education Collectively St. Maarten/ Bonaire, Eustatia, Saba), The Hague, Committee Police Education of Ministry of Interior & Police Academy of the Netherlands.
Brekelmans, T., Tomkowa, H., Vossen, B. and Peeters, H. (2005) A Competency Profile for Senior Police Officers in the Field of International Cooperation, CEPOL: Bramshill.
Bryant, R. and Peeters, H. (2007) Course Outlines, Master of Science in Policing, Canterbury/Apeldoorn: Modified Validation Programme Document.
Bunk, G.P. (1990) 'Schlüsselqualifikationen – antropologisch und pädagogisch begründet (Key Qualifications – on an Anthropological and Pedagogic Basis)', Betriebspädagogik – Theorie und Praxis, Esslingen: Deugro. 175–188; derived from: C. Baitsch, and F. Frei, (1980), Qualifizierung in der Arbeitstätigkeit (Qualifying by Working), Bern: Hans Huber.

Den Boer, M. and Peeters, H. (2007) 'A View across the Border: Higher Police Education in the Netherlands', in B. Frevel and K. Liebl (eds), *Empirische Polizeiforschung IX: Stand und Perspektiven der Polizeiausbildung (Empirical Police Research IX: State and Perspectives of Police Education)*, Frankfurt: Verlag für Polizeiwissenschaft, 115–130.

European Commission, Education & Training (2010) http://ec.europa.eu/dgs/education_culture.

Grotendorst, A., Jellema, M., Stam, L., Van Der Vegt, M. and Zandbergen, C. (2002) Leren in Veiligheid, het nieuwe politieonderwijs in maatschappelijk perspectief (Learning in Safety, the New Police Education from a Societal Perspective), Apeldoorn: Politie LSOP.

IJzerman, P. (2003) Q13: Quality in Thirteen Questions, towards a Harmonised European Space for Police Education, Warnsveld: CEPOL.

Meerdink, P., Peeters, H., Van Tongeren, T. and Hupperetz, G. (1999) Hart voor de Publieke Zaak – Het Nieuwe Beroeps- en Opleidingsprofiel Bestuurskunde/Overheidsmanagement (A Heart for Public Affairs – The New Occupational and Curriculum Profile for Public Administration), The Hague: LOBO.

Mintzberg, H. (1983) Structures in Fives: Designing Effective Organisations, New Jersey: Prentice Hall, USA.

Nijhof, W., Beukhof, G., Geerligs, J., Kicken, A., Peeters, H., Van De Pol, R. and Wijngaarden, R. (2010) Schakelen in Verantwoordelijkheid, beroepen van de politie herijkt (Switching between Responsibilities, Police Occupations Recalibrated), The Hague: Politieonderwijsraad (Police Education Council, POR).

Peeters, H. (2004) 'Meten van Werkervaring (Assessing Work Experience)', RIC §7: Relevante Initiële Competenties (Relevant Initial Competencies), Apeldoorn: Politieacademie.

Peeters, H. (2009) 'Ten ways to Blend Academic Learning within Professional Police Training', *Policing, A Journal of Policy and Practice*, 4(1): 47–55, Oxford: Oxford University Press.

Peeters, H. (2010) Toetsingskader POR na Herijking Beroepsprofielen (Assessment Grid for the POR on the basis of the Reviewed Occupational Profiles), Apeldoorn: Politieacademie.

Peeters, H. (2011) Specifieke Kwalificatieprofielen van de Politieacademie (Specific Qualification Profiles of the Police Academy), Apeldoorn: Politieacademie.

Peeters. H. (2012) Bundel Kwalificatiedossiers, Politieonderwijs 2012 (Collection of Qualification Files, Police Education 2012), Apeldoorn: Police Academy of the Netherlands.

Quinn, R. (2003) Becoming a Master Manager: A Competency Framework, 3rd edn., New York: Wiley

Stam, J.G., Grotendorst, A., Prins, B.A. and Peeters, M.H.A. (2007) 'New Look, Reforms in Police Training', in P.C. Kratcoski and D.K. Das (eds), Police Education and Training in a Global Society, Lanham: Lexington Books.

Twijnstra Gudde Management Consultancy (2007) Partners in Leren, Programma Evaluatie Politieonderwijs, Evaluatie van het Samenhangend Stelsel van Politieonderwijs (Partners in Learning, Programme Evaluation of Police Education, Evaluation of the Coherent System of Police Education), Apeldoorn: Politieacademie.

Part II

Preparing for police work

7 Police training and reform in India

Bringing knowledge-based learning to the Indian Police Service

P. Neyroud and N. Wain

Introduction

In September 2011 a bomb exploded outside Delhi High Court just three months after a similar attack at the same spot. The public and the media expressed outrage at the fact that since the 26/11 attacks in Mumbai not one case of terrorism had been successfully investigated by the Indian Police. The failures of security and prevention reignited the debate on the need to reform the Police Service, which has remained largely unaltered since the days of British Rule. The same Metropolitan Force, Delhi, came under renewed criticism just a month later when a trader from the old spice market in the city was flagged down by police and an officer shot him three times whilst trying to take some gold chains from around his neck. The death of the market trader came just one week after a truck driver was beaten to death by police because he refused to pay a 5,000 rupee bribe to the constables. These are not isolated incidents. A 2009 report by Human Rights Watch documents the ongoing corruption and violations carried out by the police in India which range from a failure to investigate reported crime through extortion to extrajudicial killing. These abuses have also provoked calls for police reform from India Against Corruption, the group led by Anna Hazare, whose hunger strike brought severe difficulties to the Congress-party-led government in late 2011.

The Hazare-led movement comes nearly 40 years on from the report of the Gore Committee on Police Training and over 30 years from the key National Commission on the Police, which endorsed Gore's recommendations on police training. The Commission was set up to respond to concerns about the Indian police system. In their first report they commented:

> In the perception of the people, the egregious features of police are politically oriented partisan performance of duties, brutality, corruption and inefficiency, degrees of which vary from place to place and person to person. The basic and fundamental problem regarding the police today is how to make them function as an efficient and impartial law enforcement agency fully motivated and guided by the objectives of service to the public at large, upholding the Constitutional rights and liberty of the people.

A key part of the Commission's recommendations focused on improving the training of the Indian Police Service (IPS), the small cadre of senior officers recruited by the Union government to provide the most senior ranks of the State Police and Union or Federal police forces like the Central Bureau of Investigation (CBI).

Progress in implementing these recommendations has been, at best, patchy, partly because of the tensions between the Union and States over responsibility for policing. But in 2010, the Congress-led Union Government pushed forward with new training programmes for 'mid-career' officers from the IPS. The Ministry of Home Affairs made a conscious departure from precedent by specifying that the programmes would be delivered by international institutions in partnership with an Indian institution and the National Police Academy. In this chapter we will discuss the development and delivery of the Mid-Career Training Programme for IPS officers at the rank of Deputy Inspector General, drawing on developments in the UK (Neyroud 2011) and Australia and placing it within the context of India.

Background and context

India is an extremely complex country to police. Described as the world's largest democracy and an emerging economic powerhouse the population has now crossed the one billion mark and the diversity of the country is such that the state officially recognizes 17 different languages and over 5,000 dialects. It is a country where its scientists have sent a mission to the moon yet there are still around 300 million people who cannot read. Whilst the numbers of police officers in the country may seem huge at 1,563,301 officers, many of these are in state agencies and the numbers include many in reserve battalions. Officially there is one civil police officer per 761 Indian people[1] but often in rural areas the number of officers can be as low as 1 per 10,000. Over 90 per cent of the civil police are in the ranks between Constable and Inspector and they have to face some significant problems, including armed insurgency, religious and caste violence and organized crime.

The policing and legislative system in India is based upon the old British colonial system. A State military model of police force, the Indian policing system is still guided by the Police Act of 1861, passed by the British in the aftermath of the Indian Mutiny or 'first war of independence'. The 'officer corps' of the Indian Police Service, the IPS, was also founded in 1861 and from the start its role of order maintenance far outweighed any responsibility to prevent or detect crime. The nature of colonial policing in serving the interests of the elite and the British Empire was such that from the outset the Force was paramilitary in nature, resembling more the model of the Royal Irish Constabulary than the Metropolitan police.

Like most colonial forces officers were recruited directly often from the military but often from the Royal Irish Constabulary, who were seen as the blueprint for imperial police forces, reinforced by the decision by the Colonial Office in 1907 requiring all senior officers from the colonies to be trained in Dublin (Emsley 2011: 51). The separate nature of the senior officer class and direct entry was reinforced post independence in 1947 with the establishment of the Indian Police Service (IPS) which is an all India service recruited trained and managed by central government and which provides the vast majority of senior officers to the states.

From the outset the police in India have been the responsibility of the state. Each of the 28 states and seven union territories has its own police force, although there are also central police agencies. Article 246 of the Constitution of India places the police under State legislature which makes police reform for Central government difficult and attempts to reform both legislation and the police have been constantly frustrated.

The head of the police force in a state is the Director General of Police (DGP). Each of the states is divided into ranges, districts and subdivisions but the basic unit of police administration is the police station. There are around 10,000 police stations in India and a medium-sized state will have around 700 to 900 stations. The Criminal Procedure Code requires all crime to be recorded at a police station and all investigative work to be carried out from there and yet, as late as last year 350 police stations in India did not have a working telephone and 108 had no form of radio communication. Whilst officers based at these stations will carry out some patrol work a number have no access to vehicles.

Typically there will be around five officers on duty at a police station responsible for actioning public complaints or record crimes on a First Incident Report (FIR). However, there will only be one who does any writing whilst at least one will act as an armed guard on the entrance. Apart from a lack of communication equipment there is often a shortage of stationery and complainants will often have to provide their own pen. Constables at these stations have no rostered rest periods and technically they are supposed to be on duty 24 hours a day and seven days a week. These conditions and lack of appropriate facilities are central to the challenges facing the Indian Police Service. The working conditions result in many officers taking short cuts such as refusing to record crimes and poor treatment of detainees in order to extract confessions (HRW 2009). Fear of not receiving attention and demands for bribes and possible abuse keep many people away from the police.

Attempts at police reform

Since the 1960s there have been many police commissions in India looking at police reform that were largely ignored. Even when a National Police Commission sat between 1979 and 1981 producing eight thick volumes on improving the effectiveness, accountability and public image of the police, very few of the recommendations were enacted. In more recent years the government put together a group to draft a new police Act for India. As a result the Model Police Act was passed by the central government in 2006 and at the same time the judgement of the Supreme Court in the Prakash Singh case resulted in a direction to all states to implement the Act. The actual case was filed by two former Director Generals of Police due to their concerns around the poor performance of the police in India. Such is the delay in the process in Indian courts that it took ten years to be heard by the Supreme Court (see Stanislas 2013).

The Model Police Act 2006 included a number of training recommendations including an absolute requirement for basic training of new officers and further training upon transfer, annual refresher courses with linkages to career development schemes and state governments to upgrade training establishments and produce a clear training policy for all ranks. Yet despite this very few states have implemented the Supreme Court judgement in full. In fact, some states have completely ignored the judgement and five years on even in those who have passed a new Act the 'new laws are as regressive, if not more so, than the archaic laws which they replace. They give statutory sanction to all the bad practice that earlier existed.' (CHRI 2011: 51). In the view of the Commonwealth Human Rights Committee, the 1891 Act has been replaced with ones which have moved the country backwards.

The fact is that most politicians in India are reluctant to lose their control over the police. Not only does this control represent an important tool in exercising power but it also serves personal interests, with many commentators suggesting that politicians often use this power to have opponents arrested or friends escape justice and that it is a common characteristic of postcolonial criminal justice systems (Verma 2011: 4; see Stanislas 2013). Such stories proliferate in the media, such as the one in the *Times of India* in 2011 suggesting that politicians and their ability to secure the most 'lucrative' positions for their 'favourite' officers had influenced the transfers of 38 police Inspectors.[2] These practices have a debilitating effect on the morale of the police, its quality of leadership and general performance (Stanislas 2013).

Police training

In the face of these challenges of size, complexity, corruption and abuse the training requirement should be a priority and yet total police expenditure on training in 2005/6 was only 1.17 per cent of the total national police budget. According to the Commonwealth Human Rights Initiative there are only 162 police training centres in India. Many of these are empty and suffer from the same resource limitations as those described in police stations. The same NGO quotes an internal report that describes poor quality military style initial training, delivered by poor trainers in institutions without basic facilities.

Constable training consists of drill, field craft, weapons and riot training, and even for directly recruited Inspectors and Superintendents such training forms a large part of the curriculum with less emphasis on leadership and people skills. Officers recruited to the IPS are trained at the National Police Academy in Hyderabad. They are direct descendents of the officer cadre established by the British. Normally a colonial police force was a two-tiered system which was racially divided with the officer class being reserved for white Europeans.

However, even prior to Independence there were moves towards employing the most educated and higher class Indians in a middle or third tier (Sinclair 2010: 27). In the early twentieth century the process of Indianization resulted in almost a third of senior officer positions being occupied by Indians (ibid.). After 1947 there was no real change in the arrangements; the structure, culture and legislative powers remained. All that happened was that these socially superior Indian classes took the place of the Europeans and there was a requirement for officers to be Indian citizens.

A significant number of highly qualified students compete for entry into the IPS every year by sitting the examinations supervized by the Union Public Service Commission of India. The competition for places is high as the group still enjoys high status in the country and it is often seen as a launch pad into a higher position within the Indian administration. Many of those serving in the IPS hold degrees ranging from medicine to computer science and a substantial number have been professionals in areas such as veterinary science and engineering.

The Mid-Career Training Programme (MCTP)

In recent years the Indian Ministry for Home Affairs (MHA) has taken a bold step to outsource the delivery of their senior officer training to not just an external organization, but a foreign organization. The government that was elected in 2009 promised to actively pursue police reform and in many respects this ground-breaking programme could be described as a visible representation of the willingness to engage others in that reform. The three programmes which make up the MCTP are targeted at officers at Superintendent (7–9 years service), Deputy Inspector-General (14–16 years service) and Inspector-General (24–28 years service) level. The MHA's ambitions for the programmes are 'to prepare the IPS officers for the next level competency' (prior to promotion) and to enable them 'to possess the necessary skills and attitudes to discharge their responsibilities effectively' (NPA 2012: 8).

The new courses superseded programmes that had suffered from poor attendance. MHA responded to this by opting for a more 'intensive' approach, with programmes that would be 'evaluated and satisfactory completion of the programme would be a pre-condition for officers to get promoted to higher positions' (NPA, 2012:9). The latter was seen as essential to prise IPS officers out of their state and union cadres long enough to attend the programme. Moreover, a further incentive was that each programme was to include a two-week 'foreign component', designed to ensure that the IPS had 'experience in international policing and management' (NPA 2102: 10).

The approach reflects the realities of Indian policing. The union has limited control over the IPS officers once they have been assigned to their cadres within the states. Their careers, unless they have been seconded to union cadres such as the Central Reserve Police Force or CBI, are closely linked to the politics of their state and the person of their DGP. The one area that the union has some control over is the regulations covering pay and promotion and it is these that the Committee under Shri Trinath Mishra, a former IPS officer, chose to use to leverage the programme. This means that the attendees are obliged to attend and must meet the assessed standard, but not that they are necessarily obliged to learn or start from a presumption that the programme is relevant to their day-to-day professional lives.

Conger (1996), in a wide-ranging assessment of the effectiveness of leadership programmes for the European Institute for Leadership, has sub-divided them into four distinct approaches: programmes that focus on personal development; skills building; programmes based on feedback; programmes designed to raise conceptual awareness. The MCTP approach is primarily pitched at skills building, with a strong emphasis on preparing officers for the next ranks. This presents some major challenges for the programme. Some skills, such as developing a strategic vision require, as Conger comments, 'a very long gestation period. Much of it comes from an immersion in one's industry combined with a willingness to challenge the status quo–a paradoxical combination' (p. 6). Conger suggests that programmes can, however, prepare students for such challenges by allowing them to reflect and rehearse such skills. This cannot, however, in his view be done in a very short programme. MCTP programmes have been set at six weeks in India and two abroad, which is a relatively long programme by modern standards, but does at least offer space for Conger's suggested approach.

Drawing on the characteristics of successful programmes in his assessment, Conger recommends not one approach but a combination of all four. He suggests that this needs to start from a clear leadership approach, which is then reinforced in all the lectures, exercises and case studies on the programme. Moreover, programmes need to make a strong link between the learning and the workplace in order to reinforce the relevance of the learning. In order to do this, it is also important, he argues, for the participants to be clear that the programme has support from the top. Finally, he comments on the importance of building a critical mass in the organization.

Mid-Career Training Programme phase IV

MCTP IV is the mid-career programme aimed at IPS officers at DIG level and between 14 and 16 years service. In 2010 the programme contract was awarded to Cambridge University. Police practitioners from several UK, US and Australian forces together with academics from Cambridge University formed the faculty to deliver the programme. The programme is the mandatory entry requirement for IPS officers to attain the highest ranks in the service, the equivalent of the UK's Strategic Command Course for entry to Chief Officer (Association of Chief Police Officers) level. The course involves eight weeks of commitment from officers of Inspector General (IG) and Deputy Inspector General (DIG).

The course agreed by the MHA and NPA with Cambridge University was designed to address five key areas: professional topics; best practices and innovations; leadership and team building; strategic management; sensitization modules (designed to raise awareness of issues such as terrorism, corruption and diversity). The course content was, therefore, focused primarily on skills building and the development of professional knowledge. These were largely delivered by the international faculty, but balanced by smaller workshop groups led by a faculty member and aimed to encourage discussion of the lectures in the context of India. In order to link the learning to personal development, all the participants were provided with a weekly assessment of their performance in multiple choice exams on the lectures and their contribution in the workshops.

The lectures were deliberately designed to mix professional presentations with matching academic contributions, so that professional issues were continuously placed in the context of sociological and criminological research. Drawing on Sherman (1998) and Weisburd and Neyroud (2010), the programme placed a very strong emphasis on evidence based policing and encouraging the participants to make the linkages between social science research and their own 'clinical' professional practice. In this the programme sought to add conceptual thinking to the process of skills building.

All participants on the programme had four personal or group pieces of work to undertake through the programme, each of which was assessed which contributed to their overall mark. Before their arrival participants were required to complete a 1,000 word pre-course assignment on a key issue in their workplace. In the two earliest courses they were required to do police station visits and report their observations. Participants have to produce a strategic leadership project in which they were encouraged to choose a topic that they would be able to put in place in their own workplace. They had to present this to their colleagues and the Cambridge faculty and produce a supporting written report. As a group, they had to undertake a 'policy project' on a area of policing chosen by the MHA. These included issues such as improving the burglary detection rate, reducing corruption and reducing road deaths. The aim of this project was for the group to work as a team to produce an outline policy or good practice approach for the whole of India. Given that such all-India approaches are rare in reality, this exercise was deliberately set in order to encourage more nationally coherent approaches.

Finally, the fourth exercise required participants to undertake a Compstat. This exercise was run by senior US police officers and with UK staff and data. The Cambridge faculty also gathered some data from Jaipur in Rajasthan and Chennai in Tamil Nadu, so that the IPS officers would experience both UK and Indian data. The process required the officers to work in teams scrutinizing each other on their tactics and their understanding of the data. The combination of international and national data during the exercise was deliberately designed to emphasize the achievability of transferring the methods and tactics to an Indian context.

Looking back at Conger's typology, the MCTP IV was carefully designed to meet Conger's challenge for a mixed-method approach, whilst also focusing on making the links between international research and practice and the Indian context and challenges. There were a number of potential weaknesses for the programme that needed to be considered. There was no clear strategy for following up the learning. Conger strongly recommends that such senior-level programmes are designed in several short inputs, with workplace projects between each module, so that the linkages between the workplace and the learning are maximized. This would have been very difficult for the MHA and NPA to accomplish, because of the reluctance of the States to release officers. Only by linking the programme to the regulations governing promotion could attendance be secured. Moreover, the process of extracting officers often resulted in very short notice of attendance, whereas Conger suggests that workplace preparation for programmes is important and the ability to leave the workplace out of the seminar room is essential. The latter was not always possible – one Inspector-General ran key parts of the recovery operation from a major earthquake from his mobile phone whilst on the course.

Training and the challenge of reform and change in the Indian Police

The MCTP IV has to be set against the challenges of reform in India. What is interesting is the question as to why with so many bright students and educated people, the Indian Police Service have so far been unable to undertake significant reform of the service. Some of that will be the political interference and influence previously described, but it may also be a reflection that it is not just politicians who fear a change in the system. What is evident, however, is the great effort that has been made by individual IPS officers within their state or department to change the system. In a recent book on Indian policing, 'The New Khaki', a former IPS officer describes these attempts to change policing as 'thousands of flowers blooming' (Verma 2010).

However many of these changes are small scale and have had limited effect not lasting beyond the tenure of the officer who is moved on. Like many police initiatives worldwide they lack a secure evidence base from which to be able to draw secure conclusions. With the advent of the Cambridge course this approach may well be changing. The course has provided exposure to and materials from UK, US, European and Australasian policing. It has come at a time of wider professional interest in testing change. Shortly before the course started, Massachusetts Institute of Technology and Rajasthan state police force undertook a major change programme. This drew on many aspects of a similar reform programme in Trinidad and Tobago (Wilson *et al.* 2011; see Harris chapter). In an attempt to overcome the challenge of police reform an IPS officer, Nina Singh, undertook a series of Randomized Control Trials to evaluate a series of interventions implemented at police stations across the state (Singh *et al.* 2009). Many of these interventions were targeted at the issues that had been highlighted by reform Commissions and included: changes to officer duty rosters to give time off, suspending transfers of police personnel, providing in-service training to improve professional and behavioural skills, and placing community observers in police stations.

The training element of Singh's research consisted of a group of Inspectors randomly assigned to undertake a professional investigative skills course at the State police academy (Harris ibid.) and another similarly selected group of officers at all ranks trained in public relations skills. The outcomes of the police training area of the experiment had a significant impact upon victim satisfaction. A post-experiment victim satisfaction survey showed that more victims were satisfied with the investigation conducted by trained officers than those untrained. In addition it suggests that those trained undertook more rigorous investigations of the reported crimes.

Singh's research was used as a major case study on the MCTP IV programme and the discussion illustrated some of the challenges of change in India. Many of the participants rejected the lessons of the research because it had been done in another Indian state, where the conditions were seen as different. In contrast, many participants were more prepared to accept lessons from the US and UK. In a sense, these lessons were less threatening and provoked less professional competition. The importance of bringing international practice into India is, therefore, combined with the challenge of how to make the links between with the Indian context.

The future

Reform in Indian policing in the near future will not be driven by politicians; it is more likely to come from the service itself. Internal reforms of training, professional development and strategic planning can start to change the culture of the organization. Research supported by sound evidence will enable the IPS to challenge traditional ways of policing and introduce more professional approach. Some Indian authors have suggested that this research should be promoted through partnerships with leading Universities (Verma 2011) much like the groundbreaking aforementioned MCTP IV course.

Both Human Rights Watch and the Commonwealth Human Rights Initiative recognize the need to improve police professionalism (Stanislas, Chapter 1). The latter believe that the State Security Commissions (SCC) established by the Supreme Court can play a role in preventing unhelpful political interference in policing and evaluate in a more scientific way police performance in the states. They recommend that the SCC undertake much more rigorous evaluations of police performance than the current review of questionable police statistics (CHRI 2010: 54).

Like most of the Court's recommendations the establishment of SCCs has been ignored by the states. But maybe the constant pressure brought by these groups and the mobilization of civil society by the media, in particular social media, can bring about change. In the wake of the bomb attack on the court at Delhi the editorial in the Hindu newspaper called on the Indian Prime Minister, Manmohan Singh and the government to 'kick-start' police reform.[3] In that article the editor calls for 'world standard institutions for police tactics and investigations' and professional competence to be the benchmark for promotion and reward. This is not going to be easy, as one of the most eminent scholars on Indian Policing, Professor David Bayley, has stated in one of his lectures on the MCTP IV 'somehow politicians have got to agree a ceasefire on the use of the police for political ends' (Author's notes).

Bayley has also argued in his lectures that India may be on the verge of a tipping point in the development of its policing. There is an apparent convergence of forces within civil society which are pushing for a better police service. The media, the Supreme Court, prominent retired IPS officers, the Indian business community and the Indian diaspora who are investing from abroad, many of whom are considering returning, all are calling for improvement. As India seeks to cement its position as a global economic superpower, Indian business community and civil society will want to operate and live in an environment where they can have confidence in the police and in which the professional competence of the police can prevent the types of terror attack like that in September 2011 in Delhi. When such groups start to voice their concerns then maybe the police reform and standards of police training that India so badly needs can be introduced. In this context, MCTP IV will, hopefully, have equipped a key group of India's most senior police officers to be able to respond to such challenges and trigger transformation within to match the calls for reform from outside.

Notes

1 Data on Police Organizations in India 2011. Bureau of Police Research and Development. New Delhi 2012. http://bprd.nic.in/showfile.asp?lid=772.
2 'Politicos "influence" cop transfers' *Times of India* 24 May 2011.
3 'Rebuild India's police forces' *The Hindu* 10 September 2011.

Bibliography

Commonwealth Human Rights Initiative (CHRI). (2008) *Police Organisation in India*. CHRI. New Delhi.
Commonwealth Human Rights Initiative (CHRI). (2011) *Police Reform Debates in India*. CHRI. New Delhi.
Conger, J. (1996) 'Can we really train leadership?' *European Institute for Leadership*, downloaded from http://europeanleadership.com/wp-content/uploads/2011/02/Can-We-Really-Train-Leadership-Conger-BAH-copia.pdf on 6 June 2012.
Emsley, C. (2012) 'Marketing the Brand: Exporting the British Police Models 1829–1950', *Policing a Journal of Policy and Practice*, 6(1): 43–54.
Human Rights Watch (HRW). (2009) *Broken System: Dysfunction, Abuse and Impunity in the Indian Police*, New York: HRW.
Neyroud, P.W. (2011). *A Review of Police Training and Leadership*, London: Home Office.
Sherman, L.W. (1998) *Evidence-based Policing*, Washington: Police Foundation, Ideas in American Policing.
Sinclair, G. (2010) *At the End of the Line: Colonial Policing and the Imperial Endgame 1945–80*, Manchester: Manchester University Press.

Singh, N., Chattopadhyay, R., Banerjee, A., Duflo, E. and Keniston, D. (2012) *Can Institutions Be Reformed From Within? Evidence from a Randomised Experiment with the Rajasthan Police*. Massachusetts Institute of Technology, Cambridge. MA. http://ssrn. com/abstract=2010854.

Verma, A. (2005) *The Indian Police: A Critical Evaluation*, New Delhi: Regency Publications.

Verma, A. (2011) *The New Khaki: The Evolving Nature of Policing in India*, London: CRC Press.

Weisburd, D. and Neyroud, P.W. (2011) *Science and Policing: A New Paradigm*, downloaded from https://www.ncjrs.gov/pdffiles1/nij/228922.pdf on 6 June 2012.

Wilson, D.B., Parks, R.B. and Mastrofski, S. (2011) 'The Impact of Police Reform on communities of Trinidad and Tobago', *Journal of Experimental Criminology*, 7(4): 375–405.

8 Fire-arms and self-defense training in Sweden

J. Bertilsson and P. Fredriksson

Introduction

To be able to make the police interventions tactically, legally, ethically and morally defendable, one must start with determine what is the best practical approach based on which the actually most common tasks are (type-tasks) including their inherent dangers (type-incidents) and to learn about what the natural human limitations are under such situations. Hence, instead of designing training programs based on assumptive conclusions from non-empirical experience only, it is motivated to highlight these matters through formalized experience collection (i.e., finding and defining type-incidents). If the formalized experience collection is detailed enough it also gives valuable qualitative as well as quantitative data about our natural human limitations in real-life incidents. This combined with knowledge about training systems, didactics and about human neurobiology and other related aspects of physiology, cognition and skill learning, is useful when designing effective training. Continuous data collection, combined with effective and fast analyses might even make it possible to deliver training aimed at solving identified current criminal practices harming police officers in a specific area.

The police organization in Sweden: brief description

In Sweden, a national police board write regulations and give funding that guide the 21 local sovereign police authorities in different matters and levels regarding equipment, organization and overall political aims in the regular police work. The local sovereign authorities are responsible for the policing within their territories. There are about 20,000 police officers in Sweden, and about 2,700 of them work in The Skåne County Police Department. Sweden has 9.5 million inhabitants and Skåne County holds 1.25 million of them. The 21 police authorities will be merged into one Police Authority directly under what is now the Swedish National Police Board in 2015. Recently, the National Police Board decided that the basic police education centers should be responsible for development of the subjects of fire-arms, use of force, self-defense and tactics. The current national project's (police conflict management) main goals, as we understand it at this point, are improved integration of fire-arms, use of force, self-defense and tactics training, improvement of the basic education for instructors and implementing a national basic education for trainers of new instructors. These intentions are a sound basis for, and make it possible to implement, a national scientific formalized experience collection.

What have been identified as problems in the present design of the education programs are that training on using fire-arms, use of physical force and self-defense, law, tactics and conflict management have so far mostly been taught and trained in separate courses without coordinating the education content within the Swedish police basic education programs. Thus, fire-arms instructors often do not know in detail what either the tactical or the self-defense instructors teach, and vice versa. Furthermore, commonly the fire-arms training only consists of training police officers in simple range shooting, which has few similarities to what actually commonly happens in real-life officer-involved shootings. All mentioned subjects actually need to be taught together as one subject where tactical principals would serve as a guide how to combine law, communication, conflict management, use of force and self-defense techniques and use of fire-arms and other tools to make a basic 'when, where and how to do' map. The aim of such training is to give the student/officer useful 'artificial' experience about matters that are too dangerous (for us, perpetrator or third party) or of police interventions that are rare.

Proposed new training and education paradigms

The administrators of any given police unit need to consider which basic type-tasks and related type-incidents the members need to be able to handle (most common and most dangerous). Thus, the administration includes providing needed equipment and training to reach a certain level of skills, and to ensure that these skills are maintained through training. Experienced instructors given specific objectives, the required resources and maybe a suggestion of how to do it, as mission tactics, would have a more solid practical, legal and ethical base to build from.

To be able to perform well when being put under an acute dangerous attack at close range, it is necessary to train the initial responses to be more or less subconscious through a Skinner-box; stimulus>response>reward training. Nothing else will do under those circumstances if we still want to have control over the response being tactically, legally, ethically and morally defendable. Knowing how to do something in the form of declarative memory does not equal a practical ability when actually forced to act. Hence, theoretical knowledge alone does not suffice.

Training principles

Systemic context-influenced training

The basic issued safety equipment for a Swedish police officer is lightweight body armor, laser-protective glasses, expandable baton, non-rigid cuffs, pepper spray and a service pistol. The pistol grip size can be adapted to the size of the police officer's hand by choosing different models and triggers. This is very important to minimize the probability of missing when forced to shoot under the influence of a very strong sympathetic stress response. Since 2004, whatever training our officers have participated in, they have trained in full gear.

Even small changes in context may have impact on the tactics required to solve what on the face of it may appear to be a similar problem, but in fact may be slightly different. To find out the best tactical solutions to different problems it is useful to change the affecting factors until you see a need to change the tactical approach. Thus, one can produce an artificial map or matrix of problems combined with its corresponding optimum solutions. For example, a perpetrator may be compliant; expected compliant; intransigent; potentially dangerous; dangerous or lethal. He may have different weapons and use different types of attacks. The distance may vary greatly and so may the available time before intervening is possible or optimum. Hence, a number of factors all play a part in what the optimal tactical solutions need to look like to be effective. In reality, to not be overwhelmed by the huge number of possible tasks and even larger number of possible related problems, one may need to select what parts require the focus, the use of type-tasks and type-incidents built on experience or, ideally, empirical data from real incidents. The most common and most dangerous tasks and incidents should be more thoroughly analyzed tactically.

At basic training one needs to decide a starting point, a basic technique or basic method that can solve a worst case scenario. The basic training student must be given a fixed exercise or example to be able to use as a foundation when learning variations and why the basic technique or method sometimes doesn't work – because most of the students don't have any realistic frames of reference in terms of violence and the use of force. The instructor (employer) must give the student a reasonably realistic picture of the reality and a basic set of skills so that he or she can survive day one at the job if such a situation occurs.

At the next level of training, that requires basic skills in handling certain threats and attacks, focus needs to be on the principle 'it depends'. This can be achieved through three dimensional training or micro-scenarios with a lot of decision-making, drilling flexibility and decisiveness.

We like to put the required skills as early as possible in a context and environment that mimics real lack of control and that demand not only a response but a graduated and as correct a response (tactically, legally, ethically and morally) as possible following the stimulus or stimuli we produce for the training officer. We aim for objectively correct responses and interventions, but we never judge an act before the acting officer or officers describe the way in which they perceived the produced stimulus. If they perceived the stimulus wrong in an understandable way and performed well in handling what they believed was the situation they will not be corrected. We do not demand super precision in the technical execution of the skill during the often more stressful testing of what they learned, if it will still do the job (the demands on execution for our instructors, however, is higher since modeling is a very important tool for teaching skills fast). The responses or skills trained actually need to be able to do the job even without perfect precision since this is one of the most common physiological limitations when under the influence of stress.

Fire-arms training

The basic fire-arms training usually only handles low-stress, two-handed, sighted static fire on static targets from seven to 25 meters. The system our chief fire-arms instructor Ulf Petersson found to best complement the basic training, to better prepare police officers for what the real-life officer-involved shootings actually looked like, was 'point shooting' as taught by the late instructors W. E. Fairbairn, E. A. Sykes and R. Applegate. If there is time enough, a static or slow threat, lower sympathetic stress response level and other circumstances that enables the use of sights, a static stance and a two-handed grip, is of course to be preferred.

We combined the 'point shooting' and 'krav maga' tactical principles and developed principles and exercises that allowed shooting with necessary precision on moving attackers in any direction while moving in any direction on the distances 0–7 meters. Additionally, we found that the precision overall was improved when doing certain exercises without the use of sights. To be able to use our inherent ability to lock our eyes at a moving object while moving and through proprioception point accurately enough we must use the one-handed grip. This ability is fundamental for humans so the time required to learn and retain it is very short. Moreover, this solution corresponds well to what several of our officers were actually forced to use, without any previous training, when attacked or chased by knife wielding assailants in real life.

It is very important to gradually build pressure making the participants continuous winners. The sessions usually end with thoroughly planned supervised fast paced multi-choice micro scenario stimulus–response–reward training for the training officers. This forces them to act on preset continuously varied stimuli (actors) with required responses on different levels, from being polite to arresting to running and shooting when hunted with knives or shot at. The environment should be continuously varied and disturbing (running and screaming people).

Scenario training: building a functional model

An important benefit of using a system is that one can choose a set of type-incidents with variations to train your officers to handle these different situations using the same approach. We have here focused part of our training on type-tasks for first responders. The first responders most commonly constitute two uniformed officers in a marked patrol car. This was selected since, according to our statistics (Petersson 2004), the first responders are the ones most likely to end up having to use their fire-arms (82 percent).

However, the police leaders on the strategic level would also benefit from knowing what basic tasks with their inherent dangers a patrol unit can handle, so that they can plan ahead more easily. This would mean that the police organization would be able to say what basic type-tasks and connected type-incidents one unit, with certain basic equipment, should be able to handle and also the minimum training needed for this. This also means that it would be much easier for any dispatcher or operational officer in charge of a communication center or incident field-command to know how many units or what kind of unit (regular patrol, traffic, SWAT, canine, explosives) is needed to manage a certain problem or situation following a rough map.

Stress inoculation

The key to a complete system that also works under stress is that the basic tactical principles are objectively effective and that the derived skills to use are simple, effective and logical. However, these learned skills must also be trained under the influence of gradually increased psychological stress to make them likely to work in a dangerous situation where many brain and body functions might be compromised (Nieuwenhuys and Oudejans 2010; Oudejans 2008). This kind of training will be beneficial in three ways. First, that there exists an available solution to a recognized dangerous problem and second that the possible early recognition of the threatening problem may make the initial stress response less strong or make the recovery from it faster. The third benefit is instilling the mindset 'I will never give up!' Through this, the ability to use well-adapted force and other solutions that may not necessitate force at all improves.

Instructor training

Until now all instructors in our county are trained to instruct in both fire-arms and use of force/self-defense integrated through tactical principles. The way to train instructors needs to be quite different than what is needed for the working police officer. An instructor needs to understand and be able to describe the system and the specific factors of different problems that we need to train for. The instructor also needs to be able to show solutions well enough without losing the most important parts, to still be effective after translation. Simplest, however, the user only needs to retain the essential part of the skill or response pattern following the basic stimulus–response–reward to be successful. A champion of the world does not necessarily make the best trainer.

The tactical principles used in our training system have evolved over the years from our personal experiences of training, by using good ideas from other instructors and by reading a lot of literature (Charles Remsberg, Dave Grossman, Eyal Yanilov, Kenneth Murray, Bruce Siddle, Rex Applegate, William Fairbairn, Alexis Artwohl, Bill Lewinski, Annika Norée, etc.) and scientific papers. Training of this kind cannot be allowed to be static but has to be adjusted when the society changes, i.e., if physical violence or the use of fire-arms increases. We continuously try to improve what we already have, not least every time we train instructors locally, in other counties or abroad.

Tactical approaches

The Swedish basic manual of tactics use the basic principles from Remsberg's *The Tactical Edge* with 'problem area' (house, car, person, forest) within which we find 'areas of responsibility' from where attacks are possible and 'focus point' an 'area of responsibility' from where an imminent threat or attack is actually executed that needs our immediate attention to handle. Also, we use the 'thought process' aiming at putting more processes (locate, decide, prepare) on the suspected perpetrator before he can perform an attack, and for our part at the same time cut our own necessary processes before we can react to a minimum. Assessing risks and threats tactically is integral, as well as the concept of control, enabling us to better answer the questions: 'Where are the risks? Can I control them or do I have time to perceive, define, decide and react? If not, what do I do?' These tactics take account of some of the basic human neurological and other physiological limitations (Remsberg 1986).

Differences between basic police training and advanced instructor training

The major differences between our way and that of the basic training by the police education facilities are as follows. In the first or second semester the course in tactics takes place. Only in the third semester do the students start to train in fire-arms and self-defense. This means that during all their tactical training the students only have to deal with compliant or semi-compliant role players. They do not get to test their skills or the benefits of the tactics when the perpetrator(s) really tries his or her best to 'harm' or 'kill' the student. This does not produce the much needed self-efficacy which increases the ability to perform better while under stress (Bergman 2012). The student needs to train in the life-saving self-defense and close-quarter shooting skills and tactics before they start to train in other tactical methods when stopping a vehicle, searching a house or utilizing force during an arrest.

It is important to say that before this level of training we prepare the officers by teaching the required skills corresponding to the aim of the training session and through small steps increase the pressure and complexity without allowing anyone to fail, lose, give up or get hurt. Instructors and Eyal Yanilov and Marcus Wynne have developed different systems that both have a very practical and time-effective way to get results fast (Sde-Or and Yanilov 2001). When the officers can handle the basic serious problems to a certain level (physical and decision skills under pressure in stimulus–response–reward micro-scenario training) they can start to train in the basic tactics skills and in even more varied and prolonged scenarios. During this phase the officer can always be tested with surprise attacks (focus points) and other threats and problems that suddenly may need to be managed to improve confidence and self-efficacy even further. When not under a surprise attack (full access to cognitive ability and motor skills) the officer uses tactical dispositions ('thought process' and 'risk and threat assessment') trying to prevent possible attacks and of course his or her 'people skills' to de-escalate the current situation if necessary.

Most of the practical solutions medical nurses (and physicians) are trained to use in their basic education is based on best practice currently known through scientific research and proven experience. It needs to answer the basic questions of what works and what doesn't, and why. This could be done concerning our subject(s) and applied to police basic education as well. It has been done before, by W. E. Fairbairn and Shanghai Municipal Police, cutting the number of officers killed by half within a year, a century ago (Fairbairn and Sykes 1942).

Systemic tactical training

The best practice in our experience to gain better control over the training processes and its contents is to adapt a system instead of collecting separate techniques and methods. In a system the strategy and tactics need to be visible through principles in the developed or chosen techniques and methods. The principles of the tactics (how and why) need to be derived from the problem, equipment, other resources, environment and natural human limitations and strengths when it comes to response time and knowledge of perception, cognition and motor control under different levels of physical and psychological stress activation for all involved on all levels. The principles of strategy need to be derived from legal and ethical aspects, resources at hand and what we want (what and why and to what level). In a system, techniques and methods can be used to exemplify and teach the tactical principles of the system and give a higher tactical understanding that can be used to understand other methods and techniques and even to build new ones. On the other hand the system and its tactical principles can be used to analyze real ongoing events to better adapt and change the methods and techniques available. The tactical principles can also be used to retrospectively analyze an actual event and to adapt new methods and techniques or to build or adapt training to improve the solution to future similar problems.

Research-supported training improvements

Human limitations and strengths

To improve the training and equipment one must consider human limitations including minimum time to identify and react to possible problems or threats. In addition, strong stress responses drastically limit our ability to perform needed motor skills and cognitive evaluations even more. At strong stress levels officers suffer deteriorated fine and complex motor performance and can only perform skills using gross motor control well. Not considering this can become dangerous. Sports, movies and military practice have problematically influenced the choices of equipment, tactics and techniques and continue to do so. Sometimes this also results in legal and ethical dilemmas. We believe that proven experience and scientific research is needed to cure our often misinformed minds. We need to know better what works or not in real-life under the influence of stress. This can be done through continuous investigations of hard-earned real-life experiences, finding out how different police tactics and techniques actually work. For police officers, training a motor skill is not sufficient. A key element is ability to apply a trained skill in real life situations, perhaps under imminent risk of being harmed or even killed if failing to perform the tasks correctly.

We as humans have individual biological strengths and limitations concerning anatomy and physiology, such as: tall/short, light/heavy, fit/unfit, different best skills etc. Even so we need a similar set of skills to be able to protect ourselves and others, as well as intervene in a justifiable way. We particularly need to consider our basic neurological limitations, especially when we perceive or anticipate pressure leading to activation of our stress response. We have a number of instinctive behaviors that can be more or less helpful in an emergency. A number of psychological factors can also be useful or unhelpful in our ability to perform optimally from a legal, tactical, ethical and moral point of view. These psychological factors like experience, education, expectations, prejudices, fears and attitudes are also important and can be affected in different ways. For us the most important way is through clever training. Clever training in our subject not only affects skills positively but can also at the same time influence other psychological factors. Realistic training in integrated hand-to-hand fire-arms and tactics has actually been shown to improve self-efficacy, which in turn improved the stress tolerance and has a documented halo effect improving overall performance in other areas of work that does not seem to have a natural connection to the defense skills in question (Bergman 2012; Nisbett and Wilson 1977; Morales-Negron 2008). The realistic knowledge of one's own tested skills gives confidence and a stronger feeling of control in other situations. It is important that very early on the training incorporates situational awareness and decision making into the exercises.

Stress response

When we start to suffer the effects of the psychological stress response the way we think and perceive starts to change. Our conflict style becomes more polarized, for example in the belief: 'I'm right and he is a bad apple'. The will to win can overpower the will to negotiate. This might be good but can also make us act with less control and maybe unwisely. We need to ask ourselves beforehand what makes us frustrated, scared or angry. Why do we react like this? The nonarguable answer is that we as organisms perceive a threat of some sort (social embarrassment, fear of failing or fear of pain, injury or death) and start to prepare for some kind of reaction (posturing, fight, flight, freeze or sometimes submission) (Grossman 1995). We find it reasonable to suppose that when it comes to fear of pain, injury or death the situations that objectively are, or are perceived as, most dangerous for us scare us the most. We therefore need to start to train and condition our students and officers to be more able to handle what objectively is most dangerous for them. At the same time we need to make them realize that they have the skills needed to improve their self-efficacy. If they feel that they have some ability to handle even the worst situations they will be able to do a better job in almost all other less dangerous situations (Bergman 2012).

Factual basis for tactics

As mentioned above our chief fire-arms instructor Ulf Petersson has interviewed all police officers who have been involved in shootings since 1985 in Skåne County, amounting to about 140 interviews. All subjects were interviewed thoroughly using an improved version of the form NYPD use after officer-involved shootings. Empirical knowledge of what kind of incidents and what they constitute is needed to be able to choose the most needed type-incidents to train for. If a computerized up-to-date system could be created we would even be able to know almost in real time what we need our officers to learn at this point and at this place. To be able to know what skills are most effective under the influence of stress one needs to have some knowledge of the more acute effects of the psychological stress response, motor skill performance under stress and, of course, a knowledge of many different optional solutions to specific problems to be able to make an educated choice about what set of skills or responses should be promoted and trained before others in the scarce training time that is available. Didactic variation to optimize solutions for different problems is also an important area for instructors.

Ethical considerations

What determines our success is experience, training our expectations and the circumstances when we intervene or react. The intervention and, if more difficult, the reaction must be legally defensible. Tactically my response must give the best objective protection possible. The individual moral code of the police officer needs to be compared with the ethical values that are established in the laws, regulations and basic value systems such as the 1948 UN declaration of human rights. If the differences between the established ethical system and the moral codes and convictions of the police officer is too far apart, it means a greater risk of overreactions or omissions that are negative for all parties, the officer, the plaintiff, the perpetrator and sometimes even the bystander.

The overall aim for our training is to provide knowledge and skills that give us the tools to act and react and, through this, mentally prepare us for different situations and scenarios. The fact that one recognizes a situation, knows a solution and has realistic confidence in one's ability to perform the required actions in time gives a feeling of greater control resulting in a lower psychological stress response and perpetuating better access to the necessary part of one's brain.

Conclusion

All more or less consciously decided actions and all more or less subconscious trained responses, need to be tactically, legally, ethically and morally defendable. However, this requires that the laws and their practice are actually adapted to natural human limitations. The Swedish laws addressing the use of force and self-defense for all citizens including police officers, to our knowledge and experience, are very well adapted to our human nature.

We hope and believe that the future both nationally and internationally will hold more scientific discussions and practical testing combined with more detailed empirical data from the streets as a foundation for the development of our subject. This would not only improve the police interventions through better training in line with best tactical, legal, ethical and moral practice, but also improve the public and political understanding of, and trust in, police professionalism.

References

Bergman, D. (2012) *Slagteknik och självtillit, Närkamputbildningens psykologiska effekter*. Diskussion & Debatt, Nr 3/2012, Kungliga krigsvetenskapsakademien.

Fairbairn, W. E., and Sykes, E. A. (1942) *Shooting to Live*, Paladin Press: Boulder, Colorado.

Grossman, D. (1995) *On Killing: The Psychological Cost of Learning to Kill in War and Society*, New York USA: Back Bay Books.

Morales-Negron, H. (2008) *Self-efficacy, State Anxiety and Motivation During Mandatory Combatives Training*, PhD-Thesis, Florida State University.

Nieuwenhuys, A. and Oudejans, R. R. (2010). 'Effects of anxiety on handgun shooting behavior of police officers: a pilot study', *Anxiety Stress Coping, 23*(2), 225–233.

Nisbett, R. and Wilson, T. (1977) 'The Halo-effect: Evidence for unconscious alteration of judgements', *Journal of Personality and Social Psychology, American Psychological Association*.

Oudejans, R. R. (2008) 'Reality-based practice under pressure improves handgun shooting performance of police officers', *Ergonomics, 51*(3), 261–273.

Petersson, U. (2004) *Use of fire-arms 1985–2004*, Statistics PPT.

Remsberg, C. (1986) *The Tactical Edge, Surviving High-Risk Patrol*, Calibre Press: USA.

Sde-Or (Lichtenfeld), I. and Yanilov, E. (2001). *How to Defend Yourself Against Armed Assault*, Dekel Publishing House: Tel Aviv.

9 Police use-of-force issues in Canada

A. Arsenault and T. Hinton

Overview

Canada is a rather large multi-cultural country with a multitude of police agencies scattered throughout its vast width and breadth making the standardization of police use-of-force training difficult. The proliferation of social media sites though has shrunk the world so that we can all see how police are performing in the 'global village' while also exposing to Canadians how their own police officers utilize force, infrequently as that may be, in their own home towns. There are obvious ethical problems in this regard that are in need of addressing in keeping with Peelian[1] Principles. The public will only remain supportive of those men and women in law enforcement if force to effect arrests is deemed to be both reasonable and necessary. Police departments, or 'services' as they are now prone to be called, face substantial community support issues as social media shines bright lights on back alleys patrolled by our watchdog police.

Once-unblemished badges are being tarnished, largely through use-of-force issues. These problems arise from public perceptions about how and why police use force. Explained or not, the term 'police brutality' finds its way into the media by those who hold even the concept of police in disfavour. The police must be held accountable for the force used against the public hence the rise of intermediate weaponry and use-of-force models. These models attempt to train officers in proper use-of-force protocols while serving as guides in court in cases where use of force is an issue. It is impossible for any model to depict what an officer should do in every situation as physical altercations during arrests are too complicated, dynamic, and fluid to be depicted in a two-dimensional, static model. Some force used by police is unjustified because police officers are merely ordinary human beings doing an extraordinary, and often thankless, job. Police officers suffer from the same human frailties that everyone has and these can be largely corrected with proper training. Few occupations are attacked if they do something or if they fail to do something. It is hoped that more emphasis will resolve many use-of-force issues.

Introduction

Most police in the Western world are familiar with Sir Robert Peel's well-known dictum that 'the police are the public and the public are the police'. This is reflected in his guiding principles which hold true to this day. One is that there is a positive and direct relationship between the maintenance of public support for police and their use of a minimal amount of force to achieve their objectives. Police forces across the civilized world are still wrestling with a means by which criminals and others in need of arrest can be dealt with in a humane and effective way. Peel also asserted that this minimum use of force by the police should be exercised as a last resort only as necessary to preserve the peace or restore law and order. This chapter will provide a brief evolution of policing in Canada, examine how use of force is delineated, outline problems relating to use-of-force issues that tear at the fabric of these basic Peelian Principles, and show how the new and innovative martial art of Police Judo can offer some solutions relating to the ethical and professional use of force by police officers.

History and evolution of policing in Canada

Canada, being a former British colony and current Commonwealth country, has a legal system that has been greatly influenced by her mother country Great Britain. Canada's first policing was introduced with a similar legalistic flavour to that evolving in England. This created many challenges in a budding Canada with huge geographical, logistical, and political issues for early constabularies. Several 'Upper' and 'Lower' Canada sites like Montreal, Quebec City, and Toronto formed police forces as they formally grew into cities in the 1830s. Within a few years of Confederation (1867), provincial police forces were set up in several provinces. Notably, there was the formation of North West Mounted Police (NWMP) by an act of Parliament in 1873 and this in turn eventually lead to the creation of Canada's truly federal police force – the world-famous Royal Canadian Mounted Police (RCMP) after their merger with the eastern provinces' Dominion Police (1868) in 1920. Today the RCMP consists of almost 18,000 employees handling all federal matters and some municipal policing functions (except in Ontario and Quebec where provincial police rule). The third level of policing are the 160 municipal police 'departments' or 'forces' (morphing into that of 'services' in keeping with the transition to community-based policing values beginning in the 1960s) providing about 70,000 police officers in total for the entire country.

The officers deployed into the city streets were essentially all beat officers (mounted members patrolled the outlying areas) until the advent of motorized vehicles. By being able to cover larger areas than on foot, there was a shift away from neighbourhood cops to those in 'prowler cars' who became slaves to the radio dispatching them from call to call as urban crime flourished.

Simultaneously, the human and civil rights movements in North America and elsewhere began to view the actions of police officers with a more critical eye. The methods employed by police for social control began to be challenged and the term 'police brutality' appeared when actions seemed excessive.

(Beahren, 2008: 10)

The RCMP's unblemished international reputation has become significantly degraded in a series of highly publicized use-of-force cases, particularly in the westernmost province of Canada, British Columbia, as the spotlight of social media and concomitant public attention was shifted away from the accused parties and onto the police who were arresting them.

The omnipotent eye of social media

And so we have modern-day police officers serving and protecting a more skeptical and demanding public, all under the watchful omnipotent eye of a variety of scrutinizing hand-held media devices like that of the cell phone camera. Over the past half-century, the police have turned to technological assistance in the form of intermediate weapons to solve the dilemma of protecting society without having to resort to lethal force. A case in point was the development of the conducted energy weapon (CEW) – the TASER (Thomas A. Swift's Electronic Rifle). Its inventor, the late NASA engineer Jack Cover, was asked by then-President Lyndon B. Johnson in response to the negative outcry following the beatings and deaths at the hands of the police at the Chicago race riots of 1965 to create a less lethal device that could incapacitate rioters.[2] As with any new weapon introduced, there came considerable and understandable consternation surrounding the fact that offenders were being killed (though rarely) by the police using these 'intermediate' weapons. Police are often 'damned if they do (TASER someone who dies) and damned if they don't' (kill them with their guns instead).

The court of public opinion can sway society to believe that TASERs are far more deadly than they seem. Take away the TASER and more shootings will result – that's why they were deployed in the first place – to save lives. Statistically this is not the case and can be argued that the media is not doing society a disservice by undermining their overall lifesaving utility.[3] There may be an over-reliance on such weapons as it is far easier to train an officer's trigger finger than it is to take a violent individual down using defensive tactic skills. There must be accountability over how these weapons are being used and this often falls back onto proper training, competent supervision, and accurate reporting standards.

Police brutality

There doesn't seem to be a week that goes by without a negative story in the press about a police 'beating', or with less fervour, an officer being maimed or killed in the line of duty. With the oversight by the media and independent review boards that are quickly becoming popular on major (critical) police incidents, comes unprecedented scrutiny. It is uncertain if there are actually higher rates of use-of-force incidents occurring or if there is merely a *perception* that this is the case.[4]

Many stories of police abuse stem from sensationalized media clips found all over social media sites like YouTube. Not all incidents labelled as 'police brutality' have been proven to be so despite the many graphic examples depicting police in violent encounters that get re-circulated in the media. Certainly one of the most common complaints against the police is not that force was used, rather, it is the degree of force that was used found to be unpalatable to the public.[5]

> There is no 'nice' way to arrest a potentially dangerous, combative suspect. The police are our bodyguards, our hired fists, batons, and guns. We pay them to do the dirty work we're too afraid, too unskilled, or too civilized to do ourselves. We expect them to keep the bad guys out of our businesses, cars, houses, and out of our face.
>
> We want them to 'take care of the problem'. We just don't want to see how it's done.
>
> (Charles H. Webb)

Public perception about how the police employ force started changing along with the inadvertent advances of media oversight beginning with the highly unpopular Chicago race riots of the 1960s, the abuse-by-baton of Rodney King in 1991, and more recently in the author's home province of British Columbia, the Robert Dziekański airport TASER death (inadvertent) at the hands of the RCMP in 2007. Collectively, these types of over-publicized and sensationalized incidents have caused the public to begin to ask a very salient question – what if the police are the problem? Incidents of police using force are a statistically infrequent event although media bias may cause the public to fear that the police are out of control. A recent study of force used by the Calgary Police found that in 827,022 interactions with the public, force was in a mere 0.07 per cent of the time; the use of force rate climbed twenty-fold to 1.5 per cent when arrests were affected (4.6 per cent of the contacts).[6]

Injury rates are obviously exacerbated through use-of-force encounters but details of such incidents have only recently begun to be tallied. It is becoming easier to determine how often police officers use force and under what circumstances they do now that mandatory Subject Behaviour/Officer Response (SBOR) reports have been made introduced across Canada. Yet, a third of all RCMP in BC failed to complete the required reporting of incidences of use of force,[7] a problem requiring immediate rectification, as such under-reporting has placed obvious statistical limitations on the collected data. The reputation of the police has been so damaged that making accurate statistical evaluations of their performance which has become important. Most Canadian provinces now have impartial civilian bodies, such as BC's newly-formed Independent Investigations Office (IIO), to oversee serious use of force incidents. If having such a quasi-police function in place appeases society, then the police can rest assured that these investigators will arrive at similar conclusions that outside investigating agencies did given that the same methods of fact-finding and rules of evidence used have remained unchanged. When police do wrong, then they should indeed be held accountable for their misdeeds.

Police use of force

Use of force is seldom pretty, especially to the public who are for the most part ill-informed on these issues. It is easy to misinform them by taking what force was used out of context via a few frames of video from a shaky and grainy cell phone camera. Further still, police officers have difficulty in describing in plain language why they had to use the force they did to the judge and jury. The ability to articulate and document use of force situations accurately and in an understandable fashion is paramount.

Police misuse of force

From the author's experience, police officers misuse force in the following ways:

1 Abusing their position for personal reasons like seeking revenge, reclaiming ego, looking for retribution, and other frailties of the human character, all of which lack proper justification.
2 Using poor judgement by initiating the use of force far too soon (fail to use tactical communication effectively) and far too heavily and are seen to be over-reacting to the situation thereby precipitating an assault and defensive action by the arrestee.
3 Using poor judgement by delaying justified use of force or use too little force for the situation, which causes them to use force desperately in order to play 'catch up'.
4 Failing to control themselves (temper, anger, fear, heart rate, adrenalin rush, etc.) resulting in a blinding (but less malicious) over-reaction to whatever threat they perceive.
5 Failing to gather or receive proper intelligence, and/or fail to filter and re-assess such information to reduce the possibility of over- and under-reaction.
6 Placing themselves, their partners, and the public at risk by using faulty tactics, requiring further use of force to bail them out.
7 Disregarding or failing to read their opponent (pre-assault cues) and the environment (their physical situation), placing themselves in unnecessary danger (by being too close to an angry person for example) resulting in otherwise preventable or unnecessary force having to be used.

8 Having too few tools in their arrest and control arsenal to effectively deal with resistive or combative parties causing any street confrontation to be overly stressful, fear-driven and otherwise inappropriate uses of force to be applied.

9 Using force inadequately by attempting unpracticed and unskilled techniques, or less commonly, they use skilled force excessively.

10 Failing to call for back-up or as a result of complacency they enter risky situations without first doing proper risk assessments.

11 Misusing their words and/or get too close to angry people causing the respondents to physically react to them (police-precipitated assault).

12 Consuming alcohol in off-duty hours and drunkenly and unwisely put themselves into service when a situation arises (possibly as a result of their own impaired actions).

There could be other reasons why police misuse force, but when such force is witnessed and reported to the public they have (and rightly so) little tolerance for such behaviour. These incidents of police abuse of force tends to obfuscate the minds of the public about the vast number of uses of force that are carried out very well. All uses of force must be justified and be justifiable.

> Police use of force is officially sanctioned, but questions remain. What is a reasonable use of force? Why and under what circumstances is one type of force chosen over another? What standards are in place to ensure that all police officers are consistent in addressing potential use-of-force situations? These are tough questions that demand sound answers if public confidence in the police is to be maintained.
>
> (Hoffmann *et al.* 2004)

In an attempt to answer to these salient questions, while serving as training aids, use of force models began appearing in North America in the 1970s and 1980s.

Use of force models

There are many dynamics that can alter an officer's perception of any given situation and how they react will vary according to their size, conditioning, training, experience, personal traits, etc. Use-of-force models have difficulty in depicting these variables, hence they cannot dictate exactly what an officer's response should be.

> Frameworks for judging the appropriate situations are laid down in policy to assist officers to make split-second decisions on use of force. But in the end it is at the discretion of individual police officers to use the force they deem necessary and be vindicated or vilified by those passing judgment after the fact.
>
> (Beahen 2008: 13)

It is incumbent upon each officer to control the factors that are within their reach but how many officers train for the 'most likely' of scenarios? From a risk management perspective, it is understandable how a 'bad shoot' (a 'least likely' scenario) can affect the officer, their victim (and family), and the Department. No officer wants to go through the trauma of criminal court and civil law suits that go with any kind of shooting, let alone an unjustified one. So annual firearms qualifications, as mandated by police employers at least as a risk management[8] measure, are the norm. The consequences of failing to at least *test* firearms skills are just too steep to ignore. From a training perspective (at least in Canada), a shooting is a least likely scenario, whereas hands-on situations can be common in many areas of patrol work, yet in-service training is deficient, as it is with police-related institutions.[9] Viewers must cringe when they watch a video of a gaggle of police officers all pulling their guns on a crack-head who needs to be physically controlled, not threatened into compliance with a pointed gun. What if a drunken sot walks towards a pointed firearm with both of his hands up high in the air in the universally acknowledged pose of surrender. Is his actual non-compliance for failing to 'Stand back!' grounds for shooting him as per any use-of force model? Can a sidearm be re-holstered and properly re-secured before a resistive suspect is physically taken into custody or can he be safely taken down with the officer's hand clutching an un-holstered gun (which would beg the question why the gun was taken out in the first place)? Some people will drop to the ground, knees shaking, when guns are pointed at them while others will advance, daring the officer to shoot them, and still others will turn tail and run away. Every call a police officer goes to is a potential 'gun call' because he or she is bringing a weapon with them; one in five officers are killed with their own firearms.[10] One in ten US police officers were assaulted in 2010.[11]

Inadequacy of models

Some departments are moving away from the various use-of-force models that are currently being used today, such as the Canada's National Use-of-force Framework (2000) and the RCMP's equivalent Incident Management Intervention Model (IMIM).

> Use of force continuums, once relied upon as the best way to train officers on the correct application of force, are slowly being removed from agency policies across the country as a result of fear of ligation when an officer works outside of the printed standards but still within reasonable guidelines.
>
> (Beahren 2008: 10)

The linear, step-type models have in many cases been replaced by these circular pie-type 'frameworks' but even these fall short of depicting what force an officer should use in a dynamic, fluid, three-dimensional situation.[12] These models are insufficient in accounting for extraneous factors such as the influences of fear, relative skill levels, body sizes, reaction times, environmental uncertainties, how rapidly fights evolve, etc. other than to refer to them as 'situational' factors, central to this model. There has been a recent trend to school the police in the 'reasonableness' of justifiable force as outlined in Canadian and US jurisprudence such as *Cluett* v. *The Queen* (1985) and *Graham* v. *Connor* (1989) respectively rather than to rely on use-of-force models to do so.

> Police officers are authorized to use such force as is reasonable, proper and necessary to carry out their duties, providing that no wanton or unnecessary violence is imposed. What is reasonable and proper in the particular circumstance, and in the particular case, will depend on all the circumstances. It is not possible to lay down any hard and fast rule, except the test of reasonableness. If the police officer in carrying out his authority acts on reasonable and probable grounds, he is justified in doing what he is required to do and in using as much force as is necessary for that purpose. [as per section 25 Criminal Code of Canada]
>
> (*Cluett* v. *The Queen* 1985)

The use of force within legal parameters is essential and this onus falls upon Force Options training officers. Poor training will result in more improper applications of force, injuries, and law suits.

Problems with police use-of-force training

It would be ideal to have all use-of-force training done in a logical and legally justifiable manner. Notwithstanding various police functions that require specialized training, standardization of training is somewhat difficult to achieve given the parochial nature of the business. This does not necessarily need to be accomplished on a technique-by-technique basis, rather the type of in-service training could be made uniform based upon the needs of each force. Many police services offer their own brand of control tactics based upon the kinds of problems that the officers encounter on the street. Realistic use-of-force training programs should be the norm without an over-reliance on intermediate use-of-force belt tools and with sufficient in-house refresher training programs to assist in the retention of essential skills,[13] even if it is just basic handcuffing.

The author has noted the following problems related to police use-of-force training:[14]

1   Recruit training instructors based the training around their background martial art rather than focusing on what control tactic skills the recruits needed to learn.
2   Instructors failed to successfully adapt their martial arts training to the realities of the street, leaving the recruits that unlikely task.
3   Far too many techniques were taught with far too little time to practice and review what was taught.[15]

4   There was no link between the teachings of the police academy and in-service training (sometimes the training was divergent).
5   The training facilities and instructors were lacking in the ability to provide environmental inoculation.[16]

The reluctance of in-service officers to commit to personal control tactics training, and a paucity of pertinent long-term training programs like Police Judo for police purposes can only be achieved if the members themselves demand such services.

Each police service has varying training standards from province to province and even city to city but these training variations pale in comparison to that which our big brother experiences, the United States, where there are an estimated 40,000 police agencies averaging less than a mere ten officers each.[17] Adding to the training disparity is the fact that smaller agencies cannot afford the time and resources of the larger agencies.

The trend hiring of women and minorities which make up our society has been experienced over the past several decades. This trend tears at the macho notion that policing is a rough, tough, dangerous job that can only be executed by large strapping policemen. Police officers are now seen to be reflection of the physical make up of society when perhaps the fact that 94 per cent of those arrested using force are men.[18] In any case, police need to be highly-trained individuals. Indeed policing has evolved from a job made up exclusively of large uneducated men into a complicated profession comprised of people of all sizes, genders, and personal backgrounds. It may be argued that what has been lost in brawn and stature has been made up by intellectual savvy and technological gadgetry designed to provide the wide mix of officers with a use-of-force advantage. This enhanced edge may not always yield the desired outcome, hence control tactics training should include the learning of techniques that the 'smaller, less athletic types' can benefit from in the field. Sadly, many officers put very little time into physical training (or their personal training ill-prepares them for the violence that they will encounter on the street). The end result is that many officers are gadget-driven; belt tools have significant failure rates, a frightening reality that can lead to poor decision-making during critical times of violent encounters. Both the officer and the offender may fall victim to panic-driven uses of force. Some police trainers are advocating tactical retreats as best practice when the best weapon, the brain, cannot find ways to talk officers out of physical confrontations.[19] The author feels that this is counter-productive when physical arrests must be made. How can an officer do their job if they are back-pedalling to avoid the use of force at all costs? This instills a dangerous mindset of retreat that can have serious consequences. Consider a recent study by Wolf *et al.* (2009) which has shown that police consistently under-utilize force (force deficit) and that, as logic would dictate, the longer the physical altercation lasts and the greater the number of 'iterations' (clashes) experienced, the higher the injury rate was by both the police and offenders involved (offenders fared worse than the police).[20]

Potential explanations for this reduction in force are plentiful. Although impossible to measure, well-trained professional officers, when faced with a resistant subject, may fear the legal ramifications of using too much force. Police officers may also rely too heavily on conducted energy weapons for subject compliance, even if the threat is at a much higher level than the device is legally accepted. Lastly, better educated and trained officers may feel that they can talk their way out of situations in which additional tactics might be legally justified.

Starting at the police academy, and as confirmed by this study's focus group, officers are told to use the least amount of force necessary to affect an arrest. As a result, officers are understandably hesitant to move immediately to the higher end of the acceptable response options and may first try lower-level techniques. The unintended consequence of this choice is that many of these techniques do not have high success rates for ending a confrontation and may serve to aggravate this situation through an escalation in resistance by the suspect. Consequently, it must be carefully stated that officers should be prepared to use decisive force at the point where verbal techniques and force de-escalation have failed.

(Wolf *et al.* 2009: 753)

Police Judo: innovative arrest and control training

Police Judo is an innovative adaptation of sport judo; moreover, it is a hybridization of the non-sporting aspects of judo with police arrest and control tactics.[21] It has a strong ethical basis developed by police for police though the collective efforts of highly experienced beat police officers[22] working in an area suffering from a plethora of social ailments. The techniques in Police Judo have been tried and tested in a high-volume crucible of violence, drug addiction, mental illness, and crime – the Downtown Eastside of Vancouver, Canada. It has proven to be a highly effective and low-risk means by which law-breakers, the mentally ill, and those individuals who are unwilling to submit to the legal request of law enforcement officers, by virtue of their intoxication by drugs and alcohol, can be skillfully taken into custody. Research has indicated that the most likely time of an assault against a police officer is at the initial point of contact and during the time of arrest, particularly after the first handcuff has been applied.[23] Police Judo is bucking the trend towards the reliance on intermediate weapons and preferential disengagement, both of which can cause problems for those officers who are minimally trained and for those offenders who need to be restrained. Wanton violence has no place in the Police Judo arsenal, but 'taking the fight' to an arrestee has many benefits. The authors are advocating the ethical use of pre-emptive force in order to minimize the amount of controlling force used and concomitant injuries resulting from violent and potentially violent arrest situations. The answer to this conundrum lies in ongoing arrest and control training in a safe and recreational environment. The solution to over- or under-reaction by a police officer during the execution of the arrest of a resistive or combative subject lies in the skills obtained in accessible, ethical, and pragmatic ongoing training. Police Judo delivers a low-risk, high-yield training program for both serving police officers as well as students aiming for a career in policing.

History

In 1882, Jigoro Kano, the founder of the ancient Japanese martial art of Judo developed tenets for a code of conduct for this discipline. How does judo tie into the evolution of use-of-force paradigms and how does it serve to help solve use-of-force training problems in the modern world of policing? These questions can be briefly answered within the light of the timeless and sage dictums of both Sir Robert Peel and Kano.

Kano espoused 'mutual welfare and benefit' (which is tantamount to respect) and 'maximum efficiency with minimum effort' as guiding principles for his martial art. Indeed looking after one's partner on the training mat is a central concept in the philosophical underpinnings of this 'gentle way' of fighting; Police Judo inculcates a level of care out inside, and *outside*, the training hall while dealing with the public. After all, no one deserves to be needlessly and roughly manhandled by the police simply because such trouble-makers were under the temporary influences of drugs, alcohol, rage, or mental illness. Are these not similar to Peel's principles relating to the judicious application of force on the public – those very citizens on which police rely for their very existence? Treating a person with disrespect is a recipe for inter-personal problems in any culture. Rude and insulting behaviour on the part of an officer gives an offender room to stand, and even to fight on, when he may have had none before. There is no greater need than now for accountability of force being used by police (as it is so often captured on video); there was no harsher testing grounds for that force being used than in the relatively rough and lawless streets of the Skid Road of Vancouver, Canada, where Police Judo was born.

America's old Wild West can attest to how the lack of a developed Criminal Code with its concomitant lawful guiding principles can lead to out-of-court gunplay, unfair trials (if any) and outright vigilanteeism. Some of the 'sheriffs' of the time have been depicted as merely guns for hire, meting out justice one bullet at a time. In the Far East, the samurai class of warriors were disbanded in 1867, resulting in ronin (master-less samurai acting as 'swords for hire'). So began a time of great Westernization for the relatively isolated feudal Japan. It was in this spirit of transformation which Japan found itself that Jigoro Kano founded judo in 1882, having removed the destructive (injurious) techniques from its less-refined, war-like predecessor, ju jutsu (jiu jitsu), so that even school kids could practice this 'gentle way' or art of self-defence. Kano spread judo to all points of the globe before his death in 1938. Police forces globally have benefited from the dissemination of this sport.

Police and other law enforcement agencies have long used martial arts in their training. All Japanese police departments have a dojo in which to train as all recruits must have a black belt in judo. It is interesting to note that ju jitsu was replaced by judo in Japan after a contest was held on June 10, 1886 at the Tokyo police headquarters dojo between the head police ju jitsu instructor and one of Kano's judo students (who was also an aiki jutsu master). It was reported that the police ju jitsu master died from his beating and ju jitsu instantly lost credibility in Japanese law enforcement circles and it was echoed by the progression of Japan from a feudal era to modern times. This did not mean that ju jitsu became totally obscure, rather, the modernization of the peaceful society demanded modifications that was best presented in judo.

(Arsenault 2006: 14)

Just as Jigoro Kano took the unsafe and destructive bone-breaking techniques meant for the battlefield from the various styles of ju jutsu and added soft mats on which to practice, thereby making judo training safe for everyone to practice, so too has Police Judo made modern safety adaptations. The practical judo techniques police use in the referee-less and mat-less venue of the street would likely be applauded by KANO, especially in light of his precept of 'mutual benefit and welfare', as well as the underlying philosophy of 'taking care of one's partner' as police officers are expected to do, no matter how aggressive, assaultive, or combative their 'partner' may be.

What is Police Judo?

Police Judo is the fusion of non-sport, street-practical judo grappling/unbalancing/tripping and throwing techniques (and other martial arts techniques) with modern police arrest and control tactics. Its practitioners train for the 'most likely' to the 'least likely' of street scenarios and is focused on pragmatic training, the development of useful force options skills through drills, recreational practice and demanding physical workouts. The program has been designed to minimize the risk of injury primarily through the removal of the competitive side of judo training, and is a program that can be practiced safely by people of all ages.

Police Judo incorporates 'low-risk' (to both the officer and the offender[24]) 'high-yield' techniques (placing the officer in a dominant position) that are morally responsible, ethically judicious, and therefore legally justifiable and defensible if applied in the correct use-of-force context. Many of the techniques have been adapted, tried, and tested by Vancouver beat cops during decades of walking the beat[25] on the rough side of the street. Few places in North America could test an officer's arrest and control abilities like the drug-addled and high crime environment from where Police Judo originated. There is a real need to put practical and effective no-nonsense tools into the hands of the police in order to keep everyone involved as safe as possible while looking as good as possible on the six o'clock news.

The goal of Police Judo is to take those into custody (with minimal risk) who have little regard for themselves, let alone the police who are trying to deprive them of their liberty. Like any difficult job, if one has the right tools, the job can be accomplished in a low-risk and highly-professional manner; failure to train can have serious and dire repercussions.

Liability issues

We live in an increasingly litigious society which encourages both genuine and opportunistic use of the law to resolve issues, especially in relation to the police. In 2001, there were an estimated 30,000 law suits against the police in the US.[26] There are so many sources of video on the street (including that of the police's own dashboard and lapel cams) putting today's officers under unprecedented scrutiny. The public has little tolerance for the witnessing of improper applications of force. Police Judo provides low-key, effective means of taking people into custody at minimal risk to all parties involved. Officers can often over-react with too much physical force during difficult arrest scenarios because the lack the confidence to go hands-on with aggressive and assaultive parties: they lack the requisite tools to do so. In order to handcuff anyone, the officer needs to 'own' them first. Police Judo provides those officers the skills and confidence to 'make the collars' in a low-risk[27] manner. It is the authors' serious contention that a reduction of needless injury and vicarious liability can be achieved through Police Judo training!

Gadget reliance

Police Judo advocates the use of hands-on force instead of an over-reliance of gadgets when the situation calls for a resistive person to be simply taken into custody. If the tools on your belt are all that an officer has, then that is all that officer can do – OC spray and pray, hope that the TASER batteries are fully charged (and that the prongs make proper contact), and failing all else, that your gun doesn't jam when desperately needed. Indeed it is sad to say that many officers have little fight to take to anyone unless it comes from their belts. 'Karate in a can', an under-charged TASER, an expandable baton that is too light to get the job done, and even the ineffective use of a firearm, do not have failure rates exceeding an officer's ability to die or be maimed. Good luck is relied on when dealing with pain-resistant, goal-oriented, and drugged people. Equipment failure is a policing reality; over-reliance on gadgets leaves officers rolling the defensive dice. Given the choice, the well-prepared warrior will opt for that weapon which will seldom fail him: his control tactics/techniques. The importance of hyper-vigilance and taking the fight to a would-be assailant, while ensuring that arrest and control tactics are sound (including the use of back-up officers), are critical aspects to a successful apprehension. Just as an officer has an array of tools on their belt, so too can an officer's tactical tool box contain reliable techniques requiring no gases, batteries, powders, or sprays which can directly deal with the 'most likely' scenarios that an officer will encounter on the street. People can fight blinded by pepper spray, or with one arm broken, while on the ground, or with a bullet in them. They cannot fight effectively if you 'own' them and can thereby prevent the access to weapons (or use of their own body weapons). With the proper training comes an ability and confidence that puts an officer in control of him/herself, the suspect, and the outcome of violent physical encounters. This advice may mean little to those timid, careless, or lazy individuals who dodge and neglect their hands-on training until that fateful day when their guns come out and the perps call their bluffs. Can officers morally justify squeezing the trigger merely by the fact that they 'opted out' of arrest and control training or that they did not keep up on that training, hence the suspect was a deadly threat to them? Recruit training in defensive tactics all too often ends upon graduation after a mere 80 hours of such training.

Constant training required

Most police officers' control tactics are in need of refinement, repeated drilling and practice in order for them to be ready to go. Would-be opponents know 'the look' and will often do themselves big favours by not testing the quality of an officer's mettle – the shiny badge and the magic of the uniform can only do so much. It is advisable for police officers to study anything that lets them get the job done and gets them home safely, but they need to TRAIN CONSTANTLY and learn from their failings. It has been said that the more you sweat in peace, the less you bleed in battle.[28]

> ...officer safety training needs to succeed in three objectives in order to provide safety for all. First, officers need to be competent in a range of defensive, restraint, and offensive techniques using their bare hands and officer safety equipment. Second, it is important to encourage a calm mind that facilitates the avoidance of harmful mistakes occurring in stressful violent situations. Third, this must all be accomplished within the parameters set down by the laws and guidelines that express a minimum use-of-force doctrine.
>
> (Buttle in Kuhns and Knutsson 2010: 33)

Intensive training will reveal why certain classical techniques don't work on bloody or sweaty wrists, why arms merely become tethers on methed-up people (lispy pun intended), why long hair was invented for the 'street hammer toss', and why your ten fingers should greedily fight to get access into the only seven natural holes in your opponent's head should a close-quarter deadly threat be encountered.

The authors believe that if officers had more tools in their control technique tool box and were adept at using them through regular practice, then there would be far fewer sensationalized stories about big burly officers wearing their black leather 'action' gloves standing around a deranged man only to have the TASER applied to him (fatally in a famous local case). There would be fewer videos like that of a semi-cooperative man on his knees being kicked in the face by a gun-wielding plainclothes officer; or of an out of control officer leaping from his cruiser to baton strike to the ground a hapless, non-reactive citizen in an otherwise calm situation. Not all police misuses of force are done with malice in mind but an ill-prepared mind can mercilessly sabotage an officer's performance under stress.[29]

On the flip side, there would be fewer officers injured and killed in the line of duty if they just knew how to effectively handle those who would do them harm. An instructive and sad story comes to mind of an officer sporting one handcuff falling to his death much to the horror of the multiple officers on the scene after being pushed over a stair railing by a mentally ill man. Why was this offender not 'owned' by the police trying to arrest him? Why was he attempting to be taken down in such a dangerous location? What were his cover officers doing to protect the arresting officer?

Most likely scenarios

Police Judo training operates on the premise that we need to practice on techniques that we would 'most likely' to 'least likely' encounter in our duties. It is most likely that we'd have to place people in handcuffs, be they compliant or not. It is least likely that we'd be attacked by multiple knife-wielding assailants rappelling out of trees so we limit our training along these lines accordingly. We also teach 'low-risk and high-yield' techniques. For example, a shoulder throw is executed by grabbing a suspect's arm, pulling him into you to upset his balance as you turn your back to him and lower your centre of gravity below his so that you can flip him over your shoulder and onto his back. This classic judo technique is indeed a 'high yield' one. If your goal is to incapacitate the perpetrator and you are justified in doing so, then this technique fits the bill. Those of you who are somewhat savvy to fighting tactics, know that there are 'high risks' to both the officer and the one being thrown. It is always risky for an officer to willingly turn his back on any opponent in close quarters, since an arrestee can grab your gun, choke you from behind, gouge your eyes out, etc. Also, it is risky for the person you are arresting, given that he probably does not know how to do a breakfall, nor are there any soft mats upon which to fall. Can you justify breaking his hip for a simple resistive arrest? We do practice this throw from a strictly defensive perspective though. Should a person grab an unsuspecting officer from behind in a chokehold, then the guy with extremely bad judgement could get a free flying lesson and likely a trip to the hospital after his hard landing. Hopefully he will tell all his friends about his bad decision; on the other hand and indicative of the environment police officers work in, maybe this would become another purported case of police brutality to feed the news channels.

Benefits of Police Judo

Police Judo is not a quick-fix, weekend seminar solution to use-of-force inadequacies, although the training can certainly begin there. In addition to supplemental training for in-service officers, the Police Judo training hall often attracts those interested in careers in law enforcement, making it an ideal place to assess and groom future candidates. Long-term training yields enhanced fitness levels, arrest and control technique development, and confidence building, with corresponding reductions in public complaints, prosecutions, and lawsuits.

The best way to influence the required changes in training habits is to introduce a paradigm shift in how officers approach training by starting at the front end of the police officer demographic, i.e. new recruits, by offering Police Judo classes in institutions which cater to students and ordinary members of the public. For example at universities.[30] Survey results from a sample of students taken from a recent Simon Fraser University Police Judo poll revealed that 91 per cent of the students were taking the programme for fitness, with 72 per cent also wanting police-specific training. And how does the program deliver? Ninety-five per cent of the students were satisfied or very satisfied with the Police Judo instruction and the same percentage reported that they would recommend the programme to a friend.[31] Police Judo offers a moral, ethical, practical, effective, affordable, and legally defensible way of taking uncooperative and violent arrestees into custody with as little risk as possible.

How is training carried out?

Although Police Judo incorporates techniques from a wide variety of martial arts including karate, jiu jitsu, aikido, and chin na, Police Judo stresses that how one trains will be how one reacts on the street so the principles of simplicity, commonality of technique, and repetitive technique drilling with practice under dynamic conditions are important training considerations.[32] Why do some police officers train with martial artists who have never even put handcuffs on anyone? The authors feel that this is a mark of desperation by those seeking relevant training; the need to adapt some form of martial art to suit their practical requirements of hands-on policing is the product of the scarcity of totally police-practical martial arts. Every police department has a few resident martial artists who have the martial arts aptitude needed to start up a Police Judo club. It is hoped that Police Judo clubs can be set up under their tutelage, for the benefit of all, as the costs to interested Departments are minimal and can be self-propagating.

Who can do it?

Anyone can train in a safe and supportive environment where the 'mutual welfare' care of our partners is observed, wherever that may be. By training in a recreational fashion at one's own pace and level, anyone from a teenager to a senior citizen can reap the benefits of Police Judo training.

There would be fewer officers hurt or killed, in the authors' view, if officers were not so gadget-driven (including the use of a sidearm to attempt to threaten offenders into compliance). How many times have you seen officers pepper spray each other, hit each other with their night sticks, or fumble their handcuffs or gun while trying to arrest a struggling offender? How many times have officers had their on-the-belt weapons used against themselves? We have all seen examples where one officer gets up off the ground slowly, while four or five officers cling to an aggressive suspect, working against, rather than with, each other. We have witnessed officers die due to their failure to 'own' or to fully control suspects before attempts were made to handcuff them.

As a final note, it is very important for officers to visualize street encounters so that they can *at least* mentally prepare themselves for street altercations. There is a time for talk and a time for action; not knowing the difference can put an officer in physical danger or in criminal/civil court.

Conclusion

How do you safely, effectively, and ethically deal with the most marginalized, pain tolerant, drug-saturated, and crime-infested people in our society[33] who may wish to do you harm while under the overly critical eye of anti-police watchdog groups or even just the viewing public? These practical questions loomed over the author and his skid road beat colleagues for several decades. Police Judo, created in the above-mentioned crucible of chaos and carnage, can alleviate many of the concerns arising from use of use-of-force issues, namely:

1   How can easily learned and practical effective tools be added to a police officer's control tactics tool box?
2   How are the ethical standards of conduct best ingrained into the police training culture?
3   How can police move away from gadget reliance?
4   How do police officers gain confidence in their abilities to physically arrest and control offenders?
5   How can use of force be made to look as least violent as possible and be done at the minimum of risk to all involved?
6   How can one best effect an arrest on a pain-resistant, mentally ill, heavily drugged, irrational person who has nothing to lose?

The answer to these questions lies in superior training. Commitment to such training by the police officers in the field is critical. As such, the author is recommending the practice of Police Judo as an adjunct to the brief use-of-force training received at the police academy[34] and to the minimal in-service training offered by many police agencies. Law enforcement is a career which carries inherent risks so a lifestyle involving use-of-force training should be pursued to mitigate such risks.

The learning of good arrest and control tactics such as those taught in Police Judo, although not a quick fix by any means,[35] offers ethical means by which officers can stay in top physical shape while constantly practicing with practical tools in their tool box. The author hypothesizes that the rate of officer[36] and subject injury rates would decline if more reliable and practiced control tactics techniques were employed.

Notes

1 Sir Robert Peel founded the London Metropolitan Police Force in 1829.
2 Jack Cover stated that he was also looking at its potential as an anti-highjacking weapon (personal communication in 1995).
3 The use of CEWs was found to be less injurious than either baton use or hands-on tactics (Butler and Hall 2008: 153) and were found to be very safe to use.
4 Seventy-five per cent of 422,000 citizens in use-of-force contacts with US police (1999 Bureau of Justice Statistics) felt that the force used was excessive (Langan *et al.* 2001: 3 in Kuhns and Knutsson 'Police Use of Force' 2010: 8).
5 Terrill and Paoline (in 'Police Use of Force' 2010) briefly examine the appropriateness of police use of force and note the loss of 'public trust and goodwill' regardless of the nature of the coercive tactics used.
6 (Butler and Hall 2008: 146) This latter figure is on par with American stats on all uses of force rates (force applied or threatened).
7 Quan, Douglas, in the *Vancouver Sun*, 'One third of the RCMP's use-of-force incidents not reported', December 1, 2012.
8 Ashley *et al.* (2000) note that it is not uncommon for departments to take a 'calculated risk' in lieu of training and just pay out damages when they arise in order to maintain their budgets.
9 A 2012 Police Judo survey of Canadian (non-police academy) institutions offering police-related hands-on instruction showed that only 10/77 schools actually offered hands-on training (66/1328 for US schools).
10 Seven out of 38 officers killed by firearms in 2010 were killed with their own guns. US Dept. of Justice/FBI 'Law Enforcement Officers Killed and Assaulted', 2010.
11 Ibid.
12 Peters and Brave (2006) state that there are over 50 use-of-force models being used. They suggest that these continuums are found to be too complicated to overly simple to use. The NUFF may be the best model in use to date.
13 Human Systems Incorporated (2010) notes that there is a total lack of research relating to the perishability of police use-of-force skills but it is thought that once well learned, a skill can be retained for years.
14 In 1986 the author visited six police departments in Australia, the Tokyo Police Academy, the Royal Hong Kong Police Academy, and the RCMP Depot in Regina to study their fitness and self-defence programs.
15 Grossman (2004) notes that warriors don't rise up in combat, rather they sink to the level of their training; they default to their training when the logic-less reptilian brain takes over (p. 73).
16 More recent advancements by Bruce Siddle and Dave Grossman on 'Warrior Science' and the physiological effects of stress on human performance make such environmental inoculation/stress acclimatization essential to the well-trained police officer. Under fearful conditions, adrenalin rules the amateur and optimally fuels the sage veteran of stress.
17 (Beahren 2006: 19).
18 (Butler and Hall 2008: 151).
19 In 1987, the *Toronto Star* newspaper featured an article on use of force training in the Toronto Police Service in which it was suggested that use of force was only to be used if one could not 'get out of there'. (Beahen 2008: 13).
20 Twenty-three per cent of suspects were injured during force encounters in comparison with only 3 per cent of officers (p. 71).
21 A wide variety of other martial arts techniques have also been incorporated, but judo is the predominant and parent martial art.

22 The principals behind this new martial art are all black belts in at least judo and most have decades of Skid Road beat patrol experience that has been guiding their adaptation of judo from 'sport' to 'street'.

23 Bruce Siddle's Pressure Point and Control Tactics Defensive Tactics Manual (pp. 2–12) mentions an unreported study that found 67 per cent of handcuffing resistance was encountered after the first cuff was applied. Many arrestees are intoxicated hence they are slow to realize the personal consequences of being handcuffed until one cuff is on.

24 Wolf *et al.* (2009) reveal that police under-utilize force which tends to cause physical arrests to last longer with more clashes or 'iterations' thereby incurring more injuries to both the police and the offender. 'These findings have critical implications for law enforcement by continuing to examine conflicts where police force is utilized, showing the importance of officers to be prepared to use decisive force at the point where verbal techniques and force de-escalation have failed' (p. 739).

25 The author Al Arsenault arrested, on average, seven people per day, such was the high volume of arrests for warrants, drug trafficking, assaults, etc. His beat has around 5,000 intravenous drug users, many of whom are committing crime or are mentally ill, in a hell-hole he calls the 'chemical gulag' where the addict's forced labour is perpetual crime in order to gain their next fix of drugs.

26 From Beahren 2008: 20.

27 Police are not in the 'safety' business. Policing can be a dangerous occupation so degrees of 'risk' are considered and managed.

28 This is an old military adage noted by Artwohl (1997). Both dynamism and stress in training are needed to induce high states of arousal that closely and meaningfully duplicate the realism of street combat (pp. 70–71).

29 Ashley *et al.* (2000) note that the greatest challenge for police is when to use force and how much should be used. Unprepared officers have lower levels of confidence leading to injuries and complaints of excessive force.

30 Police Judo has been doing this for years through three clubs (Vancouver Police Department, Simon Fraser University, and the Justice Institute of British Columbia) which allow students interested in a policing career to participate.

31 Unpublished SFU Police Judo Survey Analysis, 2010–2012, by Prof. Garth Davies.

32 The physiological response to high stress situations can be mitigated if the officer has been trained under similar stressful situations. The ground-breaking research by Bruce Siddle and Dave Grossman regarding stress acclimatization is essential knowledge for the modern police trainer.

33 Butler and Hall's 2008 study revealed that of those persons arrested using force in Calgary, a full 88.1 per cent were under the influence of alcohol, drugs, or mental illness: 11.9 per cent were in a normal condition, 9.1 per cent were emotionally disturbed, 17.1 per cent were under the influence of drugs and alcohol, 19.6 per cent were under the influence of drugs alone, and 42.3 per cent were under the influence of alcohol alone.

34 At the Justice Institute of British Columbia, Canada, municipal police recruits only receive approximately 80 hours of use-of-force training and little subsequent in-service training and recertification.

35 Mastery of a physical domain is said to take ten years and 10,000 hours to attain (Chapter 38 'The Influence of Experience and Deliberate Practice on the Development of Superior Expert Performance' in 'The Cambridge Handbook of Expertise and Expert Performance', 2006, by K. Anders Ericsson).

36 Butler and Hall (2008) noted that 34.7 per cent of officers involved in physical arrests filed compensation claims. Criminals and prisoners have more access to mixed martial arts training, weights, steroids, etc. making some more difficult to physically handle resulting in higher rates of injury.

References

Angel, H., Adams, B.D., Brown, A., Flear, C., Mangan, B., Morten, A., and Ste-Croix, C. (2012) *Review of the Skills Perishability of Police 'Use of Force' Skills*, Human Systems Incorporated.

Artwhorl, A. (1997) *Deadly Force Encounters: What Cops Need to Know to Mentally and Physically Prepare and Survive a Gunfight*, Boulder, Colorado: Paladin Press.

Ashley, S.D. and Golles, L. (2000) 'The Effect of Police Officer Confidence on Officer Injuries and Excessive Force Complaints', *Consulting in Risk Management and Training*, June 12.

Beahen, W. 'Evolution of Use of Force by Police in the Canadian Context'. Excerpts from a speech delivered at the CACOLE Conference by Dr. Beahen, June 16, 2008 for the Commission for Public Complaints Against the RCMP.

Butler, C. 'The Use of Force Model and Its Application to Operational Law Enforcement – Where Have We Been and Where are We Going?', undated report from the Calgary Police Service.

Butler, C. and Hall, C. 'Police/Public Interaction: Arrests, Use of Force by Police, and Resulting Injuries to Subjects and Officers – A Description of Risk in One Major Canadian City', Law Enforcement Executive Forum, 8(6), 2008.

Cluett v. *The Queen*, 2 S.C.R. 216 (1985).

Ericsson, K.A. (2006) 'The Influence of Experience and Deliberate Practice on the Development of Superior Expert Performance' (Chapter 38) in *The Cambridge Handbook of Expertise and Expert Performance*.

Graham v. *Connor*, 490 U.S. 386, 394 (1989).

Grossman, D. (2004) *On Combat: The Psychology and Physiology of Deadly Conflict in War and Peace*, PPCT Research Publications.

Hoffman, R. *et al.* (2004) 'Canada's National Use-of-Force Framework for Police Officers', *The Police Chief*, 71(10) October.

Kuhns, J.B. and Knutsson, J. (2010) *Police Use of Force: A Global Perspective*, Santa Barbara: Praeger.

Peters, Jr., J.G. and Brave, M.A. (2006) 'Force Continuums: Are They Still Needed?', *Police and Security News*, 22(1), January/February.

Police Judo (2012) 'A Survey of Canadian Institutions Offering Police-related Hands-on Instruction', Vancouver: unpublished report.

Terrill and Paoline (in 'Police Use of Force' 2010).

US Dept. of Justice. 2010. 'Law Enforcement Officers Killed and Assaulted.' FBI, www.fbi.gov/about-us/cjis/ucr/leoka/2010.

Vancouver Sun. 2012. 'One third of the RCMP's use-of-force incidents not reported,' December 1.

Webb, C.H. Excerpted from a talk to the Young, Fearful League of American Wussies, CSU, Long Beach, CA, www.outerzone.us/forum/showthread.php?p=20779.

Wolf, R., Mesloh, C., Henych, M., and Thompson, L.F. (2009) 'Police Use of Force and the Cumulative Force Factor', *Policing: An International Journal of Police Strategies & Management*, 32(4), 2009: 739–757.

10 How violence comes to French police

The role of violence in the socialization and training of the French police

C. Moreau de Bellaing

Since 1941, the French police has been a national police organization. This means that it is a State police organization, directly under the Home Department's ('ministère de l'Intérieur') supervision and that its 127,000 members are civil servants. Its administration, organization and, often, its missions are conceived and managed from a centralized command center in Paris ('la direction générale de la police nationale') and relayed by State representatives by region. Local police chiefs have quite a lot of autonomy in their everyday running. This centralized feature of French police is important when it comes to training: police recruitment is held nationwide, which means that a young recruit from a little village in a western region of France can be trained in a school based in Roubaix (in the north of France) and then sent to a police station in a suburb of Paris.

The French national police are divided into three main ranking categories: the 'corps d'encadrement et d'application' which includes 'gardiens de la paix' (literally 'peacekeepers'), that is to say the basic policemen; the 'corps de commandement', which encompass inspectors and superintendents; and the 'corps de conception et de direction' which corresponds to chief officers and high ranked police civil servants. There are specific access and training schools for each of these 'corps'. At least half of inspectors and of chief officers joined the directly police as inspectors or chief officers through external exams.

It is worth noting that the idea of training policemen is quite recent. It was only in the 1880s that the question of training police officers was raised in France. In fact, 'no one had ever thought, before the end of the nineteenth century, that the job of policing could be taught. The very idea was laughable'. (Carrot 1992: 187; see also Williams 1979). It was in the Police Prefecture that for the first time gave consideration to the question of training police personnel. During the early years of the Third Republic, training was not so much about initial training as a series of courses intended to provide police, often illiterate, with the basic wherewithal to do their job. In July 1883, the École Pratique de la Police Municipale was established. New recruits were required to undergo three months of compulsory training; the duration of training could go up to ten months for those who were illiterate. Three-hour classes were held in the morning after every third day – when the job allowed. The courses offered dealt with the day-to-day real policing tasks, the theoretical dimension of the teaching 'called upon common sense and the practical bent of mind of the trainees' (Berlière 1996: 73).

Setting up the school was the first step in the process of professionalization of police duties, a process that would continue throughout the twentieth century. The dynamic set in motion received a fillip with the arrival of the Prefect Celestin Hennion, who authorized the establishment of the École Pratique Professionnelle des Services Actifs de la Prefecture de Police in May 1914. The school offered a six-month course to fresh recruits and inspectors, and professional development opportunities for police. The school used new teaching aids, in particular films, to simulate real life situations and gauge the reactions of trainees. Later, in 1941, state control over the municipal police, imposed by the Vichy regime, led to massive police restructuring. What hitherto affected Paris for the most part through the Prefecture of Police was to have repercussions for the entire French police force whose members became state employees overnight. Several schools were subsequently set up for police officers, inspectors, officers and commissioners.

As police training became institutionalized, it gave rise to growing expectations and was also the object of much criticism: 'not enough training [five months], the program is bunkum, medieval teaching methods, no real preparation to handle the work, etc.: "a caricature" concluded Monate in 1974' (Demonque 1983: 29).[1] These critiques were formulated by policemen, as they emerged from the Interface study carried out in 1982 on a sample of 70,000 of the 110,000 police force at the time (Hauser and Masingue 1983). With the arrival of Gaston Defferre to the Ministry of Interior in 1981, there was clearly a strong will to improve police training. This brief overview provides us with the historical setting of the École nationale de la Police de Paris (ENPP) on which the observations of this chapter are based.

This ethnography took place in the ENPP, during which I followed two new recruits' promotions. After being assigned to a specific class, I had access to all (legal and technical) courses taught by a principal instructor. I also joined the recruits in their physical training (boxing, collective sports, endurance, police technics learning and so on) and other activities such as IT, first aid, shooting practice or typing classes. The ethnography has also been punctuated with informal situations (lunches, breaks, trips back to Paris at the end of the day). Finally, I got to follow instructors when they went to assess students while temporarily assigned to police stations during the training period.

The initial goals of the research were to produce a thin description of what being trained to be a policeman involves, with a focus on interactions in classes, between students and instructors and between students themselves. It was also the occasion to discuss van Maanen's theory which says that there is a fundamental distinction between training schools and true police work (van Maanen 1976). My ethnographic observations led me to discuss these points (Moreau de Bellaing 2010) and some others, in particular the instructors' role in training and training in the use of force. In this chapter, I intend to dwell on these last two issues. I will first investigate the role of instructors at the ENPP in order to better define what they do and the way they teach the police occupation. I will then specifically focus on training on the use of force.

Teaching the job of policing

Eighty instructors have been selected from amongst experienced officers for the Parisian site. They are organized in educational units; an instructor is in charge of one section of 30 students. The instructor and the students spend five hours a day together for eight months and this allows them to forge a bond.

The instructors are all police officers. To become an instructor, an officer has to apply to the Direction Nationale de la Formation (Training Headquarters), and if the application is accepted, the officer is then called for a series of tests. The first is a written general knowledge test of three hours duration (knowledge of policing, penal law, penal procedure, road safety code...) without any specific curriculum in the form of several short questions. If applicants clear the written test (there are usually between 200–300) they have to undergo an oral examination where they are questioned about their experience and their motivation: this is also a psychological test to gauge their personality and resilience. The candidate's employment record is in the ultimate analysis the determining criteria in the selection process (at least five years 'on the beat') as well as in the written or oral examinations with candidates being required to furnish their CV and letter of motivation to the interviewing panel. Once they have cleared these examinations, the trainee instructors join the instructor's school where they attend a 12-week training program. There they are made to learn the techniques of teaching (brainstorming, case studies, interactive presentations...) and acquire a certain oral fluency. They then take two or three classes with real students after which they are seconded on a trial basis to the schools of their choice. The instructor has a five-year tenure which can be renewed twice in a year.

The candidate's professional experience takes precedence over the potential teaching capabilities (Stanislas, Chapter 1). It is felt that these can be developed once the teaching starts. The instructor will then, to the extent that it is possible, rely on professional experience to teach the job of policing and will be required to assume four roles successively, or, more exactly, two pairs of roles.

The instructor as a teacher and a colleague

The first pair of roles associates the role of the teacher with that of the future 'colleague'. The instructor is first and foremost in charge of the course. Instructors do not merely reiterate official programs, but play the part of a teacher in the full sense of the term, building courses from official memos, answering the students' questions and providing additional bits of information when the course lacks clarity. Sometimes, the instructor may fine tune the program to the requirements of the situation. Some instructors like to integrate atypical factors in their teaching, based on topical articles and books of a polemical character. Others organize oral question-answer sessions every morning, and should these not take place on a given day, the students are made to feel they are being punished. Instructors frequently use command words while teaching with phrases such as 'Take note of this', 'Here, put'; during the training debriefing they frequently use questions to gauge the learning experience such as: 'What have you learnt? How did you react at the time? Why didn't you do that?'.

The instructor's status derives from professional experience. The instructor is competent to speak of law enforcement, and this goes hand in hand with the status of a spokesman of the institution which has been invested with the power to speak and act on its behalf. An instructor once told me 'I'm the first person they meet in the force [...] if I tell them the sky is red, they say the sky is red'. This somewhat provocative statement only illustrates the need for the instructor to build a relationship of authority with the students. In order to ensure this position as the establishment's spokesperson is respected the instructor must be acknowledged as such by the students. But authority has two sides: on the one hand, students perceive their instructor as one who uses legitimate authority and on the other hand as an officer who is required to establish police authority in encounters with the public (Skolnick 1966).[2] The display of authority is intended to ensure the necessary distance between the instructor and the students; if students take too much liberty they are severely put down and order is restored in class with a few scathing, at times vulgar or provocative, remarks. In the corridors, students are required to greet their instructor, failing which they are liable to be punished; students address their instructor mentioning the rank whereas instructors call their students by their surname. When entering a room, a student has to introduce himself (first and last names, section, rank) – should the student fail to do so, harsh punishment might be imposed. This distance is also maintained in the material arrangement (uniform, stripes, classroom layout...). On the other hand, building authority is about teaching the job through an authority management model, this being an essential element of a law enforcer's job on the street (Westley 1970; Becker 1985).

The instructor is not merely an instructor in a vertical relationship of authority. Since the overwhelming majority of students leave the school with an ENPP degree (there are very few failures), the instructor knows students are future colleagues. The relationship established between the instructor and the students cannot be one based solely on authority or hierarchy. Thus the instructor does not hesitate to give an insider's view usually reserved only for the initiated as students will soon be a part of the force. The instructor mentions problems associated with unionism, administrative procedures, competitive examinations and institutional functioning – and is perceived by the students as a future colleague. The hierarchical relationship associated with the first role described above tends to get effaced by the more horizontal concept of solidarity and 'esprit de corps' (Skolnick and Fyfe 1993). At such times, instructors get close to their students and have difficulty in maintaining the obligatory formalities (the use of the respectful 'vous' in place of 'tu') in class.

The expert and the critic

The instructor can also take on the role of an expert on issues related to law enforcement. Let us adopt a minimalistic definition of expertise as specialized, specific know-how. Such specialized know-how acquires shape in the instructor's accounts of law enforcement to the students in class. These 'battle tales' give a 'foretaste of the work on the street [...] sharing vicariously the achievements of instructor's predecessors' helps construct for the new recruits 'a common language and shared set of interests which will assist them forge ties with the organization till such time as they themselves have law enforcement experiences to communicate' (Cassan 1999: 105). Know-how is thus not just the imparting of technical skills but the ability to develop a capacity for producing standards that constitute the key building block of law enforcement.

The sharing of live experiences also has another function: it serves to bind the students to the program. The introduction of such accounts increases the concentration of the students. Very often it is the students themselves who ask for them, either to understand a specific theoretical case or simply because they are interested in the instructor's experience. When a class gets boring, students ask instructors to talk to them about their experiences on the street. 'What would you do if...? How did it happen when you were in the street?' The function of expertise in response to a request from the students is quite clear in the feedback. Thus during three different debriefing sessions, the students discussed with their respective instructors the thorny questions related to transporting dead bodies in police vehicles. In all the three cases, such a situation had occurred and they were required to carry out the task; they needed the expert skills of their instructor.

Sometimes the instructor takes the initiative using the know-how learned on the streets to deal with knotty situations that arise in conventional police work. This experience can be used as a model: on the basis of a specific case, the instructor moves from specific to general and this then may well become the guiding principle for action required in the given situation. In the class on detention, instructors constantly instruct their students: patrol continuously to keep a watch, don't place several individuals held for the same case in the same cell, always handcuff the person to be guarded in the police station, don't stand near a door or a window, leave the toilet door open when an accused goes to the toilet. All these acts, of general interest, acquire meaning in the instructor's lecture using specific examples: jumping out of a window, using a trip to the toilet to throw drugs in the pot. Using a concrete example, the police expert offers a general mode to proceed which becomes a 'law' for those who wish to do their job properly.

Equally important are the comments of the instructor when they are critical. The instructor draws from experience to highlight contradictions, criticize inconsistencies, decry certain practices and put principles in perspective. The instructor continues to draw on experience but this time to produce a series of critiques that the students ought to know about so that they do not commit the same errors of judgment. Instructors are often required to use formulations such as 'I know this is dumb, but...; well, it's stupid but...'. Such prefacing remarks usually lead to two forms of justification. These have to do either with teaching requirements and the criticism refers to legitimate assessment tests ('it's useless but could happen'; 'this article is not useful to know but it so happened last year that...'). Or else they are routines to be learnt and the emphasis shifts to testing in real life situations, as they deal with acts that have to be performed on a daily basis while enforcing the law (Reiner 1985; Parienté 1994).

Instructors may also criticize what they disapprove of at the school in front of their students. Several scenarios are possible: grievances against the hierarchy, in particular when the latter utters reprimands about student's dress during the hoisting of colors; complaints about the school's hygiene standards, poor organization, salaries. But it is when speaking about illegalities that the critical distance of the instructor becomes explicit. Instructors are often heard talking about circumstances in which they were placed in a situation of illegality. Here the ambivalence is obvious: the instructor is not just a law enforcement expert but also a citizen with a differentiated relationship with the law (Ker Muir 1977).

It is thus possible to see how the instructor, on account of the multiplicity of roles assumed, is able to familiarize student officers with the task of law enforcement. However more is required when the young recruits are taught to deal with the authorization to use force which is specific to their job.

Socialization to the legitimate use of violence

To consider police use of force as a spontaneous operation would assume that students have a natural inclination towards violence (they gravitate towards the job because they are predisposed to it) or perhaps it would mean postulating socialization to violence prior to the school which is both homogenous and commonplace (either of a psychoanalytic or sociological order, based on the endogamy of the law enforcement community). Now, the substantiation of the relationship with violence contained in the first assumption as well as the primary socialization hypothesis have not been able to stand up to empirical scrutiny; this also emerged from the findings of psychological and psychoanalytic studies on violence as well in sociological enquiries on supposed police cultural reproduction (Lhuilier 1992; Jobard 2002; Pruvost 2004). It is thus necessary to question the processes at work at the ENP by which young recruits are familiarized with violence in the course of their police training.

The transient nature of force in theoretical courses

There are very few courses which deal explicitly with the quantum and legitimacy of the use of force. There are only three exceptions to this rule. The first are classes dealing with police intervention techniques which require the use of handcuffs – a police object which directly materializes the authorization for the legitimate use of force. This is the case of the theoretical course on the sequence of interventions; other elements can be found in the courses on management of people questioned, observation of people detained in police premises and handing individuals over to courts of law or the management of drug addicts. In each class, students are systematically reminded that handcuffing as a restraining device is mandatory only if there is a real risk of escape or physical danger to the detaining officers or passersby. A series of informal rules surface in the narratives worked out by the instructor, where handcuffs are the tools par excellence for taking the detainee from a public space to police territory.

The second exception is courses which explicitly assume the delineation of conditions for using force. Thus, the educational aim with respect to identity verification provides for a multiplicity of intervention scenarios, especially dangerous situations and those of armed aggression when the young policemen are required to resort to the use of force. The legal framework within which questioning and arrests are to be carried out prescribes the forms of physical coercion to be applied, especially when the law enforcement agent intervenes in cases of premeditated violence and/or against an armed person. The course on maintaining law and order falls into the same category. Furthermore, the course that describes the relationship of the police with certain categories of the population provides an opportunity to dwell on the use of force and the need to limit it to 'the bare minimum required'. This is the place for a discussion on missions of a delicate nature in which the use of force may become necessary such as the hospitalization of mentally ill patients, supervision of minors in distress, etc. The course on serious crime deals with the methods to immobilize and neutralize 'clients' from organized crime. Lastly, there are some courses on the conditions of intervention in specific cases such as family disputes, where alternatives to force are mentioned. The calibrated use of force is however only briefly touched upon as a statement of principle, except for some examples drawn from the instructor's own experience.

The third type of course deals with the rare cases where the police use force illegitimately. The course on the 'premeditated attacks on the physical integrity of persons by law enforcement agents' is supposed to explain clearly what constitutes legitimate violence. The circumstances in which the use of force is legitimate are enumerated. Moreover, students are reminded that the use of police force is nothing 'else but violence legitimized by law, in the interest of all'. The proposition that legitimacy takes precedence over legality is clearly stated with three qualities being required for the use of force to be legitimate: the absence of any personal motive, the execution of a legal mission and the calibrated implementation of the use of force. Once again, such calibration depends on the police's assessment of a situation and is thus difficult to express as an objective requirement.

Therefore the circumstances in which legitimate force can be used are dealt with only partially in explicit courses. Sometimes instructors happen to talk to their students about cases where they had to resort to force. Sessions on situations of danger and distress can thus give rise at times to remarks on the ways for the proper use of force and, more generally speaking, the usefulness of the techniques taught at the school; however, they remain anecdotal. The use of force is only touched upon during the classes on specific police techniques but there is little discussion on the nature of its use. In this respect, legitimate violence is often of secondary importance in the argumentation. The idea is more to acquaint the students with the notion than to transmit such knowledge in a focused way. Teaching student policemen about the use of violence cannot be limited to an insubstantial textual presentation of the circumstances warranting the use of legitimate – or illegitimate – force. On the contrary, the teaching of this skill is imprecise and uncertain in nature. Whenever the question of using force is discussed, it is always in reference to the perception of the police officers in a given situation, as is the case in particular during the experience feedback meetings which take place after student officers finish their on the job training.

Giving form to violence: accounts during active service training programs

In the course of their training, students have to undergo three one-month active service training programs. They are posted to police stations and work under the supervision of officers in service. When they come back to school, their active service training is discussed during experience feedback sessions. One by one the students go to the instructor's desk from where they relate their experiences from the active service training to the rest of the class. They are questioned by their peers as well as by the instructor. The debriefing sessions are essential because it is during these sessions that students talk about their first hands-on experience and their impressions of their dealings with the public.[3]

During these exchanges, the question of the use of force by the police comes up often. It is raised particularly when there is a climate of suspicion. Some young recruits are offended by what they have witnessed, irrespective of whether the use of violence was legitimate or illegitimate. Though the limits of what constitutes legitimate violence appear to be getting drawn at the ENPP, they are never the subject of a comprehensive course that can give student policemen a reliable description of legitimate violence. Among the situations of violence that lead to a debate in the debriefing sessions, the relationship with weapons deserves special mention. Sociology and psychology have already discussed the 'emotional intensity with which students approach their first encounter with the power of the weapon' (Lhuilier 1992: 143; Reiss 1996). Instructors reinforce this, attaching great significance to the time spent on familiarizing their students with their weapon.

At first glance, the experience feedback sessions seem more favorable than the legal courses to teaching the job of law enforcement and its exclusive authorization for the use of legitimate violence. Whether a matter of concern or pride, students deal more easily with the use of force when it is placed in the context of a concrete situation. While such an approach does initiate the student into the use of legitimate violence, it must be emphasized that it is indeed a tricky process. The use of force should be commensurate with the situation, but there is no hard and fast rule to govern the conditions and limits of its use other than the vague necessity to be commensurate. The institution of policing itself has concluded that the use of force can only be understood/decided in a given situation. The answer to this necessity to study violence within a situational context is the attempt to technicalize the police use of force by imparting Intervention Gesture and Professional Techniques (GTPI).

Intervention gesture and professional techniques

The stated mission of the police hierarchy in teaching intervention gesture and professional techniques, boxing and self-defense is to rationalize the behavior of law enforcers when confronted with physical violence and, implicitly, restrict the modes in which police force is used by anticipating such modes, circumscribing them and making them routine.[4] To this end, instructors try and put students in real life situations. The procedures taught are intended to allow student officers to have acquired mastery, on graduating from the school, over a range of body techniques so that their physical intervention is well within the framework of the 'bare minimum force required' and the necessary proportionality of recourse to legitimate violence. Students learn the techniques of subduing the mentally ill and the various ways of handcuffing to prevent the accused from resisting. However, there is a practical problem, namely the impossibility of simulating in class the tense situations they will have to deal with once on they are on the job.

These courses must be designed keeping in mind the heterogeneous nature of the class composition (Gorgeon and Monjardet 1992). Some young recruits balk at the idea of sports, denigrate violent behavior and avoid such activities if possible. Willful absenteeism in the sports class is relatively widespread: all kinds of excuses – injuries, pain – are proffered to avoid it: even volunteering at the self-service cafeteria can be a way to skip some part of their combat training. To this extent, it is impossible to speak of a homogeneous socialization to the use of force. The tough nature of the self-defense courses is one of the reasons for the relatively low attendance of some students. While the intervention gesture and professional techniques or self-defense may be perceived as the result of the need to codify police interventions, the manner in which these courses are conducted in practice does not square up with the sugary sweet image of a police engaged in an irreversible process of euphemizing violence. Each self-defense course has its fair share of injuries. In some combat classes, I saw real violence where a few students landed some hard blows on their often consenting adversaries. After each round, there were some who were quick to discuss their performance and compare right hooks, black eyes and cuts above the eye. Similarly, the course on handcuffing techniques, especially tackle training (ground, wall), a core GTPI, initiates students into the use of force and the right amount to be used through its excessive application. There are students who try to outdo each other in the use force, as in the handcuffing classes where some get great pleasure from tightening the handcuffs to the maximum. At times, the handcuff marks are visible the next day, prompting criticism from a section of the students.

So, technicalization has its limitations when it comes to find a way to soften the use of force. For this reason, several students when questioned said they found the course superfluous. To conclude from this that GTPI are useless would be tantamount to ignoring the fact that the need to resort to such techniques arises in the first place because the decision to use violence is based primarily on the situation. In this respect at least, something has been learnt. Perhaps not new techniques, but rather a specific contact, even though differentiated, of the students with the use of violence that structures the job of law enforcement. From this point of view, we can observe the multiple ways in which violence is used depending on the student, those reluctant about self-defense having a different relationship to force from those with a more confrontational nature. Such differentiation should be understood as an index for describing the GTPI courses not so much as the learning of specific skills (even though this is an active function, it remains secondary) but as an amphitheatre for socializing students to the use of violence.

From this examination of the various ways in which legitimate violence is dealt with in police schools things two things emerge clearly. The first is the obvious fragmentation of legitimate violence which is neither the subject of a totalizing theory nor of an exhaustive seriation of its empirical manifestations. What matters are neither the texts nor the examples nor even the techniques, but the acculturation of the recruit to the possibility of resorting to force. The second observation falls within the Weberian conception of the State (Weber 1995). Learning to use force is not sufficient to acquire discipline not just because such violence does not exhaust the requirements of discipline, but also because the learning of its use cannot be understood under any circumstance as its codification. Before learning to use force 'properly', one has to come to grips with the fact of being able to exercise it. Now this was one of the first tasks of the ENPP: making the student aware that violence is normal without it being commonplace. This does not mean that law enforcers need to use force indiscriminately on every occasion or conversely that they will have perfected the use of calculated violence. It only implies that learning to use legitimate violence takes place in two stages: after the student has been familiarized with the use of violence, a considerable amount of work remains to be done. One still has to ensure that violence is used in a calibrated fashion.

Learning the calibrated use of violence through the framing of the situation

While the recruit initially learns about violence at the police school through a familiarization with the use of force, the need to calibrate it assumes an additional step in the training. Calibrating violence is not merely a question of how much force to use. Undoubtedly, the quantitative factor (what is the quantum of force to be used?) with the concomitant disciplinary need to learn how to determine the 'right intensity' is a determining factor in its proper implementation. But police force relies above all on its legitimacy regimes (does one need to resort to force or is there another solution at hand?), which assumes that violence is legitimate provided it is used commensurately with the requirements of the intervention. Accordingly, the commensurate use of force in a given situation is not so much about the ability to use calibrated violence as learning about a situational engagement type. Thus learning the use of calibrated force takes place through the mastery of interactional techniques which, if respected both by the policemen and the individuals questioned or checked, must ensure the legitimacy of the violence if necessary.

Submitting to authority and exercising it

Exercising authority is at the heart of the job of law enforcement. In his well-known work on the sociology of deviance, Howard Becker recalls this characteristic of the law enforcement officer: 'A good part of his activity does not consist in directly applying the law, but rather constraining people of whom he is in charge to respect him for himself' (Becker 1985: 181–182). Police training attaches a great deal of importance to this in both its complementary forms.

Authority is in the first place present as a factor in the layout of the school. Its importance can be seen in the strict control of the occupation of space and self-presentation within the police school. The conversion of the newcomer to the institution feeds on the sacralization of rituals and symbols that the students must respect. Authority as a principle has been assimilated in the school's architecture with a clear cut division between the outside and the inside and in the layout of the school: the director's office overlooks the central courtyard so that all the students can be seen; some zones are out of bounds for police recruits if they are not duly authorized to enter whereas other places require discipline in deportment while crossing these areas. The ENPP complex has also been compartmentalized on conventional lines such as status, working hours and activities like any other training institution (Foucault 1975). Differentiation is also effected through immediately identifiable physical markers. Uniforms along with strict rules and regulations are so many inescapable facts of the school. In addition to this strategy of visual display is the adherence to specific rules of etiquette and deference.

Right from the police school onwards, authority is reinforced through the constant emphasis on due respect as a prior condition for any interactional engagement. Indeed, one of the first things young recruits will have to learn on the street is imposing authority in an actual situation. So essential is this requirement that it even conditions, Becker says, the description of deviance which is then understood less as the resultant of behavior which violates the law and more as the lack of respect towards the person responsible for applying the law (Becker 1985: 182). The sociology of the US police has shown how police typologies are determined to a large extent by the reaction of the populations encountered and their capacity to accept police authority as testified by their compliant behavior during interactions (Westley 1970).

But this emphasis is not a case of authority for authority's sake. Evidently, police training cannot guarantee that those having to deal with the police will submit willingly to its authority, but the objective is to ensure as far as possible that the young recruits know how to assume and manifest police authority on the job to limit the probability of having to take recourse to coercion (Monjardet 1996). Illegitimate violence is less likely to occur to the extent the young recruit manages to win respect in the asymmetrical relationship with the public in a given situation. Training thus focuses on the possibility that the young recruits will learn to master the frameworks for the situation in which they have to intervene.

Mastering the frameworks for the situation

Situational exercises, during which student policemen are immersed in small plays enacted by other young recruits, provide an opportunity to revisit the forms of evaluation and adjustment to situations. The students being evaluated are expected to assess correctly the demands of the situation and be quick to display authority to see whether the people concerned will be conciliatory. If that is not the case, they should be able to marshal practical categorizations and adjust as best they can their action to the form the situation will take.

Admittedly, the forms of categorization can be learnt to a marginal extent by recognizing the external attributes of the people the policemen observed by van Maanen called 'assholes' (van Maanen 1978: 223). These scattered elements then enter into the establishment of typologies, but the diffused nature of this internalization does not allow one to talk of an overall mechanism – implicit or explicit – that can facilitate the deliberate learning of target population types. In point of fact, typologies have to be activated in given situations and for this they must be indexed to their formats. The production of frameworks for interaction occurs at least two other levels, the first conversational and the second that of body language.

The former, difficult to observe at the police school, can be seen in the situational exercises when the instructor observes that the students under evaluation do not hesitate to contradict each other in front of the person who has called on their assistance. At this point, the instructor insists on the need to display at least superficial unity even it means settling their argument elsewhere. The instructor motivates the recruits to treat people courteously but show flexibility as well. There is always the danger of a lack of consideration for the public.

Mastery of body techniques is the second mode of being in control of an interaction. An example allows us to illustrate this point. It has to do with 'palpation de sécurité' which we can translate into 'pat searching'. Theoretically different from a body search, a pat search is conducted in public spaces and is not as methodical and detailed as its related technique. The objective of pat searching is to check whether a person is carrying a weapon or not. This is neither a measure of constraint or coercion nor is it strictly speaking the use of legitimate violence and yet it has a strong bearing on the structuring of the intervention by physically actualizing the asymmetry between policemen and citizens. In this way, one can take control of the situation and decide whether or not to activate typologies.

The second example deals with three-way techniques which enable policemen to control the space of the intervention. The ways of maintaining distance are graded (courteous distance, security distance, defense distance); the policemen will chose any one of these to produce an actual police space commensurate with the demands of the situation. Accordingly during the situational exercises, most of the instructor's criticism has to with positioning. If while carrying out a pat search the policemen discover a firearm on one of the individuals, the young recruits get rebuked: the one who is in a safe position, slightly behind, was facing another student and the person being questioned such that the use of firearm would be impossible if required. As the three-way arrangement has not been respected, this jeopardizes the possibility for the policemen to use coercion commensurate with the level of danger of the situation. Here again, it is about controlling the manner in which force can be used through the mastery of techniques which have less to do with the use of force than with the ability to establish police asymmetry in a given situation. From this point of view, such techniques do not allow for a quantitative measurement of violence *in situ*, but rather for a proper delineation of the interactional conditions on which basis the violence exercised by policemen is deemed legitimate or illegitimate.

This is where learning the job of law enforcement meets its limitations: the uncertainty of police patrols or interventions on the street can only be simulated up to a point. This explains why so many policemen say they have learnt nothing at the school. They are both right and wrong. They are right to the extent that the ENPP cannot plunge its trainees into the immediacy of the situations in which they will be called upon to intervene; but they are wrong to the extent that their training at the ENPP gives them 11 months to familiarize themselves with the core elements of the job of law enforcement at the forefront of which is the use of force.

Conclusion

This overview of a French police school allows discussion on two main issues that matter in the sociology of the police, particularly when it comes to police recruit training. The first one is about the difference between the school and the street. Many police officers would say that what they learned in police schools is useless to them in their everyday routine of policing; and many sociologists would agree (van Maanen 1976). The observations made in French police classes lead us to temper this affirmation. Through the variety of roles, instructors have many ways to bring some 'true' police street experience in their courses; in the same manner, police students are required to do three 'internships' in police stations while they're trained. There are obviously differences between police schools and streets job; but they lie elsewhere, in the absence of uncertainty that marks police interventions on the streets.

The second issue this chapter allows us to discuss is the complexity of police use-of-force training. Occasions to teach in concrete terms what a 'legitimate' use of force is are infrequent, except for a handful of juridical courses and part of the physical training. One should ask why the use-of-force training is so inconspicuous, while its empowerment is fundamental in the definition of police occupation and missions (Bittner 1979). I could formulate a hypothesis that would require new ethnographies: it is because police use of force is always embedded in situations, and police officers are supposed to be able to understand the frames of these situations. It is only when the police officers' ability to engage with the situation 'properly' is challenged that a diagnosis of 'excessive use of force' can arise. As the possibility to evaluate the legitimacy of police use of force seems to require the necessity of understanding the interactional dynamics, the teaching of police use of force is harder than one supposes in the first place. It also needs more complicated training: what are the correct ways for a policeman to engage himself in situations so that if the use of force is needed, it will be necessarily legitimate.

Notes

1 G. Monate is one of the most important leaders of police trade unionism.
2 We may recall here the analogy given by Skolnick who brings together police work and, among others, the task of teaching.
3 Except those who have been police community support officers or have served as auxiliary police officers.
4 This rationalization of police gestures does not preclude lingering doubts about how harmless they are. Thus, these techniques come in for criticism regularly, as on the death of a 22-year-old man in Grasse in May 2008. The police officers had used at the time a spinal lock to immobilize the young man a direct consequence of which is to make breathing difficult. This neutralization technique is thought to have played an important role in the death of the young man, his autopsy revealing signs of asphyxia. Three of the seven policemen accused were given a suspended prison sentence and the four others were discharged. On excessive police use of force and judiciary clemency, see Jobard 2002.

Bibliography

Becker, H. (1983) *Outsiders*, Paris: Métailié.

Berlière, J.-M. (1996) *Le monde des polices an France, xixème, xxème siècles*, Brussels: Complexe.

Bittner, E. (1979) *The functions of police in modern society*, Cambridge: Oelgeschlager, Gunn and Hain.

Carrot, G. (1992) *Histoire de la police française*, Paris: Tallandier.

Cassan, D. (1999) *L'apprenti policier*, DEA dissertation, Sociology, Lille 1.

Demonque, P. (1983) *Les policiers*, Paris: La Découverte.

Foucault, M. (1975) *Surveiller et punir*, Paris: Tel Gallimard.

Gorgeon, C. and Monjardet, D. (1992) *La socialisation professionnelle des policiers*, Paris, report for IHESI.

Hauser, G. and Masingue, B. (1983) 'Étude auprès des personnels de la Police Nationale', in Ministère de l'Intérieur et de la Décentralisation, *Les policiers, leurs métiers, leur formation*, Paris: La Documentation Française.

Jobard, F. (2002) *Bavures policières? La force publique et ses usages*, Paris: La Découverte.

Ker Muir, W. (1977) *Police, Street-Corner Politicians*, Chicago/London: University of Chicago Press.

Lhuilier, D. (1992) 'Psychologie du port de l'arme et de l'uniforme', *Les Cahiers de la sécurité intérieure*, 9: 137–151.

Monjardet, D. (1996) *Ce que fait la police. Sociologie de la force publique*, Paris: La Découverte.

Moreau de Bellaing, C. (2010) 'De l'obligation à la ressource. L'apprentissage différencié du droit à l'école de police', *Déviance et Société*, 34(3): 325–346.

Parienté, P. (1994) 'Les valeurs professionnelles: une ressource pour l'encadrement de l'activité policière?', *Les Cahiers de la sécurité intérieure*, 16: 137–148.

Pruvost, G. (2004) '1982–2003: enquête sociodémographique sur les conditions de vie et d'emploi de 5221 policiers'. Report for IHESI, 2004.

Reiner, R. (1985) *The politics of the police*, Toronto: University of Toronto Press.

Reiss, A. (1996) 'Violences policières. Réponses à des questions clefs', *Les Cahiers de la sécurité intérieure*, 26: 177–192.

Skolnick, J. (1966) *Justice without trial*, New York: Wiley and Sons.

Skolnick, J. and Fyfe, J. (1993) *Above the Law: Police and the Excessive Use of Force*, New York: Free Press, 1993.

Van Maanen, J. (1976) *Pledging the police: a study of selected papers of recruit socialization in a large, urban police department*, PhD dissertation, University of California, Irvine, 1976.

Van Maanen, J. (1978) 'The Asshole', in P. Manning and J. van Maanen, *Policing: a View from the Street*, Santa Monica: Goodyear Publishing Company, 221–238.

Weber, M. (1995) *Économie et Société 1. Les catégories de la sociologie*, Paris: Plon.

Westley, W. (1970) *Violence and the police*, Cambridge: MIT Press.

Williams, A. (1979) *The police of Paris, 1718–1789*, Baton Rouge/London, Louisiana State University Press.

Part III

Police reform and training in developing and post-Communist societies

11 Police training and education in Hungary

F. Sándor

The expression 'police officer' ('rendőr' in Hungarian) first appeared in written language in the 1820s and in legislation in 1846. The history of the independent national police force goes back approximately 150 years. Politically, these were unsettled times that hindered the undisturbed development of law enforcement organizations (Cartedge 2011). These transformations resulted in the leadership of the police force being replaced, and significant numbers of well-trained and professional staff dismissed. Politicians at national and local level habitually interfered with purely professional issues, eventually usurping decision-making. Sometimes law enforcement organizations were used to suppress citizens on racial and religious grounds, to subdue social and ethnic movements, and the deportation of more than 600,000 Jewish people (Deak 2001).

Being a province of the Habsburg empire Hungary did not have the status of an independent state until 1867. Public administration and law enforcement bodies were supervised by foreign rule, which led to citizens turning against their presence. In the 1850s and 1860s the situation had become untenable (Cartledge 2011). The first Hungarian Ministry of the Interior was established resulting in the re-organization of the police. Previously, these tasks and responsibilities were allocated to the Habsburg government. After the Emperor withdrew his acknowledgement of the independent Hungarian government in 1848, leading to a war of independence, which ended with Hungary's defeat, the Ministry and its organizations were dissolved. Civil development begun in the first three decades of the nineteenth century had evolved slowly and was not strong enough to establish a Western European-type police force (Stanislas, Chapter 1). Elements of a feudal society survived until 1945, which prevented the evolution of modern civilian rule. Legislation (often considered unjust) that regulated the life of the country and facilitated the oppression of minorities and religious denominations, gravely distorted the operation of law enforcement and its relationship with the people.

What is called the 'Compromise of 1867', a legal agreement between the Hungarian and Austrian ruling elites, the Austro-Hungarian monarchy was established which created Hungary's own government, Ministry of Interior, and police within the dualist state. This led to the creation of an independent (albeit not unified) national police force. These arrangements operated almost uninterrupted until 2005, when they were replaced by the newly elected government, who, following the 'Scandinavian' model (see Kratocoski and Cebulak 2001), placed the police force under the supervision of the Minister of Justice. In 2009 following the new elections, the Ministry of the Interior was re-established and has been responsible for the police since then.

Following the 1867 Compromise, the police force and law enforcement was organised along several lines simultaneously; rural areas and villages under the Gendarmerie's jurisdiction. Gendarmerie units consisted of enforcement squads organized in a military fashion. Their establishment started in 1849 initiated by the Emperor's government. In 1881 the Hungarian government passed legislation setting up six gendarmerie districts to cover the whole country. Despite being reorganized several times, the Gendarmerie operated until 1945. After the Second World War the new democratic government dissolved the Gendarmerie for its participation in war crimes, and specifically in the deportation of Jews. Towns with larger populations had the opportunity to organize and operate their independent police force at their own cost. In 1886 there were 24 such settlements. Due to growing costs these police forces were phased out and state police organizations were established. A unified state police force in all the towns of Hungary was established in 1920 and operated alongside the Gendarmerie. State police units were formed in towns with smaller populations or those not wishing to have their own police force. In the capital Budapest the police was created by merging three geographical areas in 1872.

By the end of the nineteenth century the foundations of the new police force had been laid. The Budapest Board of Detectives was formed in 1886, a new police uniform was introduced in 1909, the Museum of Criminal Investigation was founded in 1908 and the first dog-training school of the Gendarmerie was established in 1910. The development of the Hungarian police also produced a few outstanding achievements. Hungary was the second country in Europe, and the first on the Continent, to introduce dactyloscopy (fingerprinting). This new identification method spread thanks to Ferenc Pekári, a former Deputy Commissioner of the Budapest Police, who learnt about it whilst a guest of Scotland Yard in 1902.[1]

In 1905 the Hungarian Border Police was established to address the ever growing cross-border traffic at the state borders with Romania, Serbia, and Russia. This agency was abolished after Hungary was defeated in the First World War. According to the Treaty of Trianon that concluded the war with conditions highly unfavourable to Hungary, two-thirds of the territory of the country was assigned to neighbouring states. The police force was completely reorganized in a much smaller country whose territory had been reduced to 28 per cent of its former size. The end of the Second World War witnessed the creation of new state organizations to replace the old ones that served the former fascist regime. Civilian democratic rule was short-lived with the growth and hegemony of the Communist Party in 1949, and its monopolization of state power (Cartedge 2011: 413–426).

Separate from the police, a special police organization of conscripts was set up. It mainly carried out the tasks of riot police and was used in public areas to support the police when needed. It operated until 1972, most of the time supervised by the Minister of the Interior, similar to the Border Guard, also comprised of regular soldiers. The latter was established with a two-fold purpose: it functioned as an armed force, also carrying out law enforcement activities. At one time the Border Guard had a staff of 17,000 and also assisted the police when needed. The Border Guard was integrated into the police force in 2007, consequently Hungary has one state police organization.

The political transformation of 1989–1990 resulted in significant changes within the police, especially its personnel. Its top leadership changed several times, as elsewhere throughout the organization. In the 20 years that followed democratization the same party was only able to establish a government in two consecutive electoral cycles which illustrates the instability of the time. Each incoming government introduced new plans for the reorganization of the police and a change in personnel. An important development during this period with significant consequences for the police was Hungary's accession to the European Union, which brought with it beneficial international relations (Benke 2001). This took the forms of substantial funding for the development of the organization, the purchase of technical equipment and in-service training for staff (see Stanislas, Chapter 1). Other developments with training and education implications has been the adoption of modern scientific methods which have become part of everyday working practices that include: using IT, setting up and searching databases, DNA tests, profiling, and conducting crime surveys.

Police organizational structure

The territory of Hungary is 93,000 sq km, with a population of ten million. The structure of the police reflects the system of public administration elsewhere (Mercer and Newburn 2009). The County Police Headquarters is located in the capital, with local administrative units in each of the 19 counties, and the National Police Headquarters as the main managing body. The Defence and Law Enforcement Committee in Parliament is responsible for passing bills related to law enforcement and meets in the event of crises. The police force is supervised by the Minister of the Interior and controlled by the Commissioner of the Hungarian National Police. The legal foundation for the police's various functions is provided by Act XXXIV of 1994 on the Police and the Decree of the Minister of Justice and Law Enforcement 62/2007 (XII 23). Established in September 2010 with a staff of about 600 people, the Anti-Terrorist Centre reports directly to the Ministry and is independent of the police. Its tasks include averting, and collecting intelligence on terrorist actions and the personal protection of the Prime Minister and the President.

The Hungarian police has approximately 46,500 staff and reports to the National Police Headquarters, headed by the Commissioner (see Boda forthcoming) who is assisted by three deputies, the Director General for Criminal Investigation, the

Director General for Policing and the Director General for Economic Affairs. The Director General for Criminal Investigation is the first deputy and responsible for the detection and investigation of crimes. Other areas of responsibility are:

- Criminal Investigation Department
- International Law Enforcement Cooperation Centre
- Criminal Analysis and Evaluation Department
- National Bureau of Investigation
- Hungarian Institute for Forensic Sciences

The Director General for Law Enforcement is responsible for the activities of the 'uniformed units' and:

- Law Enforcement Analysis and Evaluation Department
- Department of Duty and Defence Administration
- Public Order Department
- Traffic Policing Department
- Administrative Policing Department
- Border Policing Department
- Riot Police
- Airport Security Directorate (operating at the international airport of the capital and some smaller airports).

The second level of the police force is constituted by the 20 police headquarters. Their jurisdiction corresponds to the 20 public administration counties, one of which is the capital. Police stations responsible for towns and neighbouring settlements operate on the next (third) level. There are 154 such units operating all over the country. At the lowest level are police stations (of smaller settlements), offices of community police officers and border policing offices, also supervising border crossing points. Hungary is situated at the external border of the EU, therefore guarding the more than 1000 km-long Schengen external border is a major task.

Personnel and training

Police staff comprises commissioned officers, non-commissioned officers (NCOs) and civilian employees. These groups of personnel have different responsibilities and tasks which is reflected in their training. The Commissioner of the National Police also supervises four law enforcement vocational schools that provide basic training for NCOs. Only those graduating from one of these vocational schools can work as police NCOs. The faculty of Law Enforcement of the University of Public Service is independent from the police, and provides BA and MA Degree programmes for those preparing to become commissioned officers. Several other centres for further training, and a dog-handler training school, can also be found within the police organization.

The aim of NCO training is to prepare students for probationers' positions. After finishing the vocational schools students are allocated to a branch of the police service (CID, traffic, public order or border policing, the riot police). Successful candidates become professional employees of the Ministry of the Interior, and take an oath, prior to taking up their role as police sergeants. The Police Act (1994) stipulates a certificate of secondary education and graduating from a law enforcement vocational school as the condition of becoming a police sergeant, and member of the professional staff.

The job of a police officer is recognized in Hungary as a regulated profession. Police education is part of national vocational training. Legally accepted professions in Hungary are listed in the National Training Catalogue, a document that prescribes the requirements set for various professions and the number of lessons to be provided for professional courses. It also establishes which professions can be considered as similar, and relevant educational preconditions (see Peeters' chapter). There are four law enforcement vocational schools where NCOs are trained, established in former schools or military training bases. These were transformed into vocational schools in 1992–1993. Their curricula were updated and they obtained the right to issue a certificate of secondary vocational education. Managed by police colonels, these schools report to the Ministry of the Interior in terms of organization and to the Police Commissioner on budgetary matters. Training lasts for two years, starting in September and finishing in May of the second year. The admission quota is agreed by the Minister of the Interior; in September of the 2011–2012 academic year this figure was 1200 people, and 25–30 per cent of the students are women.

Accommodation and full board is provided at the schools, the cost of which is partly covered from students' grants. The curriculum is divided into five modules. After completing the first module, students are employed as professional probationer staff for one year and later confirmed in posts. Being probationers they are authorized to carry out partial police duties, a common practice in developing basic skills and knowledge and provided with the necessary uniforms and equipment. At the beginning of their studies students agree a contract with the police force, in which they commit themselves to work as professional police officers for two years after finishing their studies, in exchange for the education provided.

The structure and content of training

Hungarian citizens aged 18–35 without a criminal record are eligible to join the police and start training. After completing the various admissions procedure, clearance, and physical tests candidates receive basic training. The training described here was launched in the 2011–2012 academic year and organized around five modules. The basic training for police NCOs has changed several times in the last ten years. Post-secondary school training for NCOs was introduced in 1992, but because of the shortage of police officers a new two-year programme was run simultaneously with the earlier ten-month course.

Within police NCO training four specializations (in official terminology: branches) are border policing, public order policing, criminal investigation traffic policing. While the structure and length is the same for all of these specialisations, there are differences in the curricula. The total number of lessons is 2500. The curricula are broken down into five modules with 350–350–600–600–600 lessons, with each lesson being 40 minutes in duration. Training for the various branches is the same in the first four modules and is specialized in the fifth.

After graduating from the vocational schools police officers can attend the following additional training courses that build upon the knowledge acquired in one of the four specializations:

- police ensign – prepares students for activities requiring higher expertise, e.g. leadership of a service team
- officer attending scenes of accidents
- SOCO (Scene of Crime Officer)
- border police manager – prepares students for activities requiring higher expertise in this field
- police officer responsible for a certain area or settlement (community police officer)
- document examiner

General issues

Based on their previous studies students can choose between English and German technical language for law enforcement, and each student can learn one language. By the end of the second year students are required to obtain a driving licence type 'B', entitling them to drive a sedan (i.e. ordinary passenger car). In

Table 11.1 Basic training modules

Module 1	*Law enforcement agencies: general tasks and responsibilities, regulations.* Basic training involves intense physical stress exercises every morning, a 10-kilometre and a 20-kilometre route march and marksmanship with a pistol and with a carbine submachine gun. After finishing this module, hitherto civilian students swear an oath and are transferred to a probationer police officer status
Module 2	*Guards' and patrol members' tasks and responsibilities* prepares students for guarding facilities and escorting arrested persons.
Module 3	*Patrol members' tasks and responsibilities in squad operations* about the activities of the riot police and working in public areas.
Module 4	*Patrols' tasks and responsibilities* prepares students for the activities of police patrols.
Module 5	Consolidates and revises the knowledge acquired before and relevant for the given specialization, and supplements it in the special areas of border policing, public order policing, traffic policing and criminal investigation.

the last ten years, because of frequent shortage of police officers, training has been shortened several times so that students can be sent 'on the beat' as early as possible. To this end the '1 + 1' system was introduced in which students spend the first year at school and the second one in a police unit, finally returning to the law enforcement vocational school to take their final exams (Stanislas, Chapter 13). In 2011 a training course was conducted for 900 students covering only the first two modules due to staff shortages (Guards' and patrol members' tasks and responsibilities) six months before joining the police. Fifty Roma candidates also attended a shortened six-month course so as to increase the ratio of Roma people in the police force. Another method used by schools to mitigate staff shortage and to shorten the term of training is called 'partial vocational training', where students complete only a few out of the modules of a course, e.g. at the law enforcement vocational school. They then start working as police officers, but only in the special area relevant to their training. This partial training can later be supplemented by completing the remaining modules in order to obtain the full professional qualification required to become a police officers.

Training dog handlers

Like public order training, the training of police dogs (K-9s) receives little attention, despite their fundamental importance to contemporary police work. It is also a very unique area of activity working with live animals. The Hungarian Police employs approximately 550 service dogs and provides a range of training for working with them at its Dog Training Unit, which also houses other special courses. The dog handler profession is acknowledged in the National Training

Table 11.2 Special courses for handlers of dogs

Special courses for handlers of dogs deployed in	Duration
• general police duties (for community police officers, for patrolling and tracking tasks and responsibilities)	5 months
• tracking	6 months
• patrolling	3.5 months
• guarding	2 months
• narcotics detection	4 months
• explosives detection	4 months
• odour identifying	6 months
• public order (special training)	5 months
• criminal investigation (special training – corpse detection)	5 months
Dog training courses	
• tracking (for dog handlers who have completed the special course)	3 months
• patrolling (for dog handlers who have completed the special course)	1.5 months
• narcotics detection (for dog handlers who have completed the special course)	2 months
• explosives detection (for dog handlers who have completed the special course)	2 months
• squad operations	1 month

Catalogue. Training is carried out for various types of the deployment of K-9s such as guarding, patrolling, drugs/narcotics, explosives, and corpse detection. The outline below illustrates that the use of dogs in Hungarian policing is far wider than represented in Benke (2001: 98), who suggests they are used primarily as tools of control and intimidation.

Course for service dog handler candidates

The aim of the training is to enable the would-be dog handler to keep their future K-9 at home or place of work and to train it independently or with the help of a trainer dog handler. It lasts for one month (or for two weeks at places of duty with a trainer dog handler). Courses build on previous training, for narcotics detection, corpse detection, and tracking. The aim of the training is to enable dog handlers having K-9s younger than six years, with special abilities and appropriate classification, to carry out multiple duties after completing the course.

Further training conducted at law enforcement vocational schools

Depending on capacity, institutions are regularly used by the police force to conduct further training programmes which are not part of basic training. In the last few years vocational schools have run the following courses:

- Romanian and Serbian language courses of neighbouring countries
- document examiners course
- for officers attending scenes of accidents for the Traffic Policing Department of the army
- for customs investigators for the Customs Guard
- supplementary courses for police officers who joined the force earlier and had not yet attended the two-year training.

Higher education and commissioned police officers

In Hungary there is only one institution where students are trained to become commissioned police officers. Commissioned police officers' positions can only be filled by holders of college or university degrees (Kratocski 2007: 16–17). The first college for commissioned police officers, named Police College, was established in 1970. Training for the police and the Correctional Services started around the same time, and their training provision increased to include further specialisms such as:

- 1987: Customs Investigation
- 1991: Customs Management
- 1992: Border Policing
- 2000: Economic Crime Investigation

- 2004: Disaster Management
- 2006: Private Security
- 2008: Law Enforcement Management (MA)

The present institution, named the National University of Public Service was founded by the Hungarian government in January 2012. The University was created by integrating three institutions of higher education, namely:

- the Faculty of Public Administration of the Budapest Corvinus the University, trains officials for state and local administration;
- Zrínyi Miklós University of National Defence, maintained by the Ministry of Defence, trains army officers;
- the Police College supervised by the Minister of the Interior, trains commissioned officers for the Police, and broader areas of law enforcement.

These three institutions were merged, as of January 2012, and transformed into one university, unifying public administration, military and law enforcement training. The new organization has three faculties:

- Faculty of Public Administration (FPA)
- Faculty of Military Sciences and Officer Training (FMSOT)
- Faculty of Law Enforcement (FLE).

At the head of the University are the Rector and the Senate. The faculties are led by the Deans and the Faculty Councils. The Governing Board is the most important decision-making body, composed of representatives from the three ministries that administer and fund the University (the Ministry of Public Administration and Justice, the Ministry of Defence and the Ministry of Interior). The Board exercises power over training, economic management, and personnel issues. Both the educational institution and its specialities are accredited in the system of higher education. Bologna-type Bachelor's and Master's programmes are taught by the institution (Betcheva and Valev 2003), controlled by the Hungarian Accreditation Committee, the Ministry of National Resources (responsible for higher education) and the other ministries concerned.

The tutors' and students' rights and duties are regulated by legislation, e.g. the Act on Higher Education. The annex to this Act lists state accredited institutions of higher education, including the University. Tuition is conducted in a credit points system (Bachelor's programme: 180 credits, Master's programme: 120 credits). The Police College, the predecessor of the present FLE, joined the European Credit Transfer System (ECTS) and the European Higher Education Area (EHEA) (see Osborne and Thomas 2003). The Faculty continues to be involved in the EU's Erasmus Programme (Thomas 2003). Within its framework foreign students from various countries of Europe are received to study subjects in English. Students of the Faculty are sent on work placements and to study in other states such as the United Kingdom,[2] Spain, France, Germany, and Central

European nations. Tutors have also been involved in a wide range of travel and learning opportunities under this programme.

The tutors at the Faculty are civilian employees or professional commissioned police officers, who must fulfil the requirements for tutors set by the Act on Higher Education. Senior teachers hold scientific degrees, have achieved habilitation or are college or university professors. Police tutors are members of the staff of the Ministry of Interior. They apply for positions at the Faculty and after their term has expired they can return to the police. The institution is located on the territory of a former nunnery, and has classroom facilities, including for the teaching of special subjects, language labs, a hall of residence that can accommodate 500 persons, sports facilities and an indoors shooting range.

The Bachelor's Programme

At the Faculty three-year BA training courses are conducted both full-time and part-time for future mid-level leaders of the police force, the National Tax and Customs Administration, the National Directorate for Disaster Management, the Hungarian Prison Service and for the private security sector (see Wakefield and Button chapter). This latter programme is self-financed by the students, whereas all the others are state-funded. Quota for admission to the University is agreed annually by the Ministers concerned. The migration specialisation with a Bachelor's Programme starts in September 2012 for the Office of Immigration and Nationality. Training is organised into six semesters, after which the students have to pass a final examination and defend their degree theses. Students on full-time courses first undergo preparatory training, which is practically the same for all of the specialisations, and at the end of the second and fourth semester, and participate in a work placement of 320 hours spent at the various police units.

Students can choose to learn one of four foreign languages: English, German, Russian, or French. The most popular is English. Students can only get their degrees if they pass a state-accredited oral and written foreign language exam at intermediate level.

In Hungary there are Bachelor's programmes with a large number of various policing specializations. The currently accredited BA specializations are as follows:

Current accredited BA specializations

- Private Security (a self-financed course for would-be specialists in the private security sector);
- Criminal Investigation (+);
- Corrections (training for the Prison Service);
- Economic Crime Investigation (+) (training investigators for the area of economy and finance);
- Border Policing (+);
- Administrative Policing (+);

- Disaster Management (students are trained for the National Directorate of Disaster Management);
- Traffic Policing (+);
- Public Order (+);
- Financial investigation (training for the Tax Authority and the Customs Guard);
- Customs and Excise Administration (training for the Customs and Finance Guard)
- Specializations marked with (+) train officers for the Police.

The Master's Programme

The former Police College founded and accredited a university speciality in Law Enforcement Management. The first students started their studies in September 2008. The purpose of this course was to launch an independent MA speciality for police officers. The first training programme of its kind in Hungary, it gives commissioned police officers the opportunity to obtain a university degree in their 'own' educational institution, and being holders of the qualification be able to fill managerial positions. The developers of the curriculum were able to take into account the requirements and peculiarities of police work (see Peeters ibid.). Until that point commissioned police officers were able to obtain degrees of such a high level only at 'civilian' universities, and they usually opted for faculties of law. The number of applicants for the MA programme is usually three or four times higher than the quota.

This speciality is accredited as a full or part-time, four-semester course. For practical reasons it is being conducted only as a part-time course and is self-financed, i.e. students pay a tuition fee of HUF160,000 per semester (approximately £446.00). Applicants come from various law enforcement agencies, including the police. Classes are held at the weekends because of work demands. The course ends with a final examination where students must write and defend their theses. The condition for issuing the diploma is obtaining a certificate of an intermediate-level state-accredited English language exam. There is an entrance examination, a written test in law and law enforcement. Only commissioned law enforcement officers with a Bachelor's degree and at least three years' professional experience can apply. If their original diplomas do not accrue 50 credit points in law and law enforcement studies, the applicants must obtain them.

Policing managers' course (for commissioned police officers)

Increasing numbers of employees of the Hungarian Police are holders of 'civilian' Bachelor's degrees (typically obtained at teacher training, and technical colleges, business schools or faculties of law), but have not received specialised training at a higher education law enforcement institution. In order that they can work in mid-level management, as commissioned police officers, and get the income appropriate for such positions candidates must complete the policing managers' course (see

Neyroud and Wain chapter); also conducted at the FLE. This type of thinking informs calls for a new management qualification for the British police (Neyroud 2011: 38–39, Stanislas, Chapter 4). Graduates from the police managers' course are not given a higher education degree. Only employees of the police with a degree in civilian higher education can apply, with the consent of their commander. Thus, students already belonging to the police staff but in theory having only civilian knowledge have the opportunity to acquire the essentials of police work.[3] Almost half of the students on this programme are NCOs. This type of programme is very popular and approximately 27 courses have been run. Attendance is self-financed; it has cost HUF145,000 (approximately £404.00) in recent years. The curriculum consists of 600 lessons, 360 concerned with theory and 240 practice. Students spend 15 weeks at the Faculty, attending 360+90 lessons (theory and practical respectively), which is followed by a four-week (150 hours) field trip spent at one of the mid-level management units of the police force.

Additional information

The Faculty of Military Sciences and Officer Training of the NUPS has an accredited doctoral school (for PhD candidates) that runs doctoral training two-year part-time courses. One of the areas PhD students can conduct research in is defined as 'National Security and law enforcement'. Among the doctoral supervisors of the University, are commissioned police officers who are habilitated doctors and holders of scientific degrees. They supervise four to five PhD students (commissioned police and law enforcement officers) with writing and defending their theses. Enrolment for PhD studies is self-financed by students. The University also accepts foreign applicants.

Law enforcement research

Both the Ministry of Interior and the National Police Headquarters have their Scientific Councils. They coordinate scientific research conducted at the organizations, announce tenders for papers discussing issues of importance for the police force, organize conferences, support doctoral students and issue publications. Research is divided into sections according to the most important topics. The legal basis for the activities of the two councils is provided by the decree issued by the Minister of the Interior. In 2004 the Hungarian Association of Police Sciences was founded to coordinate the activities of those interested in law enforcement research. The Committee on Police Science was established within the Section of Economics and Law of the Hungarian Academy of Sciences in 2007. The Committee has 18 members and its aim is to coordinate law enforcement research at the level of the Academy.

Further training for police officers

By further training we mean all forms of training that are not part of the training provided by the law enforcement vocational schools or by the accredited programmes of the FLE and the NUPS. At a national level further training is organised and coordinated by the Education and Training Management Department of the National Police Headquarters. The most common form of such programmes is training courses that last for different periods of time. Several institutions within the police are maintained with the task of conducting further training.

Special examination in law enforcement

The special examination in law enforcement, the passing of which is mandatory for filling managerial positions, has existed since 2002. Candidates are prepared for it at two levels, at Leadership and Master Leadership courses. The special examination in law enforcement comprises obligatory and elective subjects and written and oral tests. The tests are preceded by a three-day training, attendance which is a condition for being admitted to the examination. All the tests need to be passed within one year from the first day of the training. Candidates who cannot pass all the tests in one year lose grades obtained from all previous tests. In such cases, candidates are provided one more year to pass all examinations without having to repeat the training. Failing to obtain the certificate of the special examination results in having to re-apply for the course again.

Passing the law enforcement special examination is mandatory to fill posts belonging to the category of head of department or higher, as defined by the Ministerial decree on the law enforcement special examination, and leadership training in law enforcement. The aim of the training is to ensure that commissioned officers, candidates for the aforementioned positions acquire comprehensive understanding of the activities of law enforcement agencies, and operation of public administration and complement and update their professional knowledge (Kratoscki and Das 2007, Stanislas ibid.).

The content of the training:

The material of the nine examination subjects (one obligatory and eight elective)

- Public administration and integrated law enforcement management (obligatory subject)
- Border policing administration (elective subject)
- Disaster management and fire protection administration (elective subject)
- Police administration (elective subject)
- Health and psychological management of law enforcement agencies (elective subject)
- Economic and financial management of law enforcement agencies (elective subject)
- Administrative management of law enforcement agencies (elective subject)
- HR management of law enforcement agencies (elective subject)
- Technological and IT management of law enforcement organs (elective subject)

Leadership training

The condition of appointment to certain higher posts is completing two more coherent training courses. Commissioned officers who have passed the special examination in law enforcement and have completed the Leadership course can be appointed Head of Department or Deputy Head of General Department (and are entitled to the corresponding income). Only those who have completed the Master's Leadership course can be appointed (or be acting holders of the positions of) Head of General Department or to higher managerial positions or other roles at this level.

Training takes place at the Law Enforcement Leadership Training and Research Institute (LETRI), an organ of the Ministry of Interior with an autonomous budget and staff of 53 (Stanislas, Chapter 1). Leadership training courses have been conducted there for 12 years and have been completed by about 1500–1600 officers. The dual functions of the LETRI are:

• to provide leadership and further training for the leaders of the commissioned staff;
• to provide the organizational background for scientific research in law enforcement.

Training is carried out in two stages, in two connected courses called Leadership (12 five-week courses a year, with four days a week and groups of 14) and Master Leadership courses (two four-week courses a year, with four days a week, groups of 14).

The curriculum covers the current theoretical and practical issues of leadership in the police force. On completing the course students are awarded a diploma.

A needs analysis and compiling a development plan form an integral part of the programme, as well as completing a significant number of assignments. Students must research a project and present it at the final examination. For a more detailed examination of different types of leadership programmes and forms of assessments used (see Neyroud and Wain chapter).

Central European Police College (MEPA)

The German name of the organization is Mitteleuropäische Polizeiakademie, a regional cooperation involving Central European countries with similar historical, social, and cultural backgrounds. The member countries are: Austria, Hungary (as founding states), Slovenia, Slovakia, Poland, the Czech Republic, Germany, and Switzerland (Pagon *et al.* 1996; see Peeters chapter). The institution was established to carry out training tasks; its primary aim is to facilitate practical cooperation in combating organized and cross-border crime, using the German technical language for policing and by acquiring new methodologies in criminal investigation and border policing (Stanislas ibid.). The training is preceded by a (German) technical language course, as the working language of the CEP is German. Member countries send commissioned officers to the CEP for training. During the training students visit member countries and their educational institutions and law enforcement agencies. Students obtain knowledge of up-to-date professional methodologies and the peculiarities of the different countries (Neyroud and Wain ibid.; Kratoscki and Das 2007). The course is completed by the presentation of a professional essay. The ability of students to establish personal relationships is of major importance, and is particularly beneficial in developing further international cooperation (Stanislas ibid.).

The Central Bureau of Coordination is in Vienna and there are national contact points in every member state. The highest authority of the organization is the Board of Directors, assisted by the Board of Trustees, which carries out organizational and executive tasks. The institution has been operating since 1992; its working language is German and it offers opportunities for further training for commissioned police officers in the following fields:

Further training for commissioned police officers

- (Main) course in criminal investigation (11 weeks+ language course – approximately eight weeks) – target group: specialists in the field of organized and economic crime.
- Integrated Border Management (four weeks+language course – approximately three weeks) – target group: police officers working in the field of border security with intermediate or advanced technical language skills.
- Professional seminars (annually 8–10) in the member countries (4–5 days) in the field of criminal investigation, public order and border security for participants with intermediate technical language skills
- Work placement corresponding to the participant's original place of duty (one week for participants with at least intermediate technical language skills)
- Language course abroad (three weeks in a German-speaking country with at least elementary technical language skills)
- German courses of 500–550 lessons – preparation for elementary, intermediate and advanced language exams, starting in February and September.
- Publications, books, periodicals, online material (search with keyword MEPA, www.mepa.net)

International training centre

The institution was founded in 1999. At present it reports to the Minister of the Interior and financed by the Ministry. Being an accredited adult education institution and a state registered language examination centre, its main tasks include:

- organizing training courses;
- recruitment, selection and preparation of officers for international missions and peacekeeping activities;

- organizing and conducting language (English, German, French, Russian, Italian, and Esperanto) courses of 50, 100, and 450 lessons;
- operating as the national contact point for CEPOL (European Police College), and hosting its national office;
- providing logistic support for the International Law Enforcement Academy (ILEA). This training institution is maintained by the US (Stanislas, Chapter 1), it operates according to the bilateral agreement signed by the Hungarian and the US governments in 1996, managed by an American Director and supervised by the US Embassy in Budapest;
- providing logistic support for the operation of the Central European Police College (MEPA).

The main courses conducted by the Training Centre are:

- peacekeepers' training
- mental-tactical training
- training the trainers
- training in crowd management (public order, public safety)
- training for undercover detectives
- witness protection
- training in complex investigation, open and covert methods and tactics
- community policing and crime prevention
- police communication with the media
- traffic safety and attending the scenes of accidents
- basic training in criminal investigation
- crime scene investigation
- training for mid-level managers
- hostage negotiation training
- training for criminal experts and research workers
- training in fighting organized (drug) crime.

Law enforcement agencies' training centre

The police force has a training centre in the capital with the following tasks and responsibilities:

- planning and organizing annual sports events for the police;
- planning international police sports events;
- special training (for operations teams, sharpshooters, motorcyclists, motor-boat drivers, off-road vehicle drivers, marksmanship instructors, trainers of tactics used when taking measures);
- conducting psychological and traffic safety training;
- management of the annual further training and sports activities of the Hungarian Police;
- cooperation with international training and sports organizations.

Conclusion

The Hungarian police training and education system represents an ongoing effort to develop a comprehensive approach to produce the highest possible quality police officers with appropriate knowledge and skills to carry out their various roles. One dimension of this has been the increasing importance of higher education as illustrated by postgraduate education as a precondition for access to higher appointments and the provision of specialist modules available to police and other public security and emergency response personnel. The Hungarian police training system is underpinned by assumptions about the professional nature of police work and formally recognized as such. Increasingly, an appreciation and exposure to working in international environments or those other than Hungary or in combination with agencies outside the country is becoming an important feature of these processes, reflecting contemporary trends.

Notes

1 Source of information: The Police History Museum. The museum was founded in 1908 and for 36 years it collected a significant amount of material from the relevant subject area, which was almost completely destroyed during the Second World War. It boasts a significant archive of films and a collection of 50,000 specialist books and periodicals.
2 De Montfort University is a member of the Erasmus Programme. Its Erasmus coordinator is Kim Sadique of the Community and Criminal Justice Department.
3 The essential difference and strength of the Hungarian system compared to the British in providing various career routes for civilian staff can be evidenced via the writer's personal experience. During his first spell of teaching at Bramshill Police Staff College, he was interrupted by an Assistant Chief Constable who enquired about his age. He then asked whether the writer had considered doing a 'proper job' commensurate with his talent, and went on to explain that based on experience he recognized a 'natural operational commander'. He then began to explore the various mechanisms open to a civilian police staff member of a particular career grade wanting to fast track through the police structure, and was joined by other senior officers in the discussion. The conclusion was there was no mechanism for that to occur, other than to take a reduction in pay to join at constable rank. How to address some of these problems are considered by the Winsor Report.

Bibliography

A rendészeti szervező szakképesítés rendőrszervező elágazás képzési programja, (Training programme for the policing manager speciality, police manager specialisation) 2009, internal publication of the Police College, Registration number: 1421–98/2009.

Act XXXIV of 1994 on the Police.

Adyligeti Rendészeti Szakközépiskola Pedagógiai Programja, (The programme of the Law Enforcement Vocational School, Adyliget) 2011, Without a registration number.

Benke, M. (2001) 'Policing In Transition Countries Compared With Standards In The European Union – Where Dreams Are Not Fulfilled' in A. Kadar (ed.), *Policing In Transition: Essays On Police Forces In Transition*, Budapest: Central European University Press.

Betcheva, R. and Valev, K. (2003) 'University Continuing Education in Bulgaria' in M. Osborne and E. Thomas (eds) *Lifelong Learning In A Changing Continent: Continuing*

Education In The Universities Of Europe, Leicester: National Institute of Adult Continuing Education.

Cartledge, B. (2011) *The Will to Survive: A History of Hungary*, Columbia University Press.

Deak, I. (2001) *Essays on Hitler's Europe*, University of Nebraska Press.

Decree of the Minister of Justice and Law Enforcement 62/2007. (XII. 23.) on the Service Rules of the Police.

Hallgatói Tájékoztató (Students' Guide for the 2009/2010 academic year) published by the Police College, 2009, Without a registration number.

Mihály Ernyes: A magyar rendőrség története, (The history of the Hungarian Police) 2002, published by the Ministry of Interior, ISBN 963 9208 13 2 Ö.

Rendőrségi Évkönyv (Police Yearbook), 2010, 2009, 2008, 2007, www.police.hu/magyarrendorseg/evkonyv/evk2010/evkonyv2010.html.

Thomas, E. (2003) 'Europe, the European Union and University Continuing Education' in M. Osborne and E. Thomas (eds).

Websites

National Police Headquarters, www.police.hu.

Law Enforcement Vocational School, Szeged, www.szrszki.hu.

Law Enforcement Vocational School, Miskolc, www.mrszki.hu.

Law Enforcement Vocational School, Körmend, www.rendeszkepzo-kormend.hu.

Law Enforcement Vocational School, Adyliget, www.arszki.hu.

Law Enforcement Leadership Training and Research Institute, www.rvki.hu.

International Training Centre, www.nokitc.hu.

Faculty of Law Enforcement, National University of Public Service, www.uni-nke.hu.

Police History Museum, www.policehistorymus.com.

Central European Police College) (MEPA), www.police.hu/kepzes/kera.

International Law Enforcement Academy, www.ilea.hu.

Hungarian Association of Police Sciences, www.rendeszet.hu.

Scientific Council of the Ministry of Interior, www.bm-tt.hu

12 A review of police education and training in China

Y. Tingyou

Introduction to police education and training in China

This chapter will examine police education and training in China, from its initial creation to current developments. Through 60 years of trials and hardships Chinese police education and training (for brevity's sake referred to as police education in most instances) continues to grow and develop. Since the reform and 'opening up' policy, approved at the *Third Plenary Session of the 11th Central Committee* in 1978, police education has made significant leaps in the past 30 years and boasts some important achievements.[1]

Chinese police education has its modern origins in the communist system of Mao Zedong where the police were seen as primarily serving the state and ruling party machinery, which was largely reflected in police training. After decades of reform, a relatively mature system of training and education has been established. Pioneering and typical examples of training practices will be presented to illustrate this process.

Despite some important obstacles, China initiated a new round of police education reform in 2008, based on its historical experience and awareness of the inadequacies in existing practice (Wang 2010). The current reform attaches greater importance to occupation-related skills training and recruitment system improvement (see Peeters' chapter), which is underpinned by an official commitment to meritocratic practices and professionalism (Wong 2011: 18). This is also an important measure of the new general orientation of the police and public services to adapt to new national priorities.

Police education in China, as elsewhere, reflects important aspects of the national education system (Zhou 2005), as well as the police organizations' own practices. In the broad sense, police education refers to the activities that can help police or students improve their overall policing abilities including increasing their knowledge and skills by means of education and training (Stanislas, Chapter 1). China's police education, in essence, is vocational, including general academic police education and in-service training. General academic police or undergraduate education places emphasis on the student's overall qualities (Stanislas ibid.), which include scientific and cultural qualities, such as being versed in the liberal arts, as well as career skills, and an appropriate academic degree or certificate is granted upon graduation and completion of studies. In-service police training mainly refers to basic skills training.

Police education refers primarily to education and training that take place in police colleges (schools) or universities, as well as in some police internship bases. Chinese higher police education and training institutions are an integral part of public security agencies or organs, and their main task is to produce qualified police professionals for public security agencies. In this regard the Chinese higher education systems shares similarities to the Hungarian system. In the 60 years of police education and training in China gradually developed into a relatively mature and comprehensive system, while retaining very important Chinese characteristics. The present system has historically passed through what can be viewed broadly as the initial foundation period and the new development period.

The initial foundation period

The Initial foundation period of Chinese police education and training broadly includes two historical stages of development and change: the creation stage and destruction/stagnation stage.

I The creation stage for Chinese police education and training (1949–1965)

Since the establishment of the People's Republic of China in 1949, its governments have attached much importance to police work. On 5 November 1949, the Public Security Ministry (PSM) of China held its inaugural meeting. In January 1950, the first police college, namely the central police cadres' school, was established. Initially police education programmes were too few to meet the demands of policing organizations in the country. In order to produce sufficient qualified police officials at all levels, a new system of police education and training was put on the agenda. All over China police schools were set up under the guidance of different police organs, not only at the national or central level, but also at the provincial and some at city level (Mawby 2005: 24). Short-term training was introduced by police schools to train their police officers.

Since then, police schools have become the primary channel for training police officers. Police education instilled an ideological foundation for police officers by focusing primarily on political education, learning the basic theories of Marxism, Leninism, and the thoughts of Mao Zedong. It also involved studying the party's principles and policies, and establishing a revolutionary outlook (Wong 2011: 6; Mawby 2005: 22–24). Training enabled trainees to clearly understand their tasks, responsibilities, and the importance of police work. According to Wang (2010) 35 police schools were established in the beginning of the founding of new China. Police schools trained newly-enrolled recruits in different cohorts and at different levels, with each phase of training ranging from three or four to six months in length. In 1956, the number of police colleges in China had increased from 35 to 52, with more than 27,000 police students.

During this stage of development, four areas were highlighted as priorities in order to improve the quality of police colleges or academies. First, in improving the quality of teaching staff by widening the selection pool. Besides leading cadres and professionals who are employed by police academies to serve as teachers, cadres with higher professional and cultural qualifications were now also included for selection. Second, was the systematic compilation of teaching materials for wider use across the country. Prior to this there was no standardization of police training educational materials. Between 1954–1957, 13 sets of professional teaching materials were compiled, and subsequently introduced. The third development priority involved re-equipping teaching and laboratory equipment, and the final involved reforming teaching methods (Stanislas ibid.). Very large classes were reduced to smaller classes, accompanied by new pedagogies such as independent (self-)learning, coaching, seminars, to include tours and internships, etc.

The basic task of Chinese police education and training during this stage was to adapt to the requirements of police work. Police education and training in this period was largely dominated by on-the-job training, including the reliance on short-term training and professional skills training (see Chappell chapter). The emphasis at that time mainly focused on political and professional education. Police cadres' schools played an important role in laying the foundations in the development of teaching material, computer hardware and software (Brew 1999). They also accumulated a wealth of valuable experience in education for later police college and undergraduate education, while meeting the needs of professional policing at that time. With the rapid development of police work, the existing on-the-job training model was unable to meet the needs of police personnel (Kratoscki and Das 2007; Stanislas ibid.).

II Destruction and stagnation stage of police education and training (1966–1977)

From 1966–1977, the repression of the Cultural Revolution brought severe disaster to China and its people (Macfarquhar and Shoenhals 2006).[2] It also brought a great deal of destruction to police education and training. All levels and types of public police colleges were severely disrupted, and all six police colleges directly under the leadership of Chinese Public Security Ministry were closed down or their senior faculty members dismissed (Macfarquhar and Shoenhals 2006: 112–117). Teachers in police colleges were persecuted or forced to do manual labour in the countryside. Police college premises were taken over for other purposes. Books, data, files and teaching facilities in police colleges were severely damaged or burnt. In-service police education and training was canceled thus bringing the police education system to almost a standstill (Wong 2011: 5).

The new development period

In the late 1970s, Chinese police education staggered into the New Development Period which can be broken down into four broad stages: the recovery, consolidation, progressive, and a new bold reform stage (see Wong 2011: 4–11).

I Recovery stage for police education and training (1978–1985)

In the middle and later stage of the Cultural Revolution, with the support of leaders such as Deng Xiaoping and Premier Chou Enlai, police work begun the slow process described by Wong (2011: 6) as 'rising out of the ashes of destruction' to enjoy a degree of recovery, and the rehabilitation including the return of hitherto ostracized police officers. However, the residual legacy of the Moa's rule still acted as an constraint to progress which was reflected in police education and training often prioritizing political education over professional policing skills and knowledge.

When the Cultural Revolution was finally put to an end, most police officers in China had received formal police education or training. According to statistics, collected by the MPS at the time (Yanji 2010)[3] police officers with junior high school or lower levels of education accounted for 60 per cent of officers. Police officers who completed university study only accounted for 3.6 per cent of all personnel. After the demise of the 'Gang of Four' (who instigated the disastrous Cultural Revolution), in 1976 Chinese central authorities introduced a new quality standard requirement, for the police to improve police academic education and its overall performance' which was seen as an urgent priority. In 1978 in all the provinces, municipalities and autonomous regions, police schools or colleges were almost fully restored and operational, and tasked with providing in-service police training. Professional vocational police classes were introduced at the same time for prospective police officers.

The desire to rebuild the police training infrastructure can be seen by the number of important activities that took place starting with the first national conference on police education and training was held in 1984. Three levels of the central, provincial and regional (municipal) police education and training management system were also established, and a scheme of police education was developed. While some police schools in China recovered many middle level and higher level police schools had to be built or re-built. Higher police college teaching plans were formulated and implemented. Many of the most important developments in contemporary Chinese police education have been shaped by these events.

The recovery of in-service police education and training

Administrative police cadres' colleges were established. The colleges recruited in-service police, who after two to three years schooling return to their original public security agencies after graduation with a college diploma. Fifty-seven adult secondary police schools were set up to train in-service police officers, which after completing their two-year course participants receive a diploma, continuing to work in their original public security agencies. In addition, in-service police officers were encouraged to participate in 'amateur schooling' in police colleges and secondary police schools, in other words in-service police-men were encouraged to utilize self-teaching in order to improve their perform-ance (Birzer 2003).

The establishment and development of secondary police schools and higher police colleges

From 1978–1985, 83 secondary police schools were established throughout the country. The educational system of higher police university also came into being. The typical examples are 'Chinese People's Public Security University' and 'Chinese Criminal Police College'. The teaching provision of these institu-tions will be outlined further on.

II The consolidation stage of police education and training (1986–1999)

The number and size of the police colleges increased and within a period of approximately ten years, various types and levels of officially approved police colleges amounting to more than 100 were in existence. A group of police train-ing schools and training bases were also established. By the end of 1996, the number of students in police schools totaled approximately 130,000 and teach-ing conditions and facilities had improved considerably.

During approximately a ten-year period multiple forms of adult academic education and training sprang up, including full-time in-service police educa-tion.[4] Chinese police officers were encouraged to utilize every option to develop themselves, similar to police officers in other parts of the world (Stanislas, Chapter 1), which included attending classes in their spare time, or via corres-pondence courses or evening and self-study classes. In addition, there was exten-sive job training, short-term professional training, promotion training and so on. In 1995 the number of police officers who finished college education amounted to 26.62 per cent from 4.2 per cent in 1984, and their overall quality and capa-city was significantly improved.

Improving the quality of police education and training[5]

The police colleges have changed the traditional tendency of focusing on know-ledge and theory while ignoring ability and practice, which is the opposite to the historical practice in many western policing traditions where police training has been viewed more in craft terms (Stanislas ibid.). In order to meet practical needs the colleges increased the number of basic professional courses, special-ized courses and skills training courses. In addition, they shortened the time spent teaching and strengthened the links between experience and practice. They also organized for students to obtain practical experience in basic public security agencies to improve their school teaching abilities and capacity to develop future students.

Enhance the faculty team in police colleges

Police colleges of different levels took measures to enhance the development of the teaching staff (see Green and Woolston chapter). On the one hand, they train in-service teachers to improve their teaching quality, and on the other recruit high quality teachers, for example by selecting professional technical cadres in police departments to teach, and by selecting outstanding graduates from police schools for four years of further academic education to become qualified teachers. The colleges also invite police experts to become visiting professors as supplement teachers.

Improve the compilation of textbooks, and materials, and police study specialisms

The Chinese Public Security Ministry (The Ministry) has published about 200 professional textbooks, using the central unified planning system to direct and coordinate activities (see Zhou 2005). Among them, there are 100 higher education textbooks, 62 junior education textbooks and about 30 kinds of in-service training materials. Police colleges also produce their own textbooks, often in cooperation with other police schools. The number of these textbooks, references, and lecture notes now available total 1,000. Police colleges also produce multimedia materials to support learning. The outcomes of these activities are the creation of a relatively comprehensive police teaching material system covering most subjects (Stanislas, Chapter 1). One dimension of this strategy is its contribution to the development of specialist knowledge by teaching institutions and improving the professional disciplines police students are able to study. Nearly 30 police majors in specialist subjects have been set up, including police management, investigation and security administration, document testing, traffic management, fire protection, and border management. These specialisms are similar to that offered to Hungarian police, public, and emergency officials (see Sándor chapter).

Promote police exchanges and cooperation with foreign countries

China actively carries out police educational exchanges and cooperation with other countries, for similar reasons to other policing jurisdictions as outlined in Chapter 1. First, it successively sends delegations to observe and study more than ten countries' police training, such as the US, France, Italy, Germany, Thailand, North Korea, Russia, Ukraine, Pakistan, and Egypt[6] (see Yang 2010). In return, it receives police delegations from the US, Russia, and China Hong

Kong. Second, China also organizes study groups of police school principals to visit the US, and take part in the international police education meetings and other academic activities. It jointly holds seminars about international legal medical examiner issues and public security with the US, Japan, and other countries. Third, China has established sister-relationships with police colleges in the US, Britain, Russia, and France, especially in the fields of teaching, academic research, and the teachers' training. To enhance teachers, and promote study abroad and in-service training, China employs more than 270 cultural and educational experts from the US and Britain, and sends about 100 teachers to study abroad a year (see Yang 2010).

Police education and training for Chinese ethnic minorities,
reinforcing the micro management and guidance for police education
and training

The MPS and other police colleges are concerned about police education and training in ethnic minorities communities and areas. Like many countries in the world China is not ethnically homogenous and has its own history of ethnic difficulties (Qi Pan and Mei Tan 1999; Acharya and Gunaratna *et al.* 2001). For example in 2009 local police had to intervene after a group of ethnic Uighurs attacked their Han neighbours (Branigan 2009). Junior and college education classes in colleges were established in order to recruit and train police personnel from these areas awarding Bachelor Degrees and college diplomas. From 1995–1999, in-service police training underwent important development. In 1999 the MPS held the second national police education meeting in Shanghai, and introduced a policy to develop in-service police training and proposed guidelines that police education must focus on both academic education and in-service training; and seek to gradually eliminate secondary vocational school recruitment. In addition, the Shanghai meeting declared that China needed to upgrade secondary vocational schools to specialist police training centres within the next three years.

In the whole police education training system, police adult education is the principal means to improve officer education and train in-service police, and is fundamental to constructing a life-long police education system (see Chapter 1). Police adult education is divided into three parts: full-time adult education, part-time education, and self-study education. In 2000, the MPS initiated the adult education recruitment reform in police colleges. Chinese People's Public Security University (CPPSU) and China's police colleges are the major drivers for adult education. China has improved the level of education of police officers by setting up schools and police colleges throughout the country. The national self-study education system has improved considerably, which has strengthened the role and expertise of police colleges who have led in this area. In 2000, over 50,000 police officers took part in higher education's self-study education (See Wang *et al.* 2008).

III The progress stage of police education and training (2001–2008)

With China undergoing a number of reforms simultaneously, in terms of its 'opening up' policy together with national economic development priorities, and implementation of aforementioned policing reforms in education, its police were confronted with an increasingly arduous set of tasks (Peiwen 2008). An important set of factors driving these changes was the desire to improve the professionalism, legal and public accountability, and effectiveness of the police in the face of economic and social change; along with an increase in crime (Wong 2012: 9–12; see Zvekic 1998). The Chinese police education and training system had to improve and entered probably its most vigorous stage of development.

The framework for this new phase of development had already been communicated in the form of MPS guidelines to improve the police which included a big emphasis on science and education strategies, to strengthen the police college education and improve the training of in-service police, in an effort to cultivate high-quality adaptable police personnel (see Chapter 1). The main task of police educational institutions set out in the guidelines was developing postgraduate education under the overall planning system; develop secondary education; strengthen graduate education; and improve postgraduate provision. All police officers according to the guidelines should have access and pass through four training processes, namely, recruitment; promotion; job/role preparation and special business; and knowledge renewal.

Police training regulation

In November 2001, the MPS issued new police training regulations to standardize in-service recruit training, professional training, and promotion training. The ordinance makes detailed stipulations about most aspects of training including: its organization and management, safety and security, and funding. Also covered by the regulations are matters related to the division of training responsibilities and tasks, training institutions and the construction of facilities, and training time and content. One of the clearest messages coming from this change was that suitability for promotion was to be based on being trained and certified.

The development of police academic education

Police academic education continued to make sound progress. By 2002 the restructuring of the secondary-level People's Police School was nearly completed. Three kinds of education forms co-exist: general police academic education, adult education, and in-service police training. The police colleges are accountable and under the leadership of the MPS, and provinces are responsible for autonomous regions. Municipalities are directly under the Central Government for academic education and professional training, while city-owned police schools serve their localities. As of 2002, there are over 400 police schools and training bases in China. Among them there are five under-graduate colleges, 29 junior colleges, nine active service colleges for frontier defence and fire-fighting, seven provincial training schools, 237 municipal training schools, and 185 county-level training bases respectively. From 2002–2005, nine three-year colleges in Hubei, Jiangsu, were successfully upgraded to graduate colleges. In 2005, the number of junior police colleges expanded to 30.

The enhancement of police higher education

Increasing the quality and capacity of police postgraduate education was also identified as an urgent priority which created new challenges for this sector. Dating back to 1993, the CPPSU started a Master's Degree programme in pro-cedural law, besides a Bachelor's Degree, which was a major breakthrough in Chinese police postgraduate education. In September 2003, it was granted the authority to grant PhD degrees. This made the CPPSU the first police educa-tional institution to award both qualifications.

In 2004, the CPPSU began to recruit doctorate candidates. Continuing to improve its provision, in 2007 it created a post-doctoral research centre in law. Established in 1948, the CPSU is the oldest and largest institution of its type and has played a vital leadership role in developing police higher education and training. At present the CPPSU has 15 departments, of law, public security, criminology, and investigation etc. It has advanced and comprehen-sive teaching and research facilities. Laboratories for DNA identification, fin-gerprint identification, security protection technology has also been introduced by the university, and boasts two key state laboratories for safety and risk evaluation, and a criminal science laboratory in Beijing. The CPPSU is a major leader in international relations and cooperates with countries such as Britain and the US inter alia.

Strengthening practical teaching in police combat training

In 2004, the MPS issued a notice on strengthening the work of practical police training for grass-roots level and frontline police officers. It proposed detailed requirements and measures regarding training content, methods, training time, personnel, organization, and so on. For example, a group of highly-regarded police instructors from Hong Kong were invited to give classes to officers and others were sent for short-term training; combining practice and research to produce learning materials (see Shiu-Hing Lo 2012). The local public security organs, who play an important role in neighbourhoods and residential areas, made good use of these instructors, adopting the 'rolling' step-by-step (i.e. cas-cading what has been learnt) training model, and establishing a combat instruc-tor teams with high technical, tactical, and teaching ability.

One of the concerns raised in the context of police higher education was stu-dents' lack of hands-on practical abilities. In order to address this deficiency many police colleges, in particular the CPPSU, have made important strides in addressing this issue. Thus, in 2007 the CPPSU's Innovation Experiment Programme for Advanced Police Talent Training was accepted as one of the quality projects of the Ministry of Education. This resulted in better integration of police classroom and practical training in order to produce the desired outcomes in improving students' understanding and capabilities. Since then over 30 practice teaching bases mixing student training, internship, teaching practice, research, and police procedural training were established to meet the needs of students, interns, police training staff, and researchers.

A typical example of an institution that takes a similar practical teaching mode approach is Shanghai Police College (SPC). SPC is a Shanghai municipal college established more than 60 years ago which has undergone even more reforms than its counterparts in the development of its police education programme. When the other police colleges in China were making every possible effort to introduce Bachelor Degree police education, Shanghai Police College was unmoved. In 2003 it introduced its second diploma police education and training programme which proved to be successful in providing police officers with a diverse knowledge base and integrated policing skills. The SPC's second diploma adopts an 'order type' training mode which gives local police discretion in what is taught according to their needs and service requirements. The thinking which underpins 'order type' training represents three conceptual shifts in emphasis from the 'subject-oriented' to 'competence-oriented', from 'classroom-centered' to 'field site-centered', from 'whether you understand or not' to 'whether you can do or not' to put police education and training more in line with the actual work and practical needs of policing.

In 2000, SPC initiated the 'Alternative Rotating Training, Job-training Combination' mechanism which organizes serving police officers and instructors into cohorts to participate in a closed training camp, where they remain, eat, and sleep, while trainees are required to be on duty to handle regular and emergency police tasks.[7] In 2003, SPC introduced a new trainer system, recruiting a large number of trainers from seasoned frontline police officers, and with proven teaching ability as instructors, contrary to the traditional British approach to tutor selection (Stanislas, Chapter 1).

SPC is the only police college under the leadership of both Shanghai Public Security Bureau and the college itself. This co-management guarantees 'the close interactive linkage' between SPC and the Shanghai Public Security Bureau. SPC's reform and development has been included in the national-level key construction projects in June 2010, and it is still unique as the only police college across China which enjoys the reputation of a national model vocational college. The 'Shanghai Police Education and Training Mode' is highly regarded by students, employers, Public Security Bureau, and the college itself. The MPS established SPC as a national training centre for police teachers' further learning, as well as for foreign police training and is certainly a banner of Chinese police education and training reform.

IV A bold new reform stage of police education and training (since 2008)

The 6th plenary session of the 2006 the Communist Party 16th Central Committee chaired by Party Leader Hu Jintao made improving the police and public security a priority as part of its 'harmonious' society vision. Since the second half of 2006, the MPS has sent several research groups to review public security organizations and police colleges around the country. Through their survey and investigation, the research groups formed a preliminary vision on how to carry out the police college education reform. With the aid of Ministry of Personnel, Ministry of Education, Ministry of Finance, and National Development and Reform Commission, this led to a new reform proposal on police education and training, namely the 2008 Implementation Plan on Pilot Work of Reform on Police College Recruiting and Training. While retaining the original forms of education and training in police colleges, the main focus was on police college recruitment and the cultivation of potential candidates. In 2008, the pilot work of reform was launched in 17 political law colleges. The reform includes the following five transformations.[8]

The shift of students. An emphasis in changing the characteristics of recruits from former high school graduates to college graduates and retired military soldiers or veterans.

The shift of examination mode. Traditionally, the entrance education examination and civil servant examination are taken separately. After the reform, the two were combined together and the content of the examination was simplified. Retired soldiers are only required to take the public subjects test in civil servant examination. Undergraduates who apply for the second degree or students who are willing to upgrade from junior college to university are required to take an additional examination on civil law.

The shift of training direction. The original non-directional cultivation of potential recruits has changed to targeted recruitment, admissions, orientation training, and targeted deployment. When candidates apply for schools, they know where they will be deployed after graduating. On entering college, they sign the target training agreement and obtain the qualification of civil servants. When the students have finished their two-year schooling and training in police colleges and become qualified graduates, they are deployed to grassroots public security organizations of county (city) level in agreement provinces, according to the agreements they have signed.

The shift in the cost-bearing. Students who have been recruited by Police Colleges do not pay for the tuition fees, which is paid by the government. Students can receive an extra living stipend which is a change from previous practice. The central government shoulders all the costs, especially for students from western regions, which greatly reduces the financial burden of these regions.

Shift in training focus. As a consequence of this pilot work, police colleges were expected to focus on professional training and career capacity training, and course design for subject majors courses. Colleges are also expected to highlight teaching practice and training content and to develop a new mode to carry out targeted administration and training, using the integrated police education approach to develop police officers of requisite quality.

The directive places a major emphasis on improving police professional competencies which is seen by the fact that practical training courses take up 50 per cent of all police college courses. It also highlights the cooperative education which is carried out by these institutions, and local public security organizations, from training programs, curricula, course-building, and assessment criteria.[9] One course is a two-year-long programme that includes a year-and-a-half in-school learning and half-a-year practice in local public security organizations. The teaching contents concentrates on practical police competencies and improving teaching methods, and practice, and combat skills combined to form an integrated training approach. Throughout the setting of courses, teachers should teach the essence of the courses and make out a training plan according to the MPS requirements. The teachers hired for these students must have practical experience and have gained at least a title of lecturer.

Since the beginning of reform, the number of students recruited annually has increased from 4,360 in 2008 to 13,000 in 2011. The junior college degree, required to gain access to university, the second Bachelor's Degree and the Master Degree are vital components of a complete police education system. The number of pilot schools has increased from 17 to 31. The number of provinces (autonomous regions and municipalities) taking part in the reform has jumped from 14 to 29. This demonstrates that the reform is an urgent requirement in pushing forward the regularization of public security agencies, and it is also an important approach to make public security education and training better serve the daily work of public security.

The reforms introduced profound changes to the public security organization in selecting educating and recruiting candidates. It has created new ways for grass-roots public security organization to recruit, train, and employ staff. It is hoped these changes will improve the quality of the whole public security sector and will reinforce the capacity of grass-root public security organizations, especially for providing the long-term, stable, talented professionals they need in the mid-western and underdeveloped areas where they play a vital role.[10] For three years, the MPS and the local public security organizations have actively carried out the aforementioned reform to ensure that their work is progressing well and developing.

Overview of police education and training in China

In China, police education and training is an important part of national education and training. It plays a fundamental role in police team construction and is the vital guarantee for future sustainable development. China's police education consists of common academic education and in-service training. The former can be further divided into categories of postgraduate, in-service education including adult education (medium level and advanced level, such as full-time specialist, undergraduate course, correspondence school, night courses, and self-taught study). Police professional training includes initial training, promotion and in-service training, specialized business and job training.

In recent years, the focus has been on improving the police political, professional, legal, scientific, and technological skills and qualities. June 2008 witnessed the start of the reform of recruit and training system in the political and law colleges, and the exploration of the new educational model which allows successful college graduates to be accepted in police training colleges and unifying teaching, studying, and practice.

The style of China's police education and training is an important aspect of understanding the development of police education, innovation, and its unique character. Its distinction lies in reflecting how police education and training is guided by police work and the teams or groups police officers work in, and how education and training renew guidance and inform educational practice.

The Chinese police education and training system

Police education and training is under the leadership of both police and educational organs, but the police sector takes greater responsibilities in matters relating to policing. Different levels of police colleges are mainly in charge of police education and training matters. Their teaching and management must embody the characteristics of police education and training policy. However, the police colleges' staffing, teaching, examinations, recruitment, distribution, the awarding of degrees, and budget are subject to the constraints of the state educational sectors. In terms of management the CPPSU and Chinese Criminal Police Universities and the other three colleges are under the direct leadership of the PSM of China, while other police colleges are under the leadership of provincial police departments. In different cities, provinces, and regions, there are still some police schools or training centres, mainly under the leadership of provincial police departments, and the rest are accountable to city or municipal and regional police bureaus.

After years of development, the police colleges combine academic education with in-service training and have built up a multi-level police education and training system, including, doctoral, postgraduate, undergraduate (the second major), junior college, and adult higher education. Moreover, senior police officer training, Hong Kong, Macao, and foreign police training are also included as part of the Chinese police education and training provision.

At present, the operation of China's police higher education system still use independent police colleges as its main element, while local ones serve as a supplement. These days, changes in police higher education tend to reflect general changes in higher education. First, in-service training and adult education are beginning to combine academic education with professional training; second, these schools' academic status have been upgraded, from secondary level education, i.e. technical secondary school education and specialty education to further education level, i.e. junior college and college education. Third, police education is moving from a system where police education courses were not directly related to police work in any practical sense to a more directly related one.

The length of schooling for Chinese police education and training

China's police academic education courses are defined by length of time in line with most countries in the world (Shengiun 1995) and specialized subjects normally last for three years, Bachelor's degree four years, Master's or doctoral degrees three years. Police in-service training lasts for six months; promotion training generally 6–20 weeks; professional training two to up to 40 weeks. Nowadays the existing forms of training include: recruit training, professional and promotion training, civil police annual training, and three-year officer training all push towards regularization and standardization of training provision.

Main features of Chinese police education and training

Police education and training's first and foremost task is to develop political quality, career awareness, and professional ethics. The specific dimensions of this are:

Distinctive professional police education and training

Police is one of the social professions, whose training should improve professionalism and business capacities, and must highlight the professional characteristic and meet the position requirements. On the one hand, it must improve the police culture and management capability, which in return gives them a sound knowledge base and high all-round quality. The police must establish a training system focused on 'professional training', which aims to improve their overall business capability and cultivate adaptability and career development potential.

Unique management mode for Chinese police education and training

China's police education and training model takes many levels and many forms. Beside junior college, undergraduate, graduate, adult, and junior high school education, it also takes short-term police professional skills training. Police colleges have multiple functions: training talent, serving society, and carrying out research. These schools provide an integrated model and contribute in bringing a new and distinctive form of combining academic service with in-service training to the business of policing.

Capability-centered education and training for Chinese police officers

China's police education and training adheres to an educational theory that capability comes first. This thinking is embodied in the core competencies and requirements of general police officer. General police officers are required to demonstrate important general requirements, namely political identification capability, law enforcement capability, and abilities to respond to emergencies and adjust mental states. The police colleges' main task is to train police officers to develop such capabilities to serve society. The police's abilities include political capacity, law enforcement capacity, security management, and investigating capacity, emergency responding capacity, ability to control criminal suspects, communication abilities, interpersonal skills, language skills, and the ability to adapt to circumstances and update knowledge capacity. For senior officers the demands are even greater. They need to enhance their decision-making abilities and capacity to motivate, innovate, and communicate effectively (Wang *et al.* 2008).

The transformation from knowledge and discipline-based education to capability is the first requirement to develop police officers. They occupy important roles in leading positions in society in addressing issues of importance and therefore must have corresponding capabilities. Of particular importance is the ability to evaluate and judge the present situation scientifically (strategic thinking), handle police work effectively, and have a clear understanding of law and appropriate policies and so on.

Conclusion

Police education and training objectives derive from the people's understanding of the role of the police in the new China. The police are to protect civil rights, to be an important force of stability and social order in the face of this responsibility and mission, and education and training plays an essential role in meeting these expectations.

From the overview of 60 years of Chinese police education and training, we can see that, compared with other developed countries in the world police education and training, the country is making steady progress and faces challenges as it has in each phase of its reform. Significant changes can be seen in the shift from a theoretical pedagogy to a focus on improving the practical capabilities of police officers. This is matched by efforts to strengthen teaching quality and capacities, and constantly develop appropriate business skills, fostering a noble morality and a pioneering spirit in improving the education and training received by Chinese police and public security officials.

Notes

1 See www.mps.gov.cn. Accessed 19 July 2005.
2 See http://news.xinhuanet.com/ziliao/2003–01/20/content_697889.htm. Accessed 26 July 2012.
3 Police Education for the 21st Century, edited by the editorial board of Police Education for the 21st Century, Chinese People's Public Security University Press, 1996, p. 198.
4 See: Police Education for the 21st Century.
5 See: Police Education for the 21st Century.

6 The writer will be hosted in England by De Montfort University's Community and Criminal Justice Department to observe their police training programmes and meet with the Department's police partners, including Leicestershire Constabulary.

7 An important challenge for police leaders in introducing system-wide change requiring the training of all key staff groups (see Cummings and Huse 1989, Waters 2007) is trying to logistically balance the requirements of emergency response organizations with being able to take officers out of the workplace for development activities.

8 See www.mps.gov.cn/n16/n1267/n3097/1721169.html: On Chinese Peoples' Public Security University Recruitment Pilot Class's Training System Reform. Accessed 26 July 2012.

9 www.mps.gov.cn/n16/n1267/n3097/1721169.html: On Chinese Peoples' Public Security University Recruitment Pilot Class's Training System Reform.

10 The model of local security organization and its relationship to the formal policing agencies reflects the co-production model of policing (Friedmann 1993) which is historically alien to British policing culture outside the Jewish community (Brogden 2005, Stanislas 2006).

References

Acharya, A., Gunaratna, R., and Pengxin, W. (2001) Ethnic Identity and National Conflict in China, Palgrave, London.

Birzer, M.L. (2003) 'The Theory of Andragogy Applied to Police Training', Policing: An International Journal of Police Strategies and Management, 26(1): 29–42.

Branigan, T. (2009) Han Chinese Launch Revenge Attack on Uighur Property, www.guardian.co.uk 7 July 2009. Accessed 12 July 2012.

Lo Hing-Shiu, S. (2012) 'The Changing Context and Content of Policing in China and Hong Kong: Policy Transfer and Modernisation, Policing and Society', An International Journal of Research and Policy, 22(2): 185–203.

Macfarquhar, R. and Shoenhals, M. (2006) Mao's Last Revolution, First Harvard University Press.

Osborne, M. and Thomas, E. (2003) Lifelong Learning in a Changing Continent: Continuing Education in the Universities of Europe, Leicester, NIACE.

Peiwan, Z. (2008) Theory and Practice of Police Training, Research Press.

Qi Pan, Z. and Mei Tan, X. (1999) Ethnic Conflict in China: Characteristics, Causes and Countermeasures, Issues &Studies, 35(5): 1999–09/01.

Wang, G., Xiuwei, F., and Fanbo, Z. (2008) Training Contents and Innovation Methods for Senior Officer's Training from the Perspectives of Trainees' Feedback on Their Needs, Core Society and Innovative Law Enforcement, Chinese People's Public Security University Press.

Wang Yanji. (2010) Sino-foreign Police Education and Training. Chinese People's Public Security University Press, Beijing.

Wong, K. (2012) Police Reform in China, CRC Press, Florida.

Zhou, J. (2005) Higher Education in China, Cengage Learning.

13 Transforming St Lucian policing through recruit training in a context of high crime

P. Stanislas

Introduction

This chapter examines the efforts of the Royal St Lucian Police Force (RSLPF) to introduce new practices in its recruit training programme and some of the important challenges faced as part of that process. Drawing on research data, it specifically examines the perceptions of key actors responsible for introducing these changes and some of the factors driving that process. Data about recruit responses to and perceptions of their basic training will also be examined. The chapter explores some of the constraints in reforming recruit training which reflect broader organizational problems limiting the transformation of a post-colonial police organization.

Background

This chapter has its origins in an interview with the then RSLPF Commissioner in 2007. The core of the interview concerned the organizational problems facing police leaders in small Caribbean countries, in the context of public concern about an unprecedented increase in violent crime and police ineffectiveness (World Bank 2007; Stanislas 2013). Established in 1831 what was to become the RSLPF is a military-type police organization characterized by an emphasis on order maintenance and law enforcement (Stanislas 2013; Harrison 2000). These institutions were not designed as crime-fighting organizations or to meet citizens' expectations (see Cole 1999). Training of recruits traditionally emphasizes military-types skills and physical fitness (Harrison 2000: 32, Onouja 2005).

The research presented here on recruit training reform is one dimension of several investigations carried out in St Lucia between 2009–2011 (see Stanislas ibid, Stanislas forthcoming) and will draw on relevant data where necessary. Appropriate ethical considerations were observed throughout the research. By the time agreement was gained to commence the research one cohort of new recruits was well into their basic training. As a consequence the research was unable to assess recruits' expectations and relevant experiences prior to the start of training (Kirkpatrick 1998). A pre-training questionnaire was issued to a second cohort prior to starting their course by civilian administrators at the

RSLPF Academy (Academy). A hurricane in 2010 disrupted the training of the second cohort of recruits, who were deployed as part of the emergency response. This created problems for the researcher in terms of being unable to re-arrange another visit at the completion of training and led to some improvisation.

Methodology

The research questions that inform this study relate to the factors driving the process of change in police recruitment training and their various impacts. Another related set of concerns regards the challenges and constraints faced by those wishing to bring about significant change in this and related areas of police human resource management practice. The data sets which this chapter utilizes are based on a mixed methods research design. The benefit of this approach is that it enables the researcher to establish respondents' responses to a number of important training-related issues and to explore their subjective perceptions (Brannen 2005). Data was obtained from two cohorts of police recruits in 2010 and 2011 by means of a questionnaire. The recruit cohort for the year 2010 consisted of 60 students and 52 for 2011. Due to cohort two not completing their training only 15 recruits were chosen from this cohort to complete the questionnaire and included in the interview stage of the research. Seventy-five completed questionnaires forms were used as the basis of the analysis, 60 from cohort one and 15 from cohort two.

The questionnaire consisted of pre-selected fixed and open questions which sought to solicit recruits' responses and experiences around a range of training-related matters. It also collected personal data on recruits in terms of age, sex, and educational qualifications. This information was also collected in the pre-training questionnaire. In-depth follow-up interviews were held with a sample of recruits (15 from each cohort) chosen systematically by means of predetermined numerical criteria from an attendance register. Effort was made to ensure female representation within the sample. The number of respondents interviewed from cohort one was eight males and seven females from 48 males, ten females, and two unknown. The second round of interviews involving cohort two consisted of ten males and five females from a total of 52 recruits of which 40 were male and 12 female.

Content analysis was used to identify themes or categories in the quantitative data obtained by the questionnaire. The data, themes, and coding derived from it was checked independently (MacQueen *et al.* 2004). In instances where it was deemed important some themes were subjected to quantative analysis. For example, to indicate how widely a view was held by respondents. This enabled issues to be explored further in the interview phase. The criterion used to apply quantative analysis was the number of respondents who raised similar issues with two being the minimum for consideration. Over and beyond this condition was the contribution of the data to broader issues pertinent to the research question and the existing literature (See Chapter 1). Originally the idea behind the research was to compare the responses of two cohorts about their basic training. Given that only one group had completed training this was not possible outside very limited areas. The data from the second cohort will only be used where valid comparisons can be made. Programme and course documents were also analysed. Finally, the researcher used participant observation methods being based at the Academy for parts of the research, and able to observe classes in process, and get a feel of the teaching conditions and the interaction between recruits and instructors.

Research findings

The 15 key findings coming from the research are:

- higher levels of educated recruits joining the RSLPF
- increased levels of education of recruits has adverse organizational consequences as well as benefits
- evidence of important improvements in the recruit selection process
- teaching syllabus reform has involved a reassessment of how time is used
- social sciences subjects have been integrated into very limited teaching areas with the body of teaching content still being legally based
- the majority of recruits were satisfied with basic training, but a significant minority were not
- the importance of teaching topics was found to be shaped by the value placed on them by tutors, other experienced officers, and recruits' own perceptions of policing priorities
- recruits expressed clear preferences about approaches to learning and teaching
- colonial policing practices were found to be a major obstacle to learning and a source of widespread dissatisfaction
- the training regime induces excessive stress amongst recruits
- the punitive culture of training can contribute to recruits internalizing attitudes with adverse consequences for how they relate to the public
- evidence of a more student-centred approach to learning, counter-balanced by approaches which are insensitive to recruit learning preferences
- traditional teaching practices and limited resources define what student-centred learning means and how it's understood
- community policing philosophy is embedded in most aspects of training
- there was little evidence of human rights matters being formally taught as a subject, but such sensitivities were demonstrated in other educational contexts.

Colonial inheritance, policing, and social change

One of the defining characteristics of colonial police organizations was the calibre of their recruits. The poor levels of education of police officers posted to the colonies was a particular concern (Cole 1999; Harriot 2000: 132). Stanislas (2013) documents the frustrations experienced by chief officers in St Lucia in their efforts to carry out rudimentary policing with inadequate personnel. Most commonly recruits failed their entrance examinations and if passing did so at the lower levels of attainment (Annual Reports 1949: 10; 1975: 35). More recently, and reflecting the process of modernization (Joseph 2011; Kratcoski and Das 2007), St Lucia has witnessed a growth in the numbers of its population receiving education at all levels (UNESCO 2010/11). These changes are illustrated in the 2002 Police Week Magazine where police managers proudly display their educational qualifications. This observation is reinforced by the Acting Commissioner:

> The St Lucia we operated in those days was a very basic society and that has changed. Quite a few of us hold graduate and postgraduate qualifications. In fact several of us in Senior Command got our degrees from England through distance-learning.

An important actor that has made its presence felt in further education in St Lucia is an independent American college which established a campus on the island in 2007 (The Voice 2012). This has increased the number of further and higher education institutions in the country to three (see UNESCO 2010/11). The improvements in education and its import for the quality of recruits coming into the force are highlighted in the remarks of a male recruit from cohort one 'Many of us could have gone onto university, including myself. Several recruits have degrees that I know of'.

The recruit's comments seem to support the analysis of recruits' educational data illustrated in Table 13.1 which found a significant amount of them possessed additional and higher qualifications than the entry requirements. The basic educational entry requirements for joining the RSLPF are the possession of five CXCs (Caribbean Examination Council) which must include a qualification in English language.

A similar pattern of findings was also evident for the second cohort of recruits which is illustrated in Table 13.2.

Table 13.1 Educational qualifications of Cohort One

6 CXEs and Over	Additional Qualifications	Associate Degrees	A Level	Diploma/Other Vocational Qualifications
14 per cent	1 per cent	36 per cent	9 per cent	14 per cent

Table 13.2 Educational qualification of Cohort Two

6 CXEs and Over	Additional Qualifications	Associate Degrees	A Level	Diploma/Other Qualifications
9 per cent	6 per cent	26 per cent	35 per cent	4 per cent

Taking the possession of at least one advance qualification (i.e. Associate Degree, etc.) as an indicator of recruits whose educational attainment exceeds formal entry requirements, 37 per cent of all recruits from cohort one possessed an Associate Degree or similar advanced qualifications. In cohort two 44 per cent of all recruits possessed Associate Degrees or other advanced qualifications. In short, a significant number of recruits entering the RSLPF have the potential to pursue graduate education, and theoretically better careers outside the police (Wayne 2010: 288).

While there is little previous research to compare changes in educational attainment of prospective police officers in St Lucia, the historic records and interviews with experienced officers indicate there has been a significant improvement, from the days when the ability to read and write was the pre-entry educational requirement for joining (Stanislas ibid.). With this in mind, the introduction of new requirements by the RSLPF reflects the improvement in education levels within the country (see UNESCO 2010/2011) and illustrated in the qualifications held by recruits.

An important set of factors in the take up of education is its affordability and availability (UNESCO 2010/2011).The Acting Commissioner touches on the importance of the American college, situated less than a mile from the Academy,[1] and its impact on providing educational opportunities for local people; and particularly important to the RSLPF (Chapter 1): 'Now we also have the College that really has made a difference because they provide what is needed right on our own door-step. They have made a real difference'.

The principal of the private college provides some background to their presence in the country:

> I had been coming to St Lucia for holidays for years and the need for an educational institution sensitive to the needs of the people was obvious. I pitched the idea about us setting up a campus and the rest is history really. Most of our students are people studying out of their own pockets, wanting to improve themselves, who did not have an opportunity because the other institutions are insensitive to their needs.[2]

Police reform programme

Around 1997 the RSLPF announced a reform programme to improve its performance. Part of this process was designed to transform important aspects of the organization, how work was structured and its ethos (Police Week Magazine 2002). The RSLPF's work culture has been described by Stanislas (ibid.) as essentially work-avoiding, characterized by low levels of technical competence and contributing to poor conviction rates. In this context the improved education level of recruits constitutes an important factor in any change strategy designed to address the aforementioned problems (See Green and Woolston chapter). The recruit selection process was one area which became the target for reform given the poor calibre of police officers entering the force, and their behaviour once in post (Stanislas ibid.).

Selection procedures

A consensus was found in other research carried out (see Stanislas ibid.) in support of changes to the RSLPF selection procedures. A female member of the public shares her view (Stanislas ibid.):

> I don't think they do background checks on people joining. I know a few of them who I grew up with, who are police, and some of the things they are capable of doing and they want to give these types of people power and a gun? That is a disaster waiting to happen.

An officer responsible for introducing new selection procedures confirms this suspicion and throws light on the institutional culture (see Stanislas ibid.) which has given rise to this problem:

> We now have a more rigorous selection system which is designed to get people of good character. Back in the day there was not much screening done to be honest. You have to start with the selection of those who were given responsibility for that task, how they were chosen and why.

The norms shaping selection and appointment of staff in the RSLPF has traditionally relied on personal patronage, with merit and more formal considerations playing little role (Stanislas ibid., Hinton and Newburn 2009: 12–13). An important feature of the new selection process involves placing pictures of new recruits in newspapers and encouraging the public to bring to the police's attention anything of concern. Given the small size of the island's population of approximately 170,000 (Stanislas ibid.), the utilization of the public as a safeguard can be seen as a progressive development in introducing transparency (Ally 2010); and a unique form of community-police participation.

Adverse consequences of higher levels of education

Improved levels of education of police officers is a source of potential friction as well as bringing a range of benefits, with implications for organizational change (Roberg 2004: 3; Mahony and Prenzler 1996: 287). Two contrasting views were found amongst police managers about the attitudes of contemporary recruits, shaped in part by their levels of education, personal confidence, and willingness to question. A critical view is provided by a senior officer: 'You find that many of the young people entering the force exhibit some of the negative values and behaviours from modern society which they come from. So it's a constant battle which has serious implications for discipline.'

The Academy's Commandant gives further illustration of how these changes have impacted on some within the organization: 'Supervisors were complaining that they could not deal with the recruits because they were more questioning, empowered, and learned to work on their own'.

For those socialized in an authoritarian-type institution these developments are perceived as a potential threat and something to be resisted (Roberg 2004: 3; Mahony and Prenzler 1996: 287). However, contrary views were found among a small cadre of reforming officers (Brew 1995). Criticizing the traditional attitude towards authority the Superintendent, who introduced many of the reforms in recruit training, reflects on his basic training which informs his support for change:

> I remember one thing that used to piss me off was regardless of your age and levels of personal responsibilities, whether you joined as a married man with a family or whatever, the instructors treated you like a little kid cursing and shouting at you. New recruits are not going to respond positively to that type of culture and neither is the public.

The latter part of the quote is particularly important given the increased sophistication of the population in the contemporary world, even in a poor postcolonial society such as St Lucia (Chapter 1) and their ability to compare local police practice with those from elsewhere. Members of the public often revealed during fieldwork that international news and American TV shows were important sources of information in informing their understanding of policing (Stanislas 2013b).

Recruit syllabus and course content reform

In 2004 responsibility for RSLPF education, training, and development passed to a new Superintendent with a degree of expertise in the area, having led a review of police training in the English-speaking Caribbean (see Jones and Satchell 2009). The Superintendent came into post with clear ideas on the changes he wanted to introduce (Cummings and Huse 1989: 164–167; Harriot 2000: 126–128). The key goals of this change strategy can be reduced to six objectives: (i) transform the authoritarian military ethos of recruit training, (ii) reduce the time spent on non-educational matters and increase time for learning, (iii) introduce a student-centred learning approach to teaching, (iv) introduce a community policing orientation throughout the syllabus, (v) introduce an awareness of human rights matters (see Chappell ibid.).

Concerns about the ethos of recruit training were expressed by many experienced officers, as well as having its supporters. The Acting Commissioner reflects on his experience of basic training:

> There was this intention of trying to force you to be a police officer and this concept that you had to be a real hard person to be a police officer. I did not like the ethos of compulsion and the military-type attitude which allowed people to be abused.

Changing the attitudes described involved the reorientation of training staff to adopt new thinking required, in this instance training sessions for trainers (Cummings and Huse 1989: 129–131). It also included the introduction of new staff and the departure of others (Harriot 2000: 127). An important dimension of tackling these militaristic norms was changing the training syllabus and how time was used. The Superintendent elaborates:

> Another important difference was in my day a lot of emphasis was spent on drills. I would say about 50 per cent of the programme was spent on drills. I cut down drills. We now spend three quarters of the programme studying police and related subjects which will help officers in the field.

The Training Inspector outlines the specific benefits of this change: 'We use that time to do human relations type subjects, sociology, psychology things that will help the officer interact better with the public'.

Recruit training syllabus

Candidates who pass the various checks and meet the requisite criteria attend basic training, which is two years long and involves six-month residency in barracks at the Academy. Part of the training consists of a two-week working attachment at a local station, and recruits are required to return to the Academy periodically for various activities until they have completed their training. Assessments are continuous and varied throughout the course and consist of weekly written examinations to more periodic assessments, and other more practically based ones, e.g. those used in weapons training. The recruit training syllabus consists of the modules illustrated in Table 13.1 which are broken down into specific topic areas. Due to lack of space only the shortest module is illustrated in full. See Table 13.3.

Several observations can be made about the accuracy of the course programme provided to the researcher. The first relates to the times allocated to topics. Interviews revealed that the times stated are inaccurate. For example while eight hours is allocated for Working with Mentally Challenged Individuals, part of the Policing Techniques Module, respondents indicated

Table 13.3 Training syllabus

Module	Module title	Hours
1	Administration	65
2	Introduction to Policing	158
3	Policing Techniques	289
4	Introduction to Criminal Offences and Investigative Techniques	194
5	Juvenile Delinquency	95
6	Traffic	106
7	Criminal Justice	116
8	Public Order	93
9	Social Studies and Community Policing	346
	Total	1,319

they received a two to three hour one-off input, and lack of time given to the topic was a concern. The programme also indicates several topics where classes had never been held. For example An Introduction to Criminology as part of Module 9, and Human Dignity and Human Rights in the same module. In the case of the latter, the absence of formal teaching on the topic does not negate that pertinent issues may be raised during other topics or discussions.[3] With these discrepancies in mind Table 13.3 should be seen more as a broad expression of intent than a precise guide to teaching activities. An omission in the hours highlighted in Table 13.3 is the time allocated for 'Other Activities' which is built into every module and illustrated in the Module 6 in Table 13.4.

Time allocated for 'Other Activities' is more or less consistent across all modules with swimming and life-saving and first aid decreasing by a couple of hours. What is particularly interesting to note is the combined time allocated to military-type practices and rituals (such as muster parade which involves domestic activities such as cleaning dormitories, kit inspections and drills) of 36

Table 13.4 Module 6 Traffic

Core subjects	Hours
Traffic Signals	4
Estimating Speeds and Distance	3
Motor Vehicle Classification	3
Driving Licence, Insurance and Related Offences	4
Careless, Dangerous Driving etc	4
Driving under the Influence	3
Causing Death by Dangerous Driving	3
Traffic Offences/Fix Penalty Tickets	8
Road Collision Scenes	8
Managing collision scenes	8
Total	48

Other activities	Hours
Swimming and Life Saving	6
First Aid	6
Muster Parade	8
Kit Inspection	6
Foot and Arm Drills	22
Weapons Training	8
Physical Training	4
Self Defence	4
Commandant's Lecture	2
Games	3
Debates	3
Total	50

hours compared to the learning time for important components of traffic policing. The allocation of time for these activities remains the same throughout all nine modules. This supports Harriot's (2000) and Onoja's (2004) observation, that even on paper military-type activities appear to have disproportionate value in the training of recruits in postcolonial policing systems.

Recruit responses and basic training

This section examines the results and the analysis of the questionnaire data, before going on to the qualitative data which assists in providing a deeper explanation of the findings. The questionnaire questions sought to elucidate recruits' responses to and perceptions of basic training. It starts with recruits' general impression of training (Q2). The majority of recruits were happy with the course. Thirteen per cent rated it very good, 58 per cent rated it good and 21 per cent rated it as average. Eight per cent of recruits rated the course below average. Q3 asked recruits what aspect of training they found most useful. Given the range of possible responses to this question content analysis was used to identify themes within the responses. These are:

*   learning basic policing skills[4]
*   learning about law and legal procedures
*   arrest and cautioning procedures
*   on-the-job training (attachments)
*   educational class-based inputs
*   self-defence and weapons training
*   other

The key finding was that recruits had greater appreciation for input that was practically related to the core aspects of police work (Werth 2009; Chappell ibid.). This finding is not surprising given the purpose of basic training which reflects recruits' own understanding of police work (Conti 2006). At this stage of their career's recruits have little real practical policing experience to shape their understanding of the relevance of all of their training (Roberg 2004: 4; Carlan 2007) and are largely dependent on their prior assumptions and the values of their tutors, or other experienced officers. The preference for practical inputs does not suggest that academic or theoretical inputs were not valued by recruits, but they had greater value when linked to the aforementioned (see Tingyou chapter). A female recruit explains:

> We need more practical stuff to support the theory taught in class. I play volley ball. You can talk about the theory of the game, but unless you get out on the court you will never learn how to play volley ball.

Another related concern was the relationship between what is taught at the Academy with practice on the ground. Reducing this gap constitutes an important challenge for advocates of police reform (Chappell ibid.). This discrepancy was often made apparent during recruits' attachment to police stations. One recruit shares his experiences:

> The training here is largely theory which we are supposed to put into practice, but when you go to stations you can see things are very different. Simple things like how to write a movement diary. So what can you do? Tell the instructors they're wrong?

What is interesting here is the recruit's bias in assuming that street-level practice is correct and what is taught in the Academy is incorrect, not vice versa. This illustrates the type of thinking associated with the informal police culture and its impact on recruit's values (Chapter 1). Concerns about the relevance of what is taught was also a factor in shaping how some recruits received the social science components of the programme (Chapter 1). While the questionnaire data found no significant response or concerns raised about this topic, when it was raised views were polarized around two contrasting positions. A more critical view is illustrated by a male recruit: 'Personally I can't see the relevance of sociology and psychology and what that has to do with policing in St Lucia, and speaking to officers I know neither can they'.

A more supportive attitude is highlighted by a female recruit: 'Sociology helps us to understand aspects of society, how people think and behave and the types of thing we can expect. I think it is a good thing in broadening our knowledge'.

This difference in opinion goes beyond syllabus content and reflects a broader attitude among police officers towards increasing the educational requirements of policing, and organizational reform (Stanislas, Chapter 4). Q4 asked recruits what aspects of training they found less useful. Content analysis was used to identify the themes in respondents' answers as follows:

- military aspects
- social sciences
- general ethos and discipline
- sign language
- self-defence
- other

Sixty-seven per cent of respondents identified military-type activities (specifically drills, muster parade, etc.) which drew the highest response, followed by 27 per cent for sign language classes as the least useful aspect of training. The response rate was 60 per cent. As the analysis of the training programme content revealed militaristic practices disproportionately took up more time than that spent teaching substantive topics; and probably far more than formally indicated as revealed in the remarks of some recruits: 'We spend more times on those things than anything else. I know the argument that we don't have a standing army so we need the military training.[5] But what time do we have for actual policing?'

A female recruit explains the knock on effect of this prioritization of the military aspects of training over the civilian:

> The problem with these things is they are at the discretion of the instructors and can mess up your whole day. We are always rushing through topics and things we should be spending more time on. If you are told you are on section duty that is your whole week messed up because that time comes from time you already do not have.

Similar sentiments are expressed by an academic tutor:

> One of the biggest problems I have with the recruit programme is the structure of the day. You have them up from four o'clock in the morning cleaning, cooking, doing muster, then drills until ten o'clock in the hot sun; and anything else. Then you send them to class for academic learning. They come in all sweaty, tired, pissed off and angry. Then you have recruits doing sentry duties, or on watch until eleven at night. That is not the environment to teach people anything.

These strong feelings about the militaristic aspects of training influenced recruits responses to subsequent questions. Q5 asked recruits was there any aspect of training they would change. Eighty-four per cent of respondents indicated yes, while 16 per cent indicated no. Q5b asked recruits to specify what aspect of training they would change. Content analysis was used to identify themes in the responses. Each theme/category has been given a number to assist quantative analysis (see Table 13.5):

The theme/category with the greatest number of responses was 9=other with 17 which consisted of nine about the military ethos of training, and four related to the conduct of instructors which is associated with the former. When these responses are added to those in the category Military Aspects of Training (3) it can be seen that 43 per cent of all respondents to Q5 would change at least one

Table 13.5 Responses to Question 5b

Theme	Frequency	Per cent
1. Time management	2	5
2. More practical training	6	14
3. Military aspects of training	5	11
4. More/less self-defence	4	10
5. Teaching approach	2	5
6. Sports and leisure	2	5
7. One to one support	2	5
8. Access to information/material	2	5
9. Other	17	40
Total	42	100.00

aspect of the military characteristic of recruit training. The response rate was 75 per cent. One example of the type of practices recruits reacted very strongly to was the punitive ethos of the training regime; a view shared by several senior officers. These findings highlight some of the features of what some authors have termed 'stress academies' (see Chappell chapter) where police recruit training is characterized by strict rule enforcement and a punitive ethos, reinforcing a militaristic model of policing; which is even more apparent in the ex-colonial RSLPF.

Learning environment

The types of pressures that recruits are placed under is contextualized by another important factor shaping their training was the learning environment, i.e. physical and other conditions, which they have to negotiate (see Tingyou chapter). Class-based learning generally takes place in the afternoon after daily physical activities which include physical training and self-defence. All class-based teaching takes place in a small classroom approximately two metres wide by four and a half meters in length. Students sit shoulder to shoulder in columns with no desk or little to write on. Neither students nor tutors have any room to move once classes start. Under these conditions listening to lectures in the Caribbean climate must be extremely difficult which is illustrated by a recruit: 'The classrooms are not conducive to learning. They're built for 30 people not 60 and it's just too hot. The air conditioning is a joke. It's not surprising so many people fall asleep during lectures'.

The sanctions used against recruits who fail to perform, breach any infraction or instruction can take extreme forms (Chappell ibid.). One recruit shares his experience of being 'locked up', in prison-type conditions for three weeks as punishment[6]:

> It affects you personally. People say that St Lucian officers are violent and aggressive and I have to relate that to the discipline and punishment which they have experienced during training; because when you're locked up it can affect you if you are not a strong person.

Another male recruit makes similar observations: 'All this negative pressure we are under, it creates a rage within recruits and you begin to see the public like a different species. I have spoken to experienced officers who said the same thing'.

One of the challenges of introducing cultural change within organizations is obtaining sufficient number of change agents of required quality (Cummings and Huse 1989). In small postcolonial countries finding people not adversely influenced by the prevailing institutional culture constitutes a major obstacle for change leaders (see Harrison 2000; Stanislas ibid.). A civilian tutor throws light on how this problem manifests in the Academy and impacts on recruits:

The problem there is many of the tutors are old school cops. They use modern phrases and terms and are more polished than their predecessors, but are essentially cops who came through that system. While they may concede some power within the classroom, the majority of recruits' time is not spent in class.

A female recruit crystallizes many of the concerns of her fellow recruits, high-lighted in the quantative findings, about the impact this militaristic culture has on recruits' stress levels and their general performance:

A lot of things people get bookings for are a complete waste of time. The amount of time we spend on rubbish that has nothing to do with policing? What time do we get to study and think? Then someone makes a mistake because they are physically and mentally exhausted and they throw the book at them. Someone really has to look into this because this is a waste of everybody's time and poor St Lucia's tax money.

Police occupational culture has traditionally been viewed as something which is positively embraced by recruits (see Chapter 1). One of the paradoxes of recruits' experience of being attached to local stations is in making sense of their treatment by instructors, the disparity between the stress ethos of the Academy and the occupational culture observed in the work environment which is eluci-dated by a recruit: 'What some of us find confusing is the instructors are busting our balls, but when we were attached to stations and you see the amount of delinquent officers there and they want to beat us up about discipline?'

Teaching methods

Changing the way recruits are taught constitutes a major feature of the new philosophy which has been introduced into RSLPF's basic training, and in line with global trends in police modernization (Kratcoski and Das 2007, Chapter 1). An essential dimension of the changes which the research tried to capture is the introduction of a student-centred approach to learning (Hesson and Shad 2007). Q10 asked recruits how effective were the teaching methods used on the training course. Thirty-two per cent of respondents indicated that the teaching methods were very effective, 32 per cent indicated the teaching methods were good. Twenty-six per cent indicated that the teaching methods were average, while 9 per cent of respondents said that they were below expectations. The findings for this question suggest that while the majority of recruits were satisfied with teach-ing methods, approximately a third of respondents believed there was room for significant improvement. The response rate for Q10 was 92 per cent.

One of the criticisms of the traditional police model of teaching has been its reliance on a didactic approach which disempowers learners (Birzer 2003: 31). Q12 asked recruits to specify what teaching methods they found less effective. The most significant finding was that 44 per cent of respondents found didactic methods which reduced their involvement less useful, which is similar to the responses for Q10 given the similarities in both questions and how they could be interpreted despite being different. A key dislike was the over-reliance on lectures or hand-outs where tutors/instructors read through most of the session. Nineteen per cent of respondents indicated lack of prior information as an important impediment to learning which forced them to sit passively through lessons. The response rate for Q12 was 90 per cent.

These findings are illustrated in the comments of recruits when speaking about the teaching methods relied on by some tutors. Most criticism was directed at police speakers/tutors from specialist departments, e.g. Traffic, who generally are not qualified trainers/teachers (Chapter 1). The general view of recruits was that Academy tutors and civilian specialists who taught on the programme were flexible and skilled educators. One male recruit shares his view on the matter:

> There are speakers who come well-prepared and are very interactive and everything is good. Then you have others who come with this attitude 'I have being doing this for 20 years and it worked then-so it will now'. No it won't. You are talking about a different generation. We are not fools who are not used to being taught.

These sentiments are also expressed by a female recruit:

> What's effective where learning is concerned depends on the topic and the individual. This is not a restaurant and you can't do everything to people's taste. But I can guarantee you this, I can speak for every student in my class about what does not work. Some fool who can't teach and doesn't care or even notice half the class are sleeping or dying from sheer fatigue because he is talking them to death.

An important aspect of adult based or student-centred learning is appreciating the variety of ways individuals learn in order to maximize learning (Hesson and Shad 2007: 22–25). A training instructor explains how this thinking informs practice in terms of its acknowledgement of the importance of learners' involvement and experiences:

> The way we impart knowledge now is different. People now have opportunity to express themselves. We do not talk at people, now we talk with the students and learn from them. We do not approach students as if they don't know anything. They know a lot and it is about bringing that out.

Building recruits' capacity to accept responsibility for important aspects of their professional development and work is another important strand of the new philosophy. The Superintendent makes this point: 'We place a lot of emphasis on the students themselves and their learning needs and making them responsible for that and other things'.

A female recruit confirms the importance of this philosophy to their training:

> Student-centred learning shapes most of what we do in how we approach our studies and general affairs. I mean we are responsible for most things from our upkeep and presentation even cooking our own meals. So it's no real stretch for us to be made responsible for our own learning.

A recruit from the second cohort reinforces this view and throws light on some of the ways this philosophy is enforced: 'From our first few study skill classes we spent a good bit of time discussing this concept and the instructors are always reinforcing and referring to it in different ways'.

Identifying the range of learning resources available to recruits is a particularly important aspect of this new teaching and learning philosophy (Sarasin 2006). Q15 asked recruits whether any learning material pertinent to their training was available on the internet. Sixty-one per cent answered yes and 39 per cent no. The response rate was 90 per cent. Interviews with recruits and independent examination revealed the majority of this material consisted of the criminal code (law), crime statistics, and basic information about the RSLPF for the public. Furthermore, there were no computer facilities for students. This represents a constraint on the learning and options available to recruits, most of whom are familiar with ITC due to their schooling (International Telecommunications Union 2004). Recruits also had no access to a library. The frustration experienced by some recruits by the lack of basic resources is illustrated by the following remarks:

> It would be very helpful if we had pcs to do our research. They said they were putting in cables in one of the other rooms to provide us with pcs, but nothing seems to have happened on that front. That was when we started training; we are now a few weeks from graduation. If you don't have access to books then you must have access to the internet.

Another explains:

> A couple of us have or own wireless pcs, but you can't get a signal from the Academy. I mean it's a joke. I can get a signal from any tourist spot or bar in town, but here in the only police academy in the country no signal.

The findings reveal an important contradiction between the traditional militaristic approach to police training and the stress aspects of it, which largely treats recruits in a childlike manner, and student-centred learning. This is compounded by the lack of learning resources that constrain the ability of recruits to maximize their learning. These tensions represent a conflict between the old and modern which is crystallized by the lack of ITC available to recruits, and their familiarity with these resources due to their previous education.

Educational content of training programme

Community policing

Community policing and human rights discourse share similarities in that while having their origins in the west, they have been embraced universally in one form or another with varying degrees of commitment (Brogden and Nihaj 2005, Marenin 2007). These subjects along with others, such as sensitivity to vulnerable groups (See Chappell ibid.) often form important components of a modern police education syllabus and are commonly linked to the introduction of liberal arts topics (Chapter 1). In the case of St Lucia, the Deosaran Report (2003) called for the introduction of community policing as a vital tool in increasing public confidence and reducing crime (World Bank 2007; Stanislas ibid.). The importance of community relations to contemporary recruit training is explained by the Training Inspector: 'We are making a greater effort to help officers fit into and to understand the community they will be working with and how to work effectively in that situation because it is crucial'.

The chief executive of the police-community partnership body is more forthright:

> We didn't have to think about community when I was a beat officer, we assumed it. We were a simple society who lived by the law and standards of decency. Today we have crime like we could not imagine. People have no trust in the police which has emboldened these young men. Nothing happens in this small country without somebody knowing, so working with the community is about survival and I know for sure recruits are being taught that.

Q17–Q28 sought to establish whether the training syllabus addressed working with the general community and the various groups that make it up (Stanislas ibid.; Jones 2003). Only a few questions will be examined here. Q17 asked recruits whether their training included any content on how to improve or maintain a good relationship with the general community (see Figure 13.1). Seventy-eight per cent of respondents indicated that the course did address these issues, with 18 per cent indicating that the course did not. Three per cent of respondents indicated 'other'. The response rate to Q17 was 100 per cent representing the highest response to any question and it is suggested reflects the status of community policing to the RSLPF. The findings to a number of questions are illustrated below in Figure 13.1.

Interview evidence also suggests that the RSLPF have been successful in developing awareness of community policing which was shared by recruits and integrated across most teaching modules. One recruit illustrates this point: 'Our communication skills class is very popular and almost every scenario used is based on some aspect of community policing'.

Another recruit is more critical, but highlights the importance of community policing in basic training: 'Community policing is a very serious issue here.

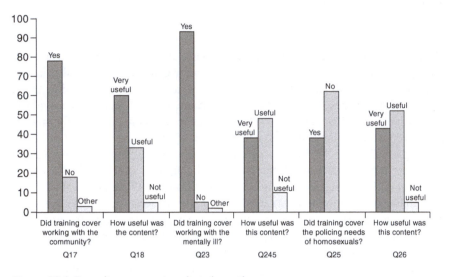

Figure 13.1 Recruit responses to selected questions.

Why else would you teach police officers sign language? It's a waste of time,[7] but you can see what the force is trying to ensure that nobody is left out'.

Similar sentiments were expressed by recruits from the second cohort: 'We have studied and talked about these issues from quite early because they are important in terms of knowledge and skills'.

A potentially significant factor for why community policing is important to new recruits is in differentiating themselves from previous generations of officers and the negative perception of many of them (Stanislas ibid.). The issue of violence, its use and practice is identified by Moreau de Bellaing in his chapter as an important topic in recruits self-identification or rejection of particular aspects and images of policing. This differentiation was a theme throughout many of the interviews and can be inferred from the remarks of a recruit from the second cohort:

> I think it's important for young officers, even outside of work. I did not join the police because I am a bad person and most of us don't want that reputation. So how we treat the community can make a difference in people realising we are public servants who serve them.

Q18 asked recruits how useful they found the aforementioned content in improving their understanding. Sixty per cent of respondents indicated that they found this input very useful, while 33 per cent indicated it was useful, and 5 per cent indicated that the input was not useful. The findings indicate that the overwhelming majority of recruits (99 per cent) who confirmed that they received an input on police community relations found the issue important.

Gender

Sexism and the degradation of women was a distinctive feature of the colonial experience which has become part of the cultural fabric of contemporary St Lucian society and manifests in a number of very apparent ways (see Country Poverty Assessment 2005–2006: 21–23). Amongst these is violence against women, sexual exploitation (See Wayne 2010: 491; Stanislas ibid.), and over-representation of women amongst the country's poorest and most vulnerable (CPA 2005–6; see Jones 2003; Wayne 2010). Q19 asked recruits whether their training contained any input on issues related to women and their policing needs. Fifty-one per cent of respondents indicated that the training did contain content relating to women, and 47 per cent indicated there was no content on this issue. The response rate for Q19 was 98 per cent. The type of input received on women's issues is elucidated by a recruit: 'We covered offences against women, such as sexual assault, rape and a range of offences.'

Another recruit shares their experience of what was taught and some of the problems encountered: 'From what I remember it was very rushed and we did not spend a lot of time on it, but I think we dealt with domestic violence and sexual assault'.

While most of the responses obtained via the questionnaire and interviews on gender matters were largely legal in character, there were some exceptions which indicated that broader education on some issues was provided:

> I remember the instructor telling the class that because of poverty many mothers are involved in using their daughters for sexual purposes and act as if they do not know what is going on, when they are clearly aware what stepfathers or their boyfriends are doing.

The odd finding for Q19 was that it received both affirmative and negative responses in nearly equal proportions replicates a pattern of responses to others questions about teaching content. This pattern of response throws light on how topics are taught, usually by specialist police officers (see Teaching Methods), and the weight (or lack of) given to them by Academy instructors, more than respondent disinterest in the topic. In this regard it is clear that some issues enjoy higher status such as community policing, compared to matters of gender and are handled in a different way and more likely to be remembered by recruits. This explanation is supported by information obtained during interviews with recruits, who often revealed contrary to their negative responses to questions in the questionnaire they had received input on specific issues. The over-reliance on a legalistic approach to teaching topics and how they are framed may not only limit recruits' understanding of the phenomenon in question, but also contributed to miscommunication in many of them misinterpreting questions resulting in negative responses.

Q20 asked recruits how useful did they find the content on women's issues. Thirty-three per cent indicated that the content was very useful and 42 per cent that it was useful, while 18 per cent indicated it was not useful. Six per cent of respondents described the input as poor. This finding indicates that while the majority of respondents were satisfied with what was taught, approximately a quarter of respondents indicated that significant improvements needed to be made to how policing issues related to women is taught. The response rate for Q20 was 53 per cent.

The mentally ill

The difference in how some social problems were addressed in recruit training is nowhere clearer than when considering the issue of policing the mentally ill. The inclusion of a lecture on working with the mentally ill, delivered by mental health professionals, is a response to the high rate of incidents involving the police and this group. These incidents are still fewer than the widely published cases of violence and sexual abuse of women involving men from every strata of society (see Wayne 2010; Stanislas ibid.). Many incidents involving the police and the mentally ill take place in public space and graphically highlight the RSLPFs potentially violent and brutal character that causes public revulsion (The Voice 2009). The importance of improving recruits' understanding of issues relating to the mentally ill (Chappell ibid.) is acknowledged by the Acting Commissioner:

> The mentally ill is an important issue for us, because most of our officers are either ignorant about those with this condition or are just basically scared when dealing with them and it has some bad outcomes. There are mentally ill people who are terrified of police. We have had an officer killed by a mentally ill man. It just takes one incident no matter how long ago for that view to take hold amongst officers on the ground.

Q23 asked recruits whether the training contained any content about working with the mentally ill. Ninety-three per cent of respondents indicated that the training did contain content on this matter and 5 per cent indicated it did not. The response rate to Q23 was 98 per cent (59). Q24 asked recruits how useful was the aforementioned content. Thirty-eight per cent of respondents indicated it was very useful, and 48 per cent indicated it was useful, with 10 per cent indicating it was not very useful. The findings indicated by the high response rate to Q23, show that recruits found the issue of policing the mentally ill and their education on the topic important. This can be placed in the context of this issue being seen as a pressing policing concern as indicated by senior officers. A female recruit describes some of the teaching on this matter:

> The people from the Ministry of Health taught us about the perceptions society has of the mentally ill, the different types of conditions people may have from depression to schizophrenia and how they manifest, and how we interact with people with these issues.

The importance of what is taught and its practical utility in shaping recruits' attitude to the topic is illustrated by the following account of an interaction between a trainee and an individual with mental health issues: 'It was very good because I remembered what we were taught when I had to deal with an old lady during our Christmas attachment, and how to approach her to calm her down and it really worked'.

Policing the mentally ill was found to be a very important subject with recruits, which may in part be informed by similar motivations already highlighted in the context of community policing of wanting to be seen as more concerned and caring (Kratoscki and Das 2007; Chappell ibid.).

Homosexuality

The issue of homophobia has become a central feature of the human rights agenda of many powerful interests with import for small Caribbean countries dependent on their economic relations with advanced western countries (see Chapter 1). Pressure around human rights also has important domestic sources such as the media and human rights lawyers in St Lucia (Ally 2011; Stanislas interviews 2010). The increasing numbers of educated senior police officers has also sensitized the RSLPF to many social issues with import for human rights. The Acting Commissioner stresses the importance of human rights to recruit training:

> Under our present training system I think we are on the right path in terms of developing sensitivity towards human rights. We need to keep emphasising the importance and value in treating people like human beings, the value of people's constitutional rights and not to trample on them.

Despite their common colonial legacy of Christianity and homophobic legislation, Caribbean countries differ in their degree of acceptance of homosexuality with some being traditionally more tolerant than others, with the French and Eastern Caribbean islands such as St Lucia being among the most relaxed on the matter (Chevannes 2000: 218). Policing attitudes to homosexuality and how they inform how police officers carry out their duties is a useful indicator of cultural attitudes to the issue (Meyer and Forest *et al.* 2004; see Chapter 1). Q25 asked recruits whether their training included any content relating to crimes against homosexual men and women or any related issues. Thirty-eight per cent of respondents indicated that these issues were covered in training, while 62 per cent said that they were not. This finding reflects similar issues already discussed above given evidence that recruits did receive input on issues about policing and homosexuality. This is illustrated in the response to Q26 which asked recruits how useful they found this content (issues relating to homosexuality) in improving their understanding. Forty-three per cent indicated that it was very useful and 52 per cent indicated it was useful, with 5 per cent indicating that it was not useful. Some examples of recruits' response to this topic are illustrated. One recruit recalls: 'We dealt with buggery and under what circumstances it is allowed and the law. Same for everyone really you can't have sex with minors and in public'.

Despite the specifics of legislation, traditional St Lucian morality on this issue which is reflected in the RSLPF's interpretation and enforcement of the law is primarily concerned with public sexual behaviour. A recruit recalls their response to the topic: 'It was really helpful in clarifying how to interpret the law on these things, which I think is in a good way'.

Another recruit comments on what he gained from this topic: 'It showed you how to act despite any personal bias you may have and keep things on a professional level'.

The reliance on a legalistic approach to a topic does not negate the type of techniques that educators can use in imparting knowledge (see Stanislas, Chapter 4) and creating an environment for broader education on any number of issues; ranging from personal prejudice, comparative attitudes to matters around equality, to professional practice. A female recruit recalls an exercise used in teaching:

> I remember we had a case study about a domestic disturbance involving male lovers and the police are called which is not uncommon. We discussed how we would address this scenario. I remember the consensus was we would handle it the same as a husband and wife domestic.

The response rate of 35 per cent (21) was one of the lowest to all questions. One possible factor in the high negative responses to Q25 of whether their training included any content relating to crimes or policing issues relating to homosexual men or women is the possibility of recruits not being interested in the topic about homosexuality or indicates their own personal bias reflecting wider societal homophobia (see Wayne 2010: 491–492) which resulted in their lack of recollection or not wanting to engage with the question (Allport 1987)

Conclusion

Efforts to reform postcolonial police organizations pose many pressing challenges which are highlighted in the St Lucian context. Key amongst these is the importance of recruiting personnel of requisite quality. The evidence suggests that the RSLPF have made important strides in this direction, aided by the general improvement of education in the country and high levels of unemployment in a small island economy. The demand for higher standards in police practice can be set against a backdrop of an organization struggling to manage the transition from a settled post-war and low crime St Lucia to a more contemporary one. As in many policing jurisdictions organizational reform has been forced onto the RSLPF (Stanislas ibid.). The modernization of the RSLPF as indicated by its greater sensitivity to recruits' learning needs and to the wider community and groups is driven by a desire to maintain public support in the face of a crisis in confidence and insecurity caused by the inability of the police to apprehend and prosecute offenders.

Despite the promotion of more adult forms of pedagogy, lack of resources disadvantages recruits in their ability to fully utilize these concepts in practice. The lack of library, computers, and other facilities constrains the means available to recruits to learn in very basic ways, never mind any particular preferences they may have. These observations highlight the relative nature of concepts such as student-centred learning and evidenced elsewhere in the context of community policing (Brogden and Nihaj 2005: 176–180). One of the major hurdles to cultural reform in recruit training in postcolonial military-type police organizations is that many problematic practices are not restricted to the classroom. These practices start first thing in the morning when recruits wake, to enforced 'lights out' at night. What takes place outside the classroom can have a very significant impact on recruit performance within it. The punitive ethos of these 'stress academies' and obsession with anachronistic military rituals undermines the progressive values being promoted as part of the reform process and diverts time from educational matters. They also contribute to a negative socialisation of individuals potentially contributing to an aggressive disposition towards the public that has long been a criticism of the RSLPF. What is particularly instructive is that many of the worst of the practices associated with the colonial model of policing was purported to have been eliminated as part of the reform which is clearly not the case.

The RSLPF reflects many black postcolonial societies which distinguish them from many white ex-colonial societies (see Cole 1999) or others which experienced subsequent major transformations and where there was a concerted effort to make a clear break with the past in psychological terms. This has not been the case in postcolonial countries, such as St Lucia, where new elites not only embrace the cultural legacy of their ex-rulers, but positively identify with it in important instances. For example the reintroduction of the khaki colonial police uniform by the new Acting Commissioner, viewed as a popularity measure, and the preferred attire of many officers which had been withdrawn by the previous incumbent due to its symbolism and excessive costs (The Star 2010). Such actions highlight the contradictory consciousness described by Freire (1970) which is difficult to square with the modernising and populist language of the RSLPF's new leadership and priorities such as tackling corruption. Their interests are interwoven and articulated through the colonial paradigm which in parts speaks not only to the lack of development in these countries, but the incremental form that it takes when the need for change is forced upon them.

Notes

1 Tutors from the College teach voluntarily at the Academy on police and correction officers recruit training programmes and in turn have access to an almost captive market for their various programmes and courses.
2 The presence of the American college and its philosophy and the positive reception it received in the country highlights the failure of the University of the West Indies and

its progressive vision popularized by luminaries such as St Lucian and Nobel Prize winner Professor Arthur Lewis (Sherlock and Nettleford 1990).

3 This is illustrated in the context of discussions about sexuality where even though the issue of human rights was not explicitly address it clearly underpins the attitudes and teaching of tutors. See pp. 20–21.

4 What is contained within many of these categories is often over or under inclusive in terms of how respondents define topics.

5 This argument is a popular one, but not based on any experience of the type of discipline, leadership, and other characteristics associated with effective military institutions. The RSLPF is neither a military nor a traditional policing organization.

6 The researcher was shown the cell mentioned by the recruit at the former's request.

7 The most common concern expressed about the teaching of sign language is recruits may forget what is taught by the time such skills are required.

Bibliography

Allport, G. (1987) *The Nature of Prejudice*, California: Addison Wesley Publishing.

Birzer, M. (2003) 'The Theory of Andragogy Applied to Police Training', *Policing: An International Journal of Police Strategies and Management*, 26(1): 29–42.

Brannen, J. (2005) 'Mixed Methods Research: A Discussion Paper', ESRC National Centre for Research Methods.

Brew, A. (1995) 'Directions in Staff Development', The Society for Research into Higher Education and Open University Press.

Brogden, M. and Nihaj, P. (2005) *Community Policing, National and International Models and Approaches*, Collumpton, Devon: Willan Publishing.

Chevannes, B. (2000) *Learning to be a Man*, Barbados: University of West Indies Press.

Cole, B. (1999) 'Postcolonial Systems', in C. Mawby (ed.), *Policing Across the World: Issues for the 21st Century*, London: Routledge.

Conti, N. (2006) 'Role Call: Professional Socialisation into Police Culture', *Police and Society*, 16(3): 221–242.

Cummings, T. and Huse, E. (1989) *Organizational Development and Change*, 4th edn., New York: West Publishing Company.

Freire, F. (1970) *The Pedagogy of the Oppressed*, Penguin Books, London.

Harrison, A. and Harriot, A. (2000) *Police and Crime Control in Jamaica: Problems of Reforming Ex-Colonial Constabularies*, Barbados: University of West Indies Press.

Hesson, M. and Shad, K. (2007) 'A Student-Centred Model', *American Journal of Applied Sciences*, 4(9): 628–637.

Hinton, S. and Newburn, T. (2009) *Policing Developing Democracies*, Abingdon Oxford, Routledge.

Joseph, T. (2011) *Decolonization in St Lucia: Politics of Global Neoliberalism*, Jackson: University of Mississippi.

Kirkpatrick, D. (1998) *Evaluating Training Programmes*, San Francisco: Berrett Koehler.

Kratcoski, P. and Das, D. (2007) *Police Education and Training in a Global Society*, United Kingdom: Lexington Books.

MacQueen, K., McLellan, E., and K. Kay (2009) 'Code Book Development for Team-Based Qualitative Analysis', in K. Krippendorff and A. Bock (eds), *The Content Analysis Reader*, London: Sage.

Mahony, D. and Prenzler, T. (1996) 'Police Studies, The University and The Police Service: An Australian Study', *Journal of Criminal Justice Education*, 18(1): 106–122.

Marenin, O. (2007) 'Policing for Democracy', in P. Kratocski and D. Das (eds), United Kingdom: Lexington Books.

Myer, K., Forest, K., and Miller, S. (2004) 'Officer Friendly and the Tough Cop: Gays and Lesbians Navigate Homophobia and Policing', *The Journal of Homosexuality*, 47(1): 17–37.

Onoja, A. (2006) 'Sustaining a Tradition of Policing Through Alienation: An Assessment of Recruitment and Training in the Colonial and Postcolonial Nigeria Police', *Afrika Zamani*, 13/14: 137–151.

Roberg, R. (2004) 'Higher Education and Policing: Where Are We Now?', *Policing: An International Journal of Police Management and Strategy*, 27(4): 469–486.

Sarasin, C.L. (2006) *Learning Styles Perspectives: Impact in the Classroom*, Madison: Atwood Publishing.

Sherlock, P. and Nettleford, R. (1990) *The University of the West Indies: A Caribbean Response to the Challenge of Change*, Caribbean: Macmillan.

Stanislas, P. (2013a) 'Policing and Criminal Administration in a Caribbean Micro State: A Case Study of St Lucia', *Police Research and Practice* (forthcoming).

Stanislas, P. (2013b) 'Postcolonial Discourses and Policing Violent Homophobia in the Caribbean and the British Caribbean Diaspora: The Limits of Postmodernity', *Interventions* (forthcoming).

Tosey, P. and Mathison, J. (2003) 'Neuro-linguistic Programming and Learning Theory: a response', *The Curriculum Journal*, 14(3): 361–378.

Van Zant, E. (2005) 'Better Policing: Tackling the Problems Besetting Police Service Means Overcoming a Long History and Great Shortage of Funds', Asian Development Bank Review.

Wayne, R. (2010). *Lapses and Infelicities: An Insider's Perspective of Politics in the Caribbean*, St Lucia: Star Publishing Co Ltd Lucia.

Newspaper articles

Ally, A. (2011) 'Francois Speaks out on Death List', 12 March 2011, *The St Lucia Star*, www.star.com. Accessed 12 March 2011.

Francois Wants to Inspire Cops, 6 June 2010, *The St Lucia Star*, www.star.com. Accessed 12 June 2010.

Monroe Give Gift of Education, 10 July 2012, www.voiceslu.com. Accessed 12 August 2012.

Police Kill Man with No Name, 7 December 2009, www.thestlucianvoice.com. Accessed 10 December.

Police Recruit Make Court Appearance, 27 February 2010, *The St Lucia Star*, www.star.com.

Reports

Annual Report of the Organisation and Administration of the Royal St Lucia Police Force 1975.

Annual Report of the Organization and Administration of the St Lucia Police Force 1949.

Crime, Violence, and Development: Trends, Costs, Policy Options in the Caribbean. A Report by The United Nations Office of Drugs and Crime and the Latin America and Caribbean Region of the World Bank, March 2007.

Deosaran, R. (2002) National Survey on Fear of Crime and Community Policing in St Lucia.

ICTs in the Eastern Caribbean: Saint Lucia Case Study, The International Telecommunications Union (2004)7.

Jones, M. and Satchell, N. (2009) Data Gathering on Police Officer and Civil Service Training in the Caribbean Region, Prepared for the Organisation of Americas States.

Neyroud, P. (2011) Review of Police Leadership and Training, HMSO, London World Data on Education, United Nations Educational, Scientific and Cultural Organisation, VII Ed 2010/1011.

St Lucia Country Poverty Assessment 2005/6, Caribbean Development Bank.

Part IV

Contemporary developments in policing and training

14   Getting back to Peel

PCSO training in England and Wales

A. Crisp

Context

Almost two decades prior to their introduction in 2002 the Home Office proposed that public sector organisations should be working towards 'economy, efficiency and effectiveness' (Home Office 1983). This new emphasis was associated with a reduction in autonomy and local accountability and focused on the crime-fighting role of the police (which included the suppression of possible civil unrest). The Police and Magistrates Courts Act 1994 strengthened government control of local police authorities, while espousing rhetoric to the contrary. The Sheehy Report (1993) and the Posen Inquiry (1995) challenged the hitherto unquestioned job-for-life culture, which had underpinned thinking about British policing indicating previously sacred matters were now legitimate topics of debate. Supplementary tensions and events led to debates about other important policing areas (Shearing and Wood 2003; Wood 2004).

The late 1990s brought a change in government and new reforms, which required the police to provide a more community-focused service whilst working under the conditions outlined by the 'Best Value Framework' (Home Office 1999).

Services, which at one time were perceived as core to 'police business' became subject to critical consideration for potential parcelling out to other bodies (Coxhead 2009). This included the expansion of an extended police family made up of members of the newly regulated security industry. Agencies within the criminal justice system, as well as within health and social care, were encouraged to adopt the principle of business rather than public service. This contributed to an appearance of accountability and encouraged the 'consumer' to 'shop' elsewhere if services were poor – as exemplified by the community of New Earswick where, after having initially sponsored a local community police patrol, they changed to a contract with a local security company because of poor police service (Crawford *et al.* 2003).

Impact of police culture on police/civilian working relationships

Research by Highmore (1993) into police/civilian integration observed a number of issues which were motivated by police arrogance and apparent feelings of superiority towards civilian staff. These images of a disenfranchised group of civilian staff were reinforced by the perceptions of officers themselves. This behaviour culminated in a sense of 'us and them' feelings towards staff and potentially reinforced by differences in pay and conditions (Highmore 1993: 47; Parrett 1998: 97). The lack of engagement, team-working, and respect in the relations between police and civilian roles was again highlighted by Cope (2004). Similar demoralising experiences were identified by Williams (2004: 4) in relation to the work of scientific support units by BCU Commander highlighting what Howgate-Graham (1947) calls 'the anti-civilian position'.

UNISON (2000) polled its police civilian staff members and found that over half of its respondents claimed to have witnessed or been subjected to bullying at work. Inappropriate practices were associated with an undervaluing of civilian staff by police managers which underlines the concerns expressed by Wachter and Hodge (2003). Similar issues were found in an UNISON survey in 2009 (Rayner 2009).

International examples

Internationally the role of 'unsworn' civilian aids for frontline policing roles is not a new idea. In the US for example, similar roles were proposed in the late 1970s (Tatum 1977). These proposals were subsequently adopted by American cities such as Orlando (the Orlando Crime Commission Report 1981), which advocated the concept of a policing auxiliary to facilitate budgetary savings and provide a more immediate response to non-emergency calls. The duties of the US 'Community Service Officer' (CSO) role is similar to its British counterpart in that their duties are linked to quality of life issues and the provision of frontline police support. Before being permitted to patrol independently officers receive 672 hours plus an additional 12 weeks of field-assessed training (Orlando Police 2012). Skolnick and Bayley (1986) noted that the introduction of new frontline civilian police roles appeared to positively augment community policing. The use of private security in the US to carry out similar functions has also been the subject of international policy transfer (de Ward 1999; Avant 2005).

The Dutch police have endeavoured to increase the numbers and responsibilities of civilian staff, sensing that they should not only perform a policing role but develop bonds between the police and the communities they serve (Merritt 2009). The introduction of Police Liaison Officers or PLOs in the Australian Police Service was seen as an opportunity to provide a more culturally sensitive support to ethnic and racially diverse groups. Whilst the role carries few policing powers, it requires PLOs to act as the primary intermediaries for police/community issues. The difference however is that these officers, in most cases, have been specifically recruited from a particular ethnic group. Native Australian PLOs were recruited to support policing initiatives in local Aboriginal communities to ameliorate some of the issues identified by the 1991 Royal Commission and similarly with the Vietnamese, Samoan, or Arab communities.

The PCSO in England and Wales

The emergence of the Police Community Support Officer (PCSO) as a result of the Police Reform Act (2002) was initially seen as part of the wider workforce modernisation agenda. This arguably provided an opportunity to assign less crucial tasks to ensure key personnel were free to undertake the more important aspects of their work.

Simultaneously the introduction of National Crime Recording Standards (2002) and the APAC's framework standardised the methods for reporting crime, and identified the associated levels of police performance in which offences would be brought to justice regardless of any mitigation, which removed the use of discretion. This acted as both the 'carrot and stick' to police managers and viewed by critics as a means to criminalise members of the community in order to meet performance targets. Whilst frontline police officers were rapidly losing their ability to apply discretion, the new PCSOs were not initially subjected to the same need to meet performance targets which meant that their relationship with communities began as a less retributive one.

The drivers for change in training

After the enforced closures of the country's five Central Police Training and Development Authority (CENTREX) (2002, 2004; Home Office, 2006, 2008) due to financial and political pressures (Home Affairs Select Committee 1999); police and partnership negotiations with local education providers begun, and with apparent reluctance in some police jurisdictions. Without clear government direction of methods of delivery of the new Initial Police Learning and Development training (IPLDP) the process was left to the discretion of local chief officers, some choosing to retain complete control and train 'in-house', whilst others sought out partners who might contribute the additional academic content recommended by Elliot and Kushner's (2003) review.

Whilst negotiations for the delivery and confirmation of content of the IPLDP and National Occupational Standards for Police Officers were carried out with some care, the training of PCSO staff was very much seen as an 'add on'. Cooper *et al.* (2006) notes the lack of time provided to develop appropriate training packages for PCSOs meant that each force had to develop their own packages which varied from force to force. Many Forces who decided to work with academic institutions on initial police training combined the requirements of the Home Office within an HE Foundation Degree framework (see Stanislas chapter), and, if the training of the new PCSO staff was included in the initial 'business' negotiations, it too was incorporated in this formal academic process. This in some cases led to successful students being awarded a University Certificate of Professional Development (UCPD). In the majority of cases the training of the PCSO was seen as something to be built on to the short local training courses of traffic wardens from whose ranks many of the first officers were recruited.

In designating the role of the PCSO, there was a provision for chief officers to choose from a range of policing powers (suited to their local needs) which would complement a series of standard powers; the training requirement was also intended to reflect these choices. The Association of Chief Police Officers (ACPO) later noted their role as:

> [C]ontributing to the policing of neighbourhoods, primarily through highly visible patrol with the purpose of reassuring the public, increasing orderliness in public places and being accessible to communities and partner agencies working at local level. The emphasis of this role, and the powers required to fulfil it, will vary from neighbourhood to neighbourhood and force to force.
>
> (ACPO 2005: 6)

The choice of a more independent, and potentially haphazard educational route, is highlighted by Miller (2005). The choice of a more formal route of training and education for PCSOs adopted by one of a number of Midlands forces constitutes the following case study.

Training the plastic police in a UK force

This 'case study' force had taken the opportunity, like many others, to initially convert their Traffic Wardens' posts into the new PCSOs' roles to receive additional funds available at the time, which made recruitment to this new role possible.

Former Traffic Wardens whose previous punitive roles traditionally put them in positions of potential conflict were expected to transform overnight into highly visible community-focused operatives with little additional training. What little training that was provided was designed to impart minimal levels of skill and operational proficiency. Initially PCSOs received basic training in their new policing powers from the force's training unit, who were at the time involved in a restructuring process. Qualified police trainers who were serving police officers appeared disquieted that they would be training these new auxiliary staff who were seen as a threat to frontline roles. They were seemingly unavailable to devise specific sessions to accommodate this new post as they were alternatively deployed on other training matters or eventually the planning and preparation of materials for the new FD. As a result, retired police training staffs were initially employed on an ad hoc basis to fill these gaps.

The early PCSOs consequently either continued to do what they had always done (i.e. focus on parking offences), or endeavoured to undertake independent learning (some with the support of local beat officers) and gain additional experience. Unfortunately for some, the lack of direction and understanding of policing powers meant that many PCSOs were unable to effectively perform their roles which fuelled police gossip about laziness or incompetence. This was not subsequently helped by negative media headlines about perceived PCSOs' failings and more seriously (and incorrectly) gross neglect of duty (BBC 2007).

By the time that the police/HE partnership led training process was launched in 2005, two types of PCSOs were in post; those who had experience but little formal training, and others who would be given additional training under the new system but had no experience. Nationally these officers were recruited on a combination of permanent and temporary contracts, and, ever resourceful, some of the more progressive officers turned to the internet for advice developing PCSO support sites such as pcsos-national.co.uk[3], which provided advice on aspects of policing powers and shared experiences.

With little formal confirmation or advice available about which aspects of the occupational competence process would apply to PCSOs, the programme structure for the UCPD was based on components which were taken from the Policing FD.

These elements focused on a number of key areas:

- Most important was an appreciation of the nature of prejudice, human rights and the knowledge, skills, and understanding necessary to work with diverse communities, remembering that without key policing powers PCSOs have to rely on communication and negotiation skills.
- To provide an appreciation of the law and an understanding of how PCSOs apply their powers in likely scenarios they might face.
- A grounding in practical policing skills linked to beat work and the knowledge of the processes and technology that PCSOs require to utilize and record or report progress. This included an understanding of data protection, techniques of problem-solving, and how to take statements and present evidence in court. The preservation and gathering of evidence in crime scenes, traffic control and offences, and railway safety were an additional component of this early training.
- Finally there was a need for these new ranks to understand their role and learn basic research skills in order to understand wider social contexts and issues impacting on their work, the criminal justice system, and aspects of victim support and multi-agency engagement.
- Personal protection and first-aid.

Due to the opportunity for graduates to convert their academic credits towards the FD, assessments were linked to Higher Education framework standards.

In 2005 the development stage of the IPLDP programme, which already had detailed lecture and training requirements and materials provided by the Home Office, the male sergeant in charge of training, an inspector, and several police trainers worked with university staff full-time on the programme content over an intensive six-month period. For the UCPD a female sergeant from the force training department was drafted to work with a representative of the University, and a civilian police trainer, to produce and finalise programme content over a four-week period.

Essential curriculum components were simplified as little time was made available for civilian members of staff to be trained, and even less time for them to produce academically credible assignments.

Table 14.1 Original structure of the foundation degree in policing incorporating IPLDP

Year 1 ──────►	'In company' period ──────►	Year 2
23 weeks based at local University including 10 Community Placement days+Completion of 4 Modules	10 weeks based at BCU[1] undertaking community policing and general duties under supervision by local practice Tutor	Based at BCU undertaking community policing/general duties+Completion of 3 Modules
1) Legislation Assessment – 2 exams 2) Occupational Competence Practical tests assessment based on 'role plays' 3) Criminal Justice Assessment – 2 academic essays and group presentation 4) Diversity Assessment – 2 academic essays	Released to single patrol after providing evidence of competence in 'PACs' (Police Action Checklist)	1) Occupational Competence Assessment – NVQ based upon IPLDP 'SOLAP' 2) Diversity Assessment – 2 academic essays 3) Criminal Justice Assessment – 2 academic essays After successful completion of academic work and confirmation of competence awarded Foundation Degree in Policing

Note
1 Basic Command Units are the area police headquarters.

Table 14.2 Original structure for the UCPD for police community support officers

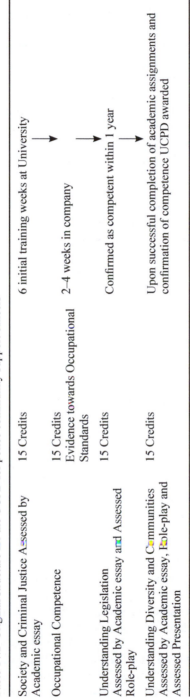

Society and Criminal Justice Assessed by Academic essay	15 Credits	6 initial training weeks at University
Occupational Competence	15 Credits Evidence towards Occupational Standards	2–4 weeks in company
Understanding Legislation Assessed by Academic essay and Assessed Role-play	15 Credits	Confirmed as competent within 1 year
Understanding Diversity and Communities Assessed by Academic essay, Role-play and Assessed Presentation	15 Credits	Upon successful completion of academic assignments and confirmation of competence UCPD awarded

The first bemused recruits to the university programme were trained at the same time that the first IPLDP student officers received their training. The PCSOs' training was six weeks, and based entirely at the University, as opposed to the student officers' six months at the University which incorporated community placements and additional study time to complete academic work. Unwin (2006) notes that in 2005 the majority of PCSO respondents to a national online survey stated that their training in post lasted one week, with only 17 per cent of respondents having trained for six weeks or more.

In view of the limited time available to initially train these officers it is not unsurprising that a survey undertaken on behalf of the Home Office found that only 38 per cent of the PCSOs studied felt that their initial training had adequately prepared them for their job (Cooper *et al.* 2006). When polled three years later a UNISON study found that the confidence in post, as a result of training had risen to 66 per cent (UNISON 2009). Altogether the student officers' training which, combined police requirements within the structure of a FD, lasted two years combining work in academic and practical field settings whilst the PCSOs were required to be fully operational after just six weeks at university. They were required to become operationally competent frontline officers and complete academic assignments in order that they might be confirmed in post by the end of their first year in post.

Whilst in their initial training, student officers and PCSOs were expected to attend university lectures and in their first weeks had similar introductory lectures and sessions which outlined their roles and explained the expectations that the service and society had of them as warranted or non-warranted officers. One of the key sessions was delivered by the Professional Standards section which dealt with discipline and codes of conduct. Elements of this session would constantly be referred back to throughout both training pathways, as would a session on occupational health and safety. University staff working on both programmes reported what was perceived as a greater tolerance for 'unsuitable' behaviours from student officers, where such behaviours were not tolerated to the same degree from PCSOs. The possible support of the Police Federation of newly recruited student officers may have had some influence on this, whilst the union representation of the PCSOs did not appear to hold the same level of sway. This bias appeared to affect a number of aspects of training.

Due to an apparent identified risk, student officers were initially not permitted to undertake practice-based role-plays in public areas around the university, because stab vests had not arrived; the police perception being that without this protection they were at risk of attack from other students or members of the community. In other similar programmes nationally this may not have been seen to be so much of an issue, as student officers undertook their college and university-focused training in uniform and performed role-play exercises in public areas without apparent concerns. The early cohorts of PCSO trainees however were told that even once they had been trained they would not be issued with stab vests as they were not required to become involved in dangerous situations. This decision was later rescinded, but the lack of personal protection for

PCSOs remained the same for some time, leaving the general feeling that their personal safety was less important to the organisation than their student officer colleagues.

Whilst the IPLDP programme evolved generally smoothly, as additional components were added to the core requirements, the training of PCSOs lurched forward as new learning requirements were introduced as a matter of expediency like a shopping list; usually as a result of a complaint, error, or concern about their role. *Roads Policing* training, which involves officers in training in safety procedures to preserve scenes of vehicle collisions and highlight potential dangers to oncoming traffic, is one example of a component brought in exogenously as a result of an incident involving a PCSO.

This process continued until September 2007 when the Wider Police Learning and Development Programme (WPLDP) brought together a national list of training requisites. These were finally recommended as core to PCSO training by the National Police Improvement Agency (NPIA) in their PCSO Review 2008 and integrated into local training.

In contrast to the experiences of student officers undergoing training in a northern university described by Heslop (2009, 2010); whilst finding the training programme to be academically and in some ways emotionally demanding, the majority of PCSO students in the case study found their time at university overall to have been agreeable, and, for some, life changing. This was greatly due to the hard work of committed civilian and police training staff who worked well together and co-taught sessions with members of academic staff in order that in the limited time available both the practice based and academic content were integrated for greater coherence (see Peeters and Tingyou chapters).

Regrettably whilst the levels of content increased, the time available to teach these additional subjects did not, which made the learning experience frustrating and stressful for all concerned (see Stanislas, Chapter 4). As the role of PCSO appeared to be less prescribed and more accessible than that of a police constable, it appealed to applicants from diverse backgrounds and non-traditional candidates to police work. As an example, some of the more mature entrants in our case study had left school without formal qualifications, did not know how to use computer based systems, and had not studied for over 40 years which made the challenge of a programme considerable.

Rowell (2010) notes the perception by a number of police managers that the basic standards of literacy of PCSO staff were poor, consequently recommending changes to required levels of educational achievement within the recruitment process. This concern is not unique to PCSO recruits: and is highlighted by this respondent in relation to police officers: 'I see recruits whose command of written English is woeful. Entry standards need to be reviewed and raised.' (Neyroud 2011: 88)

To a certain extent Rowell's (2010) findings could be initially observed within the police/PCSO relationship at university, with some police trainers, and to a certain extent new police recruits, viewing PCSO students as being 'sub-standard' or 'not quite bright enough' (Crisp 2008).[1] In some respects this perception was correct as many of the PCSO students had only basic levels of educational attainment and some had tried unsuccessfully to become police officers. In spite of this, what they lacked in academic ability was compensated for (by some) in their ability to communicate, empathise, and understand community issues. There also appeared to be a genuine sense of a 'calling to do good things' in the community. This facet appeared in recruits who joined the job to be PCSOs, as well as those who saw the role as a stepping stone to become police officers. It was particularly encouraging to see that over time graduates from the programme voluntarily return in their own time to support new recruits who were going through training in order that they might be reassured.

Amongst the former experiences of the wide range of graduates of this early version of PCSO training in the case study force area were officers who spoke many languages fluently, held a Master's Degree, formerly owned their own successful businesses, were housewife returners-to-work, and 'a cleaning lady'. Their diverse ethnic origins, gender, social status, and age seemed to more accurately represent the wider local community than the recruits to the police. This perception is supported by research evidence (Home Office 2010: 14).

Johnston (2006) notes that in the Metropolitan police areas, recruitment targets for gender and ethnicity is being surpassed by PCSO applicants who see the role in some respects as one where they might test the water to establish whether a career in the police service would suit them. 'What is striking is that many are from ethnic communities and most of them are young' (Francis 2003: 18).

New programme developments

With national developments demanded by the NPIA and additional needs identified locally; the training of PCSOs in the case study force has now significantly changed from that which was 'tacked on' to the IPLDP. The more positive development of a blended programme has subsequently succumbed to pressures to cram content into PCSO training without additional learning time. This experience is not unique to the case study programme as the role of the PCSO is easy to define, but apparently hard to encapsulate in a training programme as it appears to 'expand and contract' as required, nationally.

This leads us to ask the question, 'What is the role of the PCSO?'

In 2012 there is an acceptance by the police service nationally that the recruitment and training route of the PCSO or Special Constable will facilitate the recruitment of direct entrants to police officer IPLDP training programmes. As a result of this, our original case study programme is now WPLDP compliant and has conversion routes to the IPLDP/FD programme. Already a number of officers with a desire to become police officers have successfully progressed through this route, whilst a meaningful number have preferred to remain as PCSOs. As an ex-PCSO now a Police Officer said, 'Whilst the money is better, I don't get a chance to make a difference any more.'

Nationally, academically focused policing pre-entry requirements appear to be gaining popularity with those individuals with hopes to become police officers, and, in addition to the role of Special Constable, there is some indication that a volunteer role associated with the PCSO is under consideration.

Impact

In many areas of the country PCSOs have made a significant impact to the perception of community safety, and have been noted as being partially responsible for the fall in crime (HMIC 2004; Francis 2003: 18).

Once they were able to demonstrate their worth to frontline policing ranks PCSOs have now been seen to be of great value (Wilson 2004; Lund 2004; Cooper *et al.* 2006). This situation might change however, if frontline police numbers were reduced in their favour (Cooper *et al.* 2006).

There continues to be significant confusion over the role in both the public and police domains in spite of continued government campaigns and their promotion on TV in a fly-on-the-wall documentary series, 'Beat: Life on the street', which was commissioned by the Home Office in 2006 (Crawford and Lister 2004; Cooper *et al.* 2006).

In an evaluation by Johnstone in 2005, over half of respondents interviewed found that the presence of PCSOs had made them feel less fearful and more reassured.

Similar findings have been identified by Casey (2008) and reinforced by the results of figures from the British crime survey (2009) which indicated that PCSOs had been effective with the perception of crime in their areas of patrol going down by 8 per cent.

Research by Pamment in 2009 found that whilst Home Office Reports (2005, 2008) suggested that PCSOs were making a valuable contribution to neighbourhood policing, young offenders, who represented an important component of their expected contact role perceived them as lacking credibility as a supposed deterrent against crime. Generally however, Cooke (2004) observed that young people found it easier to talk to these 'uniformed officers' rather than the warranted police as they found them to be on a 'similar level'. providing evidence of increased confidence amongst such groups.

The cost implications of the PCSO

Initially Chief Officers, keen to secure additional resources, were more than willing to accept government sponsorship of new 'ring fenced' PCSO posts locally. They consequently found themselves in the unenviable position of having to financially sustain the role and received advice and guidance from the Home Office as to how this might be facilitated through matched funding initiatives (Home Office 2006).

The original funding situation is now more serious with the publication by HMIC of *Policing in Austerity* (HMIC 2012). This review considers the responses of forces to the impact of global recession and national policing policy and identifies the changes to local policing as a result; noting the reduction of 10 per cent of officers involved in frontline policing by 2015, and the necessary changes to police structures and processes in order to meet demands and cut costs. Shadows of the O'Connor recommendations (HMSO 2005) whilst originally 'dodged' by Chief Constables, appear to be resurfacing in our more economically overextended society; as government look to the consolidation of services in policing to secure levels of performance and save money.

This has already resulted in the loss through compulsory retirement (by the use of Police Regulation 19) of longer serving more experienced officers and will undoubtedly have a significant impact on PCSOs. Whilst initially introduced for their visible impact on the frontline the report revealed that 30 police forces surveyed had begun to move PCSOs into frontline non-visible roles which suggests 'that forces are focusing their resources on those areas of greatest harm and risk' (HMIC 2012: 37).

In response to a Freedom of Information (FOI) request for information about the cost of training for PCSOs and Police Officers in Cambridge it was noted that in the years 2007–2008 training costs for a Police Constable were £5,849.95 and for a PCSO £467.49 (FOI ref 0322/2009 2009). Based on these figures for every student officer trained for the Cambridge force an additional 12 PCSOs could be trained, which in terms of 'bodies' on patrol as a visible deterrent to offending (but most importantly without the costs of wages and miscellaneous on costs, etc.) it certainly appears to be value for money.

Conclusion

Crystal ball gazing – the future – survival of the cheapest?

In spite of initial fears and contrary to expectations, the PCSO has become an acceptable and accepted member of the wider police family. Evidence suggests that they provide a visible reassuring police presence and generate intelligence about local issues, and they have proven to be a worthy support to the office of constable – a 'Robin' to the constable's 'Batman' – who can be managed by local beat officers to improve police coverage and support to local people. Gyott (1991)[2] notes the positive professional consequences for police officers associated with the development of such managerial opportunities.

Yet both Batman and Robin were crime fighters. Could the police culture envelop these civilian staff to such an extent that their original role is eventually forgotten? PCSOs already undertake an important role in local communities, unfortunately however, there is a tradition in the police service to see the community focused policing roles as 'rubbish jobs', or the places allocated for lazier officers to hide from the 'real work' of fighting crime; automatically devaluing the work that the PCSOs have been employed to undertake.

Evidence thus far suggests that the role of the PCSO has already evolved; the future may present the serving PCSO with additional tasks but with some support provided by volunteers. The police service is driving forward strategies which will support the recruitment of volunteers in all areas, including perhaps, civilian volunteer PCSOs to help them patrol our streets.

According to a survey by UNISON, PCSOs feel that they might be in a better position to do their job properly with additional policing powers (UNISON 2009). This idea appears to be supported by Rogers (2004: 18) who notes the need for additional policing powers to enable the PCSO role to more relevantly deal with community issues relating to the maintenance of order. With the possible reduction of police officers on frontline duties, it is important that those who are left to patrol our streets have the right tools to do the job. This may require more formal policing powers to be legislated for use by the PCSOs, further training to be developed and greater personal protection, such as pepper spray, to be provided. In more recent examples of civil unrest PCSOs were deployed in some neighbourhoods close to the problem areas to reassure and support local communities, this meant however that when tensions became more difficult to handle they were left in unsettling circumstances with little protection.

There are a number of additional, perhaps unexpected, dangers in allowing the PCSOs to develop along what would undoubtedly be a route that would save money, in that already there is evidence to suggest that many PCSOs are being swept into the police culture of crime fighting rather than providing community reassurance. When this is reinforced by the lack of police or public appreciation of what the PCSO's duties actually are, the positive benefits that communities have gained since 2002 may be swept away to save money, which would be regrettable.

Notes

1 This denigration of 'fitness' was extended to the civilian and police ranks who provided the PCSO training by their police colleagues initially with the IPLDP training staff perceiving their worth as significantly different to that of their colleagues.
2 With Neyroud's recommendations for the professionalisation of the police service in mind this would seem to be a situation of mutual benefit.
3 Now called PCSO.com, www.policecommunitysupportofficer.com/viewtopic. php?f=3&t=17315.

References

ACPO (2005) *Guidance on Police Community Support Workers*, London: ACPO.
Avant, D. (2005) *The Market for Force: The Consequences of Privatising Security*, Cambridge: Cambridge University Press.
BBC News online (13 April 2012) What is the Role of Community Support Officers? www.bbc.co.uk/news/uk-17702622 (accessed 1 July 2012).
BBC News online (21 September 2007) Police defend drowning death case http://news. bbc.co.uk/1/hi/7006412.stm (accessed 1 July 2012).
Barnes, L., Pepper, I.K., and Thornton, M. (2007) 'Learning Partnerships: The key to skilled workforces', Education in a Changing Environment, International Conference,

Manchester, University of Salford, 12–14 September 2007 www.ece.salford.ac.uk/proceedings/papers/48_07.pdf (accessed 6 July 2012). www.unison.org.uk/acrobat/16771_Call_of_Duty_A4.pdf (accessed 8 July 2012).

Bradley, D., Walker, N., and Wilkie, R. (1986) *Managing the Police*, Brighton: Wheatsheaf.

Broster, P. (20 September 2007) Force hires more plastic police than real bobbies www.express.co.uk/posts/view/19606/Force-hires-more-plastic-policemen-than-real-bobbies (accessed 6 July 2012).

Button, M. (2002) *Private Policing*, Exeter: Willan.

Casey L. (2008) *Engaging Communities in Fighting Crime*, London: Cabinet Office.

Cambridge Constabulary (2009) Freedom of Information Request ref 0322/2009 2009.

Chan, J. (1996) 'Changing police culture', *British Journal of Criminology*, 36(1): 109–134.

Chan, J. (1997) *Changing Police Culture: Policing in a Multicultural Society*, Cambridge: Cambridge University Press.

Cherney, A. and Chui W.H. (2011) 'The Dilemmas of Being a Police Auxiliary – An Australian Case Study of Police Liaison Officers', *Policing*, 5(2): 180–187.

Cooper, C., Anscombe, J., Avenell, J., McLean, F., and Morris, J. (2006) 'A National Evaluation of Community Support Officers', *Home Office Research Study*, no. 297, Home Office.

Cooke, C.A. (2004) *Issues in Schoolchildren's Perception of Uniformed Police*, Hawaii, HI: American Psychological Association.

Cope, N. (2004) 'Intelligence Led Policing or Policing Led Intelligence? Integrating Volume Crime Analysis into Policing', *British Journal of Criminology*, 44(2).

Coxhead, J. (2009) *The Pluralisation of Policing: The Police Private Security and Public Consent*, Lambert academic publishing.

Crawford, A., Lister, S., and Wall, D. (2003) *Great Expectations Contracted Community Policing in New Earswick*, York: Joseph Rowntree Foundation.

Crawford, A. and Lister, S. (2004) *The Extended Police Family: Visible Patrols in Residential Areas*, York: Joseph Rowntree Foundation.

Crawford, A., Lister, S., Blackburn, S., and Burnett, J. (2005) *Plural Policing – The Mixed Economy of Visible Patrols in England and Wales*, Bristol: The Policy Press.

Crisp, A. (2008) The Training Needs and Requirements Of The PCSO, Unpublished.

Cunningham, W. and Taylor, T.H. (1985) *Private Security and Police in America – The Hallcrest Report*, Portland: Chancellor Press.

De Ward, J. (1999) 'The Private Security Industry in International Perspective', *European Journal on Criminal Policy and Research*, 7(2): 143–174.

Elliot, J. and Kushner, S. (2003) *Learning Requirement for Police Probationer Training in England and Wales: An Independent Review*, London: Home Office.

Francis, I. (2003) 'Quality Street. Community Support Officers', *Police Review*, 30 May 2003.

Guyot, D. (1991) *Policing as though People Matter*, Philadelphia: Temple University Press.

Heslop, R. (2009) Learning the 'wrong' things: a case study of police recruits trained at university, Research Thesis Leeds University (accessed 10 October 2010).

Heslop, R. (2010) 'They didn't treat us like professionals': a case study of police recruits trained at a university, www.leeds.ac.uk/medicine/meu/lifelong10/Richard%20Heslop.pdf (accessed 10 October 2010).

Highmore, S. (1993) 'The Integration of Police Officers and Civilian Staff: A study of Internal Service Quality', *Police Research group*, Home Office.

HMIC (2002) *Training Matters*, London: Home Office.

HMIC (2004) *Modernising the Police service: A Thematic Inspection of Workforce Modernisation – The Role, Management and Deployment of Police Staff in the Police Service of England and Wales*, London: Home Office.

HMIC (2005*) Closing the Gap: A Review of the Fitness for Purpose of the Current Structure of Policing in England and Wales*, London: Home Office.

Home Office (1995) *Review of Core and Ancillary Tasks*, London: HMSO.

Home Office (1999) *Best Value: Briefing Notes for The Police Service Audit and Inspection*, London: Home Office.

Home Office (2001) *Policing a New Century, A Blue Print for Reform*, London: Home Office.

Home Office (2004) *Building Communities Beating Crime (Government Green-Paper)*, London: Home Office.

Home Office (2004) 'Policing: Modernising Police Powers to Meet Community Needs' Communications Directorate: Home Office, 2004: 10.

Home Office (2005) *Neighbourhood Policing: Your Police: Your Community: Our Commitment*, London: Home Office.

Home Office (2005) *Initial Police Learning and Development Programme Central Authority Practitioner Guidance: Community Engagement and Professional Development Units*. London: Home Office.

Home Office (2006) *Good Practice for Police Authorities and Forces in Obtaining CSO Funding*, London: Home Office.

Home Office (2006) *Letter from the Home Office dated 17 July 2006: Initial Police Learning and Development Programme (IPLDP) National Qualification for Student Police Officers*, London: Home Office.

Home Office (2008) *From the neighbourhood to the national: policing our communities together (Government Green-Paper)*, London: Home Office.

Home Office (2010) *Policing in the 21st Century: Reconnecting Police and The People*, London: TSO

Howgrave-Graham, H.M. (1947) *Light and Shade at Scotland Yard*, London: John Murray.

Hughes, M. (2009) On the Beat with the civilian detectives in Manchester. in the *Independent* online 15 September 2009 www.independent.co.uk/news/uk/crime/on-the-beat-with-the-civilian-detectives-in-manchester-1787335.html (accessed 7 July 2012).

Johnston, L. (2003) 'From "pluralisation" to the "police extended family": discourses on the governance of community policing in Britain', *International Journal of the Sociology of Law*, 31: 185–204.

Johnston, L. (2005) 'From Community to Neighbourhood Policing: Police Community Support officers and the Police Extended Family in London', *Journal of Community and Applied Social Psychology*, 15: 241–254 Wiley.

Johnston, L. (2006) 'Diversifying police recruitment? The deployment of Police Community Support Officers in London', *The Howard Journal of Criminal Justice*, 45(4): 388–402.

Johnston, L. and Shearing, C. (2003) *Governing Security: Explorations in Policing and Justice*, London: Routledge.

Leake, C. (2007) 'Labours plastic bobbies to replace full time police', Daily Mail www.dailymail.co.uk/news/article-473229/Labours-plastic-bobbies-replace-time-police.html#ixzz0ZrEYklt2 (accessed 1 May 2012) cfnp.npia.police.uk/UsersOnly/.../cs_operation_comfort.doc (accessed 6 July 2012).

Loveday, B. (2004) *Literature Review for HMIC Thematic Inspection on Civilianisation*, Home Office.

Loveday, B. (1993) 'Civilian Staff in the Police Service', *Policing*, vol. 9. Summer.

Loveday, B. and Reid, A. (2002) *Going Local*, London: Policy Exchange.

Loveday, B. (1999) 'Police Accountability' in R. Mawby (ed.) *Policing around the World*.

Lockerman, D. (2010) Support for funding CSO application Dave Lockerman Housing Services Manager Broxbourne Housing Association posted 1/3/10 www.hertsdirect. org/mm/.../crimedisor100304evidlockerman.doc (accessed 8 July 2012).

Lund, S. (2004) 'Forces are choosing to pay for CSOs', *Police Review*, 12 March 2004.

Maguire, M. (2002) 'Crime statistics: the 'data explosion' and its implications' in M. Maguire, M., Morgan, R., and Reiner, R. (eds) The Oxford Handbook of Criminology: 3rd edn., Oxford: OUP.

Martin, J.P. and Wilson, G. (1969) The Police: a Study in Manpower: The evolution of the Service in England and Wales 1829–1965, London: Heinemann.

Mason, G. (2000) Bullies, The Unison Survey, Police Review (7 July 2000).

Meeting of the Select Committee on Home Affairs (2009) www.publications.parliament. uk/pa/cm199900/cmselect/cmhaff/77/7705.htm (accessed 1 October 2010).

Merritt, J. (2009) 'Pluralist Models of Policing: Legislating for Police Powers, a Cautionary Note from England and Wales', *Policing: An International Journal of Police Strategies & Management*, 32(2): 377–394.

Miller, R. (2005) 'An Evaluation of a Police Community Support Officer Scheme', *Safer Communities*, 4(1): 38–41.

Neyroud, P. (2011) *Review of Police Leadership and Training*, Home Office.

NPIA (2008) Neighbourhood policing programme PCSO Review July 2008 NPIA.

Operational Policing Review (1990) Home Office Circulars 105/88–106/88, Devon and Cornwall Constabulary.

Orlando Crime Commission Report issued on 8 October 1981.

Orlando Police Department Community Service Officers www.cityoforlando.net/police/ support_services/cso.htm (accessed 5 July 2012).

Pamment, N. (2009) 'We Can Terrorise Them! Young Offenders' Perceptions of Community Support Officers', *The Police Journal*, vol. 82.

Parrett, L. (1998) *Past, Present and Future Role of Civilian Personnel in The Police Service of England And Wales*, University of East Anglia.

Press Reith, C. (1956) *A New Study of Police History*, London: Oliver and Boyd.

Rayner, C. (2009) Workplace Bulling and Harassment in 2009: Report to UNISON www. port.ac.uk/research/cord/workplacebullying/researchreports/filetodownload,108517,en. pdf (accessed 7 July 2012).

Rayner, C. (2000) *Bullying at work in the Police Section membership of UNISON*, London: UNISON.

Rayner, C. (2010) The Police occupational Culture: Understanding negative behaviour using Interaction Ritual Chain Theory Paper to the 7th International Conference on Workplace Bullying and Harassment (with Hilary Miller), Cardiff, June 2010.

Rogers, C. (2004) 'A Uniform Approach To Order Maintenance: Can Police Community Support Officers Step In?', *Safer Communities*, 3(4): 15–19.

Rowell, P. (2010) Assessing the literacy of PCSOs: have the NPIA and MPS aligned the standard to operational requirements? MSc dissertation, University of Portsmouth. http://eprints.port.ac.uk/923/ (accessed 8 July 2012).

Royal Commission into Aboriginal Deaths in Custody (1991) Regional Report of Inquiry in New South Wales,Victoria and Tasmania. By Commissioner, the Honourable J.H. Wootten, AC, QC. Canberra: Australian Government Publishing Service.

Shearing and Wood (2003) 'Governing security for common goods', *International Journal of the Sociology of Law*, 31(3): 205–25.

Sheehy Report (1993) Inquiry into Police Responsibilities and Rewards, Cm 2280.I, II, London: HMSO.

Skolnick, J.H., and Bayley, D. (1986) *The New Blue Line: Police Innovation In Six American Cities*, New York: NY Free Press.

Tatum, G. (1977) 'Combating Crime – Full utilisation of the Police Officer and CSO (Community Service Officer)', *Concept Police Chief*, 44(4)L 46–47, 50, 87, (April 1977) NCJRS database www.ncjrs.gov/App/Publications/abstract.aspx?ID=40823 (accessed 6 July 2012).

Taylor, B. and Rogaly, B. (2004) Migrant Working in West Norfolk Report to Norfolk.

Unwin, S. (2006) Community Support officers A force for the futures. A study into the training and employment of Police Community Support Officers www.national-pcsos.co.uk/JOSSMAN2.pdf (accessed 6 July 2012).

UNISON (2000) Police staff bullying. Report no. 1777, London.

UNISON (2009) survey of PCSO opinions for channel 4 dispatches programme Sunday 20 September 2009 Cops on the Cheap Channel 4 Dispatches www.channel4.com/programmes/dispatches/articles/cops-on-the-cheap-survey-results (accessed 6 July 2012).

Wachter, V., and Hodge, A. (2003) 'A New Era for Police Managers', *Policing Today*, (9)3.

Williams, R. (2004) The Management of crime scene examination in relation to the investigation of burglary and vehicle crime. Home Office online report 24/04 http://library.npia.police.uk/docs/hordsolr/rdsolr2404.pdf (accessed 6 July 2012).

Wilson, J. (2004) 'Training Support. What Training are forces giving to community support officers across the country?', *Police Review*, 23 April 2004.

Wilson, J.Q. and Kelling, G.L. (1982) 'Broken Windows: The Police and Neighbourhood Safety', *The Atlantic Monthly*, 249(March): 29–38.

Windsor, T.P. (2012) Independent Review of Police Officer and Staff Remuneration and Conditions Final Report.

Wood, J. (2004) 'Cultural change in the governance of security', *Policing and Society*, 1(3): 31–48.

15 New perspectives on police education and training

Lessons from the private security sector

A. Wakefield and M. Button

Introduction

A coherent strategy for promoting leadership, professional standards, professional development and training should underpin any occupational discipline seeking to claim the elevated status of a 'profession'. This has become a recent focus of the United Kingdom government with respect to policing: following a detailed review by Chief Constable Peter Neyroud of existing arrangements and future needs for Britain's police (see Chapter 4). Specifically plans were announced to establish a new College of Policing in the UK Its objectives will be to:

> protect the public interest, enhance policing standards, identify evidence of what works in policing and share best practice ... support the education and professional development of staff and officers and ... motivate the police and partners to work together to achieve a shared purpose, including taking a major role in shaping the work of the higher education sector to improve the broader body of evidence on which policing professionals rely.
>
> (Home Office 2012)

Among his recommendations, Neyroud advocated the establishment of a new body to allow for 'the phasing out of a complex and convoluted governance structure for overseeing police leadership and training that has evolved over the last 100 years' (2010: 11). While acknowledging a number of key strengths in the British system, including a strong reputation in international police training, Neyroud observed a number of significant limitations. Importantly, he recognised that 'the relationship between police education and practice and higher education has not reached the level of embedded partnership that it has done in medicine or education' (p. 81), highlighting that there is much to learn from more mature professions about the strategic delivery of education and training. Other noted deficiencies included a frequent duplication of content within courses, a reliance on costly in-house training with little input from external providers, and a lack of systematic evaluation of training effectiveness. It is proposed that there needs to be a shift away from in-house, classroom-based training, towards a more flexible approach which places more responsibility for professional development on individuals, and more emphasis on partnership with further and higher education.

While recognising the insularity of the current arrangements, it is notable that the review itself looks inwardly at the police service's leadership and training strengths and weaknesses, and not outwardly towards effective models or lessons learned in other sectors. It appears to mark, for the police service, the beginning of a well-trodden 'professionalisation' journey that numerous occupational disciplines have followed. As the College begins to take shape in 2013, its architects should take note of arrangements and issues in other occupational disciplines, including those involving similar skills and competencies such as the military and the private security sector.

Private security is the focus of this chapter, a sector that confronts well publicised limitations associated with typically low profit margins in the commercial sphere, while also striving for improvement as a route to competitive advantage in an increasingly wide-ranging and complex market for security. It comprises those employed to deliver the security function within public or private sector organisations ('corporate security', also referred to as the 'end user'), as well as the vendors of such goods and services, supplying governmental, corporate or private clients ('commercial security', also referred to as the 'supplier'), and indeed it should be noted that the terminology 'private security' is far more commonly employed by external observers of the sector than those within it. In the forthcoming sections we consider the development of security practitioners at the management and operative level in turn, with reference to arrangements in the UK. The discussion is framed around the dual processes of professionalisation and regulation, the former concerned with the raising of individual standards at the management levels of security practice, and the latter about establishing minimum collective standards among frontline operatives.

Developing the security manager

This first section considers the extent to which security management can be considered a profession, beginning with a discussion of the characteristics of security managers. We examine the core elements of a profession as they apply to security in order to assess its maturity in this respect. These elements are identified as being the presence of defined standards and ethical codes, an established knowledge/evidence base, recognised associations, measurable competencies along with appropriate certification programmes, and an educational discipline (Simonsen 1996).

The 'typical' security manager?

Former police, military and intelligence personnel have traditionally made up a large proportion of security managers, and continue to do so. Thus, private security is very much a sister discipline to the police, at least at the management levels. Research studies carried out in the UK (Hearnden 1993) and US (Armstrong Whiting and Cavanagh 2003) suggest that somewhere between 60 and 75 per cent of security managers derive from these public sector disciplines. They are occupations with condensed career timelines, with many retiring early and seeking new opportunities, as well as relatively limited scope for interorganisational mobility (McElroy *et al.* 1999). Security is a popular second career choice for those coming from such backgrounds, and the obvious functional overlap between public and private security ensures that their skill sets are valued in the private sector. Indeed, as public and private security evolve hand in hand, in response to a common threat environment, public security personnel working in emerging specialist areas may well find opportunities to pursue similar specialisms in the private sector.

In the UK, austerity budgets are now challenging the tradition of policing being a career occupation. At the time of writing, at the close of summer 2012 and London's Olympics and Paralympics, substantial redundancies are anticipated (BBC News, 29 June 2012), and it is possible that growing numbers of outgoing police officers will consider a security career. At the same time, increased outsourcing of police functions to the private sector could well become a tempting strategy for police leaders being required to 'do more with less', as may be a shift towards greater multi-agency working. Both trends are likely to strengthen the association between the police and private security even further, and illustrate the transferability of knowledge and skills between the two disciplines.

The respective value of different disciplinary backgrounds or routes into private security is frequently debated. As Briggs and Edwards (2006) observe, it is unsurprising that security employers rely so heavily on individuals with public security backgrounds, given the wealth of training and experience they gain that is rarely available elsewhere. Indeed the continuous flow of well-trained, former public sector personnel into private security has perhaps become so taken for granted as to limit the appetite for professional development within this sector. Noting, 'the absence of any formal or recognised qualification for security management, and … the paucity of knowledge about corporate security within most boardrooms', Briggs and Edwards point out that 'this is a pretty logical form of quality control for companies to adopt' (p. 79). Yet they are not alone in arguing that a greater diversity of new entrants to the profession, including more emphasis on business and strategic skills, is important for its future (see also Gill *et al.* 2007; Button 2008).

Many of the key considerations are synthesised in a model proposed by Gill *et al.* (2007). Summarised in Table 15.1, it is based around two hypothetical types of manager, described as 'traditionalists' (associated with police and military expertise), and 'modern entrepreneurs' (associated with a business centred approach), intended to convey two extremes on a continuum rather than representing particular stereotypes.

The model usefully captures the realities of contemporary security practice whereby, in an increasingly complex and risky business environment, it should

Table 15.1 Security 'traditionalists' versus 'modern entrepreneurs'

Traditionalists	Modern entrepreneurs
◄———————————————————————————————————►	
Security is:	*Security is:*
• A discrete service function	• Part of the business process
• A necessary cost on bottom line	• Integral to all activities and embedded in
• Associated with police and military	culture and process
expertise	• Managed strategically
• Delivered through command and control	• Measured in terms of return on investment
• Measured using traditional indicators	• More reliant on business acumen than
such as arrest rates	security knowledge

be aligned as closely as possible with the corporate objectives it serves, and act as a business enabler. Good business skills are vital when corporate chief security officers need to act primarily as business people, and those running commercial security companies face an increasingly competitive marketplace as well as an increasingly complex and regulated business environment. Such skills are often lacking in public sector personnel and may need to be learned.

At the more tactical and operational levels of security practice, core public security skill sets such as protective security, investigations and intelligence remain central to the services being provided. This dependence on the skills, experience and even reputations of former public sector employees is reinforced by private security's limited track record in developing its personnel, a topic of further discussion below.

Defining security professionalism

Evetts *et al.* define a profession as 'the main form of an institutionalization of expertise in industrialized countries' (2006: 105), and associate professions primarily with knowledge-based occupations that are typically grounded in university education and vocational training and experience. They highlight the importance of expert knowledge in today's world, characterised by uncertainty and risk. While knowledge, provided by human capital and advanced technology, has always been central to economic development, advanced industrial societies are today more dependent than ever before on the production, distribution and application of knowledge. Investment is now predominantly directed towards knowledge assets, such as research and development, software, human capital and organisational capital (institutionalised knowledge), than physical assets such as buildings and machinery. Thus, as Evetts *et al.* observe, professionals are heavily involved in assessing and managing risks (such as legal, financial or health risks) and helping customers deal with uncertainty.

Larson's (1977) concept of the 'professional project' refers to the combined efforts of occupational collectives to define themselves, raise their professional status and insulate themselves from the wider labour market. For example, a study by Howe (1986) documented social workers' efforts in the 1970s and 1980s to construct their tasks as professional and intellectually complex in nature, and even to 'ditch the dirty work' – shifting the focus from the less glamorous aspects of the activity towards the more sophisticated. Larson herself was critical of such efforts, seeing them as motivated solely by self-interested aims to monopolise the labour market and win the spoils of doing so, but today professionalism is largely seen as having great normative value. Indeed, Evetts *et al.* draw attention to the wide ranging use of the 'profession' concept today: in advertising to attract customers, in company mission statements to motivate employees, by occupational groups wanting to be labelled as professionals, and in management literature and continuing professional development (CPD) programmes.

Private security suffers from frequent public portrayals that it is *un*professional. Notably, Briggs (2005) describes the security community as 'secretive and closed', operating on a 'strictly need-to-know' basis. Consequently, she argues, they are held back by security professionals' general lack of engagement with public debates, so that 'non-security experts have set the tone of debates and their perceptions and assumptions have been allowed to go unchecked' (p. 34). The activities of the private sector, as a result, tend to gain most attention in the media and politics when something goes wrong. The shortage of security officers and the low calibre of many of those employed by G4S in its poor handling of the security guarding contract for the London Olympics (*Guardian* 2012b) cast the UK commercial security sector in a highly negative light in a media story that played out for some time, while the government's arguably equally poor management of the procurement arrangements gained relatively little attention. Similarly, the most extreme cases of misconduct concerning armed private security personnel operating in hostile environments overseas, such as the Blackwater shootings of Iraqi civilians or the drunken shooting by a British Armourgroup contractor of two of his colleagues following an altercation (*Guardian* 2012a, 2011) have intensified social concern about this segment of private security and the need for its regulation.

As Briggs (2005) argues, this is an issue that the sector needs to address by engaging with the media in a much more open and meaningful way. The real picture, falling largely under the public radar, is that the scope of security practice is expanding and diversifying in the same way as policing, defence and intelligence work in response to the greater priority now being attached to counter-terrorism, protection of the critical infrastructure and contingency planning at home, and the opportunities opening up around the globe, particularly in settings with high security risk. In fact, Borodzicz and Gibson (2006) argue that the disparate nature of contemporary professional security makes it difficult to define, with many of its activities carrying other labels, while it ranges from:

> the management of situational crime through crisis management, consequence management, business continuity management, resilience management, internal audit, health and safety functions to insurance, counter-terrorism,

kidnap and rescue, private information brokering, security consultancy, and the increasingly critical cyber security and protection of critical infrastructure.

(p. 181)

An increasingly complex and diverse field of practice, private security has had its own 'professional project' for some time, driven by the demand for a widening range of skill sets, and the continuing supply of security practitioners seeking to differentiate themselves within the labour market. McGee (2006) argues, however, that the sector suffers from its 'esoteric' nature, pointing to the considerable variation between organisations in the security manager's job, the lack of a clear, common understanding as to the role – or potential contribution – of a security department, the absence (at the time of writing) of a set of competencies reflecting the needs of industry and forming a basis for professional qualifications, and the absence of a 'discernable theoretical core' to bind the profession together (p. 124).

Despite these limitations, Simonsen had already argued that security management *could* be considered a profession. He presented the following typology of a profession, drawn from the wider sociological literature, and argued that these five core elements were present in security:

1   Defined standards and a code of ethics;
2   An established knowledge base including professional journals;
3   Recognised association(s) as a forum for discussion and development of the profession;
4   A measurable set of competencies along with appropriate certification programmes; and
5   An educational discipline preparing the student in the profession's specific functions and philosophies.

In the remainder of this section, we discuss the degree of professionalisation that characterises security today with reference to Simonsen's five categories.

Defined standards and a code of ethics

As Simonsen (1996) recognises, uniformity of standards is difficult in security given the breadth of the field. Standards are documents setting out requirements, specifications or guidelines, for the purpose of ensuring that goods or services are fit for purpose, providing reassurance to customers through certification, supporting international trade by enabling suppliers globally to work to common specifications, and supporting business efficiency by maximising quality, reliability and productivity.

The most prominent standards organisation is the International Organization for Standardization (ISO), while numerous regional organisations (such as the British Standards Institute [BSI], the American National Standards Institute [ANSI] and the European Standards Organisations CEN, CENELEC and ETSI) and sector specific bodies also exist, and seek to be compatible with ISO standards. Popular standards include the ISO 9000 quality management family of standards, concerned with organisational performance, the ISO 31000 risk management standard supporting effective corporate governance and, in the UK, among the vast array of security specific standards, BS 7858 concerning the security screening of individuals and BS 7499 for the training of security officers. The member and trade associations of the UK security industry play a major role in determining security standards with, for example, ASIS International closely involved in the development ANSI security standards, and the British Security Industry Association (BSIA) and the Security Institute represented on BSI committees. Standards differ from regulations in that they are voluntary, although they become mandatory if required in a government or business contract, for example.

Defined codes of professional ethics serve a very different function, applying to individual practice. Their value is in setting out professional standards, promoting integrity, and acting as a basis for codes of conduct and related disciplinary processes to provide a means of professional regulation. One example of a code of ethics applying to the security profession is provided by ASIS International (2010), while the UK's new Chartered Security Professionals Registration Authority (CSPRA) has opted for a compliance based approach to cover the Chartered Security Professionals in the form of a code of conduct (Chartered Security Professionals Registration Authority 2012). Yet the mere existence of ethical standards does not convey that an occupational discipline is professional: what matters is the extent to which these are embedded in professional practice. In private security, ethics and integrity are fundamental personal qualities, because of security practitioners' responsibilities to protect and the trust being placed in them to do so. It is doubtful that the majority of practitioners with a public security background leave their public service values at the door when moving into the private sector, so potentially the sector could make much more of these core strengths and their symbolic value by placing, through its member associations, ethical values more firmly and visibly at the core of professional practice.

An established knowledge base including professional journals

The security discipline is young: relevant academic literature remains relatively scant and academic courses relatively few in number, although a gradual increase in provision is occurring in both areas. Compared with longer established professional disciplines such as medicine and law, the body of research-based knowledge is highly limited, hindering the sector's ability to identify and promote best practice and introduce it to students on university courses. There are only two academic journals targeted directly at the security profession (*Security Journal* and the *Journal of Applied Security Research*), core literature is primarily grounded in criminology and international relations and skewed by academic agendas, and research-active academics with a direct interest in private security are few in number.

Recognised association(s) as a forum for discussion and development of the profession

ASIS International, the leading global member association for security professionals, continues to do much at the global level to promote standards, training, education and research, promoted through its chapters around the world. Numerous other professional bodies represent segments of the sector, including national collectives such as the UK's Security Institute, the Australasian Council of Security Professionals, the South African Institute of Security and the Canadian Council of Security Professionals, each of which share with ASIS a focus on raising professional standards, acting as a voice for the sector on policy matters, and providing a range of member benefits.

There are many others, too numerous to mention. Those in the UK alone include industry specific groups such as the Pharmaceutical Industry Security Forum, the Institute of Hotel Security and the Association of University Chief Security Officers; occupational sub-groups such as the Association of Security Consultants, the Institute of Information Security Professionals and the Association of British Investigators; and other distinct groups such as the Risk and Security Management Forum (for corporate heads of security) and EPIC (Ex-Police in Industry and Commerce). The security sector has a well evidenced capacity to come together collectively, identify its boundaries and promote common aims. Yet the diversity of bodies and interest groups may be a limiting factor in its advancement, undermining the ability to demonstrate a critical mass. And as argued above, it is largely failing to engage meaningfully in public discourse, remaining a somewhat secretive and closed community, leaving it especially vulnerable to media and political criticism.

The existence of so many different professional bodies raises the question as to where the demand for them comes from. They clearly fill a niche in enabling knowledge sharing, networking and personal development in the generalist and specialist areas that they cover. Certainly, in private security, strong personal networks are a necessity as a means of gaining the intelligence that enables it to function effectively, and such networks rely on positive working relationships and trust between members.

A measurable set of competencies along with appropriate certification programmes

The Chartered Institute of Personnel and Development (2011) observes how competency frameworks have gained a growing importance within human resources practice since the concept of competencies emerged in the early 1980s. In that decade, training, skills and managerial excellence came to be seen as the key to competitive advantage, leading to the creation of a National Vocational Qualifications (NVQ) framework in the UK, and the establishment of occupational standards in the UK and US. Skills for Security is one of a number of Sector Skills Councils created in the UK to represent employers in addressing skills needs. This has created an array of National Occupational Standards for security intended to guide employers and training providers. The establishment of the Register of Chartered Security Professionals in 2011 launched a further set of competencies to cover the strategic and senior operational levels of the profession, intended to be generalisable across all areas of security.

With respect to certified training, the reliance of the private security sector on public security skill sets, discussed above, is perpetuated by the absence of any kind of compulsory training standards (Button 2011), such experience being highly valued in their absence. There are certain types of licences for security managers, but most security managers do not require these and none have a specialist training requirement. Furthermore, many security managers do not possess any specific security vocational training qualification. There are courses such as the ASIS Certified Protection Professional (CPP), with a strong reputation in the United States and among American employers, and the Security Institute's Certificate and Diploma courses (which took over from the International Institute of Security's courses when these two institutes merged in 2008), run from the UK by distance learning and attracting overseas as well as home students. Yet in the UK, the absence of any common expectations concerning security training (or education) at the management level means that the key agents for cultural change and professional development do not have to have an academic or professional qualification, and many do not.

This arguably conveys to lower ranks, and the wider labour market, that higher qualifications are not necessary for entry to, or progression within, security. Furthermore, employer schemes that train security personnel on the job, such as graduate trainee positions or apprenticeships are relatively rare, although Skills for Security (2012) has done much to promote the latter. Indeed, there is support for change, in the form of the championing of education by the professional bodies, most recently conveyed by the presence of an educational route to CSPRA registration among the two entry pathways. Chartered Security Professionals also have to commit to participation in an annual continuing professional development (CPD) programme, in line with other chartered bodies, in recognition of the need for individuals to maintain the occupational relevance of their knowledge, skills and competencies in a fast changing world.

An educational discipline preparing the student in the profession's specific functions and philosophies

As previously observed, security is a young academic discipline, the knowledge base remaining scant in the absence of a significant body of specialist researchers. Good quality security education is dependent on such a knowledge base, as well as regular communication between the universities providing academic courses and stakeholders in the security profession to determine curricula that are appropriate to their requirements. In the UK, this does not yet happen in a formalised manner, as occurs in a number of more established disciplines such as engineering and psychology, whereby the chartered bodies associated with those professions accredit university degrees that comply with their recommended curriculum frameworks. On the positive side, the number of security related degree courses serving the sector is slowly growing, indicating that there is increasing demand for a security education.

University curricula in security management have thus evolved in a less formal way, although the establishment of security's own chartered professional body provides a structure within which accreditation of university courses would be able to evolve. One model that proposes a set of subject benchmarks for a security curriculum is advanced by Brooks (2010), who identifies 13 core 'knowledge categories' in corporate or organisational security. To establish his 'integrated science of security framework', depicted in Figure 15.1, he conducted a survey of the content of 104 university security-related degree courses, and used his findings to adapt an existing framework devised in a partnership project by the Australian government and security industry (Bazzina 2006).

The model distinguishes between 'core security knowledge categories', ranging from 'risk management' and 'BCM' (business continuity management) to 'industrial' (industry specific security), and 'allied supporting concepts'such as law and criminology. Brooks' approach in developing the framework was commendably thorough, although the relevance of his findings is limited by the constraints of his methodology, based on the supply of (overwhelmingly American) degree courses and their existing curricula, as opposed to an assessment of the demands of the (international) marketplace.

Access to security education within the UK is being made easier and cheaper by means of the increasing use of accredited prior learning across the education and training sectors. The government now employs three qualifications frameworks (the National Qualifications Framework for qualifications awarded by government regulators, the Qualifications Credit Framework for vocational qualifications and the Framework for Higher Education for university qualifications) which adopt common levels from entry level to level 8, and enable the mapping of vocational qualifications to educational qualifications. The purpose of this is to make a student's progression through the vocational and educational systems

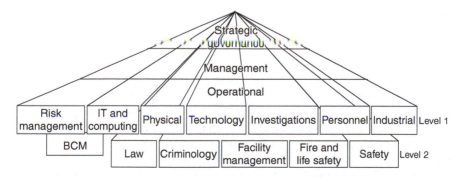

Figure 15.1 Brooks' (2010) integrated science of security framework.

more streamlined, as it enables them to demonstrate more easily the level of attainment they have reached and sometimes to transfer credits to higher level courses. Universities increasingly recognise vocational qualifications in their admissions criteria for degree courses, and can sometimes exempt students from certain course modules through accredited prior learning (APL) schemes. Such mapping is of value to the quality control processes associated with both, as it defines the minimum and maximum standards associated with each level of qualification.

Summary

The security sector has many champions and has come a long way. Yet its breadth, and the plethora of security functions, makes it difficult to consider as a single unit (Simonsen 1996). Private security's 'professional project' has consequently been hindered by a lack of overall co-ordination and common purpose, and has a long way still to go. The sector's reliance on the prior training and experience the majority of candidates have gained in the police, military or intelligence services limits accessibility to the sector across the labour market as a whole, and the value being placed from within on higher vocational and educational qualifications as well as employer training and development schemes. This has made progression pathways in security management unclear. There is greater consistency in the training of frontline security operatives, due to the requirements of the sector's regulatory regime, to which we now turn.

Developing the security operative

As previously observed, the standards and training of lower level security operatives became a very public issue in the UK in July 2012 when G4S, the world's largest security company, failed to meet the terms of its contract with the London Organising Committee of the Olympic and Paralympic Games (LOCOG) with respect both to the number and quality of personnel they were able to mobilise for such a large event. This episode highlighted a number of problems with the management of security at the Olympics that were not limited to the actions of G4S. Prominent, however, among the issues demonstrated was the importance of selecting adequate candidates and establishing and maintaining a sufficient level of training at the frontline of security, not least when working to an official terrorist threat level of 'severe'.

The UK was relatively late in comparison with other developed countries in introducing statutory minimum standards to its security sector, and the quality of baseline training of security operatives needs to be considered as part of the wider debate about the adequacy of such regulation, and what minimum standards *should* look like. In 2001, after many years of campaigning, regulation of the private security industry in England and Wales was introduced with the Private Security Industry Act 2001. The legislation was subsequently extended to the rest of the UK and, amongst many other requirements, paved the way for statutory minimum standards of training in some, but not all security occupations (Button 2008).

The legislation was introduced for a number of reasons: to stamp out criminality, to improve accountability and to raise standards, particularly those of training, to name the most important (Button and George 2006). The situation before licensing, for some occupations in the security industry, had been very mixed in terms of standards: generally low voluntary industry training standards complied with by the majority prevailed, combined with some pockets of excellence exceeding these, but there were also significant numbers of personnel not even receiving basic industry training (House of Commons Home Affairs Committee 1995; George and Button 2000). This varied between different security occupations, which will now be illustrated.

Baseline training before and after the Act

Table 15.2 illustrates the situation before and after the 2001 legislation for the principal security occupations. For security officers the standards have not risen significantly, but those minimum standards are at least now compulsory. Thus, in the security guarding sector there has at least been a levelling off at a slightly higher level for all officers (increase of 16 to 26 hours' mandatory training), bar those employed 'in-house'. Indeed, the absence of compulsory licensing for in-house security officers (those employed directly by organisations rather than by commercial security companies) is a controversial feature of the legislation, although some do voluntarily become licensed.

The biggest success for licensing and training has arguably been for door supervisors. Surveys of this sector of the industry have indicated perceptions of generally positive change by both suppliers and operatives (Security Industry Authority 2007; Security Industry Authority 2010; National Doorwatch 2011), although problems with the regulation of training have been highlighted (Panorama 2008; Curran 2008; Richards 2009). Both in-house and contract personnel require licences in this sphere of the security industry, and the current regime has replaced a mix of standards that existed prior to the legislation. Before the Act, some local authorities operated compulsory registration schemes linked to their licensing powers which in most cases set basic training, although frequently of only a few hours. There were also many areas that did not have door registration schemes (George and Button 2000; Lister *et al.* 2001). Following the Act, all door supervisors require a licence and the training provision amounts to 38 hours.

For close protection officers (CPOs), regulation could be viewed as actually having lowered standards. Prior to the legislation, the sector was dominated by former police and military CPOs who would have undergone extensive training well beyond current industry standards. To become a CPO was a difficult job to secure without that type of background. There were some other private courses, such as those of the International Bodyguard Association, but they were not undertaken by significant numbers. Subsequent to the Act, CPOs are required to complete compulsory minimum training and, at 146 hours, it is the most demanding of all mandatory training courses. This falls well below police and military standards of training, however, and the advent of SIA mandated training has encouraged more training providers to offer the courses, arguably leading to a dumbing down of overall standards. Survey research by White and Smith (2009: 65) indicated that a higher than average number of respondents in this sector compared with others in the survey perceived a decline in wage levels, skill levels and quality standards in general *after* its regulation.

There are also SIA licences for cash and valuables in transit, public space surveillance (CCTV), key holding and vehicle immobilisers.

The private investigation sector (along with precognition agents, who interview witnesses in Scotland on behalf of defence solicitors) was included in the 2001 legislation, but the provisions have never been implemented. This would look likely to change following the revelations concerning the conduct of some private investigators in relation to the Leverson Inquiry and the House of Commons Home Affairs Committee Report on Private Investigators (2012). It remains to be seen whether licensing, if introduced, will extend to compulsory training qualifications for investigators. The lack of intervention means that training norms for private investigators remain similar to those before the 2001 Act, whereby most private investigators do not have a specific training qualification, many coming from public investigatory bodies such as the police and relying upon their past training. Some, in the absence of such backgrounds, learn on the job. A minority undertake one of the training courses offered by the main professional bodies, the Institute of Professional Investigators (IPI) and the Association of British Investigators (ABI). Following the SIA legislation the ABI has become more interested in training, picking up on preliminary work by the SIA for the licensing of this sector which was never implemented in order to create a level 3 qualification in professional investigation (Association of British Investigators, n.d.). Nevertheless, take-up of such qualifications is still low in the sector.

Security consultants were another occupation included in the 2001 legislation. As with private investigators, the provisions for licensing have never been effected, but unlike the latter there is little prospect of the legislation been implemented. Security consultancy is an occupation which provides advice on a wide range of security issues. Expertise may be drawn from a diverse range of security disciplines which have their own training and qualifications structures. Before the 2001 Act there were no specific security consultancy courses attracting national recognition. Post 2001, Skills for Security introduced a level 5 Certified Security Consultant course accredited by the Institute of Risk Management and Buckinghamshire New University. Control Risks in partnership with Leeds City College also offer a Security Managers and Consulants foundation degree. The extent of take up of these awards is difficult to determine with limited research taking place, but typically security consultants do not possess specific qualifications in security consultancy.

There are also some general problems and issues applying to all of the security industry training. In the sectors where there is compulsory training,

Table 15.2 The state of training for key security occupations pre- and post 2001 legislation

Security occupation	Pre-2001	Post 2001
Security officer	Voluntary industry training standard of two days off the job. Most big companies complied 'most of the time'. Significant element not complying.	Compulsory training. Level 2 Security Guarding Qualification. SIA minimum of 26 hours. *In-house officers exempt.*
Door supervisor	Various local authority-led standards. Very mixed picture, but significant numbers with no training.	Compulsory training. Level 2 Door Supervision. SIA minimum of 38 hours.
Close protection officer	No industry standard course. Many CPOs coming from police/military roles with prior training. Some courses available at time through Task International and International Bodyguard Association	Compulsory training. Level 3 Certificate in Close Protection. SIA minimum of 146 hours. *In-house officers exempt.*
Private investigator	No national standards. Institute of Professional Investigators offered course, with limited uptake. Most private investigators using past experience training from police and related careers and on-the-job training.	*Licensing of private investigators not implemented.* Same structure exists plus addition of Association of British Investigators training course.
Security consultant	No dedicated courses	*No compulsory training implemented.* Level 5 Certified Security Consultant course Level 5 Security Managers and Consultants course

Sources: George and Button (2000); Security Industry Authority (2012b:24).

there have been regular exposés ranging from instances of poor practice to those of outright fraud amongst some of the training providers. Much of this stems from the system that was introduced, which allows training companies to determine whether a candidate has met the required minimum standard. Evidence has emerged of training companies failing to take seriously the administration of examinations testing what are already very basic standards (for example, allowing cheating or giving hints for answers) (Panorama 2008; *Guardian* 2012c). The structure created would be the equivalent of allowing driving instructors to administer the driving test rather than an independent government agency, a situation that would never be tolerated since it would undoubtedly lead to many candidates been passed when they should not. This is being allowed to happen with security officer training, however, undermining those companies who do follow the rules, and exacerbating already minimum standards.

It is also important to note that the compulsory training standards in comparison to most European countries and some Canadian and Australian states are lower (see Sarre and Prenzler 2005; Button 2007a; Prenzler and Sarre 2008; Palmer and Button 2011). In many European countries the minimum standards for entry occupations such as security officers are in the hundreds of hours of training before working in the industry is allowed (Button 2007a). There are also frequently standards for specialist roles, supervisors and managers in these regimes too (Prenzler and Sarre 2008). Other than the USA, where minimum training standards are generally very low or non-existent, the UK is behind many industrialized countries.

The new regulatory regime?

The UK security industry now faces a degree of uncertainty over the future of regulation for the private security industry. With the passage of the 2001 Private Security Industry Act, a consensus had emerged on the benefits of regulation and any debates concerned only the shape of it (White 2010). This seemed to be shattered by the country's new Conservative/Liberal Democrat coalition government in October 2010, when a review of Government 'quangos' ('quasi-automonous non-governmental organisations', that is, arm's length public bodies of which the SIA is one) was published in which the SIA was marked among a number earmarked to be dissolved, and replaced by a 'phased transition to new regulatory regime'. In fact, security press journalists had received a press release the evening before suggesting the SIA was to be abolished completely, with the industry deregulated, but this was quickly changed to the statement above (SMT Online, 2011). A hastily mobilised organisation called the Security Alliance (consisting of the sector's leading representative bodies, the British Security Industry Association, the Security Institute, UK ASIS Chapter and the Worshipful Company of Security Professionals) has, however, been effective in championing the case to keep the SIA or a version of it.

Proposals have begun to emerge to put flesh on the 'new regulatory regime' (Security Industry Authority 2012a), but its development was placed on hold through the immediate period of preparation prior to London's hosting of the Olympic Games, which placed a heavy reliance on private security personnel. Amongst the changes being discussed, it is possible that the emphasis on licensing will shift from the individual to businesses, which 'could' mean:

> ...that the terms and conditions of business licensing will also include a requirement for the business to ensure a registration process is carried out for employees that confirms their identity, address history, right to work, qualifications and a criminal record check.
>
> (Security Industry Authority 2012a)

There may thus be a risk that the new regime will not have compulsory training standards, which would be a major step backwards. But even if they do remain, if the requirement for licensing individuals moves from the regulator to the company there will be opportunities to cut corners in the companies by not completing all that is required. The pressures of the highly competitive security market will invariably push some to bend or break the rules as has been frequently exposed in the training providers (as discussed above). Such opportunities for cutting corners with individual licensing are limited under the current regime. Whether there will be any shift in the government's position following the storm over the G4S handling of the Olympic security remains to be seen.

Summary

In contrast with the more senior levels of the security sector, statutory minimum training standards exist in the UK for security officers, door supervisors and close protection officers and other types of frontline operative. There is no doubt that statutory regulation of private security in the UK has raised standards. The lack of independent oversight of training is a concern, however, and it is difficult to estimate the extent to which the bending of rules by training providers occurs. With the future shape of regulation in the UK still to be confirmed, it is difficult to know what the future will hold, but the proposed shift towards licensing by businesses is an area of concern, as it would reduce independent oversight still further.

Statutory requirements are of course not the only drivers of quality at the frontline of security. Pay levels, working conditions, the prospect of interesting work and the potential for advancement all impact on the appeal of a security operative career (Wakefield, 2003). The continuing promotion of professionalism in security by the sector's member associations, particularly with respect to the upper levels of security practice, should be seen as a positive trend all round. Lower ranking officers need to be able to see what they can aspire to, in order for quality applicants to take an interest in security. The growing number of security managers valuing education, higher level vocational training and continuing professional development can only be positive for the sector as a whole.

Conclusion

Private security naturally operates very differently to policing, being driven by market forces as opposed to the requirements of a bureaucratic organisation. Policing, as a frontline public service, places a strong emphasis on training and development in order to prepare officers formally in the basics of the job, specialist tasks and management functions. This serves the private security sector very well, as it relies heavily on the prior training and experience of its ex-police, ex-military or ex-intellgence services entrants.

There is a substantial supporting industry in security training and education which, in the UK, ranges from the mandatory level 2 training for different categories of frontline security operative, to more advanced vocational training up to level 5, to university degrees. These arrangements are piecemeal in that, other than the baseline training of security operatives, there is no standard approach to training or education, no general expectation of practitioners to hold specific qualifications, and limited investment by employers in the training and development of their personnel. The accreditation of many vocational courses in accordance with the Qualifications Credit Framework makes them meaningful and aids student progression through the educational/training system, but there remain areas of training and education where standards could be improved. At the lower (level 2) end, these concern the integrity and regulation of some training providers. At university level, specialist courses are limited in number and the relationship between the universities and the sector's professional bodies could be much closer, in order to ensure that curricula reflect the specific knowledge and skill sets ideally required of a twenty-first-century security practitioner.

Neyroud's (2010) review suggests that the current limitations of police development and training are at the other end of the spectrum, being too standardised, rigid and insular. He calls for an approach that places more onus on the individual police officer to steer his or her own professional development, and engages far more extensively with further and higher education. Those in security have relatively little access to training and development other than that initiated by themselves, although the growth of security related higher education courses is evidence of a healthy demand for this. What the security sector perhaps also lacks is a clear strategy for training, development and leadership, akin to the Neyroud review, which its professional bodies could develop, as a means of encouraging employers to place more emphasis on developing its personnel, and making progression pathways clearer to those interested in security careers.

References

Armstrong Whiting, M. and Cavanagh, T.E. (2003) *Corporate Security Management: Organization and Spending since 9/11*. New York: The Conference Board.

ASIS International (2010) *Code of Ethics*. Alexandria, VA: ASIS International. Retrieved 27 September 2012, from www.asisonline.org/membership/resources/codeofethics.pdf.

Association of British Investigators (n.d.) *The ABI Academy*. Retrieved 27 September 2012, from www.theabi.org.uk/training.

Bazzina, M. (2006) *Security Standards and Support Systems Report: A Collaborative Project Between the Commonwealth Attorney-General's Department and Standards Australia*. Sydney, NSW: Standards Australia International.

BBC News (2012) *Met Police: 'Clarity' sought over post-Games 'job cuts'*, 29 June. Retrieved 27 September 2012, from www.bbc.co.uk/news/uk-england-london-18646809.

Borodzicz, E. and Gibson, S.D. (2006) 'Corporate security education: towards meeting the challenge', *Security Journal*, 19(3):180–195.

Briggs, R. (2005) *Joining Forces: From National Security to Networked Security*. London: Demos. Retrieved 27 September 2012, from www.demos.co.uk/publications/joiningforcesbook.

Briggs, R. and Edwards, C. (2006) *The Business of Resilience: Corporate Security for the 21st Century*. London: Demos, available at: www.demos.co.uk/publications/thebusinessofresilience (accessed 27/9/12).

Brooks, D. (2010) 'What is security: definition through knowledge categorization', *Security Journal*, 23:225–239.

Button, M. (2007a) Assessing the regulation of private security across Europe. *European Journal of Criminology*, 4, 109–128.

Button, M. (2008) *Doing Security: Critical Reflections and an Agenda for Change*. Basingstoke: Palgrave.

Button, M. (2011) 'The Private Security Industry Act 2001 and the security management gap in the United Kingdom'. *Security Journal*, 24, pp. 118–132.

Button, M. and George, B. (2006) 'Regulation of security: new models for analysis.' In Gill, M. (ed.) *Handbook of Security*. Basingstoke: Palgrave.

Chartered Institute of Personnel Development (CIPD) (2011). *Competence and Competency Frameworks*. London: CIPD.

Chartered Security Professionals Registration Authority (2012) *Register of Chartered Security Professionals Code of Conduct*, London:CSPRA. Retrieved 27 September 2012, from www.csyp-register.org/about.

Curran, V. (2008) 'Door supervisors – a cause for concern?' *Professional Security*, 8 February. Retrieved 27 September 2012, from www.professionalsecurity.co.uk/news/news-archive/door-law/.

Evetts, J., Mieg, H.A. and Felt, U. (2006) 'Professionalization, scientific expertise, and elitism: a sociological perspective' in K.A. Ericsson, N. Charness, P.J. Feltovich and R.R. Hoffman (eds) *The Cambridge Handbook of Expertise and Expert Performance*. Cambridge: Cambridge University Press.

Gill, M., Burns-Howell, T., Keats, G. and Taylor, E. (2007) *Demonstrating the Value of Security*, Leicester: Perpetuity Research and Consultancy International (PRCI).

Guardian (2011) 'Briton Danny Fitzsimons jailed in Iraq for contractors' murders,' 28 February. Retrieved 27 September 2012, from www.guardian.co.uk/world/2011/feb/28/danny-fitzsimons-jailed-iraq-murders.

Guardian (2012a) 'Blackwater guards lose bid to appeal charges in Iraqi civilian shooting case,' 5 June 2012. Retrieved 27 September 2012, from www.guardian.co.uk/world/2012/jun/05/blackwater-guards-lose-appeal-iraq-shooting.

Guardian (2012b) 'G4S boss discovered Olympic security guard shortfall only a few days ago', 14 July. Retrieved 27 September 2012 from www.guardian.co.uk/sport/2012/jul/14/london-2012-olympic-security-g4s.

Guardian (2012c) 'G4S staff 'cheat' on tests to run x-ray scanners at Olympic Games'. 23 July. Retrieved 27 September, 2012 from www.guardian.co.uk/uk/2012/jul/23/g4s-x-ray-olympic-games.

Hearnden, K. (1993) *The Management of Security in the UK*. Loughborough: University of Loughborough.

Home Office (2012) *Police Professional Body* (press release 16 July), London: Home Office.

House of Commons Home Affairs Committee (HAC) (1995) *The Private Security Industry*. Vols I and II. HC 17. London: HMSO.

House of Commons Home Affairs Committee (HAC) (2012) *Private Investigators*. HC 100. London: The Stationery Office.

www.professionalsecurity.co.uk/news/news-archive/door-law/.

Larson, M.S. (1977) *The Rise of Professionalism: A Sociological Analysis*, Berkeley, CA: University of California Press.

Lister, S., Hadfield, P., Hobbs, D. and Winlow, S. (2001) Accounting for Bouncers: Occupational Licensing as a Mechanism for Regulation. *Criminal Justice*, 1: 363–384.

McElroy, J., Morrow, P. and Wardlow, T. (1999) 'A career stage analysis of police officer work commitment', *Journal of Criminal Justice*, 27(6):507–551.

McGee, A. (2006) *Corporate Security's Professional Project: An Examination of the Modern Condition of Corporate Security Management, and the Potential for Further Professionalisation of the Occupation*, MSc thesis, Shrivenham: Cranfield University.

National Doorwatch (2011) *National Doorwatch Consultation Survey*, Lincoln: National Doorwatch.

Neyroud, P. (2010) *Review of Police Leadership and Training*, London: Home Office.

Palmer, R. and Button, M. (2011) *Civilian private security services: their role, oversight and contribution to crime prevention and community safety*. Expert Group on Civilian Private Security Services, Oct 12–14. Vienna: United Nations Office on Drugs and Crime.

Panorama (2008) Britain's Protection Racket. Retrieved 27 September 2012 from http://news.bbc.co.uk/1/hi/programmes/panorama/7195775.stm.

Prenzler, T. and Sarre, R. (2008) Developing a Risk Profile and Model Regulatory System for the Security Industry. *Security Journal*, 21: 264–277.

Richards, R. (2009) 'Door thought', *Professional Security*, 20 May. Retrieved 27 September 2012 from www.professionalsecurity.co.uk/news/news-archive/door-thought/.

Sarre, R. and Prenzler, T. (2005). *The Law of Private Security in Australia.* Pyrmont, NSW: Thomson.

Security Industry Authority (2007) *The Impact of Licensing on Door Supervision and Security Guarding*. London: Home Office. Retrieved 27 September 2012, from www.sia.homeoffice.gov.uk/Documents/research/sia_ds_sg_research.pdf.

Security Industry Authority (2010) *The Impact of Regulation on the Door Supervision Sector*, London: SIA. Retrieved 27 September 2012, from www.sia.homeoffice.gov.uk/Documents/research/sia_ds_impact.pdf.

Security Industry Authority (2012a) *Future of Regulation – Factsheet*, London: SIA. Retrieved 27 September 2012, from www.sia.homeoffice.gov.uk/Documents/sia-future-factsheet.pdf.

Security Industry Authority (2012b) *Get Licensed: SIA Licensing Criteria*, London: SIA. Retrieved 27 September 2012, from www.sia.homeoffice.gov.uk/Documents/licensing/sia_get_licensed.pdf.

Simonsen, C. (1996) 'The case for: security management is a profession', *International Journal of Risk, Security and Crime Prevention*, 1(3):229–232.

Skills for Security (2012) *Apprenticeships in the Security Sector – Overview*, Worcester: Skills for Security.

SMT Online (2011) 'The SIA's future: how the private security industry was nearly 'quangoed', 19 October. Retrieved 27 September 2012, from www.info4security.com/story.asp?sectioncode=10&storycode=4125992.

Wakefield, A. (2003) *Selling Security: The Private Policing of Public Space*. Cullompton: Willan.

Wakefield, A. (2006) The Security Officer. In, Gill, M. (ed.) (2006) *The Handbook of Security*. Basingstoke: Palgrave.

White, A. (2010). *The Politics of Private Security*. Basingstoke: Palgrave.

16 Police training in America

Changes in the new millenium

A. Chappell

Introduction

Scholars have often referenced three eras when discussing changes in American policing over time: the political era, the reform era, and the community era (Kelling and Moore 1988). The political era, which spanned the 1800s and ended in the early 1900s, saw police who walked the streets and knew citizens well. Known for their 'watchman style', political era-police officers were connected to and engaged with their communities. They focused on keeping the peace, maintaining order, and catering to those in political positions. Police officers in that time had wide discretion and little supervision, which led to allegations of corruption and abuses of power.

Emerging in response to the problems that plagued watchman style police, the reform era espoused the 'professionalization' of the police and a 'legalistic' style of policing (Wilson 1968). Police agencies evolved into bureaucratic, legalistic entities with policies and procedures in place to control discretion and increase officer supervision. Legalistic police were aggressive law enforcers who, in the interest of equality, often neglected cultivating relationships with community residents. Police began to be formally trained as part of professionalization. Importantly, advances in technology made it possible for officers to patrol from police cars which led to a narrow focus on rapid response to calls for service. However, this damaged the relationship that had existed between the police and the public because officers were taken away from the neighborhoods and essentially policed from a distance.

In the 1960s, the US experienced significant social unrest, as well as a strained relationship between the police and the public. Increases in allegations of abuse, especially of minority citizens, combined with rising crime rates led to a crisis of legitimacy for the police (see Stanislas 2013 for British experience).

The community era

In an attempt to repair the broken relationship between the police and the public, the community era was born. Defined by its 'service' style, community policing aimed to rebuild partnerships with community members and solve the problems that caused criminal incidents (Kelling and Moore 1988; Wilson 1968). The idea was that community members should be involved in the identification and solution of problems that caused repeated criminal incidents. If the root problems could be solved, crime – and thus calls to the police – would decrease. Community-oriented policing and problem-solving became the dominant philosophy – if not practice – of police departments, and by 1997, most large police agencies had personnel assigned to community policing (Bureau of Justice Statistics 2000).

The 2001 terrorist attacks highlighted the lack of communication between federal agencies and questioned the extent to which local police agencies should be involved in counter-terrorism. Indeed, immediate changes occurred in some of the largest police departments. According to the former president of the International Association of Chiefs of Police (IACP): 'The fight against terrorism begins in our own backyards – our own communities, our own neighborhoods – and police chiefs need to prepare themselves, their officers, and their communities … against terrorism' (Glassock 2001). In the wake of 9/11, police departments have created departmental counter-terrorism units, added new responsibilities to their workload, and revised training (see NYPD chapter). Funds for community policing have decreased while funds for homeland security have increased. Given that history suggests that resources drive priorities, some have speculated that policing has moved into a new 'era' of sorts – one defined by homeland security (Oliver 2006).

Counter-terrorism has had a significant impact on the daily operations, and thus training, of many large law enforcement agencies such as the NYPD, site of the 9/11 attacks and recognized 'model' American police agency. The extent to which homeland security has impacted smaller departments is less clear, but with the federal government administering much of the training on such issues, many officers even in small agencies have received some counter-terrorism training. The current chapter is couched within the assumption that American policing is somewhat in flux – possibly moving toward a new era of policing but still unclear how it will materialize. Scholars agree that regardless of the extent to which homeland security will be integrated into police operations and training, community policing is here to stay (White and Escobar 2008).

Police education and training

Police reformers have long promoted higher education for police officers. In the early 1900s, Vollmer called for a college-educated police force. Later, the 1967 President's Commission on Law Enforcement and Administration of Justice and the Law Enforcement Assistance Administration (LEAA) recommended college degrees for all police officers. This led to the proliferation of criminal justice programs at American colleges and universities (Carter and Sapp 1990). Despite continued calls for a college-educated police force, currently only approximately 16 percent of police departments have a college requirement while the majority only require a high school diploma. Only 1 percent of all police departments require a four-year college degree, 9 percent require a two year degree, and 6 percent require 'some college' (Bureau of Justice Statistics 2010). However, improvements have been made. Even though the percentage of departments 'requiring' a degree is low, an estimated 25–30 percent of officers holds a 4-year college degree (Mayo 2006) and upwards of 65 percent has completed some college (Carter and Sapp 1990). In Virginia, approximately 33 percent of patrol officers had a two year degree or higher in 2007 (Chappell and Gibson 2008). The proportion of college-educated officers tends to be higher in larger police departments, but recruitment challenges – finding qualified candidates – make it difficult for departments to increase their educational requirement (see Fridell *et al.* 2002).

Concerns about college-educated police officers beg the question: Are college-educated police officers better at their jobs? Many studies have been conducted on this topic, and the findings are equivocal (Walker and Katz 2005). Some studies have shown that college education is beneficial for police work. For example, some studies show that college-educated officers are less likely to resort to use of force to resolve conflicts (Paoline and Terrill 2007; Worden 1990); others suggests that they have fewer citizen complaints and better supervisor evaluations (Roberg and Bonn 2004). College-educated officers also tend to be older and more mature, have better writing, communication, and critical thinking skills, and have a better knowledge of the criminal justice system (Worden 1990). It is also likely that college-educated officers have had more experience with diverse populations and exhibit more tolerance (White and Escobar 2008). Some research indicates that college-educated officers are less authoritarian and cynical (Regoli 1976; Roberg 1978) and have more flexible value systems (Hays *et al.* 2007). Further, commentators contend that as the public becomes more educated, police will need a higher level of education to keep pace and to maintain legitimacy. In sum, proponents of higher education for police officers believe that it is necessary for the development of values needed to exercise discretion fairly and equitably in a democratic society (Paterson 2011).

Some research suggests, however, that college education has little or negative impact, or is not necessary for the tasks of a police officer (see Worden 1990). There is a concern that requiring a college degree further complicates recruitment, limiting the pool of qualified applicants and disproportionately impacting minorities (White and Escobar 2008). Some research also suggests that college-educated officers may be more likely to become bored on the job (Eskridge 1989). Additionally, some argue that policing requires experiential knowledge, or 'on-the-job' training, rather than formal education (Roberg and Bonn 2004). Given the increased sophistication of community policing, technological advances, and future changes and challenges in policing, a college education is likely to continue to be a valued attribute of police personnel.

In the US, education and training are generally administered separately (Schafer and Boyd 2007), with education preparing students to succeed in a variety of occupations/professions by teaching students how to 'learn' and exercise critical thinking skills (Carter *et al.* 1989), and training focused on systematically building a specific skill set for a particular job. However, although police training – which is required in virtually every department – is distinct from the [higher] education contemporary training curricula include a variety of topics that go beyond skill building, as highlighted in Chapter 1. Indeed, recent developments in policing have led to more training and education in a wider range of knowledge areas that go beyond police 'mechanics'. For example, legal training, communications skills, and cultural diversity are more readily taught and understood as academic areas rather than skill sets. Due to the addition of knowledge areas, police training may be more effective if administered in an educational medium, by instructors who are skilled teachers rather than police trainers who are generally veteran officers. As training topics become more cognitive rather than task oriented, the distinction between education and training will be less clear (Chappell *et al.* 2010).

Academy training

Despite the obvious connection between police training and policing itself, changes to training practices have historically lagged behind changes in actual policing philosophies and practices (Chappell and Lanza-Kaduce 2004). In the political era, police officers learned how to do their jobs informally from seasoned officers. Allegations of corruption and abuse led to a series of reforms in the 1900s; one such reform was the introduction of formalized training requirements. However, as recently as 1965, only 15 percent of all police departments administered any training to their new recruits (White and Escobar 2008). At present, virtually every department requires some training, and training is generally required throughout an officer's career.

There are three types of training that occur for police officers: academy (recruit) training, field training, and in-service (on the job/continuing) training as highlighted by Berlin in Chapter 2. Academy training is administered either by a police department at the state, county, or municipal level, or by a college or university geared toward vocational training, such as a community college. Although police training facilities are sometimes operated by higher education institutions, it is important to note that police training is generally considered a vocational program rather than an academic program. States decide on the number of hours and requirements, and there is wide variation (Marion 1998). Nationwide, the average number of academy training hours is 761, or 19 weeks (Bureau of Justice Statistics 2009). In some cases recruits are hired prior to the academy and paid to attend (training is paid by the hiring department). In other cases, recruits pay their own way through the academy with hopes of being recruited after they have been trained and certified. Police officers are required to pass standardized state examinations in order to acquire their certification and begin work as a police officer (Chappell *et al.* 2010).

Reform-era recruit training focused primarily on the technical and mechanical aspects of acquiring physical skills, such as marksmanship, driving, defensive tactics, and first responder (Alpert and Dunham 1997), while neglecting 'softer' subjects like communication and problem-solving (Birzer 1999). Many academies, or police training centers, continue to train this way today. Recruits spend 90 percent of their training time honing physical skills even though only 10 percent of their job duties will require these competencies (Germann 1969; Mayhall *et al.* 1995). Since the widespread adoption of community policing, many training facilities have updated their curricula to more accurately reflect the daily task of police officers and increased coverage of topics such as problem-solving, crime prevention, community building, and interpersonal relations.

Although they vary by state and facility, typical academy curricula augment physical skill building exercises with the following topics: legal training, report writing, diversity, conflict management, community policing/problem-solving, and emergency preparedness. Other special topics, such as domestic disputes, hate crimes, and special populations (juveniles, mentally ill, elderly) may also be covered. Some topic areas are known as 'high liability' areas (e.g., driving, firearms training, defensive tactics, and first responder). This highlights the fact that police departments and officers can be held liable for 'failure to train' in the event that something bad happens and there is evidence of inadequate training. Indeed, liability has had a significant influence on training, leading to the standardization of curricula, examinations and certification (see Ross 2000). Certificate and licensure are developed and administered at the state level and exist to protect officers, municipalities and states from liability. While standardized training regimens protect officers and departments from lawsuits, they present problems for knowledge areas that are not so easily standardized (e.g., diversity).

As previously outlined police training is a socialization process that converts the recruits' values, beliefs, and behaviors. Recruits are exposed to a mix of formal and informal lessons in training. Not surprisingly, the formal and informal lessons may not converge; attitudes and beliefs learned from the training staff and policing peers may undermine the formal academy lessons.

Police trainers are crucial to the socialization of police recruits. They serve as mentors who model the accepted norms and behaviors in policing, often shared through experiential knowledge, or 'war stories'. According to Van Maanen (1973), war stories are delivered differently from the formal teachings. The environment is more egalitarian and recruits are allowed to take a break and join their superiors in laughter and fun. Research suggests that lessons transmitted in this environment may be more easily learned than information from a formal lecture. For example, one study showed that despite formal instruction in cultural effectiveness, informal messages were both sexist and racist (Marion 1998). A significant challenge confronting community policing training is that police trainers – many of whom are veteran officers trained before community policing was fully adopted – may not espouse the philosophy. Research shows that if trainers do not buy into the philosophy, it is unlikely to be effectively transmitted to recruits (Ford 2003).

Instructional methods (or delivery) in police training have been a focus of attention in recent years. Traditional training in the paramilitary police organization relied on a top down pedagogical style characterized by passive listening. In contrast, adult learning scholars advocate andragogy, which is interactive, self-directed learning with the instructor as a facilitator of the learning process. Andragogy is appropriate for adult learners and is more consistent with ideals of complex contemporary policing (Birzer 2003). Similarly, model police training programs have moved toward scenario-based training approaches. The idea is that scenarios better prepare officers for real life situations that in class/lecture formats cannot address. Contemporary training also incorporates video scenarios and interactive video programs that simulate real life police work and allow trainees to practice responding to unique situations in 'real time' (Schafer and Boyd 2007). Andragogy and scenarios, however, are less amendable to standardization and thus propose challenges in terms of testing, certification and liability in a bureaucratic environment (Schafer and Boyd 2007).

A model police training program

Training was slow to catch up with community policing, but now over 90 percent of police academies claim to be teaching recruits about the philosophy of community policing. The quality and quantity of that training varies widely even in the most innovative departments. Many large police departments, such as those in California, Florida, and Illinois, have paved the way toward the institutionalization of community policing through training. In Florida, the entire academy curriculum was revamped in the early 2000s to reflect community policing in a scenario based approach called Curriculum Maintenance System (CMS). Similarly, the Los Angeles (California) Police Department has updated their training which was the subject of an analysis by the RAND Corporation (Glenn *et al.* 2003). Below, we summarize that analysis to illustrate the new wave of police training the US.

The training philosophy of the LAPD is based on the assumption that training should reflect the working conditions of police officers. Recruits must not only learn content, but they should also learn how to interpret it and put it into practice. Importantly, they must adopt the practices so that they can be prepared and able to act quickly in unpredictable situations. Scenario based training helps concepts become second nature so that they are available when situations demand them. Glenn *et al.* (2003) discusses four elements addressed earlier by Berlin in his chapter that are fundamental to successful training and describe how each is integral to the LAPD training experience. They are 1. Contextualized learning, 2. Integration of topics throughout the curriculum, 3. Scenario building, and 4. Debriefing.

LAPD's new training regime reflects what the author's experienced in Florida in their observations of CMS recruit training. Florida's new curriculum included 40 hours of scenarios, debriefings, 'threading' of themes throughout the curriculum, and improved delivery methods. Scenarios were well received by the recruits; they captivated recruits' attention, which contributed to their effectiveness. We found that recruits were much more alert and involved in the scenario-based academy versus the former traditional academy. Scenarios brought the classroom lessons together and illustrated their relevance. For example, one exercise required recruits to consider how they would speak to a victim and a suspect, write a report, and follow proper arrest procedure in one scenario, which reflects the way policing naturally occurs in the field.

While traditional (reform) training focused on the technical and mechanical aspects of police work, community policing training aims to 'provide officers with a level of understanding which will allow them to effectively employ problem-solving and community engagement techniques in their daily work' (Peak and Glensor 2004: 166). This understanding is fostered by andragogy and scenario based training. However, while academy training can provide the foundation, it is imperative that the lessons are reinforced in the field.

Field training

After the completion of academy training and certification (i.e. passing state exam), recruits enter the field and complete a subsequent training program, known as field training. The majority of field training programs are administered by the hiring department, but some are operated by the training academy. Field training resembles an apprenticeship as the recruit goes 'on the street' with senior officers known as Field Training Officers (FTOs) who mentor and teach the recruit the norms and procedures of policing in that particular agency (Haberfield 2002). The San Jose Field Training Officer (FTO) program is the most widely recognized program of its kind. It began in 1972 in response to an incident in San Jose, California in which a rookie officer was badly injured and a citizen was killed due to the rookie's lack of training. The San Jose police department decided that rookies needed to have an 'information bridge' mentoring stage to transfer their knowledge from academy to the field.

The FTO model lasts approximately four months and consists of four week increments of training followed by an evaluation period (Haberfield 2002). Training occurs on each workday shift in various areas of the agency's jurisdiction. Recruits are assigned to different FTOs for each period in order to gain exposure to a variety of policing styles. Each FTO follows a specific curriculum; they are responsible for both teaching and evaluating the trainee on a particular set of skills and abilities. Generally, trainees' share of the police work increases as they progress through the FTO program; by the time they reach the final (evaluation) phase, the FTO acts solely as an observer and the trainee is responsible for 100 percent of the police work.

The FTO model was developed prior to the widespread adoption of community policing by American police agencies. It is likely that it is not well suited for reinforcing community policing lessons that may have been learned in the academy. Because field training occurs immediately after the academy, it is an ideal time to expose recruits to community policing and problem-solving in practice, thus linking training with practice (Haarr 2001). The effects of high quality academy training may dissipate if departments do not reinforce the lessons learned in the academy in field training (Mastrofski and Ritti 1995; see Haarr 2001).

Because the San Jose FTO program was not developed to teach community policing, the Police Executive Research Forum (PERF), the Office for Community Policing Services (COPS), and Reno, Nevada Police Department worked together to develop a new field training program known as the Police Training Officer (PTO) program. The PTO model incorporates adult learning principles, problem-solving, community relations, and shared responsibility (COPS office 2001). First implemented in 2001, it has since been tested and adopted by agencies in several states (Pitts *et al.* 2007). As of 2007, fewer than 60 agencies in Canada and the US use the PTO Program as the training method for newly hired officers. A recent study conducted on the understanding about and utilization of the PTO program by US law enforcement agencies found that while there remains to be a lack of awareness and understanding of the PTO program, impacts on program graduates have been positive. In particular, officers completing the PTO program were more likely to use creative, non-traditional solutions to problems, they felt empowered and confident, and they put considerable effort into following up with community members to proactively solve problems which led to increased community confidence in the police department. Evidence also suggested that this information and ability was retained and committed to long term memory (Rushing 2010). Wider adoption and implementation of the PTO program is the next step toward institutionalizing community policing in the US.

Both academy and field training have been making strides toward institutionalizing community policing and problem-solving. Progress has been slow, however and challenges continue, particularly in the current economic climate. Funds for community policing have decreased significantly in recent years as the war on terror has escalated, and funds for homeland security have increased (Oliver 2006). Given American policing's historic militaristic roots, the focus on counter-terrorism may present new challenges for community policing.

Continuing challenges: the paramilitary structure and culture

Military service has been a recruitment focus since Peel's original police force, and North American police agencies have long been organized in a paramilitary, bureaucratic fashion. Paramilitary, bureaucratic organizations are characterized by specialization, division of labor, vertical authority structures, and extensive rule systems (Willis *et al.* 2004). Even in the community era, police departments continue to be highly specialized, bureaucratic entities (Kraska and Cubellis 1997; Maguire 1997). Some research suggests that recent developments like CompStat (New York City's effort to hold officers and precinct commanders responsible for crime and quality of life issues) have extended the bureaucratic structure, and the proliferation of SWAT units, even in smaller departments, signifies an increase in paramilitarism. The recent shift to homeland security and counter-terrorism has also contributed to increased militarism in police agencies (Chappell and Lanza-Kaduce 2010).

Police training academies have followed suit. The most recent data suggest that the majority of recruits continue to be trained in 'stress academies', characterized by the incorporation of paramilitary drills, intense physical training, group punishments, and other militaristic rituals (Bureau of Justice Statistics 2009; Lundman 1980). Stress academy advocates believe that this approach promotes self-discipline which leads to better time management skills, increased likelihood of completing tasks, and rule-following. State, municipal, sheriff's, and county training academies are more likely than college/university academies to report having a stress orientation; however research has shown that even some college/university academies that report using a non-stress approach still promote a paramilitary environment and adopt 'boot camp' like rituals (see Chappell and Lanza-Kaduce 2010). For example, they focus on appearance, marching, punishment, and unquestioning obedience of commands from superiors (Schafer and Boyd, 2007; see Stanislas, Chapter 13).

The emphasis on chain of command, group punishments, and physical/emotional stress found in paramilitary organizations works to increase solidarity with one's peer group. In fact, researchers argue that few organizations instill the same degree of occupational identification as do the police (Britz 1997; Skolnick and Fyfe 1993). The police subculture helps recruits cope with the rigidity and intensity of training as they learn that they must count on each other for survival. It also fosters an 'us vs. them' mentality, as there is a shared perception of the dangerousness of police work and a related focus on officer safety that can only be understood by other police officers. Militaristic rules and discipline strengthen the cohesion and instill the belief that officers are isolated from citizens.

Community policing does not jibe with the paramilitary environment that continues to predominate in most police academies. Paramilitarism and community policing are antithetical (Stanislas, Chapter 13). While community policing advocates equal partnerships between the police and the public, the paramilitary structure fosters top down hierarchical relationships. Indeed, the police structure and culture have been recognized as the most significant obstacles to the institutionalization of community policing. Community policing requires a structure that facilitates flexibility and autonomy to engage in creative problem-solving (Skogan and Hartnett 1997). Scholars have long discussed flattening the bureaucratic structure to facilitate horizontal communication and increase line officer discretion, but because hierarchical centralized bureaucracies are resistant to change (Gaines *et al.* 2003; Hannan and Freeman 1984), little progress has been made.

The paramilitary academy espouses beliefs inconsistent with the goals of community policing (Ford 2003). Although most police departments are now teaching the philosophy of community policing, recruits may be more likely to learn the values and behaviors associated with the informal paramilitary culture if they differ from the formal teachings. That is, there is a tension between the formal lessons that espouse community policing, and the informal lessons that reinforce traditional ideals of policing in the academy. Evidence suggests that even in academies that purport to teach community policing – but maintain elements of the paramilitary structure – the most salient lessons are those associated with discipline, obedience, and chain of command (Chappell and Lanza-Kaduce 2010; Stanislas ibid.).

The federal government is now providing a significant amount of training on terrorism/emergency preparedness through the Department of Homeland Security's National Incident Management System (NIMS). Local police training hours for homeland security, terrorism, and emergency preparedness have also increased significantly. Local police agencies are revising training curricula to include topics such as intelligence gathering, task forces, and weapons of mass destruction in their curricula (Bureau of Justice Statistics 2009). While little research has been conducted on new training curricula reflecting changes after 9/11, some departments such as New York Police Department now require all of their recruits to receive training in counter-terrorism and intelligence.

Although the tension between the paramilitary culture/bureaucratic structure of American policing and community policing has existed for some time, there is reason to be concerned that the tension will result in a shift back toward legalistic/reform policing (Diamond and Bucqueroux 2012). The militaristic, subcultural emphasis on crime-fighting may be legitimized in a time of terror and war. Thus, community policing may be up against newer, tougher challenges. The war on terror and associated federal initiatives send the message that a militaristic, aggressive approach is appropriate and this belief may extend beyond terrorism to domestic crime and disorder issues.

Despite the widespread adoption of community policing, there is some evidence that these fears are materializing. For example, Kraska has written extensively about the proliferation of SWAT units, even in small towns with low crime rates (Kraska and Cubellis 1997). Other research has noted the use of war-like tactics in handling disorder and petty offenses, such as drugs and homelessness, often under the umbrella of 'zero-tolerance' or 'quality of life' policing. Research suggests that 'stop, question, and frisk' practices have increased in many large cities, such as Philadelphia and New York. A recent report found that such stops tripled between 2003 and 2009 in New York (Jones-Brown *et al.* 2010). These tactics have not gone unnoticed by citizens. In fact, New York has seen a significant increase in citizen complaints for stop, question, and frisk practices, and many cities have seen increases in allegations of racial profiling of Muslim and Arabic residents since 9/11 (Bornstein 2005; Thatcher 2005). This evidence heightens concerns that departments are moving toward the use of 'war like' approaches to handle domestic problems, such as drug interdiction, homeless/vagrants, and other disorder and petty offenses in place of problem-solving and community policing.

The advances in community policing that police agencies have made in the past few decades are more important than ever. A return to the militaristic model of policing will not be beneficial in the fight against terrorism, nor will it be helpful in fighting domestic crime. Further, the problems that accompanied reform era policing and inspired the shift to the community era, such as hostility and distrust toward the police, will likely re-emerge. Police officers should build partnerships with the community, enlist the assistance of law abiding community residents, and increase trust so that they can rely on citizens to be trusted inform-ants (Stanislas ibid.). Otherwise, they risk alienating those who are the eyes and ears of the community who may have the knowledge to help solve crimes, including threats to homeland security. Communication and diversity lessons learned in the academy and in the field – often under the umbrella of community policing – are imperative: officers who can communicate well will be better pre-pared to defuse conflicts, obtain better information from witnesses and suspects, and avoid the use of force. A sophisticated officer who is sensitive to cultural differences because of diversity training will be in a better position to gather information about all types of criminal activity. Especially when the stakes are high, police must see the community as partners rather than enemies.

According to Chappell *et al.* (2005: 84–85):

> ...Expertise, rather than the symbols of power and coercion will be the basis for partnerships in community outreach.... Traditional policing that emphasizes top-down authority relations, where police have 'ownership' over crime problems, needs to give way to community involvement and partnerships. Success will depend on training that teaches and demonstrates how to share power and authority, how to gather information and sugges-tions, how to work through conflict to build consensus, and how to cooper-ate and coordinate with others.

Newer training approaches, as illustrated by the LAPD and Florida's CMS, are relevant to counter-terrorism. Like other crime problems, counter-terrorism is not easily standardized. Incorporating real-life scenarios, improving delivery, and contextualizing learning will improve officers' ability to think on their feet, multi-task, and use critical thinking skills in the event that a disaster occurs. Cre-ative, empowered officers who have been trained in problem-solving techniques will be more effective in the face of a tragedy. Thus, homeland security policing and community policing are complementary; both rely on collaboration between police and the public, and both benefit from training that incorporates adult learning methods (Chappell and Gibson 2009).

Finally, we must keep in mind that while counter-terrorism is important, the daily tasks of policing have not changed much. Police still spend the majority of their time maintaining order, serving citizens, and keeping the peace. Our domestic crime problems are complex and require critical analysis and multi-dimensional responses that go beyond militaristic drills and covert actions. Police officers will be more effective if the lessons from community policing become second nature; this can be done through training. Progress has been made in the community era as training has evolved to better reflect the daily tasks of police officers. We should be concerned that a significant shift toward homeland security will have a cost in terms of personnel and training time toward what is likely to be a 'very narrow slice of police work' (Schafer and Boyd 2007: 383).

Conclusion

American policing, and thus training, is going through a transitional period. Although community policing is now considered the way of doing business in most police departments, it has been a long and arduous battle for the 'hearts and minds' of police officers – one that has not been easily won (Lurigio and Skogan 1994). Certainly, training has been identified as necessary in the institutionalization of community policing and has been slow to catch on. To continue making progress, training academies must continue to embrace an approach that is appropriate to policing in a democratic society. Through training, local police agencies can ensure that officers continue to learn and value the skills that are not only most useful in the identification and solution of domestic crime problems but also in the war against terror.

Bibliography

Alpert, G.P. and Dunham, R.G. (1997) *Policing Urban America*, Illinois: Waveland Press.

Birzer, M.L. (1999) 'Police Training in the 21st Century', *FBI Law Enforcement Bulletin*, 16–19.

Birzer, M.L. (2003) 'The Theory of Andragogy Applied to Police Training', *Policing: An International Journal of Police Strategies and Management* 26(1): 29–42.

Birzer, M.L. and Tannehill, R. (2001) 'A More Effective Training Approach for Contemporary Policing', *Police Quarterly*, 4(2): 233–252.

Bornstein, A. (2005) 'Antiterrorist policing in New York City after 9/11: Comparing perspectives on a complex process', *Human Organization*, 64: 52–61.

Britz, M.T. (1997) 'The Police Subculture and Occupational Socialization: Exploring Individual and Demographic Characteristics', *American Journal of Criminal Justice*, 21(2): 127–146.

Bryant, C. (1979) *Khaki-collar Crime*, New York: The Free Press.

Bureau of Justice Statistics, (2000) *Local Police Departments, 1997*. Washington, D.C.

Bureau of Justice Statistics (2009) *State and Local Law enforcement Training Academies, 2006*. U.S. Department of Justice, Office of Justice Programs, Washington, D.C.

Bureau of Justice Statistics (2010) *Local Police Departments, 2007*. U.S. Department of Justice, Office of Justice Programs, Washington, D.C.

Carter, D.L. and Sapp, A.D. (1990) 'The evolution of higher education in law enforcement: preliminary findings from a national study', *Journal of Criminal Justice Education*, 1: 59–85.

Carter, D.L., Sapp, A.D., and Stephens, D.W. (1989) *The State of Police Education: Policy Direction for the 21st Century Washington DC*, Police Executive Research Forum.

Chappell, A. and Gibson, S. (2008) *Commonwealth of Virginia Law Enforcement Survey: Results*. Report made available to Virginia Police Departments.

Chappell, A.T. and Gibson, S. (2009) 'Community Policing and Homeland Security: Friend or Foe?', *Criminal Justice Policy Review*, 20(3): 326–343.

Chappell, A.T. and Lanza-Kaduce, L. (2004) 'Integrating Sociological Research and Theory with Community-Oriented Policing: Bridging the Gap between Academics and Practice', *Journal of Applied Sociology/Sociological Practice*, 21(2): 80–98.

Chappell, A.T. and Lanza-Kaduce, L. (2010) 'Police Academy Socialization: Understanding the Lessons Learned in a Paramilitary-Bureaucratic Organization', *Journal of Contemporary Ethnography*, 39(2): 187–214.

Chappell, A.T., Lanza-Kaduce, L., and Johnston, D.H. (2005/2010). 'Police Training: Changes and Challenges', pp. 53–70 in Roger G. Dunham and Geoffrey P. Alpert (eds.), Critical Issues in Policing, 6th Ed. Prospect Heights, IL: Waveland Press.

Congressional Budget Office. (2004). *Federal funding for homeland security.* Washington, D.C.: Congressional Budget Office.

Dantzker, G., Lurigio, A., Hartnett, S., Houmes, S., Davidsdottir, S., and Donovan, K. 1995. 'Preparing Police Officers for Community Policing: An Evaluation of Training for Chicago's Alternative Policing Strategy', *Police Studies*, 18(1): 745–770.

Diamond, Drew, and Bucqueroux, Bonnie. 2012. Community Policing is Homeland Security. www.policing.com/articles/terrorism.html.

Eskridge, C. (1989) 'College and the police: A review of the issues', in D.J. Kenney (ed.), *Police and policing: Contemporary issues*, 17–25. New York: Praeger.

Ford, R.E. (2003) 'Saying one thing, meaning another: The role of parables in Police Training', *Police Quarterly*, 6: 84–110.

Fridell, L., Murphy, J., Jordan, T., and Vila, B.J. (2002) 'The Cop Crunch: Identifying Strategies to Deal with the Recruiting and Hiring Crisis in Law Enforcement', *Annual Meeting of the American Society of Criminology*, Chicago, IL (Paper Presentation).

Gaines, L.K., Worrall, J.L., Southerland, M.D., and Angell, J.E. (2003) *Police Administration*, 2nd edn, New York: McGraw Hill.

Germann, A.C. (1969) 'Community Policing: An Assessment', *Journal of Criminal Law and Police Science*, 60: 89–96.

Glassock, B. (2001) 'Letter to IACP colleagues', *International Association of Chiefs of Police*, Alexandra, VA.

Glenn, R.W., Panitch, B.R., Barnes-Proby, D., Williams, E., Matthew, J.C., Lewis, W., Gerwehr, S., and Brannan, D.W. (2003) *Training the 21st Century Police Officer: Redefining Police Professionalism for the Los Angeles Police Department.* Santa Monica, CA: RAND.

Haarr, R. (2001) 'The Making of a Community Policing Officer: The Impact of Basic Training and Occupational Socialization on Police Recruits', *Police Quarterly*, 4: 402–433.

Haberfield, M.R. (2002) *Critical Issues in Police Training*, Upper Saddle River, NJ: Prentice Hall.

Hannan, M.T. and Freeman, J. (1984) 'Structural Inertia and Organizational Change', *American Sociological Review*, 49: 149–164.

Hays, K.L., Regoli, R., and Hewitt, J.D. (2007) 'Police chiefs, anomia, and leadership', *Police Quarterly*, Vol. 10, No. 1:3–22.

Jones-Brown, D., Gill, J., and Trone, J. (2010). *Stop, Question, & Frisk policing practices in New York City: A Primer.* John Jay College of Criminal Justice: www.jjay.cuny.edu/web_images/PRIMER_electronic_version.pdf.

Kelling, George and Moore, Mark (1988). 'From Political to Reform to Community: The Evolving Strategy of Policing', in *Community Policing: Rhetoric or Reality*, eds. Jack Greene, and Stephen Mastrofski. New York: Praeger.

Kraska, Peter and Cubellis, L.J. (1997) 'Militarizing Mayberry and Beyond: Making sense of American Paramilitary Policing', *Justice Quarterly*, 14: 607–629.

Lundman, Richard (1980) *Police and Policing: An Introduction*. New York: Holt, Rinehart and Winston.

Lurigio, A.J. and Skogan, W.G. 1994. 'Winning the Hearts and Minds of Police Officers: An Assessment of Staff Perceptions of Community Policing in Chicago', *Crime and Delinquency*, 40: 315–330.

Maguire, Edward (1997) 'Structural Change in Large Municipal Police Organizations During the Community Policing Era', *Justice Quarterly*, 14: 547–576.

Marion, Nancy (1998) 'Police Academy Training: Are We Teaching Recruits What They Need to Know?' *Policing*, 21: 54–75.

Mastrofski, S.D. and Ritti, R.R. (1995) 'Police Training and the Effects of Organizations on Drunk Driving Enforcement', *Justice Quarterly*, 13(2).

Mayhall, P.D., Barker, T., and Hunter, R.D. (1995). *Police Community Relations and the Administration of Justice*, Englewood Cliffs, NJ: Prentice Hall.

Mayo, L. (2006) 'College Education and Policing', *The Police Chief*, 73(8): 20–38.

McGarrell, E.F., Freilich, J.D., and Chermak, S. (2007) 'Intelligence-led policing as a framework for responding to terrorism', *Journal of Contemporary Criminal Justice*, 23: 142–158.

Office of Community Oriented Policing Services (COPS office) (2001) *PTO: An overview and introduction. A problem-based learning manual for training and evaluating police trainees*. U.S. Department of Justice.

Oliver, W.M. (2006) 'The fourth era of policing: homeland security', *International Review of Law Computers & Technology*, 20: 49–62.

Paoline, Eugene A., III and Terrill, William (2007) 'Police Education, Experience, and the Use of Force', *Criminal Justice & Behavior*, 34(2): 179–196.

Paterson, Craig (2011) 'Adding value? A review of the international literature on the role of higher education in police training and education', *Police Practice and Research*, 12(4): 286–297.

Peak, K.J. and Glensor, R.W. (1999) *Community Policing & Problem-solving*. Upper Saddle River, NJ: Prentice Hall.

Pitts, S., Glensor, R., and Peak, K. (2007) 'The Police Training Officer (PTO): A Contemporary Approach to Post-Academy Recruit Training', The Police Chief, August 2007, pp. 114–121.

Regoli, R.M. (1976). 'The effects of a college education on the maintenance of police cynicism', *Journal of Police Science and Administration*, 4: 340–345.

Roberg, R.R. (1978) 'An analysis of the relationships among higher education, belief systems, and job performance of patrol officers', *Journal of Police Science and Administration*, 6: 336–344.

Roberg, R. and Bonn, S. (2004) 'Higher education and policing: where are we now?' *Policing*, 27: 469–486.

Rosenbaum, D.P. and Lurigio, A.J. (1994) 'An inside look at community policing reform: Definitions, organizational changes, and evaluation findings', *Crime and Delinquency*, 40: 299–314.

Ross, Darrell (2000) 'Emerging Trends in police failure to train liability', *Policing: An International Journal of Police Strategies and Management*, 23(2): 169–193.

Rushing, Patricia (2010) 'A New Strategy for Training Police Officers – the PTO Program', CALEA Update Magazine | Issue 102.

Schafer, Joseph A. and Boyd, Sandy (2007) *The future of education and training for policing. Policing 2020: Exploring the Future of Crime, Communities, and Policing*, ed. Joseph Schafer. Futures Working Group, U.S. Department of Justice, Federal Bureau of Investivation.

Skogan, W. and Hartnett, S.M. (1997). *Community Policing, Chicago Style*. New York: Oxford University Press.

Skolnick, Jerome and Fyfe, James (1993) *Above the Law: Police and the Excessive Use of Force*. New York: The Free Press.

Thatcher, D. (2005) 'The local role in homeland security', *Law and Society Review* 39: 635–676.

Van Maanen, J. (1973) 'Observations on the making of policemen', *Human Organization*, 32: 407–418.

Van Maanen, J. (1978) 'Epilogue: On Watching the Watchers', in *Policing: A View from the Street*, P.K. Manning and J. Van Maanen (eds), 309–349, Santa Monica: Goodyear.

Walker, S., and Katz, C. (2005) *The Police in America: An Introduction*, New York: McGraw-Hill.

Weisburd, D., Mastrofski, S., McNally, A., Greenspan, R., and Willis, J. (2003) 'Reforming to Preserve: CompStat and Strategic Problem-solving in American Policing', *Criminology and Public Policy*, 2: 421–456.

White, M.D. and Escobar, G. (2008) 'Making good cops in the twenty-first century: emerging issues for the effective recruitment, selection and training of police in the United States and abroad', *International Review of Law Computers & Technology*, 22: 119–134.

Willis, J., Mastrofski, S., and Weisburd, D. (2004) 'Compstat and bureaucracy: A case study of challenges and opportunities for change', *Justice Quarterly*, 21: 462–496.

Wilson, J.Q. (1968) *Varieties of Police Behavior*, New York: Atheneum.

Worden, R.E. (1990) 'A Badge and a Baccalaureate: policies, hypotheses and further evidence', *Justice Quarterly*, 7(3): 565–592.

17 Conclusion

P. Stanislas

Policing legitimacy, society and change

The issue of police education and training for many different yet related reasons is an increasingly important one in the policing world. Demands for higher standards are often driven by controversies or problems that highlight deficiencies in existing practice and deeper underlying issues. In advanced and developing societies alike these problems are often highlighted in government commissions, official reports or the media. Deficiencies in practice may be brought to wider attention from external international agencies, or governments, in conjunction with local and foreign-based activists. The motivation for change in police training and education come from demands for more effective or efficient policing responses in a changing world. In Berlin and Chappell's chapters they show how policing has gone through several phases of reform driven by the changing perceptions of police legitimacy and the police's authority and its relationship with citizens.

Reiner (1992) illustrates this in the British context and maintains that the legitimacy of the police in the contemporary world differs in some important ways from that which existed in the post-war period. One dimension of this change is the greater diversity of the British population with immigration from the ex-British Commonwealth countries. This has contributed to both conflict and a greater awareness of policing issues and concerns of hitherto excluded minorities, such as ethnic communities, women and other vulnerable groups in society such as gay men and lesbian women (Stanislas, Chapter 1). These values and sensibilities shape societal standards and impact on the training and education of police officers in advanced policing jurisdictions, as highlighted in the chapters of various contributors such as Wyatt and Bell in Canada, Green and Woolston in Australia, and Stanislas in Britain. These values are also communicated to the outside world, contributing to debate and potential change in police practice in various ways.

This can be seen by the issue of homophobia, and its relationship to definitions of human rights (Cheah 1997, Stanislas 2013), and its impact in differing ways on small developing Caribbean countries such as Jamaica and St Lucia as highlighted in Chapters 1 and 13. Homophobia has also been highlighted in countries of East Africa, such as Uganda, which has been largely fed by American Christian fundamentalists, who have sought to exploit Christian support in poor black countries to promote their views about homosexuality (Raghavan 2010). These views are often rooted in an anti-western critique similar to that described by Stanislas (2013) in the Jamaican context. Prejudice towards sexual orientation in the Caribbean was brought to the region by white Christian colonialists, and codified in law and made the responsibility of the police to enforce. The consequences of this process of change and its contemporary manifestations are evident in the case of Jamaica which has witnessed the growth of a particularly virulent strain of homophobia in the search for scapegoats for society's ills. These attitudes have penetrated the police service and have led to calls for improved education of Jamaican police on matters related to homophobia and respecting social diversity (Chapter 1). In St Lucia a more relaxed attitude exists towards homosexuality and respecting the private, and aspects of public, lives of citizens and is reflected in the training and education provided to police recruits. Gay men and lesbian women may gain some additional succour from the general culture of weak law enforcement in contemporary St Lucia (Stanislas forthcoming) which provides them with a degree of protection from prosecution if breaching the colonial laws of the country. This of course has to be balanced against their needs for police protection or justice requirements if victims of homophobic crime, albeit not common (Stanislas interviews 2010), or if subject to selective law enforcement as in instances or attempts to blackmail (Long 2003).

This process of social and cultural conflict and change, highlighted by greater sensitivity to sexuality in many parts of the world, reinforces the observations made by Kratcoski and Das (2007) and reflects developments in access to education and greater awareness of the world via improvements in technology. This has increased expectations around police behaviour and has important implication for the training, education and development of police officers. A case in point being the increasing use of internet based programmes. Technology and its widespread use, such as social media and mobile camera phones, as explored by Arsenault and Hinton, has serious implication for police accountability and professional conduct, while empowering citizens in new ways. It is perhaps a signs of the times, and a potential insight in things to come, that the same types of technology which the police in many jurisdictions around the world are using to improve their capabilities are the same tools which can be used by members of the public, community groups, and social justice campaigners to improve their own capacity to monitor and hold police and law enforcement agencies to account. Technology also provides new means for offenders to commit crime as seen in the growth of internet based crime (Bowling and Sheptycki 2012: 110).

The call for reforms in police training has received a significant boost with the rise and popularity of democratic models of policing with the community policing era during 1980s. This started in the US before becoming an important set of themes in British discussion after nationwide rioting. The search to reduce these types of tensions has played a significant role in contributing to changes in policing strategies and how police officers are trained and in laying the groundwork for contemporary discourses about reform. In other countries the poor and unsatisfactory treatment of significant numbers of the population has contributed to the search for solutions which has seen the community policing model, and issues which it seeks to address, being embraced around the world in nations undergoing transition in the former communist and developing world. In China and Hungary ethnic tensions and the desire to reduce them has played an important role in the authorities wishing to build and maintain sound community relations and adopting practices which would not be out of place in Canada, Australia, and other advanced policing jurisdictions. Stanislas highlights the importance of community policing philosophy to the training of new recruits in the Eastern Caribbean country of St Lucia, which came about due to widespread dissatisfaction about policing and specifically the police's inability to effectively respond to an unprecedented rise in violent and other crime. Much of this crime is transnational in character driven by the international drugs and gun trade involving highly organized criminal gangs and their intermediaries, such as lawyers, and underpinned by systemic corruption (Bowling 2010; Stanislas forthcoming).

The professional model of development of policing and liberal democratic societies

A crucial characteristic of the professional model of policing is that it is based on efforts to specify, make explicit and standardize, in short objectify, the key competencies, skills and knowledge base required to carry out police work, in a desire to move away from the subjectivity and traditional practices evolved by police practitioners. It also calls into question the selection and preparation of police trainers who occupy a vital role in the learning process. The matter of how police trainers are chosen is one that has exercised most police organizations around the world in one way or another. Police trainers are not simply teachers, they are also future professional colleagues, leaders, and representatives of the police as an institution as Moreau de Bellaing and others remind us. The French approach to the selection of police recruit trainers, the most important in the police training and education system, reflects popular practice in most western and developing countries up until relatively recently. The notion that the most important resource required by trainers is practical experience is a widely shared view, and not an unreasonable one, has given way to a new awareness about teaching and training as a distinct discipline requiring specialist skills and education. In many countries the development of teaching and training as a profession is closely linked to important changes in vocational education (Jarvis 1992, 2010).

The increased focus on the calibre and development of police trainers is clearly evident in the Australian and Chinese instance. In the former police and academic training staff of the New South Wales Police undergo annual accreditation checks to ensure they obtain and maintain the required level of technical proficiency. The Chinese authorities have paid a lot of attention to the issue of preparing trainers and teachers involved in policing and clearly understand the importance of these roles and their requirements in the contemporary world. China, as outlined by Tingyou in her chapter, provides some of the most innovative approaches in preparing and developing police training and teaching staff. Shanghai Police College for example has introduced a range of initiatives which include Alternative Rotation Training, and enhanced training. Other institutions have introduced experiential teaching centres that feature some very original practices which characterize the Chinese approach to training and underscores the importance China places on maximizing the development of its police trainers.

Training in the use of force

One of the unique functions of the State police organization is illustrated in the training and expectations surrounding the use of legitimate force. The use of force and the protection of citizens from its arbitrary use is often a signifier or feature of particular types of policing systems; whether it is expectations around advanced or weak liberal democratic, or former communist systems or more modern communist systems such as the Russian Federation. The Chinese experience highlights a response to a basic problem which is fully explored by Arsenault and Hinton in their examination of use of force training in Canada, with relevance for many police organizations around the world, i.e. the poor level of training and support provided to police officers in the use of force. While not used often in the careers of most police officers worldwide in the course of their daily work. However, when force is required and the way it is used can become a crystallizing factor for how that police organization is perceived, way beyond the immediate confines where the incident took place. The Chinese appear to place significant weight on updating and refreshing their officers in a number of basic skill areas, including unarmed combat and use of force training, as highlighted in Tingyou's chapter; similar to other nations with ancient histories of martial arts expertise as seen in the basic training of South Korean police officers, public order officers, and more specialist personal protection officers (Public Intelligence 2011).

A common if not universal set of assumptions shared by significant sections of the world's population is the notion that policing requires the use of force in controlling or apprehending people who would prefer not to be. Therefore the realization that the police are inadequately trained in such matters in many instances must be an issue of concern. This is in part a potentially important factor for a long history of deaths in police custody, of black people in particular, in specific circumstances in countries such as Britain (see Jasper 2011). The writer's experience as an unarmed combat and use of force instructor, from the non-state sector[1] and working experience within the police service, reinforces this concern about the relatively poor levels of training and competence of British police officers and the training received. These matters are often not resolved by issuing officers with more or better protective equipment.[2] The use of questionable restraint methods for example has contributed to deaths in police custody as in the cases of Shiji Lapite and others who died of asphyxiation (Jasper 2011; Hannan *et al.* 2009). These restraint techniques are often an adaptation used by police officers, due to the ineffectiveness of the initial training received, or lack of practice in using the techniques taught to achieve competence in their use in real life situations. In the case of the killing of paratrooper Chris Adler, it appears he died as a consequence of an appalling catalogue of uncontrolled violence at the hands of the police (Jasper ibid.). High levels of deaths in police custody can be found in many parts of the world, such as in British Columbia in Canada which had the highest numbers of deaths in custody in the country (MacAlaister *et al.* 2012).The importance of the distinction between the training environment and real life events is detailed by Arsenault and Hinton, and Bertilsson and Fredriksson in their respective chapters and why it is very difficult to replicate simulations that closely resemble the latter. This also helps to explain the value given to informal on-the-job learning amongst police officers, and the importance of the working occupational culture discussed in Chapter 1.

Concerns around the use-of-force training and practice in the developing world are even more pressing and brought to light by the writer's interviews and observations of use-of-force instructors at work in several Caribbean countries (Stanislas Interviews 2010; Stanislas 2013). It is not uncommon to find basic self-defence and control procedures being taught with little protective or safety equipment, like mats to practice throws. Very often the equipment used by recruits belongs to instructors. Under these conditions it is understandable why recruits are unable to effectively learn self-defence techniques. Learning to throw someone, for example, requires somebody hitting the floor or being struck with some frequency before a degree of competence is achieved; and for the appropriate amount of mental and physical conditioning to take place. While the lack of training and training resources may be a factor in the way conflict is handled by police officers, in this and similar parts of the world, the importance of force and the ability and willing to use it was highlighted by ex-Trinidad and Tobago police officer, and PhD student, Michael Mathura at a symposium on police reform. He informed those present that his basic training involved learning the use of five firearms, to include a shot gun and mini and maxi Uzi machine guns. In St Lucia basic recruit training involves the use of three weapons, including M16 machine guns. What really highlights the priorities of police leaders in this part of the world was illustrated by Mathura, when he recalled that in ten years of service, apart from firearms refresher training, he attended no other training courses. The majority of this training is technical in character, regarding gun mechanics, how to use weapons and tactical issues. Very little of this time is spent on educational matters around the ethical use of force. The willingness to use these weapons was experienced by the writer while accompanying Caribbean police officers on duty. Of particular note was the speed at which many officers escalated their response in interactions with members of the public if challenged. Police officers were often prepared to use the threat of force, in the face of not unreasonable questions from citizens, which goes some way to explaining the high fatality rate of the public in many of these countries at police hands (Manning 2007; Stanislas 2013). It is not uncommon to hear or read reports in Caribbean countries of unarmed people being shot and killed often for fleeing from the police due to fear of being caught and beaten for being in possession of a joint of marijuana, or some other very minor offence; or none at all.

Another problem with the use of force in these types of countries is the indiscriminate use of guns in public and the killing of innocent passer-by which the Jamaican police in particular have earned notoriety for (Manning 2007). The human rights implication of this type of use of force by the police requires little elaboration here, but goes beyond these matters to include the safety of police officers themselves. The precarious nature of life in many countries and that of police officers can be illustrated by a personal experience. During the writer's fieldwork in St Lucia within a couple of days of starting three people had been shot, and two of those killed were police officers. The first officer lost his life in what many in the public and police believed was an accidental shooting by another officer, although this was not the official view. The second officer was killed several days later after plain clothed units of officers made what was described by witness accounts as a poorly coordinated attempt to apprehend an individual wanted in 'connection' with the killing of their colleague.[3] This resulted in police officers opening fire and killing another police officer, while the suspect took cover and returned fire before being wounded. The tragedy of these events was prevented from becoming worse by the courageous intervention of residents who witnessed the incident and refused to comply with the instructions of the officer, suspected of shooting his colleague, to evacuate their homes and verandas. Fearing for the safety of the wounded man residents refused to comply with the police instructions, believing he would be murdered in order to resolve an inconvenient set of problems.[4] The type of post shooting investigations outlined by Bertilsson and Fredriksson and others (Punch 2011) are not carried out in most developing countries, and not in a way that would command any confidence. In the St Lucian instance, police failed to interview witnesses at the aforementioned incident, a not uncommon practice, and still had not months after the writer had left the country.

The issue of police use of force goes beyond training in the right responses and methods, but starts at the selection or pre-selection stage (Chapter 1) and the types of personalities recruited or deemed appropriate for policing and their attitudes to force. These issues are not inseparable from matters around dominant types of masculinities and policing style, as touched on in Chappell's chapter, and the marginality of women and their cultural influences (Loftus 2012; Lancester-Ellis 2013). In short the type of police organization, how it is perceived by the public and what it deems as important, as Berlin reminds us has a significant bearing on the types of people who want to join and serve in them. Historically, it has been suggested that authoritarian-type personalities are attracted to militaristic or paramilitaristic view of policing as discussed by Chappell in her chapter on the US, and Moreau de Bellaing in the context of France. Similar matters are examined by Fanon (1967) in his work on colonial French policing. Fanon was particularly interested in the role of black and other indigenous officers who constituted the bulk of the French colonial police who apparently gained personal satisfaction, or experienced little discomfort or psychological conflict, in the use of violence against their own communities or other colonized people. The notion that personality types are attracted to particular forms or areas of policing is recognized in the popular characterization of President Putin by his critics as an archetypal KGB recruit, particularly the organization's reliance on fear and intimidation as a method for gaining compliance. This image of Putin is not one he appears to find particularly troubling, as indicated in his official biography where he appears to have gained a degree of satisfaction in recounting his fighting prowess and physical toughness and his ability to dominate and impose his will on much older and bigger boys (Geesen 2012: 49–51).

Arsenault and Hinton highlight the number of legal liability issues and financial implications of failings in use of force by police officers in many advanced liberal democratic societies. With strong legal and court systems, in terms of injuries to the public and to police officers, the loss of work time and the potential legal consequences are important matters for police leaders and the healthy and efficient running of their organizations. The use of force is an area which is crucial for police legitimacy, as Bertilsson and Fredriksson remind us, where informal practices or attitudes have to mirror as closely as possible public and political expectations. There is little tolerance for a significant gap between these worlds in advanced democratic societies, albeit this is less the case in weaker democratic countries or authoritarian systems. Use of force training relies heavily on the experience of officers and is informed to a significant degree by the social science discipline of psychology, research findings, and incident feedback data as utilized in the jurisdiction of Sweden and other western policing systems. Use of force issues is an area where policing outcomes are more likely to be shaped by the individual personality of the officers involved than most others, thus highlighting the limits of formal training (Chapter 1).

Partnership relations

The reliance and development of partnership relations involving the police, higher education and other stakeholders is an important set of practices to be found in countries around the world depending on the type of society and policing system. Improvements in police training have also been accompanied by the changing relations of the police with other stakeholders (Chapter 1). This approach to training has widened the participation of important actors in the processes and can involve partners operating at a local, regional, national and international level as illustrated by Neyroud and Wain in their chapter. As Peeters highlights in his chapter based primarily on experiences in the Netherlands and the Dutch Caribbean, academics and other professionals, along with external education and training providers such as universities occupy a critical role in the various processes involved in training and educational design and delivery. First, in helping to identify core policing competencies. Second, in developing training and education profiles and finally identifying how these competencies and knowledge can be met. A good illustration of this type of collaboration can be seen in the development and implementation of the Associate Degree in Policing Practice (ADPP) in New South Wales in Australia and the management of the process by the Contract Agreement Performance Review Committee (CAPRC). This thinking is also seen in the British Neyroud review of police leadership and development requirements, which promises to have a significant impact on reforming the training and education of police personnel in England and Wales (Neyroud 2011).

Most chapters in the book highlight various types of partnership arrangements and demonstrate their importance in contemporary policing, and no doubt will play a significant role in many areas of private security provision and its development. This is illustrated in the Hungarian instance by Sándor in his chapter. See Boda (forthcoming) and the Wakefield and Button chapter. In China police partners from other policing agencies outside the country, such as Hong Kong or local community security organizations, are important players in developing and delivering police training. The most important driver of partnership relations in this area in China are government ministries, with the Ministry of Public Security and Education being the most important in bringing together agencies and institutions in delivering and improving police education and training in the country. Partnership or consortia arrangements are particularly pronounced in some western countries such as Britain and Canada which are relatively open societies, albeit with different structural and administrative arrangements. Most advanced countries such as Australia have longer histories of partnership working within their domestic or local regions as highlighted by Green and Woolston. The test of these arrangements is their ability to withstand changes in key personnel, such as police leaders, and the financial health of the country and their ability to add value to the training and education of police recruits (in this instance).

This echoes the experiences in parts of Britain and the US and illustrates the importance of points made by Stanislas in Chapter 4 about the need for universities to be able to clearly demonstrate in empirical or other terms their worth and the importance of research and evaluation of police training. These are important set of challenges for researchers and universities engaged in these, and related areas of work and reinforced by Bayley's observations (2011). He persuasively argues that many universities have to do much more than appeal to the intuitive superiority of their services and products, given the poor levels of practice that exists in many of them in a variety of areas. Some examples of these are in the areas of human resource management, attitudes to diversity, basic management or teaching practices. One of the inferences that can be drawn from Bayley's observations is police organizations seeking to enter partnerships with universities need to be prudent in considering their prospective partners' track record in a range of areas rather than uncritically assuming they are sources of good practice. Universities' competence may well have to be demonstrated in newer ways, other than applying modern marketing techniques to highlight traditional virtues and criteria, while masking old and problematic practices. In short, police leaders are not alone in their need to give honest and sober assessments of their organization's performance and capabilities and introduce change where possible if they are to maintain and obtain their desired levels of legitimacy.

The increasing entrepreneurial nature of universities and institutions of higher education in many parts of the world has been cited as an important consideration in understanding the willingness of many of them to enter the area of police education and training or participate in various partnership arrangements (Teixeira 2006; Wimshurst and Ransley 2007: 120). This is particularly important in the tough commercial world of the higher education sector in many countries, as the US and British experience suggest that the policing sector, especially in the area of recruit training, is an uncertain and precarious market. Either in terms of the funds available for recruiting new officers, and or the lack of commitment of chief officers to the idea of institutions of higher education being involved in this area. The experience of the Law Enforcement Education Programme in the US is particularly instructive here (Froyland 2005). It appears that institutions with track records in policing and criminal justice education and training or those able to establish programmes quite early have been able to sustain their partnership and enjoy contract extensions. De Montfort University in Leicester, England, for example has enjoyed several contract extensions initially starting in 2006 and extended to 2018 for police recruit and Police Community Support Officer (PCSO) training, while many university providers have not been as fortunate. The good and close working relationship between the Leicestershire Police and the university enabled them to effectively plan around a range of important challenges such as stoppages in recruitment, the deployment of academic and other staff, in a way that maintained continuity and build capacity during periods of uncertainty. This was only possible due to the strong commitment to university-based education from successive chief constables and their adoption of a long-term view shaped by their beliefs in the real benefits of this approach and the capacity of the university to provide what is required.[5] An important consideration in informing this commitment is the quality of teaching, an understanding and familiarity of practical policing of academic and other staff on the programme; and most importantly the working relations between them and police trainers seconded from Leicestershire police based at the university. These police trainers not only play an important role in providing teaching expertise on the training programmes, and not uncommonly called on to carry out police duties when required, are invaluable sources of information in informing the decisions of police leaders. As Richard Heslop (2011) elucidates the relationship between academic staff, police officers, and police trainees is by no means an easy one and can have important consequences for how university-based programmes are assessed by police leaders.

An important set of considerations when thinking about university police partnership arrangements is the types of resources and facilities that the university possesses in meeting the wide range of requirements needed for police training and education. Canada has a unique model of private colleges that can boast a number of police standard shooting ranges, driving and other practical training facilities not found in most non-State institutions anywhere in the world, and enjoys the endorsement of police leaders and other bodies in the country as a recognized police training establishment. Atlantic Police College spent large sums of money in upgrading its facilities in becoming one of Canada's premier police training and education establishments. Post-secondary institution Holland College, a leading Canadian police training and education provider, also provides programmes for other law enforcement agencies along with the fire and emergency services. This highlights the importance of the leadership of educational and training establishments in having the appropriate vision and being able to meet the financial challenges involved in equipping their institution. In China the Chinese People's Public Security University (CPPSU) has introduced state of the art facilities in the areas of DNA analysis, fingerprinting, and security protection technology. These examples perhaps point the way in which universities and other educational or training institutions who want to increase their appeal to police leaders need to consider, with import for private sector interests, especially in the new priority areas such as internet-based security and crime. The example of the relationship between the private sector Canadian Police Knowledge Network and the Canadian policing authorities is a sound demonstration of the important role private sector interests can play in meeting policing needs in a way which is providing significant benefits in the area of internet-based police education.

International partnerships and police development funding

The professional model of development which underpins much of popular thinking about contemporary police training globally, particularly in wealthy and advances economies requires a considerable amount of financial and other resources. In particular, its emphasis on life-long learning has been criticized as being problematic for the conditions in postcolonial countries (Harriot 2000: 186–190; Mercer and Newburn 2007: 3). Cost aside many policing systems in developing and Eastern European countries have been described in dysfunctional terms and suffer with major problems around corruption, work motivation, and accountability. In short these are problems which go way beyond matters of simply training (Chapter 1). Western donor countries have provided significant amount of resources for police training and related matters for former communist countries which is driven by the desire to transform police organizations and societies, weaken traditional adversaries, and bring them into their spheres of influence. The transformation of the Hungarian police outlined by Sándor demonstrates how national developments and transnational assistance have helped to produce the modern policing system in that country, which provides a useful lesson for those undertaking similar reforms.

These political and strategic considerations are not for the most part as salient in the relationship of donor nations with many developing countries, who while able to obtain a range of support for training from international donors (Bayley 2006; Mercer and Newburn 2007), the amount they can expect pales in comparison to that which is enjoyed by former communist societies in transition (Zvekic

1998: 206; Brogden and Nijhar 2005: 193–198). Shared international concerns around security matters, such as anti-US terrorism, in developing nations may contribute to changes in this pattern of international funding for improving their policing and security systems and alter this pattern of resourcing. Countries such as Nigeria, Africa's most populated nation, which is plagued with a number of complex policing problems contributing to local and transnational crime and serious problems of violence and regional security issues with global implications. At a recent symposium Professor Gus John, calling on his decades of experience working in Nigeria, recounted the long neglect, discriminatory treatment and human rights abuses against the Muslim communities of the northern region by the Federal government and its police and security services. This has created the conditions for radicalization and the emergence of the anti-Federal government and anti-western Islamic terrorism of the Boko Haram movement and other groups (see Pflanz 2013; Gray 2013). The significance of the militant Islam in West Africa and beyond and its consequences for the stability and security, as highlighted in Mali, was detailed by Abraham Jatto in a paper produced by Nigerian Air Vice Marshall Damaballa head of 'Operation Rainbow'.[6] Jatto outlined how the discovery of significant deposit of oil in Guinea, and other parts of the region, is creating a potential point of convergence for militant Islamic forces to launch terrorist attacks.

One of the problems that the Nigerian central government and the West face as described by Professor John is that it is directly and indirectly implicated in numerous 'wars of terror', one involving the facilitation of the ruthless production of oil and gas and State crime, including human rights violations against local tribes and activists in the oil rich Delta region. The latter was brought to international attention due to the killing of Oguni activists Ken Saro-Wiwa and eight other colleagues (White 2011). This episode exposed the role of western commercial and political interests and private security companies in protecting the interests of companies such as Mobil, Chevron, Shell and others and their links with corrupt elements in the Nigerian government, police and military. Jatto and John both described the desire to increase oil production output figures is insensitive to any opposition and costs to human lives or the environment. Many of the concerns discussed about policing and security reform in Nigeria, and other similar countries, reflect those outlined by Acacia Development Association (2013)[7] who maintains that major international funding for police and security reform in Nigeria is inevitable given the global consequences of Al Qaeda inspired groups switching their operations to the more vulnerable Sub-Saharan African states. The shared worry is that most of this funding will not go to making much needed improvements in local policing systems serving the majority of the population, but will be used in improving the military and policing capabilities in anti-terrorism work, and support private security providers protecting largely foreign interests in the country. It is important to stress that unlike many other developing countries Nigeria is not a poor country in terms of resources, without the capacity to independently generate significant sums of money which can be used to modernize its policing systems and society as a whole or at least achieve far more than it has. The problem in Nigeria as in many corrupt political systems around the world is one of political leadership. This is illustrated in the controversy surrounding what has been dubbed the 'security vote' in Nigeria where millions of naira are dispensed to State governors on a monthly basis by the Federal government to be used on local security matters at their discretion. How this money is spent does not have to be publicly disclosed. Rather than 'security vote' monies being used to purchase equipment or recruit more personnel or to launch crime-fighting initiatives, such as 'Operation Rainbow', it is widely believed it finds its way into the personal funds of politicians and their associates (Iriekpen 2012; Premium Times 2012).

A question which needs to be addressed in postcolonial countries is what type of police education and training is required to tackle many of the unique issues experienced in parts of the world, such as St Lucia and similar countries. A central theme in the work of scholars such as Fanon (1967) and Freire (1970) inter alia is the project of decolonialization, starting with tackling the psychological and social conditioning and colonial cultural legacy found in these societies. How this manifests can be seen in the contradictory actions of the new progressive and reforming St Lucian police Commissioner as highlighted in Chapter 13. One of his first actions in post was to reintroduce the old colonial British khaki uniform, despite what it represents and its greater financial costs, as part of move to gain support from rank-and-file officers who purportedly prefer the colonial uniform on sartorial grounds. With this in mind, there is a need for policing and training models which are explicitly designed to tackle colonial conditioning. Part of this process must be informed by and reflect the best pre-colonial cultural traditions of countries, rather than importing models that have no roots in the history and culture of nations like Nigeria or St Lucia which does not directly address the psychological damage caused by colonial rule (see Brogden and Nihaj 2005). An example of this can be observed in attitudes towards sexual diversity and homosexuality. Anthropologist Gregerson (1982) notes that most pre-colonial African societies shared more complex and inclusive attitudes to matters around gender, sexual and social identities than the binary and exclusive notions found in the west. It is the latter which gave birth to particular forms of gender and sexual oppression that today are being reconstructed in racial terms to problematize African and black people, and their countries' attitudes towards sexuality by the now enlightened west. The project of radical decolonization of the mind requires a body of research about the pre-colonial practices of these countries, as well as the ability to integrate best practice from these traditions with those from the international policing community, in creating sustainable models of police training. In this regard, China provides a useful model of how a country and its policing systems consciously go about maintaining important aspects of its heritage and identity, while drawing from international sources. From the rise of Moa, and the creation of modern China to the present day, fundamental to the thinking of China's leaders is the shared belief that Chinese institutions remain Chinese and must reflect the best of its ancient civilization and cultural practices. These themes and the pride associated with this project are clearly articulated in Tingyou's chapter on China.

The US and Britain while important countries in funding international police reform and development, as well as spreading practice, are not the only western powers with influence on police training matters outside their own borders. Countries such as Australia is among the countries which have long provided policing support to its neighbours and the small islands historically associated with it, such as the Solomon Islands (De Heyer 2007). Australia is a respected player in world policing albeit often in a less visible way (see Neyroud 2011). By the same token so is Canada, whose status and influence is increasing in places where its name is not naturally associated, such as the English-speaking Caribbean in countries like Antigua and St Vincent and others. Canada has a strong working relationship with many Caribbean governments and their trans-national security organizations, and has provided training of all types to the Caribbean police (Bowling 2010: 153). Germany is another country that plays a very important role in training in its sphere of influence, as Sándor highlights in his chapter. Germany is a key player in the transnational arrangements at the heart of the Central European College (MEPA) where it provides a range of training to member countries such as Hungary, Slovenia and the Czech Republic (see Pływaczewski 2007). Its importance for many central European nations can be seen by that the fact that the working language of these transnational institu-tions is German and German-language courses are popular and widely provided by policing agencies in these countries. Germany is also a popular country for police secondments.

The economic problems being experienced in many rich donor countries is bringing critical attention to foreign aid with potential import for this pattern of public spending (Kirkup 2013). Debates about the reduction of foreign aid in Britain coincided with India deciding to reject British development aid on the grounds that aid received is derisory in amount to that needed to sustain development, especially compared to its economic growth and annual returns (Gilligan 2012). In the US the government, who is faced with equally tough economic conditions, is fighting to fund its foreign policy goals and is being forced to make budget cuts in order to protect key priorities, such as continu-ing the war against international terrorism outside the homeland (Provost and de Frietas 2011). Under these general conditions police reform in many poor developing countries, is more likely to continue to take incremental form with the adoption of specific features and practices which are associated with the professional model of development or in segmented areas such as counter-terrorism activities.

This incrementalism is illustrated both in India and St Lucia where evidence of professional development model influences can be seen which have been grafted onto highly dysfunctional police organizations. In the former the training of middle-ranking officers consists of advanced practices and is transnational in its delivery and content and the learning opportunities it provides. At the same time in parts of India the response of the police is so poor or non-existent, as contextualized by Neyroud and Wain in their chapter by the high population to police ratio, citizens have formed their own civilian police to act as a deterrent and catch suspects in the wake of major increases in crime (Sashtri 2012). St Lucia on the other hand has witnessed important changes in the training and education of police recruits, in terms of the educational profile of its officers in line with modern trends associated with the professional development model. This is contextualized in an organization where recruits lack access to basic equipment such as handcuffs and radios. The types of challenges that these countries face are different as are many of their basic characteristics. St Lucia is primarily a tourism-based economy, with a small and relatively homogenous population, and has a single police force and limited economic resources. India, on the other hand, is the world's largest and most ethnically diverse population, and possesses numerous police organizations, and has regional and global ambitions. At the same time, its internal divisions and severe social inequalities are summed up by Neyroud and Wain when they cite India's ambitions in sending a man to the moon, while the majority of its population are illiterate or lack schooling.

Post- and new communist policing and professional development model

One of the defining features of the communist model of policing is the supremacy of politics and political ideology in supporting the communist state, and the ruling Communist Party, in cementing allegiances and defining the role of their policing organizations. These ideas about the state and its protection inform police work priorities and to a significant degree how they are carried out and how personnel are trained to perform them. This can be seen in the criminalization of political opponents, critics, journalists and civil and human rights groups in some of these societies. This is still a feature of modern communist governments such as Russia under Putin and the priorities of the FSB, i.e. the new KGB (Gessen 2012; Harding 2012). The Russian civilian police, the *militsia*, have become the focus of political attention due to the public's lack of confidence in them, not helped by a deep-grained low level corruption associated with it (Zagorodnov 2011). President Dmitry Medvedev called for a review of the *militsia* and one dimension of his intended reforms was to explore the possibilities of significantly increasing police salaries, combined with the introduction of tougher measures to protect citizens' rights, such as having access to lawyers at police stations. Russia's elites seems torn between the desires to hold onto the past glories of Russian supremacy and reconciling this with competing and more contemporary liberal ideas around the economy and civil liberties. Other communist systems have moved forward in developing society and their policing organizations in a more orderly and potentially harmonious manner.

The Hungarian policing system represents one of the standout examples of former communist systems, along with others, such as in the Republic of Georgia (Shahnazarian 2012), which adopted an almost unprecedented approach in dismissing all serving police officers as part of its move towards a more democratic approach to policing. A professional model of development informs most aspects of Hungary's human resource strategy and thinking about policing. As Sándor highlights in his chapter the police occupation in Hungary is unique in it is official designation as a profession, along with its subsequent specialism such as police dog handlers, which like other professions require a clear route of academic qualifications and other forms of recognized training to enter and practice. The notion of lifelong training and education is central to the Hungarian system from entry ranks right through to senior management, which requires advanced educational qualifications, to obtaining PhD and research qualifications for its most senior leaders. The Hungarian system typifies Peeters's model of occupational competencies and the type of education, skills and experiences required at the three levels of policing, i.e. that of implementation, management and governance. The Hungarian approach shares Peeters's view about the role of senior police leaders and their changing and future roles and the type of skills and resources required to effectively carry of them out (see Boda forthcoming). This can be seen by the introduction of research qualifications such as doctorate degrees and their importance, a view shared by the Chinese in establishing police research centres and introducing similar qualifications, and in line with thinking elsewhere (Neyroud 2011: 95–96).

In China policing has undergone a long series of upheavals and reforms from the creation of the Communist State in 1949, and in this respect the development of police organizations are intrinsically tied to the building of the new Chinese nation-state and changes in this project to meet contemporaneous demands. The training and education of the police has been underpinned by these events, and seen by the early priorities of the government in increasing the numbers of police officers and training establishments to enable the police organization to effectively carry out its basic task of policing the country. One of the important and impressive features of the development of the police organization, and clearly highlighted in police training and education reform in China, is the role of the central planning system in driving the process of development in the building of training and education infrastructure. This system also played an important role in promoting training standards, content and educational materials, in transforming a very rudimentary system with an emphasis on political education to a very unique system of police training and education.

China has developed a comprehensive system which combines a vocational and academic approach to police training and education, some of which resemble thinking and practices found around the world and associated with the professional development model around lifelong learning and the role of higher education and academic qualifications in that process. Improving the professionalism of the police is an important priority of contemporary Chinese governments, as part of its goals of improving police accountability and performance. These priorities have been brought about due to the increase in crime, with greater democratization and wealth, and demands for a more professional policing response. Other aspects of the training and education of police officers in China are very unique, such as its experimental workshops where groups of officers can combine theory, skill development, teaching practice and research under their own control, introducing a degree of autonomy and creativity uncommon in world policing. The additional support provided in areas such as improving teaching abilities or unarmed combat training is another distinguishing feature of a very Chinese approach. China places high value on the international education of its police and related personnel in terms of developing best practice, not surprising given its status as one of the most important world superpowers. Like Hungary, China is an important source of knowledge about police training and education with import far beyond their own borders.

Problems and issues

The issue of financial costs of development activities is a major constraint in the adoption of the professional model in developing nations. The issue of costs are also matters of concern in many traditionally wealthy countries responsible for popularising this approach to police human resource management. It has spurned discussions around the adoption of pre-employment or post-employment models of training and who is fundamentally responsible for the initial training of recruits and who pays for it in part or whole (see Chapter 1). Many of the strands of this discussion can be found outside that debate. For example, in New South Wales the possession of certificate in swimming is part of the initial entry requirements for joining the police service, while in St Lucia swimming is taught as part of basic recruit training. Some interesting examples of pre- and post-employment models of police training are outlined by Wyatt and Bell in their chapter on Canada, which includes post-employment models where recruits have to pay for specific elements of the programme such as tuition. The Canadian and US experience suggests the introduction of the pre-employment training model in some regions or states while potentially causing some initial disquiet to traditionalists, as is the case in Britain (Chapter 1), has become an accepted mode to recruit and prepare new police officers in societies where the profession commands respect and is seen as an attractive and meaningful career.

Police budgets are increasingly coming under strain. This can be seen in the US and Britain where economic challenges have contributed to constraints on public spending and the reduction of staff and training programmes. In the case of the former, new priorities around terrorism and homeland security are having an important influence on training priorities. As Chappell highlights these concerns have resulted in greater attention on matters relating to intelligence, response and enforcement training activities which threaten to undermine the community policing dimension; one of the most important developments in recent police history. Berlin indicates that community policing in the US has obtained such political importance that very few police leaders would openly challenge the narrative which informs it and feeds its popularity. This, however, should not mask the fact that many police leaders have never fully bought into the community policing philosophy and approaches to training which inform it. With this in mind Chappell's fears are real in that the national priority around protecting the US homeland, and the training priorities around it, will undermine the gains made over the years in community-based policing.

The issue of counter-terrorism has become an important issue of concern in India after the attacks in Mumbai and seen in the way Indian officers are being trained and educated for senior leadership roles. This has required a break with the traditional way police leaders have been prepared for their roles which is detailed by Neyroud and Wain. Whether this new priority will have broader implications in improving the general training of Indian police, and recruits in particular, is too early to tell. Probably, more important to police officers in these parts of the world is the poor pay and conditions and the status of policing, when compared to their counterparts in wealthier countries. Associated with this, and highlighted in Chapter 1, is the low levels of investment in training and developing police officers in India.

While these things are relative, and police officers in many parts of the developing world such as St Lucia earn more than average citizens, but less than other public professionals. This is something not lost on the general public, as sympathetic as they are to the low pay of their police compared to the Caribbean police in countries such as Barbados or the Bahamas. The public in St Lucia still have a reasonable set of expectations about the type of policing they have a right to receive in a small liberal democratic country; albeit not surprised when they are not met. In wealthy countries the notion of well-paid police officers not complying with the standards, practices and expectations of other public professionals is one likely to cause a strong public reaction and a persuasive basis for calls for reform. This suggests whether by design or default, or different levels or comparative development, many of the issues and debates which have contributed to the popularization of the professional mode of development and its adoption, in part or whole, can be found in different types of societies around the world.

The changing nature of contemporary policing

Another important development in world policing is the growing recognition of police auxiliaries which can be found in many countries, under various names, and introduced for a range of reasons. For example, in Australia auxiliary police officers have been an important means to increase the ethnic representation of local policing and make it more responsive to the needs of aboriginal and other communities. In England, the growing importance of, and recognition given to, police auxiliaries have been driven largely by concerns around public spending and costs and the desire to reduce them. As Crisp indicates in her chapter, the anxieties felt by sworn officers and their union representatives to the emergence of PCSOs in Britain are very real. Chief constables have discretion in how they deploy this new member of the extended policing family; and the legal powers granted to them in order to carry out their defined roles. It is not a stretch of the imagination to see police auxiliaries taking on a wider set of policing responsibilities to meet short-falls in sworn officers. Despite a barrage of criticizm towards PCSOs from some sections of the media and amongst serving officers, their popularity and evidence of community acceptance has strengthened the hand of police decision-makers in expanding their presence and areas of responsibilities. This has already been seen with some auxiliaries being given specific tasks and roles in the context of anti-terrorism policing. By the same token, the training and development of police auxiliaries is going to constitute an important issue in this context, given the requirement for improved preparation to carry out these additional tasks.

The private sector has become an increasingly important topic in discussions about policing for several reasons. First, the greater rationalization of police organizations in many advanced policing jurisdictions, and the desire to reduce costs has created greater opportunities for private security providers to enter areas historically associated with the State and its policing organizations. Boda (forthcoming) maintains that clearly identifying the core areas of State policing activity, and their primary responsibilities, is likely to be a major area of debate for the foreseeable future and a shared concern of police leaders worldwide. In many developing countries private security firms have always played a significant role in the public and private safety, given the inadequacies of State police organizations (Andrews 2011; Stanislas forthcoming) and have a particularly important function in troubled countries with high levels of crime and violence such as Jamaica and South Africa (Zinn 2012; Harriot 2008). They have been invaluable partners in the successful staging of major international events such as the 2007 Cricket World Cup in the Caribbean, as they have in the recent Olympic Games in London albeit with less controversy (see Wakefield and Button). Second, increased awareness around risk, especially in the area of business-related activities, has sensitized operators about the importance of taking appropriate steps to reduce the possibilities of a range of criminal or other risks. This has created a market for a range of services for individual property and home owners, such as guard dogs and guard dog training found, in most Caribbean and Latin American countries and other parts of the developing world these days (Sheptycki 1998: 490–492).

As Wakefield and Button have highlighted in their chapter, ex-police and military personnel constitute the primary source of recruitment for those working in the private sector in particular areas, and efforts to expand this labour pool continue to face important challenges. In the developing world police officers moonlighting for the private sector has contributed to the crisis in policing in many countries. In St Lucia entire police stations have been found empty while officers ply their trade in the private sector during paid duty time, often utilizing police equipment and resources for these purposes (Stanislas forthcoming). In this sense the public sector in countries like St Lucia and Antigua, where the practice of 'ghost workers' became institutionalized under the successive administrations of the Bird family (International Monetary Fund 2004),[8] can be seen as subsidizing the profit-making private sector to a far more significant degree than simply training future private sector employees.

One of the problems the private sector face in many countries and regions of the world is the lack of clear 'industry' standards and the low mandatory requirements introduced by government, for instance, in places like England, the US, and the Caribbean (see Andrews 2011) compared to many countries in Western Europe in terms of the training and education needed to work in this sector. Wakefield and Button highlight the case in the highly specialized area of close protection work as one example of how government legislation has lowered the standards required to work in specific areas. Emerging domestic professional bodies, such as the British Security Industry Association, have invested considerable effort in developing and validating some training courses. However, they are unable at this point in their evolution to enforce these training requirements or compel its members to comply with them. The professionalization project in the area of private sector security provision is very much a work in progress. A lesson that can be drawn from the State policing sector is that countries with the greatest amount of regulation generally have higher standards and requirements around training and education, such as Australia and China, even though the aforementioned illustration of close protection work presently seems to contradict this.

The issue of regulation is particularly pressing in the developing world in many areas such as background screening of prospective personnel and who can own or set up private sector security companies. Harriot (2008) has written extensively about the role of criminal 'dons' in Jamaica and their influence in the private security field and corrupt relations in obtaining major government contracts. Other areas of concern relate to the conduct of private security staff in places such as South Africa[9] and Nigeria where many of these organizations have a bad reputation given their association with violence. The transnational character of some of these private security firms again raises concerns about the lack of regulation in most parts of the world. The Guardian journalist Harding (2012) in his examination of Russia's self-exiled new bourgeoisie estimated the amount of London property owned by this group in 2006 was worth £20 billion. Many wealthy émigrés are fleeing disputes with powerful figures in Russia, if not the government, and live in fear of reprisals. An example of this was the machine gun attack on ex-banker German Gorbuntsov in East London in 2012. These types of anxieties have led to the creation of private security companies staffed almost entirely by former Russian elite and secret services personnel operating in Britain (see Harding 2012). In the English Caribbean it is the strong Eastern Caribbean dollar, compared to the weak Jamaican dollar, which has led to an influx of Jamaican private security companies and their personnel, to countries such as Antigua where they can be found working in areas such as facilities management and protecting commercial premises (Andrews 2011). In both these examples given the weak system of regulation that exists, neither the existing professional bodies nor government have any real influence on how these private interests conduct their affairs in their countries. The ability of private security companies to operate transnationally or set up operations in foreign countries simply complicates the problems for those seeking to improve and regulate the domestic private security sector.

One of the problems the private security sector face, especially from some sources calling for greater regulation, is the potential for double standards, which indicates that this sector is not playing on a level field. This is an important observation made by Wakefield and Button. In countries like Britain, which has strong State policing traditions, the resistance to the increasing presence of the private sector in less discrete areas is likely to increase. The lack of regulation of the private security sector will no doubt constitute grounds for these objections. The police and ex-police officers who appeared to be falling over themselves to criticize the security company G20's arrangements for the London Olympic games, and some of the observations made and the narrative being appealed to, that the State police organization is superior to its private sector counterparts, is based on a misleading and highly selective representation of British policing and how it has been experienced by significant sections of the population.[10] For example the murder of two middle-aged parents in Nottingham took place while they were supposedly under 24-hour police protection (Bowcott 2012). The levels of incompetence revealed in the MacPherson inquiry gave the impression that nobody within the police organizations under scrutiny had ever worked on a murder inquiry before, or understood rudimentary police practice (Chapter 1). Even the area of the types of people who are recruited to the police, or allowed to remain in its employ, has come under scrutiny. Greenwood (2012) highlights that approximately 1,000 police officers in post had criminal records, with many offences being carried out whilst in office.[11] It is sufficient to say if the history of abuse, deaths in custody, racism and other forms of unacceptable police behaviour is taken into account, against the minuscule number of officers disciplined, dismissed or subjected to legal proceedings, the police may not be the best comparator for private sector standards. Professional, highly regulated, and unionized police forces are as much reproducers and defenders of bad practice as they are models of good practice to be used as a measure for others. In this regard, the private sector does not have to adopt a defensive posture when asserting its claims and right to be seen as a serious potential partner in many areas of public and private policing.

Under the correct leadership the private sector can provide alternative and superior models of practice and standards which allow communities and other potential users of their services to make sound informed choices where possible. The role of the private sector in policing is not completely sanguine, apart from the well-documented concerns around equality of access and a host of other matters; one specific worry is their influences on police practice in areas such as weapons technology, such as the development of Tasers and their increasing use around the world. Balancing the safety of officers and the public against the adverse consequences of gadget-reliant policing are serious matters forcefully articulated by Arsenault and Hinton in their chapter that should not be taken lightly. The sheer number and presence of private sector weapons and other technical manufacturers, and their representatives, and exhibits at the International Associations of Police Chiefs annual meetings, and their role as sponsors of such prestige events, demonstrates their importance and influence on global policing.

An important feature of contemporary society is the importance of expert knowledge and its relationship to research and practice, which is even more pressing in emerging fields such as the various areas of private security provision. For Wakefield and Button increasing the knowledge base of private security practice is a crucial step in the development of this sector, in particular in expanding the type of content and courses available at university and other levels of education and training. Expanding the knowledge base helps institutions to increase their offering in these and related areas, and helps to popularize the importance of the private security sector as an area of work and research. The hope is this will contribute to the growth and greater professionalization of the sector. At present the small numbers of universities around the world that teach courses or programmes on private sector security and related matters can be found in Britain, Hungary, South Africa and Jamaica to name a few. As long as the private sector is going to be an important actor in public and private protection and safety matters, and the evidence suggests that it will be for the foreseeable future, the education and training of their staff will continue to be an issue of discussion.

Issues around training, education and development lay at the heart of most discussions around the performance of police and private security personnel and the organizations that employ them in various capacities, the equipment and technology they utilize and how they respond to change. As the book highlights in various ways these issues, along with the agencies and personnel involved in the field of training and education practice and research, are international and transnational in character, as are the ideas and practices which inform them. Regardless of financial climate, as important as it is, or policing styles, strategies or whether technological change increases the number of gadgets modern police will rely on, training and education will remain a fundamental activity within policing organizations. For this reason developments and trends in this area will continue to attract critical attention and it is the hope of this book to increase research activity to inform these discussions. The study of police training and education provides ways of understanding organizations at different levels of analysis, historically and contemporaneously, as well as a means to compare them. Perhaps more importantly, it potentially provides a window into the future of policing domestically and globally.

Notes

1   Many groups cannot rely on police protection and in some cases the police may be adversaries or facilitate the actions of those hostile to them (Stanislas 2013:16–18, White 2011:6–7). A recent example of this is the policing of environmental groups that has highlighted concerns about under-cover policing. The inability to rely on the State led to the creation of forms of non-State policing systems and is illustrated in the Jewish and Black communities in parts of Britain (Stanislas 2006).

2   This is the view reached by the author after speaking to key stakeholders involved in use-of-force training in his police organization, including Police Federation representatives who shared the concerns about the poor training and lack of ongoing refresher support received by frontline officers.

3 One of the police practices which apparently contributed to this incident was plain clothed officers habitually not announcing they are the police when approaching people they want to speak. It is common practice for police to inform suspects who they are only after physically grabbing hold of individuals wanted for questioning or during physical struggles. It is therefore not surprising that many people run, especially small-time criminals fearing attacks by rivals.

4 The response of the local people interviewed was not driven by any sense of wanting to defend a small-time local criminal, but due to a sense of outrage and injustice about how poor people are used as the 'usual suspects' by the police to cover up their incompetence, corruption and often criminal behaviour and associations.

5 While many academic staff who teach on various police programmes find it very difficult to assess the benefits of such programmes in terms of their outcomes outside the confines of the classroom and share a critical disposition on the matter. There are police managers who can cite important and significant changes in officer attitudes and understanding of issues relating to community engagement, greater sensitivity and understanding of societal needs and how to respond appropriately.

6 The paper was presented at the symposium held in February 2013 at De Montfort University entitled 'Developing the Community Security Sector in the Emerging and Developing World'.

7 Acadia Development Association (2013) Global Security and Security Sector Development in Africa, www.acadiadevelopmentassociatesllp.blogspot.co.uk, February 2013, accessed 28 February 2013.

8 One of the distinguishing features of the corruption of the Labour Party rule was ghost employment for party loyalists and personal associates on an unprecedented scale. The writer knows people from Antigua who ran their own businesses for decades while drawing a monthly state salary often for senior positions they were never qualified for in the first instance.

9 Louis Theroux: Law and Disorder in Johannesburg BBC 2013, available from YouTube. The documentary highlighted some of the major problems with particular types of private security companies that operate in South Africa, which includes the casual use of ritual beatings and violence.

10 A retired police colleague aptly cites one of the greatest weaknesses of the British police is a penchant for believing its own propaganda that bears little resemblance to how it actually polices, or how police organizations actually operate. This is definitely the case in police criticisms of G20. Nowhere is this mythology more pronounced than when British police participate in international development work abroad promoting ideas such as community policing.

11 The writer came across similar findings while leading a review of his force recruitment processes, over a decade earlier. What was very clear was black and ethnic minority recruits were held to a higher standard as none of them had any convictions and came from exemplary backgrounds. The same was found in terms of disciplinary actions and how white officers benefited from being able to breach professional expectations with less concerns about formal sanctions. Contrary to the popular beliefs that minority applicants or officers benefited from preferential treatment in important areas, the review team found it was the reverse.

References

Acadia Development Association (2013) http://acaciadevelopmentassociatesllp.blogspot.co.uk/ February 2013, accessed 26 February 2013.

Andrews, D. (2011) 'Jamaica's Top Cop Urges Strict Regulation of Private Security Companies', www.kaieteurnewsonline.com, 21 October 2011, accessed 12 March 2013.

Bayley, D. (2006) *Changing the Guard: Developing Democratic Policing Abroad*, New York: Oxford University Press.

Boda, J. (forthcoming) Interview with Police Lieutenant General Dr Jozsef Bencze.

Bowcott, O. (2012) 'UK-Wide Witness Protection Programme to be Launched in 2013', www.guardian.co.uk, 28 December 2012, accessed 3 January 2013.

Bowling, B. (2010) *Policing the Caribbean, Transnationalism Security Cooperation in Practice*, Oxford: Oxford University Press.

Bowling, B. and Sheptkyci, J. (2012) *Global Policing*, London: Sage Publications.

Brogden, M. and Nijhar, P. (2005) *Community Policing: National and International Models and Approaches*, Devon: Willan Publishing.

Cheah, P. (1997) 'Posit(ion)ing Human Rights in the Current Global Conjuncture', *Public Culture*, 9(2): 233–266.

Den Heyer, G. (2007) 'Stabilising the Solomons: A Regional Response', *New Zealand International Review*, July/August, 32(4).

Fanon, F. (1967) *Black Skin, White Mask*, London: Penguin Books.

Freire, P. (1970) *The Pedagogy of the Oppressed*, London: Penguin Books.

Geesen, M. (2012) *The Man Without a Face: The Unlikely Rise of Vladimir Putin*, New York: Riverhead Books.

Gilligan, A. (2012) 'India Tells Britain: We Don't Want Your Aid', www.telegraph.co.uk, 12 January, accessed 3 February 2013.

Gray, S. (2013) 'British Hostages Among Seven 'Killed' by Nigerian Jihadists', www.times.co.uk, 10 March 2013, accessed 10 March 2013.

Greenwood, C. (2012) 'The criminals in uniform: Almost 1,000 officers with convictions from drug dealing to perverting justice are still in the police', www.dailymail.co.uk, 3 Jan 2012, accessed 3 January 2012.

Gregerson, E. (1982) *Sexual Practices: The Story of Human Sexuality*, Mitchell Beazley: London.

Hannan, M., Hearnden, I., Grace, K. and Bucke, T. 'Deaths in or Following Police Custody: An Examination of Cases 1998/9–2008/9', Independent Police Complaints Commission.

Harding, L. (2012) *How One Reporter Became an Enemy of the Brutal New Russia Mafia State*, London: Guardian Books.

Harding, L. and Elder, M. (2012) 'Attack on Russian Banker in London Leaves Trail of Clues Back to Moscow', www.guardian.co.uk, 30 March, accessed 10 March 2013.

Harriot, A. (2000) *Police and Crime Control in Jamaica, Problems of Reforming an Ex-Colonial Constabularies*, University of the West Indies Press, Barbados.

Harriot, A. (2008) *Organized Crime and Politics in Jamaica*, Canoe Press, Kingston Jamaica.

Heslop, R. (2011) 'Reproducing Police Culture in a British University: Findings from an Exploratory Case Study of Police Foundation Degrees', *Police, Practice and Research*, 12(4): 1–15.

High Commissioner, Hungarian National Police, in B. Baker and D. Das (eds) (2012) *Interviews in Global Leaders in Policing, Courts and Prisons*, Volume Four, CRC Press/Taylor Francis, Florida.

Hinton, M.S. and Newburn, T. (2009) *Policing Developing Democracies*, Abingdon: Routledge.

International Monetary Fund (2004) Staff Country Reports (Antigua and Barbuda).

Iriekpen, D. (2012) 'Nigeria: Plugging the 'Security Vote' Leakage', 16 October, www.allafrica.com, accessed 13 March 2013.

Jarvis, P. (1992) *Perspectives on Adult Education and Training in Europe*, National Institute of Adult Continuing Education.

Jarvis, P. (2010) 'Adult Education and Lifelong Learning', *Theory and Practice*, 4th edn., London: Routledge.

Jasper, L. (2011) 'Deaths in Custody Cuts Deep in the Psyche of Black Britons', www.guardian.co.uk, 15 December, accessed 23 February 2013.

Kirkup, J. (2013) 'Why Foreign Officials Could Not Spend £500m Quickly Enough', www.telegraph.co.uk, 12 January, accessed 3 February 2013.

Kratcoski, P. and Das, D. (2007) *Police Education and Training in a Global World*, Lexington Books.

Lancester-Ellis, K. (2013) 'Personal Perspectives: Challenges for Women in Policing Within the Caribbean', *Pakistan Journal of Criminology*, 5(1).

Loftus, B. (2012) *Police Culture in a Changing World*, Oxford: Oxford University Press.

Long, S. (2003) 'More Than a Name: State Sponsored Homophobia and its Consequences in Southern Africa', *Human Rights Watch*.

MacAlaister, D., Jones, G. and Kara, F. (2012) 'Police Involved Deaths, the Need for Reform', Vancouver, BC: BC Civil Liberties Association.

Manning, G. (2007) Police Excesses Worst in 2007, Jamaican Gleaner, 30 September, www.jamaican-gleaner.com, accessed 5 April 2012.

Pflanz, M. (2013) 'Nigeria: Extremists gun down nine women giving polio vaccines to children', www.telegraph.co.uk, 8 February, accessed 8 February 2013.

Pływaczewski, W. (2007) 'Polish Police Training System and the Current Crime Threat', in P. Krotoscki and D. Das.

Premium Times (2012) '36 Governors Seek Increased 'Security Votes' State Police to Combat Boko Haram', www.premiumtimesng.com, 25 June, accessed 17 March 2013.

Provost, C. and de Frietas, W. (2012) 'US Foreign Aid and the 2012 Budget: Where will the Axe Fall', www.guardian.co.uk, 7 November, accessed 3 February 2012.

Public Intelligence (2010) 'South Korea Debuts Unbelievable Martial Arts G20 Security Force', www.publilcintelligence.net, 4 October, accessed 5 June 2012.

Punch, M. (2011) *Shoot to Kill: Police Accountability, Firearms and Fatal Force*, Policy Press: Bristol.

Raghavan, S. (2010) 'Gays in Africa Facing Growing Persecution, Activists Say', www.washingtonpost.com, 12 December, accessed 4 February 2013.

Reiner, R. (1992) 'Policing a Postmodernism Society', *The Modern Law Review*, 55(6): 761–781.

Shahnazarian, N. (2012) 'Police Reform and Corruption in Georgia, Armenia, and Nagorno Karabakh', PONARS Eurasia Policy Memo No. 232, September 2012 Centre for Pontic and Caucas, accessed 12 October 2012.

Shastri, P. (2012) 'Civilian Policing in India', *The Times of India*, 17 July, www.indiatimes.com, accessed 29 September 2012.

Sheptycki, J. (1998) 'Policing, Postmodernism and Transnationalism', *British Journal of Criminology*, 38(3).

Stanislas, P. (2006) 'Models of Organisation and Leadership Behaviour Among Ethnic Minority Communities and Policing in Britain', PhD Thesis, London School of Economics. Stanislas, P. (2013) 'Postcolonial Discourses and Policing Violent Homophobia in the Caribbean and the British Caribbean Diaspora', *Interventions, Journal of Postcolonial Thought*, 35(2).

Stanislas, P. (2013) 'Police and Criminal Administration in St Lucia: A Case Study of a Caribbean Micro State'. *Police Practice and Research*.

Teixeira, P.N. (2006) 'Markets in Higher Education: Can We Still Learn From Economics

Founding Fathers?' Centre for Studies in Higher Education, University of California, Berkley, Research and Occasional Paper Series CSHE 406.

White, R. (2011) *Environmental Criminology: Towards an Eco-Global Criminology*, Routledge: Aberton.

White, R. (2011) *Transnational Environmental Crime*, Routledge: London.

Wimshurst, K. and Ransley, J. (2007) 'Police Education and the University Sector: Contrasting Models from Australian Experience', *Journal of Criminal Justice Education*, 18(1): 106–122.

Zagorodnov, A. (2011) 'Russia's Police: A new force to be reckoned with', www.telegraph.co.uk, 24 February, accessed 16 March 2013.

Zinn, R. (2012) 'Framework for an Effective Community Safety Network', *South African Journal of Criminology*, 25(2).

Index

Page numbers in *italics* denote tables, those in **bold** denote figures.

Acacia Development Association, Nigeria 299

academies and institutes, for police training: Atlantic Police Academy (APA), Canada 83–5; Central European Police College (MEPA) 188–9, 190, 301; Charles Sturt University (CSU), Australia 42–4, 46; Chinese Criminal Police College 197; Chinese People's Public Security University (CPPSU) 197, 199, 202, 298; Department of Professional Improvement and Specialization (DPIS), Crotia 3; Dutch Police Academy 107; École Pratique Professionnelle des Services Actifs de la Prefecture de Police, France 159; European Police Academy 10; European Police College (CEPOL) 190; Holland College, Prince Edward Island 83; International Law Enforcement Academy (ILEA) 190; Justice Institute of British Columbia (JIBC), Canada 75, 82; Manchester University 63; Masindi Police Training School, Uganda 3; National Police Academy, Hyderabad (India) 118, 120; National Police Training Centre, Warrington 63; National University of Public Service, Hungary 183; Ontario Police College (OPC), Ontario 80, 81; Police Academy of the Netherlands 90; Seneca College, Canada 83, 85–6; Shanghai Police College (SPC) 202; University of California, Berkeley 57; *see also* police academies

Accreditation for Prior Learning (APL) Bureau, the Netherlands 110

accredited prior learning (APL) schemes 263–4

American National Standards Institute (ANSI) 259, 260

anti-terrorism operations 34

ASIS International 260, 261; Certified Protection Professional (CPP) 262

Associate Degree in Policing Practice (ADPP), Australia 42, 44, 296

Association of Chief Police Officers (ACPO) 122, 240

Atlantic Police Academy (APA), Canada 83–5

Australasian Council of Security Professionals 261

Australia, police training in: assessment methodologies 48; Associate Degree in Policing Practice (ADPP) 42, 44, 296; Associate Degree program 42; challenges associated with 50–3; Contract Agreement Performance Review Committee (CAPRC) 49; course structure of ADPP 44, *45*; courses committee, responsibilities of 48–9; curriculum for 48; Diploma of Policing Practice (DPP) 42–3; diversity of NSW Police Force and 52–3; Facilities Maintenance and Infrastructure Committee (FMIC) 50; Fitzgerald Report (1989) 43; funding arrangements for 50; history of 42–4; indicators of success of 53–4; involvement of HEIs in 61; management structure of 48–50, **49**; model of collaboration with CSU 46–8; offer of employment 44; partnership with CSU for 43, 46–8, 54; politics, influence of 50–1; probationary

constable, expectations of 53; quality
assurance 48; Research Development
Advisory Committee 50; Teaching
Development Advisory Committee 49;
teaching staff, availability of 51–2;
tertiary education for 43; Wood
Commission (1997) 42–3, 61
Australian Federal Police 42
Australian Universities Quality Assurance
(AUQA) 54

Bayley, David 58, 68, 126, 238, 296
Becker, Howard 168
'Best Value Framework' (Home Office
1999) 237
Bratton, William 33
Briggs, R. 256, 258
Britain, university-based police education
in: advantages of 60; Commission for
Racial Equality 64; *Comprehensive
Spending Review* (2010) 66; creation of
57; degree education for police officers
63; development of training programmes
63; discrimination and diversity, issues
of 64; empirical evidence and
methodological challenges 60–2;
foundation degree in policing 64–5;
historical and international context of
57–8; knowledge-based training 63;
military model and police training
academies 58–9; modernization,
professionalization, and HEIs 65–7;
National Police Training Centre,
Warrington 63; Neyroud Report (2011)
66–7; professionalization of occupations
and 59–60; quality of teaching and
learning in 65; universities and police
education and training 62–4
British Security Industry Association
(BSIA) 260, 268, 307
British Standards Institute (BSI) 259
Brooks, D. 263
Budapest Board of Detectives 176
*Bureau of Justice Statistics State and
Local Law Enforcement Training
Academies, 2002* 30
business continuity management (BCM)
258, 263

Cadet Training Program, Canada 75,
78–80
Canada, police training and education in:
aboriginal police 76; applied police
learning 81; Atlantic Police Academy
(APA) 83–5; Cadet Training Program
78; Canadian nation state 72; CAPRA
operational model 78; college approach
83; Federalist government and 72–3;
Field Coaching Program 79; First
Nations Policing Program (FNPP),
Canada 76; future of recruit training 87;
Justice Institute of British Columbia
(JIBC) 75, 82; Ministry of Public Safety
Canada 77; municipal police agencies
75; municipal police training (British
Columbia) 81–2; national e-learning
projects 87–8; National Federal police
force 75; North-West Mounted Police
(NWMP) 77, 139; Ontario Police
College (OPC), Ontario 80; police
organizations in Canada 73; Police
Sector Council (PSC) 87; police training
curriculum 82–3; police use-of-force *see*
use-of-force, by police; policing service
delivery models 74–5; practical training
81; pre-employment or post-
employment models 74; provincial
policing (Ontario Provincial Police) 75;
qualifications 73–4; Royal Canadian
Mounted Police (RCMP) 74, 75, 77–81,
139–40; selection process, for police
officers 72, 73; Seneca College 85–6;
Stl'at'imx Tribal police 76
Canadian Council of Security
Professionals 261
Canadian Police Knowledge Network
(CPKN) 85, 87; programs delivered by
88
Caribbean Examination Council (CXCs)
212
Carlan, E. P. 61
Central Bureau of Coordination, Vienna
189
Central Bureau of Investigation (CBI),
India 118, 121
Central European Police College (MEPA)
188–9, 190, 301
Central Police Training and Development
Authority (CENTREX) 239
Central Reserve Police Force (CRPF),
India 121
characteristics of professions, similarities
between *91*
Charles Sturt University (CSU), Australia
42–3; Division of Marketing 46; School
of Policing Studies 44
Chartered Institute of Personnel and
Development, UK 261

Chartered Security Professionals Registration Authority (CSPRA) 260, 262
Chicago race riots (1965) 140–1
China, police education and training in: basic task of 195; capability-centered 206–7; Chinese Criminal Police College 197; for Chinese ethnic minorities 199; Chinese People's Public Security University (CPPSU) 197, 199, 202; combat training 201–2; compilation of textbooks and materials 198; consolidation stage (1986–1999) 197–9; creation stage (1949–1965) 194–5; destruction and stagnation stage (1966–1977) 195; distinctive professional police education and training 206; faculty team in police colleges 198; initial foundation period 194–5; in-service 196–7; length of schooling for 206; main features of 206; new development period of 196–204; new reform stage (since 2008) of 203–4; overview of 204–7; police academic education, development of 200–1; police exchanges and cooperation with foreign countries 198–9; police higher education, enhancement of 201; progress stage (2001–2008) 200–2; Public Security Ministry (PSM) 194, 198; quality of 197–8; recovery stage (1978–1985) 196–7; regulations for 200; secondary police schools and higher police colleges 197; Shanghai Police College (SPC) 202; unique management mode for 206
Chinese Criminal Police College 197
Chinese People's Public Security University (CPPSU) 197, 199, 298; Innovation Experiment Programme for Advanced Police Talent Training 202
Chou Enlai 196
citizen satisfaction, with the police 26
close protection officers (CPOs) 265, 269
Commonwealth Grant Scheme (CGS), Australia 50
Commonwealth Human Rights Committee 120
Commonwealth Human Rights Initiative 120, 125
communist policing, professional development model 302–4
Community Oriented Policing Services (COPS), USA 36

community policing 28, 279, 282–3; advances in 284; communication and problem-solving skills 29; CompStat and 34; curriculum for 29; entrance-level training in 28, 29; generation of 26; guidelines for content of 29; human rights discourse and 225; implementation of 31–2; institutionalization of 26; median hours for 29; police-community relationship 33; principles of 34; problem-based learning 30; quality of life issues and problems 34; Royal St Lucian Police Force (RSLPF) 225–6; topics associated with 29
Community Service Officer (CSO) 238
competencies of policing, categories of 92, 95, 98
CompStat management process: criticisms of 34; elements of 33; integrating with community policing 34; 'zero-tolerance' policing 34
conducted energy weapon (CEW) 140, 147
Conger, J. 122–4
Constitution Act (1982), Canada 72
contemporary policing 36, 42, 59, 63, 181, 279, 296, 298; changing nature of 305–9; occupational status of 65
continuing professional development (CPD) programmes 258, 262, 269
Contract Agreement Performance Review Committee (CAPRC), Australia 49, 296
corruption, in police forces 9, 25, 117
counter-terrorism, issue of 258, 275, 281–4, 301, 305
Cover, Jack 140
Cowper, T. 59
criminal justice system 2, 237, 276; degree programme in 61; role of policing within 5
criminal victimization 2
Cultural Revolution, China 195–6
curriculum development and content 28; in security management 263; for training in community policing 29
Curriculum Maintenance System (CMS) 279
cybercrime 3

Das, D. 2–3, 5–6, 290
Deng Xiaoping 196
Deosaran Report (2003) 225
Department of Professional Improvement and Specialization (DPIS), Crotia 3

distance learning 5, 10, 79, 212, 262
Dutch Police Education Council (POR) 90

École Pratique Professionnelle des Services Actifs de la Prefecture de Police, France 159
Erasmus Programme, European Union 183, 191n2
Essex Constabulary 63
European Credit Transfer System (ECTS) 183
European Higher Education Area (EHEA) 183
European Institute for Leadership 122
European Police Academy 10
European Police College (CEPOL) 112n6, 190
European Qualifications Framework (EQF), for lifelong learning 93, 95, 112n8
European Standards Organisations 259

Fairbairn, W. E. 131–2, 134
Federal Bureau of Investigation (FBI), USA 10; National Academy for the training 25
Field Training Officers (FTOs) 280–1
fire-arms and self-defense training, in Sweden: basic police training and advanced instructor training 133–4; ethical considerations in 136; factual basis for tactics in 136; fire-arms training 131; human limitations and strengths for 134–5; instructor training 132; new training and education paradigms 129–34; police organization and 128–9; principles of 129–32; research-supported improvements in 134–6; scenario training 131–2; Skåne County Police Department 128; stress inoculation training 132; stress response, effects of 135; systemic context-influenced training 129–30; systemic tactical training 134; tactical approaches for 132–4
First Incident Report (FIR) 119
First Nations Policing Program (FNPP), Canada 76
Fitzgerald Report (1989), Australia 43
Freedom of Information (FOI) 248
French police, training: accounts during active service training programs 165–6; calibrated use of violence 167–70; centralized feature of 158; École nationale de la Police de Paris (ENPP) 159, 161, 168; École Pratique Professionnelle des Services Actifs de la Prefecture de Police 159; expert and the critic 162–3; instructor as a teacher and a colleague 160–1; Intervention Gesture and Professional Techniques (GTPI) 166–7; legitimate use of violence 163–7; mastering the frameworks for the situation 169–70; professionalization of 159; ranking categories 158; submitting to authority and exercising it 168–9; teaching the job of policing 160; transient nature of force in theoretical courses 163–5
funding, police development 298–302, 304
Future of Higher Education, The (2003) 64

'Gang of Four' 196
Gillis, Lisa 79
Gore Committee on Police Training, India 117
'Great Recession' of 2008 36

Hamm, Leonard 29
Harriot, A. 2, 218, 307
Hazare, Anna 117
Heslop, Richard 68, 245, 297
higher education: benefits of, for police recruits 60; role in police training 23
higher education institutions (HEIs) 57, 59; Community Orientated Policing programme 61; involvement in police education 61; relation with police organizations 60
Highmore, S. 237
Holland College, Prince Edward Island 83–5, 298
homeland security 34, 36, 275, 281–5, 304
House of Commons Home Affairs Committee Report on Private Investigators (2012) 266
human and civil rights movements 140
human resource management 2, 3, 67, 210, 296, 304
human rights abuses 2, 299
Human Rights Watch 117, 125
Hungarian policing system 302
Hungary, police training in: Bachelor's Programme 184; basic training modules *180*; Border Guard 177; Budapest Board of Detectives 176; Central European Police College (MEPA) 188–9;

Hungary, police training *continued*
'Compromise of 1867' 175; course for service dog handler candidates 182; Dog Training Unit and 181; further training for police officers 186–7; general issues related to 180–1; higher education and commissioned police officers 182–4; Hungarian Association of Police Sciences 186; international training centre 189–90; law enforcement agencies' training centre 190; Law Enforcement of the University of Public Service 178; law enforcement research and 186; Leadership and Master Leadership courses 187; leadership training 188; Master's Programme 185; Museum of Criminal Investigation 176; National University of Public Service 183; organizational structure of police force 177–8; partial vocational training 181; personnel and training 178–9; Police Act (1994) 179; policing managers' course 185–6; 'Scandinavian' model 176; special courses for handlers of dogs *181*; special examination in law enforcement 187; structure and content of 179–80; training conducted at law enforcement vocational schools 182; training dog handlers 181–2; Trianon, Treaty of 176

Incident Management Intervention Model (IMIM), Canada 144
Independent Investigations Office (IIO), British Columbia 142
India Against Corruption 117
Indian Ministry for Home Affairs (MHA) 121
Indian Police Service (IPS): attempts at police reform 119–20; background of 118–19; Central Bureau of Investigation (CBI) 118, 121; Central Reserve Police Force (CRPF) 121; challenges facing 119; Criminal Procedure Code 119; Director General of Police (DGP) 119; extrajudicial killing 117; First Incident Report (FIR) 119; future aspects of 125–6; Gore Committee on Police Training 117; Mid-Career Training Programme (MCTP) 121–2; Mid-Career Training Programme phase IV 122–4; Model Police Act (2006) 119–20; National Police Academy, Hyderabad 118, 120; National Police Commission 119; Police Act (1861) 118; police

training 120–1; policing and legislative system 118; State Security Commissions (SCC) 125; training and the challenge of reform 124–5
Initial Police Learning and Development training (IPLDP) 239, 241, *242,* 244–6, 249n1
Institute of Professional Investigators (IPI) 266
institutional racism 8
intelligence-led policing 35
International Association of Police Chiefs 9, 36, 275
International Bodyguard Association 265
International Law Enforcement Academy (ILEA) 190
International Organization for Standardization (ISO) 259, 260
International Specialized Police Training Centre, Poland 10
International Victimization Crime Survey (IVCS) 2
Internet 5, 10, 224, 241, 290, 298

Johnson, Lyndon B. 140, 246
Judo, Police (innovative arrest and control training): as art of self-defence 148; benefits of 152–3; code of conduct 148; constant requirement of training 151–2; eligibility for 153–4; history of 148–9; Kano, Jigoro 148–9; liability issues 150; likely scenarios for application of 152; meaning of 149–50; 'mutual benefit and welfare,' precept of 148, 149; and over-reliance of gadgets 150–1; techniques in 147, 149; training process 153
Justice Institute of British Columbia (JIBC), Canada 75, 82, 88

Kano, Jigoro 148–9
Kratcoski, P. 2–3, 5–6, 290

Larson, M. S. 257–8
Law Enforcement Assistance Administration (LEAA), USA 275
Law Enforcement Education Programme (LEEP), USA 59–60
Law Enforcement Leadership Training and Research Institute (LETRI), Hungary 188
Lawrence, Stephen 63
laws and legislation: Constitution Act (1982), Canada 72; Model Police Act (2006), India 119–20; Police Act (1994), Hungary 179; Police Act (1861), India

118; Police and Magistrates Courts Act (1994), UK 237; Police Reform Act (2002), UK 239; Private Security Industry Act (2001), UK 264, 268
leadership, training in 188
learning, problem-based 37
Leverson Inquiry 266
London Metropolitan police 8, 155n1
Los Angeles Police Department (LAPD) training program 30, 284; approach to training 31; training philosophy of 279
Loveday, B. 66

McGee, A. 259
MacPherson Report (1999) 7–8, 63, 308
Major Cities Chiefs Association (MCCA) 36
Manchester University 63
Mao Zedong 193–4
Maple, Jack 33
Maryland Police and Correctional Training Commission 28
Masindi Police Training School, Uganda 3
Medvedev, Dmitry 302
military model, of police training and education 58–9
militsia (Russian civilian police) 302
Ministry of Public Safety Canada 77
Mishra, Shri Trinath 122
Model Police Act (2006), India 119–20
Museum of Criminal Investigation, Hungary 176

National Crime Recording Standards (2002) 239
National Federal police force, Canada *see* Royal Canadian Mounted Police (RCMP), Canada
National Incident Management System (NIMS), USA 283
National Police Academy, Hyderabad (India) 118, 120
National Police Improvement Agency (NPIA) 245
National Police Improvement Association, UK 66
National Use-of-force Framework (2000), Canada 144
National Vocational Qualifications (NVQ) 261
the Netherlands, police training in: Accreditation for Prior Learning (APL) Bureau 110; assessment of work experience in 107–10; curriculum for

107; Dutch Police Academy 107; Dutch Police Education Council (POR) 90; generic and specific competencies 93–107; occupational and qualification profiles, competencies in 91–2; operational criminal investigation competence *104*; operational emergency response competence *99*; operational law enforcement competence *101*; strategic criminal investigation competence *106*; strategic law enforcement competence *103*; tactical criminal investigation competence *105*; tactical emergency response competence *100*; tactical law enforcement competence *102*; work experience *109*
New South Wales Police Force (NSWPF) 9, 42–3, 54, 291
New York City Police Department (NYPD) 25, 34, 136, 275
Neyroud, Peter 254, 270
Neyroud Report (2011) 66–7
North-West Mounted Police (NWMP), Canada 77, 139

Ontario Police College (OPC), Ontario 75, 80, 81
Ontario Provincial Police (OPP), Canada 73–5, 77, 81
'on-the-job' training 195, 218, 276, 293

Palmiotto, M. J. 28–30
Peel, Robert 139, 148, 155n1
Peelian Principles 138–9
Petersson, Ulf 131, 136
police academies: characteristics of 58; ethos of 58; importance of 58; topics and percentage of *35*; types of *24*; *vs* university-based police education 60–2
Police Academy of the Netherlands 90
Police Act (1861), India 118
Police and Magistrates Courts Act (1994), UK 237
Police Community Support Officer (PCSO): cost implications of 247–8; De Montfort University, England 297; drivers for change in training 239–40; emergence of 305; in England and Wales 239, 297; Freedom of Information (FOI) 248; impact on community safety 247; new programme developments 246–7; training the plastic police in a UK force 240–6; University Certificate of Professional Development (UCPD) 239

police development funding 298–302, 304
police education and training:
   characteristic of 4; competency-based
   systems of evaluation 7; content of 58;
   curriculum development and content for
   28; definition of 4–6; education
   qualifications for 15; historical and
   cultural factors 15; importance of 6–7;
   in-service training 14; institutional and
   organizational culture(s) and 7–9;
   instructional methods in 279; learning,
   problem-based 30; legislation and 14;
   limits of 12; Los Angeles Police
   Department 30; military model of
   59–60; of police officers 2, 6; pre-
   employment model of 3; sharing of
   experience and learning 9–10;
   stakeholders and key actors in 10–16;
   target for 14–15; 'them and us,' notions
   of 58; trends in future 15–16; in United
   States *see* United States, police training
   in
Police Executive Research Forum (PERF)
   36, 281
police leadership and training 67, 254
police legitimacy and authority, public
   perception of 25
Police Liaison Officers (PLOs) 238
police officers: Association of Chief Police
   Officers (ACPO) 240; effectiveness of
   university-based learning on 62; impact
   of higher education on 61–2, 67, 182–4;
   importance of higher education for 57;
   National Occupational Standards for
   239; professionalization of occupations
   59; selection process in Canada 73;
   training and education of 2, 6; training
   in Hungary 186–7; type of education
   received by 59
Police Officers Standards Commissions
   (POST) Academies 24; training material
   34
police profession: competencies,
   categories of 92; distinctive core
   processes of *92*; equivalence of levels
   92; generic distinctions, typology of *94*;
   professionalization process *see*
   professionalization of the police
police racism 63, 64
police recruits: attitude towards higher
   education 61; benefits of higher
   education for 60; Community Orientated
   Policing programme 61
Police Reform Act (2002), UK 239

Police Training Officer (PTO) program 25,
   281
police violence, history of 2
police-community relationships 26, 33–4;
   impact of police culture on 237–8;
   international examples of 238;
   partnership relations, development of
   295–8
policing: CEPOL's competency
   framework 92; competency levels *96–7*;
   foundation degree in 64–5; historical
   evolution of 25; intelligence-led 35;
   international partnerships 298–302;
   legitimacy, society and change 289–91;
   liberal democratic societies and 291–2;
   movement for reform and higher
   education in 57; operational level of 95;
   police development funding 298–302;
   problems and issues associated with
   304–5; 'professional crime fighting'
   approach 25; professional model of
   development of 34, 291–2; reform era
   25; teaching the job of 160; tertiary
   education for 43
Policing in the 21st Century (2010) 66
Posen Inquiry (1995) 237
private security 255; baseline training
   265–9; professional project 264;
   security manager 255–64; security
   operatives 264–9
Private Security Industry Act (2001), UK
   264, 268
problem-solving techniques 284
professional ethics, codes of 260
professional journals 10, 259–60
professional project: Larson's concept of
   257–8; private security's 264
professionalization of the police 59–60; in
   changing attitudes and behaviour of
   police officers 59; emerging
   professionalism 59; full professionalism
   59; higher education for police recruits,
   benefits of 60; Neyroud's review of
   66–7
Public Safety Canada 76–7

'quality of life' offenses 26, 34, 282
'quangos' 268
Quinn, Robert 98, 110

Rainbow, Operation 299–300
Rand Corporation 31, 279
Register of Chartered Security
   Professionals 262

Reiner, R. 289
residential-based police training courses 65
risk management 144, 260, 263
Roads Policing training 245
Rowell, P. 245
Royal Canadian Mounted Police (RCMP),
  Canada 74, 75, 77–81, 139–40
Royal Commission on the Police (1960),
  UK 62–3
Royal Irish Constabulary 118
Royal St Lucian Police Force (RSLPF):
  background of 209–10; colonial
  inheritance, policing, and social change
  211–13; community policing 225–6;
  Deosaran Report (2003) 225;
  educational content of training
  programme 225–6; educational
  qualifications *212*; gender issues 227–8;
  higher levels of education, adverse
  consequences of 214–15;
  homosexuality, issues about 229–30;
  human rights discourse 225–6; issue of
  policing the mentally ill 228–30;
  learning environment in education and
  training of 221–2; methodology of
  training of recruits 209, 210–11;
  methods of training in 222–4; recruit
  responses and basic training 218–22;
  recruit syllabus and course content
  reform 215–16; recruit training syllabus
  216–18; reform programme, for
  improving performance 213–14;
  research findings, on training-related
  issues 211; selection procedures 214
Russian civilian police 302

Secret Policeman documentary 63
security framework, Brooks' integrated
  science of **263**
Security Institute, UK 260–2, 268
security management, university curricula
  in 263
security managers: knowledge base,
  including professional journals 260;
  meaning of 255–6; professionalism of
  257–9; standards and a code of ethics
  259–60
security operatives, development of 264–9
security professionals: association for 261;
  compulsory training standards 262;
  educational discipline preparing the
  student as 262–4; National Occupational
  Standards for 262; National Vocational
  Qualifications (NVQ) 261;

professionalism, definition of 257–9;
  security managers *see* security
  managers; state of training for *267*
security 'traditionalists' *versus* 'modern
  entrepreneurs' *257*
self-defence training 16; in Canada 7
Seneca College, Ontario 83; basic police
  training program *86*; college English 86;
  program description 85–6
Shanghai Municipal Police 134
Shanghai Police College (SPC) 202;
  'Alternative Rotating Training, Job-
  training Combination' mechanism 202
Shanghai Police Education and Training
  Mode 202
Shanghai Public Security Bureau 202
sharing of experience and learning 9–10
Sheehy Report (1993) 237
Simonsen, C. 259
South African Institute of Security 261
State Security Commissions (SCC), India
  125
Stl'at'imx Tribal police, Canada 76

Teixera, N. P. 60
Thomas A. Swift's Electronic Rifle
  (TASER) 140, 141, 150, 151
Trianon, Treaty of 176

Union Public Service Commission of India
  121
United Nations 2
United States, police training in 275–7;
  academy training 277–9; budget cuts,
  impact of 36; community era of 275;
  community policing *see* community
  policing; curriculum development and
  content for 28–9, 31; entrance-level
  training 27; environment for 31; Federal
  Bureau of Investigation (FBI) 10; field
  training 24, 280–1; higher education,
  role of 23; historical development of 23;
  Law Enforcement Education
  Programme (LEEP) 59–60; methods
  employed for *30*; model police training
  program 279; 'on-the-job' training 36,
  276; paramilitary structure and culture
  281–5; percentage of academies *28*;
  police academies, types of *24*; political
  era of 274; President's Commission on
  Law Enforcement and Administration of
  Justice 275; problem-solving techniques
  284; proliferation of SWAT units and
  282, 283; recruit training 25; reform era

United States *continued*
25, 274; role of 23; scenarios used for
31; standards of conduct 25; State and
Local Law Enforcement Training
Agencies 31; state and local training
academies 24; topics included in *27*
University Certificate of Professional
Development (UCPD) 239, 241, *243*
University of California, Berkeley 57
university-based police education:
effectiveness of 62; *vs* police academy-
based education 60–2
US Bureau of Justice Statistics 23
use-of-force, by police: brutality, incidents
of 140–2; concerns around 293;
financial implications of failings in 295;
inadequacy of use-of-force models
144–5; Incident Management
Intervention Model (IMIM) 144; legal
liability issues 295; misuse of force
142–3; models of 143–4; National

Use-of-force Framework (2000), Canada
144; Police Judo (innovative arrest and
control training) 147–51; policing in
Canada, history and evolution of 139–40;
problems with 145–7; protocols for 138;
public perception about 141; social media
and 140; Subject Behaviour/Officer
Response (SBOR) reports 141; training in
292–5

Van Maanen, J. 159, 169, 278
'verbal judo' 29
Vollmer, August 25, 57, 275

war against international terrorism 301
Wider Police Learning and Development
Programme (WPLDP) 245, 246
Wood Commission (Australia) 42–3, 61
Wood, Justice 42–4, 46

'zero-tolerance' policing 34, 283

Lightning Source UK Ltd.
Milton Keynes UK
UKHW020500080421
381413UK00014B/565